Sacred

World Religions

Fernand Comte

Chambers

EDINBURGH   NEW YORK   TORONTO

Published 1992 by W & R Chambers Ltd
43–45 Annandale Street, Edinburgh EH7 4AZ

First published in France as *Les Livres Sacrés*
© Bordas, Paris, 1990
© English text edition W & R Chambers 1992

British Library Cataloguing in Publication Data

A catalogue record for this book is available from the British Library.

ISBN 0 550 17010 3

Cover design   Blue Peach Design Consultants Ltd
Typeset by Alphaset Graphics Limited, Edinburgh
Printed in England by Clays Ltd, St Ives, plc

Acknowledgements

Translated from the French by Alison Twaddle
(Translation of Bible passages from the *Today's English Version* and the *Jerusalem Bible*)

Chambers Compact Reference Series Editor   Min Lee

Illustration credits

Other titles in
Chambers Compact Reference

Catastrophes and Disasters
Crimes and Criminals
50 Years of Rock Music
Great Modern Inventions
Great Inventions Through History
Great Scientific Discoveries
Masters of Jazz

Movie Classics
Musical Masterpieces
Mythology
The Occult
Religious Leaders
Saints
Space Exploration

To be published in 1993

Great Cities of the World
Movie Stars

Operas
World Folklore

Contents

*Nothing can ever be too beautiful or too
precious to protect the Word of God.
Imperial Bible cover, bound by Hans von Reutligen c.1500
Museum of the History of Art, Vienna*

Introduction

Has anything in the story of humankind had a more revolutionary impact than the written word?

The simplicity of the materials used, its standardization over wide areas, and the permanent nature of its messages have ensured that it has played a fundamental role. More than anything else, it has a certain magic: it speaks to man, enshrines his laws, records his history, it reaches out to another, often finer world, reveals unknown aspects of things, and holds within it mysteries hidden for centuries. It affords man a means of exploring the treasures of his heritage.

Its hesitant beginnings are so far in the past and its subsequent expansion throughout the world is so much taken for granted now that its initial amazing impact is rather lost on us today. The Ancients, spellbound by it from the start, dared not credit a human with its invention: to the Hindus it was a gift from Brahma to men; the Chinese believed that Fuxi drew the first trigrammes; to the Norsemen Odin was the discoverer of the runes; the Egyptians held Thot to be the first of the writers; even the Hebrews knew that the tablets of the Law were 'written by the finger of God' (*Exodus* 13, 18). Such an invention could only have come from heaven, first having been at the disposal of the gods. So too the first books could only be, in some way or another, the works of the gods.

Each civilization has its own particular way of attributing the origin of its own earliest works to its gods. For Muslims the *Koran* is the exact literal replica of an original which is kept in heaven for eternity. Muhammad was simply the passive instrument of its revelation; the book was the perfect embodiment of the divine Word. For the Hindus the *Vedas* would have been 'heard', from Brahma himself, by the Rsi who recorded them without alteration. For Christians the Bible is inspired by the Holy Spirit and therefore contains no errors of a religious kind, but the human authors of the different texts were free and intelligent instruments in the hands of God. And for others the books which comprise the canon, or agreed texts, of their Scriptures are very ancient works often attributed to the founders or other great figures of their faith and containing the fundamental doctrines of their religion.

Numerous civilizations have their sacred text, whether it be for reading the future (the *Sibylline Books*) or to gain the protection of mysterious powers (the *Vedas*), to discover in it the will of God (or *Torah*) or to become part of a story of Salvation (the Bible), to nourish one's love of the divine (the *Koran*) or to achieve a religious way of life (the *Tibetan Book of the Dead*). All humankind's extraordinary strivings are inscribed here, from the most irrational superstitious practices to the highest expressions of authentic mystical experiences. It is all there, but is not always received as it was intended. The faith of the believer informs the book, giving it its authority and sometimes its very meaning.

This characteristic is a factor common to sacred writings; they are made sacred by their author and they are made sacred by their appointed task. The texts aim to authenticate the origins of the faith, show its early clarity, and express the purity of its message. They are certainly the best witnesses to what the ideals of life were or still may be, expressions of the unknown and of the hopes of men across the centuries, themes so often distorted by external influences, unfortunate deviations, and the shortcomings of the faithful.

This book is intended to cover these important and enduring landmarks of the world's religions. Unfortunately, in a work of this size, it is impossible to cover every aspect in detail but an attempt has been made to give an overview of each text and,

1

as far as possible, to convey something of the essence of its inspiration. At the risk of diminishing the value each has in the eyes of its adherents, every sacred text, regardless of where it came from or into which civilization it was born, is, in one way or another, the reflection of a religious experience sufficiently extraordinary to have endured for centuries, or indeed millennia, and to have communicated a particular view of the world both visible and invisible to succeeding generations.

Perhaps this journey into the realms where the divine speaks to humankind will open up that mysterious world where people look for the meaning of life.

Ancient Egypt

The basis of Egyptian religion is not a dogma but an official form of worship celebrated by the king in person, the son of gods and a god himself. Apart from that associated with the king there is no personal religion and it is only in these terms that the ka, or personality of each person has any value. Yet little by little, at the end of the New Empire religion begins to break away from the supervision of the crown: a new fervour is seen in devotion, gifts of goods, independent of the role played by the monarchy, bear witness to the sincerity of the act.

Learned writings show that the acts of worship are now developing a spiritualist trend. God, and not the gods, whatever name he is given can be reached through personal prayer and good works: 'The one loved by God is he who obeys' (*Teachings of Ptahhotep* XIV, 6). God appears as a shepherd who looks after his own, especially the weakest ones. He punishes the wicked: 'God knows the evil man and strikes him for his faults until he bleeds' (*Merikare* 49–50). So a morality emerges, a morality personified by the goddess Maat. Maat is the key word in Egyptian religion: it stands for good behaviour, justice, and retribution. It is of little importance whether it is seen as a goodess or a theological idea, but it serves as a vehicle for a high spirituality.

A definite idea of God

During the history of the various Egyptian dynasties, gods (such as Ra, Amon or Ptah) often associated with different capital cities, creation legends from Heliopolis, Hermopolis or Memphis, priests from such and such a temple, rituals for kings, for the dead or for particular people, developed. But a certain idea of God was always maintained and it seemed, for some, to be a kind of monotheism or belief in one god. There also remained a deep and abiding religious feeling which had some connections, certainly historically, with that followed by the heroes of the story of Israel.

The number of inscriptions in temples is astonishing; on their walls can be found detailed written descriptions of the ritual to be observed, the prayers to be said or sung, the acts to be performed. The Egyptians placed an incredibly high value on the written word: what was written was, in a way, fulfilled and if the ceremony was described on the wall, it essentially meant that the sacrifice was perpetually being made, for unlike actions, the written word had permanence.

The Egyptian Book of the Dead
The book of emerging into daylight

The rites of salvation

Hymns, magic formulae, and rituals for obtaining blessing after death are gathered together in the Book of the Dead.

Anxiety in the face of death was a big issue for the Egyptians. Consequently, during the time of the Pharaohs, magic formulae and prayers had been devised with the intention of evading life's final test. A number of these documents have been found grouped together in a collection called the *Book of the Dead*. They were usually written on papyrus, a kind of parchment, and illustrated with richly-coloured sketches.

The collection is rather confused: the hymns are not of equal importance, the instructions given are not equally valuable, and the inspiration behind them varies in spiritual depth. In it can be found magic formulae, procedures for avoiding the traps set by evil spirits, and notes on the geography of hell as well as prayers of high spirituality and very moving confessions.

The judgment of souls

The dwelling place of the dead is Osiris's domain. The dead person is led into the hall of the God-Judges by Anubis. It is there that the 'weighing of the soul' or psychostasis takes place. The heart of the deceased is placed on one side of the scales and into the other side goes a feather or a statuette of Maat, the symbol of fairness. Osiris presides over this surrounded by 42 judges. Thot is the clerk who writes down the result. The deceased must turn his attention to his heart which is the seat of his personality and then to the judges whose names he claims to know, for this would give him power over them. Before this tribunal the man on trial exonerates himself from all the sins he could be accused of.

The geography of the lower regions

The realm of the dead is situated in the subterranean world, where the physical part of the individual has already been laid to rest. The text describes it as a fantastic double, or mirror image of Egypt. The 12 regions of the kingdom have their corresponding zones there, each with its god, its capital, and its inhabitants: gods, spirits,

---

Confession of innocence

'I did no evil against men, I did not illtreat any livestock, I did nothing offensive before Maat, I did not try to know what was yet to be, I did not stand by and see evil done ... I did not curse God, I did not make any poor man poorer, I broke none of the divine taboos, I did not get any servant into trouble with his superior, I poisoned no one and made no one cry ...'
(*The Declarations of Innocence*, C Maystre)

The book's effectiveness

'The man who knows this book on earth, or has it written on his tomb, can emerge into the light in whatever way he wishes and take up his place without meeting any opposition; he is given bread, beer, and a large piece of meat from the altar of Osiris; he may go to the field or reed ... Down there he is given barley and wheat; he will flourish as he did on earth, doing as he wills like the gods.' (*Book of the Dead* 72)

---

and souls of the dead. Running through the geography of this underworld is a replica of the Nile with the boat of Ra (the Sun) floating along surrounded by divine servants. And each of the dead attempts to sail with the king in order to be reborn at daybreak.

The voyage is not easy: there are various reefs in the course of the passage. The most terrible is the serpent Apopis, the forces of evil incarnate. The battle between the crew and the monster, which represents the struggle between Good and Evil is necessary for the equilibrium of the cosmos. Ra conquers it by changing into a beetle and is reborn with the day.

The description of the nocturnal voyage is very precise: it is divided into 12 parts relating to the 12 hours of the night. The king, once admitted to the stellar world (Douat) following judgment and ritual purification, joins Ra on his heavenly journey. It is at the seventh hour that Apopis appears. Each part is accompanied by comments, stories, and prayers.

The *Am-Donat* or 'Tale of the journey into the beyond' has itself had quite a journey through history. Firstly written on royal tombs it told of the voyage of the god-king. Then mere mortals came to the king to beg his favours, and they installed their statues in the royal tombs. Finally, the Am-Donat was democratized, it was written on the tombs of ordinary people, on coffins and on papyrus. Resurrection was now within everyone's reach.

The writings of wisdom

The most famous are the texts of the Pyramids and the texts of the Sarcophagi (tombs). A spiritualization of the religious cult can be seen: there has been a move from contractual religion to selfless love of God, and the notion of reward has diminished with the passage of time and has been transformed into a vision of God which brings its own blessing. 'Today death is before me like the end of rain, like the homecoming of a man after an expedition...' (Dialogue between the desperate man and his son)

The Egyptian Book of the Dead: sacrifice to Osiris.
The god is wearing the atef headdress made from two ostrich plumes and in his hand he carries the whip and sceptre which symbolize supreme power.
Funerary papyrus. New Empire. Louvre, Paris.

Baha'ism

The Baha'i phenomenon sprang from a meeting, at Shiraz in southern Persia (modern Iran), between Mulla Hussayn-i-Bushru'i, a student of Muslim theology, and a young man, Siyyid' Ali-Muhammad who was his host for the evening. The discussion lasted all through the night and at the end of their long meditation on humankind's religious quest, Siyyid' Ali-Muhammad declared himself to be the Bab — the way by which one might reach God.

This was in 1844 when the Bab was 25 years old. Already noted for his natural piety and goodness, he praised the virtue of love, attracted many disciples, and called himself the bearer of a new religion from God and herald of the saviour foretold in all the religions of the past. In September 1844 he made his pilgrimage to Mecca and proclaimed his divine mission. He sent missionaries throughout Persia and many were converted. This caused him to fall foul of the Muslim hierarchy and he was imprisoned and executed on 9 July 1850.

A new prophet

After his death the repression continued. The community found itself in a disastrous situation; the Bab's chosen successor, overcome with fear, fled into the mountains; none of the original 18 disciples survived. It was then that a new prophet appeared. Mirza Hussayn-'Ali, who would later become Baha'u'llah, was born into a noble Persian family. He had no formal education but from his infancy he had a great feeling for religion. He did not know the Bab, never read the Bayan, the book written by the prophet, but by God's grace he was the apostle of his ideas and while in a wretched prison in Teheran he received the 'supreme Spirit'.

He then began to have an exceptionally powerful influence and crowds of Shi'as and Sunnis as well as Christians flocked to hear him. Again the authorities went into action. He was exiled to Baghdad and his belongings were confiscated. For a time he withdrew to the mountains of Kurdistan, but, on his return, his spiritual influence was rekindled and continued to grow. Before a further exile in Constantinople, he announced to a few very close followers that he was 'The one whom God will reveal'.

Such was the birth of a religion which stands in the tradition of the prophets of Judaism, Christianity, and Islam, and for which the Bab is the divine revelation marking the end of the Adamic cycle and Baha'u'llah is the one marking the start of the Baha'i cycle.

The Bayan

The exposition

The precepts of the religion

A book heralding the one promised by God, the Bayan sets out the principles of the new religion founded by the Bab.

In the middle of the 19th century there was a great religious upsurge amongst the Shi'as in Persia. The coming of the hidden Imam, the Promised One, who was to renew the faith before the end of the world was urgently awaited. Some religious groups were spreading the belief in the impending arrival of this messenger. One such group, called the Shaykhi, had even sent out members throughout Persia in search of him. Siyyid' Ali-Muhammad was on this mission when he met the Bab on the night of 23 May 1844.

Consequently, the Bab was accepted as the herald of the messenger. From that moment, gripped by inspiration, he began to write. He would continue writing all his life despite the inconveniences of constant travelling and the dangers of continual persecution. It was in prison in the fortress at Chihriq (the mountain of Sorrow) at a time when his prestige and popularity were growing, when visitors both humble and important flocked to him, and the conditions of his imprisonment were particularly harsh and cruel, that he put the finishing touches to his major work, the *Bayan*.

'The one whom God will reveal'

The *Bayan* claims to be the reference book for the new religion: it warns of the coming of 'The one whom God will reveal', sings his praises, and establishes the laws and precepts which are to apply during this period of waiting. These instructions abolish the requirements of Muslim law concerning prayer, fasting, marriage, divorce, and inheritance in order to establish others, and they give a less material and more spiritual interpretation to the concepts of hell, paradise, and resurrection.

In future, prayers would be said facing the home of the Bab, divorce would be more difficult, only taking place after a year-long reflection and with the consent of both parties, and above all, the whole of life was to be surrounded by love, a pure and selfless love which has no hope of reward and no fear of punishment. The *Bayan* demands equal respect for men and women, and aid to the poor and distressed by means of a common fund organized within the life of the community.

In addition to this moral code there is a high priority given to elementary education, a great emphasis on calligraphy and other manual skills, and a spiritual significance given to the number 19. This has resulted in a calendar made up of 19 months of 19 days each, instead of 12 months of 29 to 30 days as in Islam.

The Kitab-i Akdas

The most holy book

The revelation of God

Baha'u'llah set about making the Kitab-i Akdas the fundamental book of the religion.

Baha'u'llah probably began to write the *Kitab-i Akdas* during his exile in Akko (Acre), after suffering great persecution as a disciple of the Bab and having proclaimed to his followers that he, Baha'u'llah, was in fact the very one foretold by the prophet, 'the one whom God was to reveal'. That was between 1871 and 1874. He had already written to various heads of state throughout the world putting forward his ideas and seeking recognition for his mission promoting peace and unity among men.

Baha'u'llah did not actually write, but made his pronouncements in ringing tones as he paced up and down in his narrow room. All the while there were secretaries feverishly taking down this torrent of words which they would later try to put into order. His speech was in fact a kind of mystical or poetical improvization; this was the master living his faith for all to see and expressing his concerns for the community he led.

The doctrine of the Unity

The book recalls his spiritual development, especially the unforgettable mystical experience he had in prison in Teheran, where he was prevented from sleeping by the heavy chains shackled around his hands, feet, and neck. It was then that the voice of God made itself heard; it announced that

soon people would come to him in their thousands. That marked the beginning of his prophetic mission.

In the Kitab-i Akdas he established the fundamentals of the faith, namely the existence of a totally unknowable God: 'every path leading to him is barred', the notion of creation co-eternal with the creator, and the revelation of God through the prophets from Adam, Zarathustra, the founders of Judaism and Christianity, and Muhammad to the Bab and Baha'u'llah himself, who embodies, for his time, all the prophetic religions which have gone before.

The first divine decree is therefore faith in God, which in fact means faith in him as he is revealed in his prophet. This faith makes one eternal and so continues after death. Heaven and hell are not places but symbolic words signifying the believer's journey towards God and the unbeliever's road to destruction.

The whole doctrine is directed towards that Unity which finds its expression in the truth, and reconciles science to religion and all religions to each other; the Unity of the societies where discrimination is condemned and ultimately the Unity of the whole human race.

The call

'In truth, We will help you, and you and your pen will be the means of that help. Fear nothing ... You are safe. Soon God will raise up the treasures of the earth, that is men who will help you for love of you and your name, through which God gives life to the hearts of the Wise!' (*Kitab-i Akdas*)

Buddhism

Unlike Vedism and Hinduism whose origins are lost in the earliest times, Buddhism takes its origin and essential beliefs from an Indian prince living in the 6th century BC.

Siddharta Gautama, called the Buddha, was born in Kapilavastu, in northern India. All that is known of his life comes from more or less legendary stories. As a child protected by a father anxious to give him nothing but the best in life, he escaped from his palace and was shocked by what he saw of disease, age, and death. At the age of 29, he decided to find a solution to all these problems.

He tried in turn the Brahminical teachings of Hinduism, the discipline of yoga and extreme asceticism, the punishment of the physical body in search of spiritual release, all without being convinced. He then immersed himself in a period of deep meditation. This extreme concentration led him to the discovery of the 'four noble truths' concerning suffering, the origin of suffering, the cessation of suffering, and the path which leads to the cessation of suffering: he had found Enlightenment.

Emergence of the sangha

Having become a wandering priest he went from village to village trying to share his discoveries and his experience. Disciples flocked to him, adopting his way of life. A community (sangha) grew up, consisting of men who followed the path set out by the master and spread his teachings. When the Buddha left this world in his parinirvana, thousands had given up everything to share his frugal life.

'On the seventh day after the master's death, Mahakashyapa called together at Rajagriha 500 arhats (those striving to achieve nirvana), who had overcome domination by their passions. All these thera (elders), the experienced men of the faith, handed over to thera Upali the exposition of the vinaya and to thera Ananda all the other branches of the Dharma (doctrinal duties). All those present repeated in song what they had said.' (*Mahavamsha* III, Mahanaman). This was the first Buddhist council.

The century which followed was a period of great expansion for Buddhism. The monks at Vaisali had become accustomed to receiving gifts of gold and silver, and as such gifts were forbidden by law, a second council was called at Vaisali itself to try and regulate these practices. Seven hundred arhats took part in this. Other differences later led to the council of Pataliputra in 245BC. However, it was not until the council of Ceylon in 35–32BC that the canon or agreed text of Buddhist scriptures was fixed.

Buddha preaching
The Buddha seated in the virasama position, the right leg concealing the left, a position which suggests concentration, and the right hand raised, a gesture called dharmacabra which indicates preaching.

The Vinaya

The basket of discipline

The monastic rule

As true Buddhists the monks are the ones capable of giving extraordinary importance to the observances of the rule.

The community or sangha is governed by the rules set out in the *Vinayapitaka*. This book is a mine of information of all kinds on the life of the first Buddhists. It is made up of fairly long tales criticizing the bad monks, those of the 'gang of six' who cunning, sensual, and indiciplined, had all the vices.

The first part, the *Bhikkuvibhanga* concerns the monks and lists the 227 faults condemned by the Buddha: fornication, murder, theft, and the pretence at holiness are punished by permanent exclusion from the community; masturbation, contact with a woman, racy talk, encouragement to fornicate, acting as a procurer, the setting up

---

The *Tripitaka*

The canonical texts of Buddhism are divided into three huge works known by the name of 'Triple Basket' (*Tripitaka* or *Tipitaka*): the *Vinayapitaka*, the *Suttapitaka*, and the *Abhidhammapitaka*.

Liberty

'Just as the great ocean has only one taste, the taste of salt, so this Dharma and this discipline has only one taste, that of liberty.' (*Vinaya* 11, 237)

---

of unorthodox groupings, slander, and dissent are punished by temporary exclusion; meeting a woman, scandal, and the possession of objects acquired unlawfully have penalties which vary according to the seriousness of the case.

The Buddhist canon

The *Bhikkuvibhanga* goes on to give 90 penances related to faults such as lies, slander, insults or consorting with women, thieves or heretics etc, then it gives the formula for confession; this is the Patimokkha which is considered to be the oldest text of the Buddhist canon. Finally the work ends by setting out the rules of behaviour and the procedures for the settling of quarrels.

The second part, the *Bhikkhunivibhanga* concerns nuns and is similar in structure to the *Bhikkuvibhanga*. However, there are many more faults denounced here and the text appears to be much more severe towards women than towards men. It should be remembered that the Buddha hesitated for a long time before creating communities of nuns.

In both of these sections each fault to be condemned is first illustrated by a vivid lively tale full of humour. Then the atmosphere changes: the style becomes dry and stereotyped, this is the legal language stating the rules which must be applied.

The book ends with the rules concerning worship, dress, traditions; there are accounts of dissensions and schisms, and the means of resolving them, as well as a number of judicial rulings on particular cases: the rehabilitation of guilty monks, the settling of disputes, the duties of the different grades of monks, exclusion from ceremonies and the instruction and ordination of nuns.

The Sutta (Sutra)

The word of Buddha

Discussions about this and that

'And so at a particular moment, records Ananda, I felt the disciple very close.'

The *Suttapitaka* is a prose work which is supposed to have been recited by Ananda at the time of the council of Rajagriha. It is made up of numerous accounts, the sutta or sutra, each of which can stand alone and some of which are long, some short, and some very short indeed.

Each one is placed in specific context: 'At that time the blessed one was living in the Park of the bamboos at the squirrel grounds near to Rajagriha. Then young Sigala, the son of a rich man of property came out ...' (*Sigalovada-Sutta-Dighanikaya* XXXI), and provides the master with an opportunity of explaining some aspect of his thoughts.

Since the synod of Ceylon, c. 32BC it has been the accepted practice to divide the Sutra into five parts.

The Dighanikaya

The first part, the *Dighanikaya* or 'collection of Long Pieces' begins with an explanation of what Buddhist research is: in it are set out the disciplines which help in the mastering of different arts, occupations, and professions. Then they are all roundly condemned. The enlightened person 'gives no great importance to this knowledge. For, within himself, he values another kind of knowledge, the knowledge that this earthly life will be interrupted and will cease, the knowledge of total peace through liberation' (*Dighanikaya* I).

For the Buddhist, true knowledge is that concerned with feelings and emotions, the bitterness and sweetness of them, how they begin and end. True discipline lies in avoiding involvement with them, in breaking free from their spell and escaping them completely.

The *Dighanikaya* strives to be persuasive; so in the section entitled *Brahmajala* or 'Brahma's net', it denounces many philosophical errors. It moralizes and describes the duties of the Buddhist (*Sigalovada* or the 'Address to Sigala') and exalts the virtues of monks (*Sramanyaphala* or 'Fruits of the religious life'). It is edifying and sings the praises of different Buddhists (*Mahavadana* or 'Great Achievements') and especially of Siddharta in his final moments (*Mahaparinirvana*). Finally it is doctrinal, and sets out the 32 major and 80 minor signs which distinguish the Buddhas (*Lakkhama*).

The Majjhimanikaya

The *Majjhimanikaya* consists of the Buddha's medium length speeches: very often these

---

The wounded man

'A man was seriously wounded by a poisoned arrow. His friends and relations fetched a surgeon to take care of him. But the wounded man said: "No, don't touch the arrow. Before you remove it and tend my wound I want to know who shot this arrow. What is his name? What is his caste? Where does he live? Is he tall or short? What is his colouring? What sort of bow did he use? I want answers to all these questions before you begin to treat me"' (*Majjhimanikaya* II)

---

are in the form of incantations in which the same phrases are tirelessly repeated to make a particular idea penetrate not only the brain, the intellect, but the very depth of the being. It is meditation certainly, but meditation in communion with the thought, life, and harmonious rhythm of the Enlightened One.

The subjects tackled vary enormously: the original cause, fear and terror, blessings or damnation. In most cases the Sutra ends with these words: 'The blessed monks delight in the words of the Bhagavat.' However in one instance in the *Mulapariyayasutta* are the words: 'The monks do not delight in the words of the Bhagavat.' The venerable Rahula explains this unusual ending by the fact that this passage was addressed to the Brahmins who had just been admitted to the community, eminent scholars who were proud of their knowledge of the Vedas. But their way of learning was too literal and was incapable of leading them to a deep under-

standing of the Buddha's doctrine and so it would be distressing for them to meet with an obstacle like this.

Buddhism is not a doctrine which can be learnt from books, it is a practice, a discipline of life. 'Consider then monks: a monk experiencing a pleasant sensation knows: "I am experiencing a pleasant sensation"; experiencing an unpleasant sensation he knows: "I am experiencing an unpleasant sensation" ... he remains considering the appearance and disappearance of things in the sensations: "so much for sensations". He goes through this introspection only for purposes of understanding, for reflection, and he remains free with no attachment to anything in the world: He remains simply considering sensations' (*Satipatthanasutta Majjhimanikaya* X).

The Samyuttanikaya

The Samyuttanikaya is another collection of sermons of varying lengths on a wide range of topics. This is one of the collections which contains the famous Benares sermon on the wheel of the law, the Buddha's first discourse given straight after his enlightenment which set out the fundamental beliefs of Buddhism for those who had been his fellow monks during his period of physical self torture as an ascetic.

'O monks, learn that all existence is simply suffering, birth is suffering, old age is suffering. The same goes for death, for union with what one does not care for or separation from what is held dear or the impossibility of satisfying a desire ... At the root of all this sorrow lies the thirst for existence, the thirst for the pleasures experienced through the five external senses and the internal sense' (*Samyuttanikaya* V).

The Buddha goes on to explain his own experience of enlightenment, that experience which opened his eyes and led him to peace, the Middle Way 'which gives the vision, the knowledge, which leads to peace, wisdom, awakening and nirvana (the ultimate goal of freedom from the cycle of reincarnation). The Middle Way avoids the two extremes which are 'craving the pleasures of the senses which is base, vulgar, earthly, ignoble and creates its own bad consequences, and giving oneself over to

Conscience

'Oh monks, that which we call conscience, thought, intellect, appears and disappears in an ever-changing cycle just as night follows day. Just as a monkey playing about in a forest or wood grasps one branch and then lets go of it as he reaches for another, so that which we call conscience, thought, intellect, appears and disappears in an ever-changing cycle, just as night follows day.' (*Samyuttanikaya* II)

Illness

'Bhikkhus, there are two sorts of illness, physical illness and mental illness. It would seem that there are some people who have the good fortune to be exempt from physical illness for a year or two ... But Bhikkhus, there are very few in this world who are exempt for a single instant from mental illness, with the exception of those who are exempt from all mental blemishes (that is to say, the arhats).' (*Anguttaranikaya*)

mortification which is painful, ignoble and creates its own bad consequences'. The Middle Way is the noble eightfold path 'that is: the right view, right thoughts, right speech, right action, right means of living, right endeavour, right attention, and right concentration' (*Sacca-Samyutta* II, 1).

The Anguttaranikaya

This so-called supplementary collection is also very old. It betrays efforts to systemize the doctrine and uses a rather dry style, a more disciplined organization and a great many classifications.

It contains this piece of advice from the Buddha, something quite exceptional in the history of religions: 'It is right for you to experience doubt and perplexity ... do not allow yourselves to be guided by relationships, traditions or what you have heard said. Do not allow yourselves to be guided by the authority of religious texts or by simple logic ... When you know for yourself that certain things are unfavourable, false, and bad, then renounce them ... And, when you know for yourself that certain things are favourable and good, then accept and follow them' (*Anguttaranikaya*).

In effect the Buddhist is not directed from outside, by what he is told or what he feels or by what he understands. Extinction (nirvana) is an internal experience, independent of words and things, and then 'having willed, the enlightened person acts by means of the body, the word and the instrument of the mind' (*Anguttaranikaya*).

He is on 'the Middle Way': 'One thing is considered childish according to mystical experience, namely: an immoderate laugh where the teeth are shown. If you are happy in a way which is acceptable according to the Dharma (or code of behaviour), a smile is all that is required for showing this' (*Anguttaranikaya* I, 260).

The Khuddakanikaya

These are minor texts although they make up by far the most voluminous of the nikaya. They bring together works more or less closely related to the sutta and act as illustrations for them. The *Khuddakanikaya* gathers together 15 collections which differ greatly in style, importance, and subject matter. The first, the *Khuddakapatha*, is simply a collection of appendices to the sutta.

The second collection, the *Dhammapada*

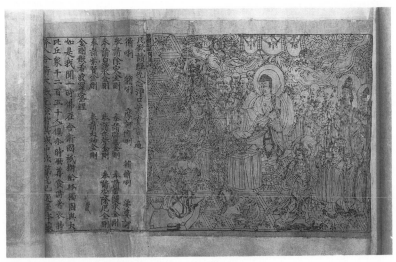

Buddha, surrounded by Bodhisattva (aspiring Buddhas).
*Wood carving of the **Sutra of the diamond**.*
Coll. Sir Aurel Stein.

or 'Verses of the Dhamma' is the best known and the most poetic. It has 423 stanzas of four feet, arranged in 26 chapters according to subject matter, which covers a wide range of topics: vigilance, flowers, the holy, old age, pleasure etc. These writings contain the essence of the Buddha's moral teachings.

The third collection, called the *Udana* is composed of maxims written in verse. The fourth, the *Itivuttaka* are words attributed to the Buddha. The *Suttanipata* are stories punctuated by long philosophical arguments: 'When the waves rise up, the fearsome waves which surround those who are overwhelmed by age and death, do they find an island? That is what I have to teach you ... There where there is nothing, where no attachment to anything exists, that is island, and that alone: that is what I call nirvana, the end of age and death' (*Suttanipata* 1093–4).

The *Vimanavatthu* is a collection of moral tales where virtue is always rewarded. The *Petavatthu* is its exact counterpart and gathers together stories where vice is always punished. So the first evokes heavenly dwellings (the paradise of the just), the second the ghosts who remain at the mercy of transmigrations (passing into another state or death): the intrinsic and inexorable justice which governs retribution for actions.

The *Theragatha* and the *Therigatha* bring together poems by some of the Buddha's leading disciples and by nuns famous for their virtue. All these verses — there are some 1279 in the first work and 522 in the second — are of great literary merit, but often use rather obscure language. They include some of India's finest religious poems.

The *Jataka* makes up the largest collection. This groups together accounts given by the Buddha himself of his previous existences, those of his disciples or just those of the people he was speaking to. It tells how Siddharta followed a long path through several existences before reaching Buddha status: being a pious monarch, he made a vow never to refuse anything that might be asked of him; thus he made a gift of an elephant invaluable for the prosperity of the land and lost his throne, then he was asked to give up his children who were made into slaves, and later even his wife. However, the maker of these demands was a god come to test him and everything turned out well in the end (*Jataka* 547).

The *Niddesa* is simply a kind of index of the sutras and a commentary which would have been compiled by Sariputta, one of the first disciples. The *Patisambhida Magga* is a theoretical treatise on doctrine. The *Apadana* are accounts in praise of the kindness of the first disciples, in short a sort of golden legend. In the *Buddhavamsa*, Buddha recounts his own life and that of the Buddhas who have gone before him.

Finally, the *Cariya Pitaka* or 'basket of behaviour' repeats 35 of the themes in the *Jataka* emphasizing the fact that during his previous lives the Buddha acquired the 10 great perfections: generosity, goodness, sacrifice, wisdom, steadfastness, patience, truthfulness, resolution, kindness, calmness of spirit.

Flowers

'The man who likes gathering pleasures like flowers is overtaken by death which will carry him away like a river bursting its banks carries away a sleeping village. He who eagerly gathers the flowers of pleasure is surprised by death before being satisfied. Wise is he who lives in his village as the bee gathers nectar, without damaging the flower's colour or perfume.' (*Dhammapada* 47–9)

Pain

'All counterfeit tendencies are fleeting ... and everything of a fleeting nature ends in pain. All that is pain is free from Self and what is free from Self is empty.' (*Udana vagga* XII, 5–8)

The Abhidhamma (Abhidharma)

The basket of doctrine

Comments and arguments

Abhidhamma is where the psychologies and theories of various factions meet, clash, and pit themselves against each other in order to arrive at the most essential part of the doctrine.

The *Vinayapitaka* which sets out the precise rules of monastic life was not pointless: the Buddhist monks were particularly fond of controversies and intellectual speculation. These discussions were even inflamed on occasion by pride, jealousy or economic competition and political intrigues. Since the 4th century BC the community had been divided into sects, each of which had their own interpretations of the doctrinal and disciplinary teachings of the Buddha.

Each group would therefore do its best to go into some point of doctrine to clarify and sharpen its arguments. It was a question of supporting its own opinions and refuting the position held by its opponents. This led to a great intellectual upsurge. Soon there appeared summaries of doctrine, and various types of catechism setting out dogma in dry systematic formulae. Each faction had its own version.

An explanatory work

At the council of Ceylon, c. 35–32 BC, which led to the final establishment of the canon of the Scriptures, there could be no question of leaving aside these debates between the various factions which had done so much to increase the understanding of the

doctrine. So without any real attempt at sorting out the different schools of thought all of these documents were gathered together to form the third collection of the *Tripitaka*.

The *Abhidhammapitaka* is therefore made up of statements, which seem artificial, cold and impersonal, concerning various questions often left unanswered by the other two parts of the *Tripitaka*. It is a tight coverage of Buddhist philosophy, a work of subtle and contradictory interpretation with various points of detail leading to long lines of reasoning. Many a schism or split amongst the believers has had its origin in this book.

The *Abhidhammapitaka*, also called 'the basket of reflection on the law' comprises seven books which strive to 'classify systematically the physico-physical phenomena' (*Histoire du bouddhisme indien* (*History of Indian Buddhism*), Lamotte). It instructs us in the state of the sciences in every department from grammar to medicine. Those involved in controversies turned to it in search of arguments but at the same time they were weaving together threads of understanding and a kind of Buddhist system was emerging.

Obviously things did not stop at that. There were to be commentaries on the *Abhidhammapitaka* and commentaries on the commentaries.

Heretics

'The monks of the Great Assembly have distorted the teachings. They have broken up the original writings and have compiled them differently. They have taken one chapter from its original place and put it somewhere else. They have altered the meaning and doctrine of the five nikaya.'
(*Dipavamsa* V, 32)

The Bardo Thodol

The Tibetan Book of the Dead

The journey beyond death

This guide is for all those wishing to break through the barrier of death, making it an act of liberation.

Buddhism was introduced to Tibet in the 8th century by Shantarakshita, but he failed to take into account the traditions and customs of the inhabitants and they soon drove him out. Another attempt was made later by Padmasambhava. He proved to be more sensitive and diplomatic. He did not make an all-out attack on the ancestral beliefs of the people but integrated them fairly successfully into his doctrine. And so Tibetan Buddhism has some particular characteristics of its own.

Buddhist orthodoxy

In a religion which is passed on mainly from a master to his disciples, differences in interpretation tend to be more pronounced. Conflict soon arose between the teachers from India, who insisted on the necessity of good works in successive lives in order to achieve enlightment, and the reachers from China who emphasized physical and mental activity, the main obstacle to the recognition of one's true nature in a Buddha.

King Khri-sron Ide-bean decided to establish orthodoxy once and for all. He brought the adversaries together, there followed long debates lasting more than two years, and the Indian gurus won the day. Then the Chinese were driven out of the country, the monastries looted, and the monks scattered. It was a full scale persecution. In the chaos of their defeat these outcasts and hermits, men on the run, hid their writings and books wherever they could, in caves or among the rocks. These were the 'treasure books' or gterma-texts.

Again and again over the centuries documents were hidden like this in troubled times. But from time to time some of them have come to light and with these discoveries the teachings of the past have been revived in a new generation of followers. Their task has been not only to make known what they have found, but to be true disciples, and their reactions, comments, and contributions are all inspired as if the guru were present and encouraging them. The respect in which these revelations have subsequently been held, the recognition which the community has given to them and the value of the ideas they expound have guaranteed them undisputed status as sacred works.

The *Bardo Thodol* was discovered in this way in the 14th century by Karmalingpa on Mount Gampodar. But the core of this work was written by Padmasambhava, the person who really introduced Buddhism to Tibet. Karmalingpa entrusted it to his son, charging him to pass it on to one person only and so on for three generations. During the

The intermediate states

'Our son, you are now going to test out three intermediate states, that of the hour of death, that of the truth within and that of destiny. Until yesterday you were in the bardo of the moment of death and, although the light of the Truth within appeared to you, you did not recognize it. So you must wander here once more. Now, however, you are going to experience the intermediate state of the Truth within and that of your destiny. Mark with care all that I show you.' (*Bardo Thodol* II)

ensuing centuries, the book took on great authority among various Buddhist groups in Tibet.

A ritual?

The *Bardo Thodol* appears as a ritual to be followed at the time of death. But it is more than a formal ritual; it is a method which can be adopted to enable a dead person to free himself from rebirth and attain Buddhahood. The procedure can be long or short according to the readiness of the person concerned. The intermediate state between death and the next rebirth, the *Bardo*, can last several days, or even weeks: some Tibetan Buddhists say between 20 and 49 days.

For this reason funeral rites in Tibet last for seven weeks. The passage of the soul from one life to the next can be greatly helped by a lama, or some other friend of the deceased, performing the different beneficial services of the *Bardo Thodol* on his behalf and in communion with him.

The path to Buddhahood

Three stages are given. The first is the *Chikai Bardo*, the state of consciousness which corresponds to 'the moment when external breathing stops and internal breath is not yet broken'. The text points out that this state may last as long as it takes to eat a meal. The dead person does not know that he is dead, he is astounded to find the world suddenly so different, he is no longer flesh and blood, and can take himself off wherever he wishes without hindrance. What he has to do is gain the vision of the 'clear primordial light' (the light which has existed from the beginning of creation). This is his first chance of reaching nirvana. If he does not succeed he goes on to the second stage.

In the course of the *Chonyid Bardo* he is brought before peaceful deities who represent knowledge, wisdom, equanimity, dis-

crimination, the fulfilment of actions and who release different states of being, from the state of god to that of anti-god by way of the human state. After this, however, he will meet wrathful deities who represent his own karma (his fate determined by his actions), the weight of his deeds. At this stage he may win the compassion of the Buddha and Bodhisattva (aspiring Buddhas-to-be), but if he does not manage to do that, he continues on his way to another birth and arrives at stage three.

The *Sidpa Bardo* is the most perilous. Confronted with his failures the dead man 'experiences a deep personal fear. He feels deprived of his body, pursued, hounded, at the mercy of the cold and the storm, and he looks for a refuge. Winds, darkness, flames, avalanches, furies, and demons are unleashed upon him and force him to plunge into any available womb.' According to the book the mental body experiences a deep longing to have a material body once more. The aim of the prayers is to prevent the new incarnation from taking place in unfavourable conditions.

The lesson of the *Bardo Thodol* is that man need not be overcome by worry and distress in the face of death, but should stay serene and vigilant at all times. It puts forward the idea of man taking responsibility for his destiny and the search for freedom. It is a religious book but the experiences which it describes also make it a mystical work.

The mental body

'What does the previous and future body of flesh signify? The previous one means that you have a body of flesh and blood formed by your past tendencies. But it is radiant and also possesses characteristic signs of the golden age. It is called the mental body, for it is the one appearing in the bardo. It shows what is contained in the mental.'
(*Bardo Thodol* III)

The Milindapanha

Milinda's questions

The Buddhist catechism, a method of instruction through set questions and answers

King Milinda picks his way through the questions he asks on the different religions of his time.

Milinda is the Sanskrit name of a Greek who built himself a kingdom in the north of India around the second century BC. He reigned for about 30 years in the ancient city of Sakala. An intelligent man, acquainted with all the philosophical doctrines of his day, he often felt the need to exchange ideas with scholars passing through his city.

All the people spreading the religions of that time, particularly the Brahmins, were invited to come and debate with the king. He would argue with them in the manner of Socrates and Plato and they would soon be

Permanence of the self

'A betrothed girl had been bought from her father whilst still a little girl. The buyer thought that when she was older she would be his wife. He left on a journey. The girl grew up and having reached marriageable age was due to take a husband. Her father was in a difficult situation; in the end he gave her to a second suitor who became her husband. But then along came the first man who insisted that the woman be given back to him. But the husband replied: "This woman, whom I have married, is not your betrothed. The little girl of long ago is not the same as this adult woman who is now my wife. It is true that we are at one and the same time identical and non-identical to ourselves."' (*Milindapanha* II, 2–6)

reduced to silence and then sent away disappointed. At this time the Buddhist monk, Nagasena, was going from village to village; he had a great reputation in the land. Rumours of his expected arrival in Sakala reached the king who was anxious to see him.

A Buddhist asceticism

As soon as the monk arrived, Milinda posed the question of the non-existence of the self, one of the principles of Buddhism: how can we assert such a thing when each feels himself, on the contrary, to be the same yesterday and today or today and tomorrow. Nagasena then set about his reply. He used rational arguments, parables, examples from history, stories, legends, in short every possible form of persuasion. Following the question of the self came other questions concerning reincarnation, the Karma, the law etc. In fact the whole of Buddhist teaching was covered and closely argued during these sessions.

When all his doubts were resolved by Nagasena, the king, his mind at ease and full of admiration for Buddhism, handed the throne over to his son and withdrew from the world. He became an arhat following the eightfold path. In time he was known as a just man and saviour.

The *Milindapanha* is written in a brisk and lively style. The dialogue does not flag as critics of the Buddhist doctrines are disposed of one by one and the teaching is clearly set out. It bears a similarity to the style of the treatises of Greek philosophy. The core of this book seems to have served as a summary of the doctrine for the Greek and Eurasian populations in northern India.

Central America

The Maya religion of the classical era (3rd–10th centuries) is chiefly known through its works of art. These reveal the presence of a sun god (Palenque), a corn god (Copan), a snake god (Yaxchilan), and a rain god (Chac), whose Mexican equivalent is Tlaloc. If Hunab Ku was the creator god, who ruled over all the gods, Itzamma was the god of the sky, the civilizing god. In all the civilizations of this region, gods were ambivalent, sometimes doing good and at other times doing evil.

The passage of time was particularly important for these peoples. They used ingenius types of calendar to measure it: they held that each person's fate could be determined from the date of their birth. In the Aztec society the length of a man's life was bound up with the fates. Among the Mayas, time was marked out by the erection of standing stones. The Katun was a period of 7200 days: at the beginning of each Katun a stone was erected; after a quarter of the Katun, another stone was erected, with another at the halfway point and another at the end. These stones are masterpieces of sculpture; they bear various date signs, the phases of the moon, the positions of the stars and planets. The heavenly bodies seem to have figured very prominently in the inscriptions: the planet Venus, the Pole Star and many others are represented, each one corresponding to a particular god.

Some stones describe human sacrifices but these were probably rare. In the main, it was animals that were sacrificed and the usual offerings made to gods were of incense. However, the faithful occasionally cut their limbs or their tongue in order to give their blood to the gods. There were many ritual dances, dances involving masks and costumes, with each dancer representing a god.

Several Central American civilizations have left books. These are usually in the form of long strips of parchment or paper, folded like a fan, on which signs have been drawn or painted. Many of these books were destroyed at the time of the Spanish conquest; this was part of the Christian missionaries' desire to remove all traces of idolatry, 'because there were none of them', said Bishop Diego de Landa, 'which did not contain superstition and devilish lies'. Those which have come down to us are made up of religious themes; they are concerned with rituals or methods of foretelling the future. The ancient Mexicans held the office of scribe in very high esteem.

The Tonalamatl

The Book of Days

A tool for telling the future

To the Central Americans, knowledge of the calendar and knowledge of destiny were one and the same thing.

One of the main functions of Central American socieites was that concerning the interpretation of signs. It was performed by the Tonalpouhque among the Aztecs and by the Chilam for the Mayas. These were highly respected figures, whose task was to keep the calendar, read it, interpret it and discover from it the fate of each person at their birth, and pinpoint the best times for taking personal or public action, in short to regulate their lives.

One example of this *Tonalamatl* or calendar has come down to us. This is the codex *Borbonicus*, now held in the library of the Assemblée Nationale in Paris. It consists of a manuscript of paint on paper made from bark. Folded concertina style, it is made up of sheets, each one covering 13 days. Each sheet is dedicated to two divinities, and each day is symbolized by signs, birds, numbers or other emblems. It would require a specialist to read this kind of document.

The white lords

'They taught fear and came to wither the flowers; so that their flower might live, they have damaged and destroyed the flower of others ... They will know the meaning of what is said here when they read it.' (*Book of Chilam-Balam*, Chumayel)

Three cycles

In this region, the calendar is by no means a simple thing. It depends on the interaction of three astronomical cycles: the ritual cycle of 260 days, the solar cycle of 365 days, and the cycle of Venus which is 584 days. Thus the date of an event can be simultaneously pinpointed in each of these three cycles and it is only every 56 years that the first two come into conjunction and only every 104 years that there is conjunction between all three cycles.

This correlation, together with the reading of signs and images written on the *Tonalamatl*, which also give indications as to directions and places, allows the priest to tell the future. Destinies are in effect decided in an uncompromising way by factors of time and space even before the people are actually born. Consequently, the indicators which are used to foresee natural phenomena are also used to determine the fortunes of particular individuals or enterprises.

The Chilam knows his secrets and, in order to bring about a certain outcome, he will fix the dates of social events and might, for example, suggest waiting a few days before naming a child born under an inauspicious sign. But time marches on inexorably and there is really little hope of escaping its hold. The gods themselves are subject to it. So, the sign 1 *acatl* marks the fate of Quetzalcoatl, the god of Plants, and because of that he must appear in the east in the form of the morning star.

The soothsayer-priests, masters of writing, seem to have set down their revelations in writing. Some *Books of Chilam-Balam* came to light after the terrible destruction during the conquest. These are disjointed and rather roughly handled later copies of collections which must have been the records of the tradition.

There are known to be 18 more or less exact translations of these actual chronicles and records of the time: they are named after the place where they were discovered; the most notable are the Mani *Book of the Chilam-Balam*, and those from Titzimin, Chumayel, Tuniz etc.

These accounts are generally written in very stark language. They are more like chronological references than real narratives and more like catalogues of past events than predictions of what is to come.

Moreover, there are few contradictions between the different Chilam-Balam books. It is in fact the calendar of events which follows the ritual calendar and the astronomical calendar of the *Tonalamatl*.

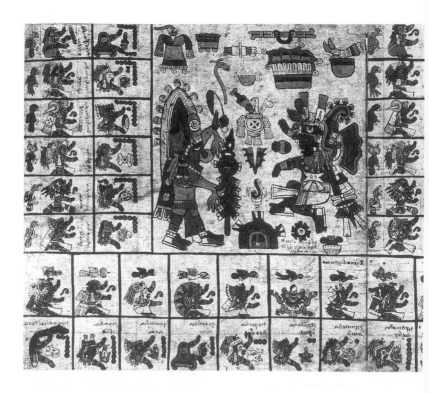

*This page of the **Tonalamatl** shows how complicated it is to read. The only things to go on here are the two divinities depicted in the centre, who govern the 13 days related to this drawing.*

The Popol Vuh

Collection of writings

Accounts of our origins

How the world was created, how civilization developed, and how the Quechua became a nation.

The origins of the *Popol Vuh* are rather vague. Our only knowledge of it comes from copies made under the influence of the colonizing Spaniards: the exact text was not finally established until the 19th century. However, experts do recognize that it is very ancient in origin: it concerns the heroic and mythical saga of the Quechua Indians of Guatemala. Its discoverer, Brasseur de Bourbourg, refers to it as their sacred book.

The *Popol Vuh* gives an account of the Creation: 'In the beginning Hurakan wanders in thick, empty darkness over a great mass of water.' He creates the earth by giving a great shout. Then the gods hold a meeting. They decide on the creation of

'They had not slept, they remained awake, great moans came from their hearts and stomachs while they waited on their knees for the break of day ... Then the sun began to rise in the sky, and the animals, great and small, were filled with joy, all those which were still in the valleys climbed to the tops of the mountains, and together they all turned and looked towards the place where the sun was rising. Then the pumas and jaguars roared. The Queletzu was the first bird to sing. All the animals rejoiced, the eagles and the kites flapped their wings.' (*Popol Vuh*)

animals, but man presents some difficulties; there is no model for this type of superior being, capable of 'saying the name of gods, sustaining them and feeding them' by their prayers and offerings. So they begin by making shapes out of earth, but these can neither speak nor move and they crumble with the rain.

A second attempt is made using wooden dolls to which the gods give life. The creators are satisfied at first and these 'Humans' people the face of the earth. But the men of wood, deprived of reason and memory, became shallow and irreverent and the gods send a flood to destroy them. Some of them are supposed to have survived the disaster, fled deep into the woods and given birth to a race of monkeys.

Only the third attempt is successful: it is achieved with white corn and yellow corn on which men were to feed themselves. The gods make four men out of a paste of corn and these four are the ancestors of humanity: they are so handsome, so good, so intelligent, and so wise that the gods soon take umbrage. They are afraid that they may have created rivals for themselves, and send a vapour to dull their minds and make them lose knowledge.

The book goes on to tell of the adventures of two brothers, Hunahpu and Ixbalanqué. They are conceived as the result of a spell by the virgin-mother Xquic, and they have to go through numerous tests laid down by the evil spirits of Xibalbay. But their knowlege of sorcery gets them out of the situation and, after a long story, filled with stormy episodes and told with remarkable imagination and imagery, they become the Sun and the Moon.

The *Popol Vuh* then records the origins of the Quechua people, their different dynasties and their conquests.

Christianity

If Christianity is accepted as a direct descendant of Judaism, it could be seen not merely as a continuation of it, but as its culmination. This idea was so strong that Christianity had some difficulty in establishing its distinctive nature. For years Christian observances were additions to ones which were strictly Jewish and to outsiders Christianity simply appeared as a sect of Judaism. It was the work of Saint Paul and the communities from pagan backgrounds which were decisive in making the distinction between the two religions.

The fact remains that the 'Law and the Prophets' whose origin is uniquely Jewish, have kept all their authority within the new religion and their divine inspiration and sacred nature have never been called into question. The differences between the Hebrew Bible and the Old Testament as Christianity knows it can be explained historically by the fact that the agreed texts, or canons, of the Scriptures of these two religions were not established until long after the founding of Christianity. So Christianity has included in its holy books works that Judaism did not have in its official list, such as those of *Tobit, Judith* the *Maccabees* etc. However, these books remain essentially Jewish and have been covered in the section on Judaism.

The most notable difference perhaps lies in how each tradition interprets this literature. Christians only see the Old Testament as the forerunner of the Good News brought by Jesus Christ, they only read the *Torah* through the mirror of the Gospel and sometimes hold that there is an important break between the old and new patterns of salvation. The common expressions of Old Testament and New Testament, Old Covenant and New Covenant, are not without significance.

Thus, without disregarding the Law and the Prophets which maintain their fundamental worth, the Church has placed the Gospels, the *Acts of the Apostles*, the *Epistles*, and the *Revelation* of John on a higher plane. These are the books which, though full of quotations from the old texts, bear witness to the earliest days of Christianity, establish its origins, and document its basis. They are the supreme authority, always having the last word after Abraham, Moses, Isaiah or any other prophet. They are the word of the Son of God incarnate, something which nothing else could ever claim to be. The Gospel is the ultimate Revelation.

The new Church

The New Testament is, moreover, very well arranged, as if the hand of God had a part in it — or was perhaps responsible for it all. It falls into three distinctive parts. The first is made up of the four Gospels: they describe the life of Jesus, his teaching, and his redeeming work. This is the foundation, not only of the new Church, but of the new humanity. These events constitute the establishment of a new relationship with

24

God, one which has changed from submission to love. From the moment of the Resurrection everything is fulfilled but not necessarily understood.

The second part concerns the beginning of the history of the Church. This comprises the *Acts of the Apostles* and the *Epistles*. It covers a time of learning, of transformation, of testing and maturing which will last until the end of time. It stands in the intervening period between the two advents of Jesus Christ, that of his earthly life and that of his proclaimed coming in glory. During this time there is to be no cosmic upheaval or radical change, but rather the sharing of an understanding, the introduction of humankind to the new order of relationship with God, the task of making redemption real in time and place. It is the time for faith to be nurtured and to grow.

Finally, *Revelation* evokes paradise. In enigmatic and mysterious terms, using strange and fantastic images, and an abundance of rather obscure symbols, Saint John brings us to the final act: the end of time, the cosmic catastrophe, the final defeat of the powers of evil, the victory of the God of Love, the resurrection of the body and the last Judgment. The story of salvation is now at an end. We have passed from the earthly Jerusalem, so often unfaithful to her God, to the celestial Jerusalem, eternal and blessed.

The Old Testament traces the whole history of the chosen people from the Creation to the coming of the Messiah: the New Testament represents the history of humankind from the coming of the Messiah to the end of the world. For the Christian, time is divided in two: before and after Christ. All that has gone before proclaims, prepares for, and indicates what is to come, but remains of lesser importance. All that follows the death and resurrection of Christ, the salvation and redemption of man, the spread of the believers throughout the world and the life to come, is of a different order, quite distinct from anything that has gone before.

In a way Christianity is a religion of the Book, as Islam acknowledges. The writers of the holy books were inspired, that is to say they were free and intelligent instruments in the hands of the Holy Spirit expressing the Word of God which has made itself heard throughout history. For this reason the Bible has great authority in the tradition of the Church.

The four evangelists *with their traditional symbols drawn from Revelation: a man for Matthew, a lion for Mark, a bull for Luke, and an eagle for John.*
The Hautvillers Miniatures *in the 'Gospels of Hebron' (9th century).*
Bibliothèque municipale, Epernay.

The Gospel according to Matthew

The Jewish Gospel

The role of Christ and of the Church

The story of Jesus is told as good news intended to encourage and sustain the Faith.

The first Gospel is usually attributed to Saint Matthew, the tax collector Jesus called to be an apostle. He may perhaps have been responsible for one of the sources of this Gospel and might well have written an earlier version in Aramaic. He is not, apparently, the author of the Greek version which is the only one that has come down to us.

Whatever the case, the author (or authors) quote freely from the Jewish Scriptures, use expressions common in Palestine without explanations and are perfectly familiar with the customs of the region. Matthew's Gospel is directed at the Jews. Its aim is to show that Christ enters their long history of salvation and is indeed the Messiah promised by the Prophets.

The calling of the disciples

'As Jesus walked along the shore of Lake Galilee, he saw two brothers who were fishermen, Simon (called Peter) and his brother Andrew, catching fish in the lake with a net. Jesus said to them, "Come with me, and I will teach you to catch men". At once they left their nets and went with him. He went on and saw two other brothers, James and John, the sons of Zebedee. They were in their boat with their father, getting their nets ready. Jesus called them and at once they left the boat and their father, and went with him. (*Matthew*, 18–22)

Who is Jesus?

The wish to prove that Jesus is the Messiah is apparent in the very first lines: the genealogy covers the whole history of the Jews from the time of Abraham. There are also the exceptional events surrounding the child's birth: Mary's conceiving while a virgin, the visit of the wise men and the flight into Egypt to escape King Herod's jealousy. The holy family then settles in Nazareth and the prophecy is fulfilled that 'He will be called a Nazarene'.

So Jesus lives a life similar to other men until the moment of his baptism by John in the Jordan. It is then that one of the first manifestations of the Trinity, the threefold God, occurs: heaven was opened, the Spirit of God came down like a dove and the voice of the Father declared: 'This is my beloved son, with whom I am well pleased'. It is as if Jesus was being enthroned as Messiah.

From that moment the Gospel goes on to make it clear just who Jesus is. He is the Son of God, as we have seen, but he is also man with all the trials which that involves. Satan makes no mistake about that as he confronts him and tries to bring him down. Three temptations folow one another: the first two challenge Jesus to make God act, firstly to provide him with bread after fasting and then to save him from a fall: the third is nothing less than an invitation to idolatry. Jesus unwaveringly replies by quoting the Law of Moses.

The Sermon on the Mount

Strengthened by this newly acquired authority Jesus is able to call his disciples and begin his teaching. It is in the Sermon on the Mount that the first Gospel gathers together the fundamental doctrines. He speaks, first to his disciples, the salt of the earth and the light of the world, then to the crowds who flock to him. Jesus seems to be all powerful in his words.

He is quite shocking in his extremism. In a country which has struggled for centuries to have a land, to be independent, to set up a kingdom, addressing a people which glorifies its heroes, Jesus states authoritatively: blessed are the poor, blessed are the meek, blessed are the persecuted, blessed are the hungry. It is the exact opposite of what makes men powerful. Of course there had been Isaiah and the suffering servant, there had been Jeremiah and Ezekiel. But never before had it been said with such force and conviction that salvation lay in weakness.

The Kingdom of Heaven as he declared it was decidedly different from what many of his listeners had in mind. Yet Jesus did not come 'to abolish the Law but to fulfil it', and in order to fulfil it he explored it in depth and drew out the very essence of it. In the past your ancestors were told: do not commit murder; I tell you: whoever is angry with his brother will be brought to trial. It was said: do not commit adultery; but I tell you: whoever looks at a woman wanting to possess her has already committed adultery in his heart.

The Beatitudes

'Happy are those who know they are spiritually poor; the kingdom of heaven belongs to them. Happy are those who mourn; God will comfort them. Happy are those who are humble; they will receive what God has promised. Happy are those whose greatest desire is to do what God requires; God will satisfy them fully. Happy are those who are merciful to others; God will be merciful to them. Happy are the pure in heart; they will see God. Happy are those who work for peace; God will call them his children. Happy are those who are persecuted because they do what God requires; the kingdom of heaven belongs to them. Happy are you when people insult you and persecute you and tell all kinds of evil lies against you because you are my followers. Be happy and glad for a great reward is kept for you in heaven.' (*Matthew* 5, 3-12)

The miracles

'The crowd was amazed at the way he taught.' He spoke with such authority that they sensed that he was no ordinary prophet. From one who preached with such assurance within himself about such essential questions, anything could be asked, even miracles, and they were not long in coming: there followed the miracles of the leper, the centurion's paralysed servant, the two blind men, the people possessed by demons, the stilling of the storm etc. Here Jesus showed himself to be all powerful in his actions.

But he had pity on the crowds 'who are like sheep without a shepherd'. So, having called the twelve disciples 'he gave them authority over unclean spirits, with power to drive them out and to heal all kinds of sickness and disease', and he sent them out to preach that the kingdom of heaven was near. This was the time for Jesus to give his advice: 'Speak freely and without fear, whoever declares himself for me before men, I will declare myself for him before my Father in heaven. But the task is demanding: whoever loves father and mother more than me is not worthy of me; beware of men, you will be persecuted.'

The parables

Opposition was already mounting: the Pharisees, jealous of his authority set traps for him, maligned him, and looked for a way to get rid of him. Then Jesus shows a sterner side: 'I have not come to bring peace, but a sword'. He rails against the towns which saw his miracles but did not believe. Then he states that the kingdom belongs to the simple, the poor, and the children who have no say in the world, and not to the powerful ones who do, and he thanks his Father for this. The kingdom is not of this world.

Then, he begins to speak in parables: those who have ears to hear, let them hear. It is true that one must be open and have a certain receptiveness if one is to understand the mysteries of the kingdom. For there are mysteries: it is a question, not of the realities of this world within the grasp of every one of us, but of the realities of another world, a spiritual world and the parable allows for the comparison of the one with the other.

Parables about the sower, the weeds, the mustard seed, the yeast, the hidden treasure, each reveal one aspect of the kingdom of heaven: it is the word sown like a seed which does or does not take root; it is the good seed — or the subjects of the kingdom — mingled with weeds — or the subjects of the Devil — it is the mustard seed, the smallest seed of all, which grows into a tree, an image of the future spread of the kingdom. Similarly with the yeast and the treasure etc.

But relations between Jesus and the powers that be grew worse. Herod became enraged and had John the Baptist executed. During this time the crowds continued to flock to Jesus. He fed them all with five loaves and two fishes, walked on water to strengthen the faith of his disciples, appeared in glory to three of them, and confirmed Peter as the head of his Church: 'You are a rock and on this rock I will build my Church'.

The Passion and Resurrection

Jesus had already declared on three occasions that he would have to suffer and die. Yet he went up to Jerusalem, made a trium-

Jesus condemns the Pharisees

'How terrible for you, teachers of the Law and Pharisees! You hypocrites! You lock the door to the kingdom of heaven in people's faces and you yourselves don't go in, nor do you allow in those who are trying to enter! How terrible for you, teachers of the Law and Pharisees! You hypocrites! You sail the seas and cross whole countries to win one convert; and when you succeed, you make him twice as deserving of going to hell as you yourselves are! How terrible for you blind guides! You teach: If someone swears by the Temple he isn't bound by his vow; but if he swears by the gold in the Temple, he is bound. Blind fools! Which is more important, the gold or the Temple which makes the gold holy? ...'
(*Matthew* 23, 13–18)

phal entry into the city, cleared the Temple of merchants who had turned it into a robbers' den, and comforted the priests and elders of the people who were again questioning his authority. As far as they were concerned he was frank and direct: 'How terrible for you scribes and Pharisees, you hypocrites! ...' If the crowd was with him, the 'Princes of the Temple', the Pharisees and important men of the land resented him. Gradually a plot was hatched against him.

After that events moved quickly, Judas agreed to hand Jesus over to the high priests. Jesus called his disciples for a farewell meal and instituted the Eucharist or holy communion, saying as he took the bread: 'This is my body, do this in remembrance of me'. Then Jesus spent a night in Gethsemane agonizing over what was to happen. There he was arrested, brought before the Sanhedrin or Council of the Temple, and judged by Pilate, the Roman governor, whilst Peter repeatedly denied all knowledge of him; he was mocked, insulted, beaten and finally crucified on the hill of Golgotha: that was on the Friday.

Buried that same evening by Joseph of Arimathea, who gave his own tomb for the purpose and guarded by armed soldiers to prevent any trickery, by the Sunday he had disappeared, the tomb was empty: he had risen from the dead. He later appeared in Galilee to the eleven disciples (Judas having killed himself) and said to them: 'Go to all the nations, and make them my disciples: baptize them in the name of the Father, the Son, and the Holy Spirit.'

This is where the Good News ends and the history of the Church begins. The *Gospel According to Matthew* marks the transition from the Messiah proclaimed by the Prophets to Jesus, from the Old Testament sealed by Moses to the New Covenant sealed in Christ, from the salvation reserved for the chosen people to its extension to include the whole world (represented by the tax collector, the prostitute, the centurian). This book demonstrates the role of Christ and that of his Church.

Saint Matthew's Christ is serious, dignified and priest-like. The first Gospel is the only one to mention the power given to Peter over the church to come.

The Gospel according to Mark

The testimony of Peter

The Good News

Jesus is revealed as the Messiah, but insists on secrecy until the Resurrection.

The *Gospel according to Mark* is the oldest of the Gospels. It would have been written between AD 63 and 70. The author was probably one of Saint Peter's disciples who had not seen the events he was reporting but took down in a slightly untidy fashion the words spoken by his master in the course of his preaching. Examination of the text seems to suggest that he was speaking to a non-Jewish audience since there are very few quotations in it from the Law and the Prophets.

The Nazarene

What we have here are recollections from preaching, so the author's main interest is the public life of the Lord. Mark begins with the preaching of John the Baptist. He omits all that happened before this. There is no mention of the birth, nor Bethlehem, nor Jesus's boyhood in Nazareth, nor his parents. It is as if his consecration occurred at a stroke when he received God's full approval at the moment of his baptism by John.

Mark calls Jesus the Nazarene, the Master or again the Son of Man, but never the Saviour. Jesus preached firstly to the crowds in Galilee announcing that the right time had come, he healed many people, and spent time with fishermen and tax collectors. The numbers following him were so great that he had to go away into isolated places: 'and they came to him from all over the country'.

His teaching went against the opinions of the scribes and Pharisees who had devoted themselves to reducing the laws and customs to lifeless, minutely detailed rituals. Jesus reminded them of the spirit which lay beneath the letter of the law: the Sabbath or holy day, is made for man, not man for the Sabbath. This was something new, a prophet at work, and there was no question of the crowd not being attracted to this kind of authority.

Some took him for the Devil, others for the Son of God. Even his family (his mother, brothers, and sisters) wanted to stop him, but he declared that his family were the people who listened to and received him. He spoke in parables to be understood only by those 'to whom the mystery of the kingdom of God has been given'. Then questions began to be asked and doubt set in: 'who is he to speak like this? Isn't he the carpenter's son, the brother of James, Joseph, Judas, and Simon?'

The doubts grew with his requests for silence and secrecy: all were asked to keep silent; the demons who called him the Son of God, the people who had been miraculously healed, the synagogue official whose daughter he had raised from the dead. Even his disciples were told to say nothing. This was probably because more words could

---

The purpose of the parables

'When Jesus was alone, some of those who had heard him came to him with the twelve disciples and asked him to explain the parables. "You have been given the secret of the kingdom of God", Jesus answered, "but the others, who are on the outside, hear all things by means of parables, so that they may look and look yet not see; they may listen and listen, yet not understand. For if they did they would turn to God and he would forgive them."' (*Mark* 4, 10–12)

not reveal his true identity. The person of Jesus was a great mystery which would only be revealed by his Passion (his sacrifical death) and Resurrection.

The making of the disciples

The twelve disciples, chosen for the mission did not fully understand everything themselves: they asked about the meaning of the parables, they were gripped by tremendous fear during the stilling of the storm and were astonished to see him walking on water. And yet they had followed him at his first call, they searched him out whenever he went away and had enough confidence in him to go and preach in his name. They listened to him, questioned him and had great admiration for him.

Gradually their commitment grew and their faith strengthened. They felt themselves bound to him, committed to his message and drawn into his mystery. The veils had not been lifted entirely but the greatness of the Son of Man and the trust placed in him had become obvious facts. So much so that when Jesus posed the question: 'Who am I?' Saint Peter, speaking for them all, unhesitatingly replied: 'You are the Christ.'

The drama of the Passion

Jesus went to Jerusalem. It was an indisputable triumph: mounted on a she-ass he rode along whilst crowds of people cast their cloaks down in his path or strewed the road with branches taken from the fields. Everyone cried out: 'Hosanna! Blessed is he who comes in the name of the Lord! Blessed is the coming of the kingdom!'

It was inevitable that the chief priests and Pharisees would take offence at this. Every day they would come to him and try to cause trouble for him. There were questions about his authority, about the taxes due to Caesar, the resurrection of the dead, and the law of God. Jesus outsmarted them at every turn and recalled the greatest of the commandments: 'Love the Lord your God with all your heart, with all your soul and with all your strength; and the second commandment, which is similar is: Love your neighbour as yourself.'

But things were coming to a head: Jesus rebuked the scribes for chasing after personal honours and praised the offering of the poor widow. He spoke of the destruction of the Temple and the coming of the Son of Man. Then the high priests and the scribes looked for a way to have him killed and Judas, one of the twelve Apostles, offered to deliver him to them when the chance arose.

But Jesus knew everything that was going to happen. During the Passover meal, the Jewish religious feast Jesus shared with his disciples, he spoke of Judas's betrayal: 'It would have been better for that man if he had never been born.' Then, he instituted the Eucharist, the symbolic meal of bread and wine, saying that it should continue to be celebrated by the disciples after his death. Later, on the way to the garden of Gethsemane he predicted Peter's denial despite the disciple's protestations.

Then his agony began. Jesus prayed: 'If it is possible, let this cup be taken from me ... but let your will be done.' During this time the Apostles were sleeping a little way off. Three times he woke them and said: 'Watch and pray.' But they failed to do so and soon the traitor arrived and Judas gave him the kiss of betrayal. The soldiers took hold of him and led him away.

Appearing before the Sonhedrin, the Jewish court, he declared himself to be the Son of God thus provoking great anger in the high priest who considered such a declaration to be blasphemous. He was then

---

The disciples

'Then Jesus called the crowd and his disciples to him: "if anyone wants to come with me" he told them, "he must forget self, carry his cross and follow me. For whoever wants to save his own life will lose it; but whoever loses his life for me and for the gospel will save it. Does a person gain anything if he wins the whole world but loses his life? Of course not! There is nothing he can give to regain his life. If a person is ashamed of me and of my teaching in this godless and wicked day, then the Son of Man will be ashamed of him when he comes in the glory of his Father with the holy angels."' (Mark 8, 34–8)

taken before Pilate, the Roman governor and condemend to be crucified. Sacrified on Golgotha and buried in the tomb of Joseph of Arimathea, he rose on the third day and appeared first to the women at the tomb, then to the Eleven, to whom he said: 'Go and preach to all nations.' Finally he ascended into heaven to rejoin his father.

The style of Mark's Gospel

There are few differences between the accounts given by Matthew and Mark of the Passion and Resurrection. However, each of them tells the story in his own way. Throughout his Gospel Mark avoids expanding on what is said. He shortens discussions and records actions, facts, and the words of the Lord. He is not afraid of repeating the same expressions several times, as a means of improving understanding. His writing seems to express the mind of the community which grew up around Peter.

The Synoptics

The three Gospels of Saint Matthew, Saint Mark, and Saint Luke report the same facts. Their similarities in recording the same speeches, the same parables, the same miracles, and the same events are such that they must be looked at together under the name of the synoptic Gospels.

There are some differences between them however: the order of events is not the same; some accounts are found in one version without appearing in one or both of the others, speeches are shortened or expanded in varying degrees, quite apart from the differences in interpretation, vocabulary, style, and atmosphere. We are indeed dealing with three distinct texts and where sacred works are concerned the question arises as to which one is correct.

For a long time the Church sought to lessen these differences by trying hard to harmonize the facts at the cost of some rather unwieldy distortions and allegories. Later on various methods were used to try and explain this phenomenon: a common source, an original protogospel (earlier version), which had been lost, oral traditions into which variations had crept among the different communities, or the notion that Mark's Gospel, the shortest one, was the first and that the others had been inspired to complement it, correct it or give it a new form more appropriate to the audience at which it was aimed.

Whatever explanation is accepted, it seems clear that each of the Gospels possesses a theological aim: Saint Matthew is intending to show that Jesus is the Messiah foretold by the Scriptures: hence the numerous quotations scattered throughout his text. Saint Mark structures his whole account around the Good News, the revelation of that which was hidden: witness his constant reminders about the messianic secret. Finally, Saint Mark underlines the universality of the gospel message: he therefore leaves out any discussion of opposition between the old Law and the new Law, or between the justice of the Pharisees and Christian justice etc.

All this is epitomized in the different treatments given to the parable of the light which must not be hidden under a bushel: Saint Matthew stresses the role of the disciples, the light of the world who are to shout the Good News from the rooftops; Saint Mark points out that 'there is nothing now hidden which will not be brought out into the open'; and Saint Luke has the light placed on a lamp stand so that those who come in (the pagans) will see the light.

> **The widow's mite**
> 'As Jesus sat near the Temple treasury, he watched the people as they dropped in their money. Many rich men dropped in a lot of money; then a poor widow came along and dropped in two little copper coins, worth about a penny. He called his disciples together and said to them: "I tell you that this poor widow put more in the offering box than all the others. For the others put in what they had to spare of their riches; but she, poor as she is, put in all she had — she gave all she had to live on."'
> (*Mark* 12, 41–4)

The Gospel according to Luke
The influence of Paul

The universal Gospel

Concern for historical exactness and the companionship of Paul lie at the root of the third Gospel.

Saint Luke writes as a historian: he has consulted eye witnesses of the events, referred to the accounts which had already been written, and conducted a detailed investigation. He wishes to offer his readers a serious basis for the doctrine proclaimed in the Church. Unlike the other Gospels, Luke's account does not end with Jesus's Resurrection but continues into what might be called volume two, the *Acts of the Apostles*, covering the spread of Christianity throughout the then known world. His account is written with the aim of demonstrating the universal nature of the doctrine.

Saint Luke was the first historian of the Church and wrote in the style of that time, namely without stating his sources and without giving indisputable evidence or concerning himself with a precise timetable of

---

The *Magnificat*
'My heart praises the Lord; my soul is glad because of my Saviour, for he has remembered me, his lowly servant! From now on all people will call me happy, because of the great things the mighty God has done for me. His name is holy; from one generation to another he shows mercy to those who honour him. He has stretched out his mighty arm and scattered the proud with all their plans. He has brought down mighty kings from their thrones, and lifted up the lowly. He has filled the hungry with good things and sent the rich away with empty hands ...' (*Luke* 1, 46–53)

---

events. He is under the influence of Saint Paul, the Apostle to the Gentiles, whose discipleship was based on the evidence and conviction that Christ's message is meant for all people of every nation and in every age.

The Gospel of the childhood

A greater importance is given by Luke to Jesus's infancy than is seen anywhere else. He was addressing himself to a Hellenistic or Greek-influenced culture where the Jewish Scriptures were unknown; he therefore felt the need to give details of the extraordinary phenomena which had surrounded the preparation for the Messiah's public ministry. No doubt the women, who feature prominently in this third Gospel, were privileged witnesses of these events. The fact remains that he writes at length about this period.

John the Baptist is the first important figure in the third Gospel. Saint Luke records the announcement of his coming by Gabriel, the affliction suffered by his father, Zechariah, because he did not believe the angel's words, his birth to an old and previously barren woman, Elizabeth, and the visit of the neighbours, his circumcision, and Zechariah's song of praise. In a parallel account he tells of the Annunciation, the message of Jesus's coming delivered to his mother by this same Gabriel, and the words of Mary's acceptance, the birth of the Messiah and the visit from the shepherds, the circumcision, Simeon's song of thanksgiving, and Anna's prophecy. The two accounts come together in the middle of the passage in the Visitation, when Mary goes to see her pregnant cousin, Elizabeth. This episode contains both the greeting addressed to the Lord's mother and also the *Magnificat*, her hymn of thanksgiving.

Finally the supremacy of Jesus is again emphasized by the epistle describing his being found in discussion with the Jewish teachers, when, at the age of only 12, he amazed his audience by his intelligence and his pertinent answers.

There can be no doubt that this parallel is intentional. Each event in John the Baptist's life corresponds to one in the life of Jesus, but while the first was completely focused on the second — he was to get the Lord's people ready for him — Jesus was declared at the Annunciation to be the son of the Most High and at his circumcision was recognized as a 'light to reveal your will to the nations'.

Within these few pages are found hymns and prayers which are still used in the Church today: the 'Hail Mary', the *Magnificat* or Hymn of the Virgin, the *Benedictus* or Hymn of Zechariah, the *Nunc Dimittis* or Song of Simeon. Were these taken from some of the sources consulted by Luke or do these prayers have their origin in this third Gospel? Basically this is of little importance but there is an evident correlation between the third Gospel and the words of the liturgy, the form of public worship.

The account continues with the preaching of John the Baptist and his imprisonment. Then Saint Luke turns to the life of Jesus: his baptism, the temptation in the desert, and above all, the proclaiming of his mission in the synagogue at Nazareth, the town where he had spent his unremarkable childhood. Using the text from Isaiah which he had been asked to read: 'The Spirit of the Lord is upon me because he has chosen and anointed me', he declared that this prophecy had been fulfilled there and then in him. But his audience did not accept this, they drove him out, and wanted to have him killed. 'A prophet is not without honour except in his own country.' Then Jesus walked through the crowd without being harmed.

The preaching

Jesus began his ministry with numerous miracles. Three of them are recorded: in Cpernaum he healed a man possessed by an evil spirit, he healed Simon's mother-in-law, and he gave the fisherman an unusu-

ally large catch. Simon was amazed at this phenomenon and threw himself at Jesus's feet. The Messiah said to him: 'Don't be afraid, from now on you will be catching men.' And leaving everything behind, they followed him.

Luke then continues with the same episodes covered by the other evangelists: sermons, parables, and miracles. Perhaps he lays rather more stress than the others on God's goodness towards sinners: he likes to recount moments of forgiveness and to show the Lord eating in the homes of sinniners; on his tenderness towards the poor and humble and, conversely, on his severity towards the rich and powerful: he is the only one to record the parable of the rich man and Lazarus, the Pharisee and the publican; and on his care for women and foreigners, groups which were rather scorned in Judaism. Luke alone points out the number of women who followed him, together with the parable of the Good Samaritan and his visit to the house of Martha and Mary.

Luke speaks just as plainly when it comes to the conditions imposed on Christ's disciples: if anyone comes to me without loving me more than his father, his mother, his children, his brothers, his sisters — and, adds Luke — his wife and his own life, he cannot be my disciple. He has a particularly strong aversion to money: the poor are fortunate, it is for them that the Good News is intended, they will walk right into the

Martha and Mary

'As Jesus and his disciples went on their way, he came to a village where a woman named Martha welcomed him in her home. She had a sister named Mary, who sat down at the feet of the Lord and listened to his teaching. Martha was upset over all the work she had to do, so she came and said, "Lord, don't you care that my sister has left me to do all the work by myself? Tell her to come and help me!" The Lord answered her, "Martha, Martha! You are worried and troubled over so many things, but just one thing is needed. Mary has chosen the right thing, and it will not be taken away from her."' (*Luke* 10, 38–42)

kingdom of God: by contrast the rich are unfortunate, they amass wealth for themselves and not for God, they are cut off from the poor, and consequently from the kingdom of God.

The ascent to Jerusalem

Saint Luke's account is geared to the ascent to Jerusalem. He mentions the goal of the journey: 'We are going up to Jerusalem', and large crowds joined him on the road. It is there that everything the prophets have written about the Son of Man will be fulfilled for 'it is not right for a prophet to die other than in Jerusalem' (*Luke* 13, 31). And on three occasions Jesus himself foretells his Passion, his death, and his Resurrection.

This journey is marked by increasing dramatic tension. The opposition forces harden against him: Samaritans refuse to receive him, the Pharisees step up their attacks on him and Herod wants to have him killed. During this time Jesus becomes more severe and more insistent: there are outbursts against faithless Jews, against Jerusalem, against the Pharisees and lovers of

---

The faith of the pilgrims on the Emmaus Road

'And we had hoped that he would be the one who was going to set Israel free! Besides all that, this is now the third day since it happened. Some of the women of our group surprised us; they went off at dawn to the tomb, but could not find his body. They came back saying they had seen a vision of angels who told them that he is alive. Some of our group went to the tomb and found it exactly as the women had said, but they did not see him.

'Then Jesus said to them, "How foolish you are, how slow you are to believe everything the prophets said! Was it not necessary for the Messiah to suffer these things and then to enter his glory?"' (*Luke* 24, 21–36)

---

money, and there are the conditions imposed on the Apostles, the sending out of the 72 disciples and the calls to repentance.

The conflict reaches its height and the idea that has been present since the opening pages — the salvation of the poor and humble, and the exclusion of the rich and the established — is wonderfully illustrated in the three parables about forgiveness: the lost sheep which is sought by the shepherd until it is found, the lost coin which the woman rejoices over when she finds it, and the prodigal son whose return to his father's house is an occasion for celebration. The kingdom of God does not follow the normal laws of the world.

The mystery of Easter

It was not customary at that time for a hero to triumph through his death. But Jesus was not exactly the usual type of hero. An innocent victim, he committed himself to the supreme sacrifice. Keeping his composure, he saw all those around him crumble away: after the triumph of Palm Sunday the crowd called for his death; even Peter denied him. But he remained resolute, declaring before his judges that he was the Son of God, and relying only on weapons of gentleness, a gentleness which was capable of bringing about a reconciliation between Herod and Pilate, and of pardoning the sins of the thief on the cross.

The true triumph came afterwards. Luke lingers over the Resurrection longer than any of the other evangelists: two angels announce it to the women at the tomb, but the Apostles are still not convinced, Jesus appears to the disciples on the Emmaus Road as they are returning home crushed by their prophet's failure. But they do not recognize him until the breaking of bread as they share a meal. He disappears just after this and they run to tell the Good News to the Apostles. They know it is true, they have seen him, they eat with him, and receive their final instructions from him before he ascends into heaven.

The Gospel according to John
The testimony of the one that Jesus loved

The Word is made flesh

John writes as a theologian and reveals the Holy Spirit at work in the earthly life of the Word of God.

There had already been a certain amount of excitement in the Church, the Good News had spread far beyond the frontiers of Palestine and there had been many experiments in Christian living by the time the fourth Gospel was written, probably around the year 100. It was within Saint John's group of followers, if not by John himself that the text was finalized. It must have been the result of a long process of research and development in their thinking and preaching.

The *Gospel according to John* is very different from the Synoptics: here we have no Gospel of the infancy, no parables, no curing of the possessed. Most of the miracles recorded here are peculiar to this Gospel and each one is intended to convey, not only Jesus's power over the elements, but also some fundamental theological significance. Most space is given over to the speeches and conversations. The fourth Gospel is more concerned with doctrine than with events.

It is not that facts are unimportant, quite the contrary. But the author's specific aim is to show how they fit into the whole history of salvation, to uncover their meaning and, at each stage of Jesus's life, to provide a key to understanding it. So, at the very beginning of the book, the Messiah is declared to be the Word of God, 'who was in the beginning with God, who was God', and, 'everything was made through him'. The supreme greatness of Jesus at last revealed!

This prologue is like a summary of the history of the world. Nine stages are suggested: the Word in God, his action in the Creation, his role as light of the world, the message of John the Baptist, the coming of the Word among men, the gift of divine sonship, or the right to become God's children, the incarnation of Jesus as a man, a further testimony from John and Jesus's return to be with his Father. There is a rhythm to this opening section with moves along with clarity and liveliness beginning with God, then turning to men and finally back to God again. The whole of the rest of the Gospel develops this rhythm.

The signs

John the Baptist's testimony is clear and direct: 'A man is coming after me, but he is greater than I am because he existed before I was born' (*John* 1, 30), and he describes him in unequivocal terms: 'I am not good enough even to untie his sandals' (*John* 1, 27). John the Baptist understands his own role: 'He must become more important

The first disciples

'The next day John was standing there again with two of his disciples, when he saw Jesus walking by. "There is the Lamb of God", he said. The two disciples heard him say this and went with Jesus. Jesus turned, saw them following him and asked: "What are you looking for?" They answered "Where do you live, Rabbi?" (This word means teacher) "Come and see", he answered. So they went with him and saw where he lived and spent the rest of that day with him.' (*John* 1, 35–9)

while I become less important' (*John* 3, 30). And it is John, the forerunner, who points out the Messiah to the first disciples.

John had baptized with water, Jesus would baptize with the Spirit. His conversation with Nikodimos is enlightening on this topic: 'No one can see the kingdom of God unless he is born again' (*John* 3, 3). Later on he speaks of being born of the Spirit. But Nikodimos questions him further so the Lord explains that he is speaking about the things of heaven, not those of this world, that have been sent by the Father so that people might believe in him and have eternal life.

The meeting with the Samaritan woman gives him an opportunity to clarify his thinking: 'If only you knew what God gives and who it is that is asking you for a drink, you would ask him and he would give you life-giving water' (*John* 4, 10). The inexhaustible gift of God! In response to the question of this woman, who would be regarded by orthodox Jews as a heretic, Jesus explains that God does not limit his blessings to the Temple of Jerusalem and Mount Zion but wants to be worshipped in spirit and in truth. Have done with petty divisions, what is important is to be honest.

This is the sign of water, the water of baptism which refers also to the baptism in the Spirit. The second sign is that of bread. After the feeding of the five thousand, Jesus declares that he is the bread of life, an allusion to the Eucharist: 'I am the living bread that came down from heaven. If anyone eats this bread he will live for ever. The bread that I will give him is my flesh, which I give so that the world may live' (*John* 6, 51).

Christ's claim to have rights and prerogatives which were considered to be God's alone raised some strong protests, the improbability of his declarations led to a widespread lack of understanding among those who heard him and his appearance as the founder of a new religion provoked increasingly fierce opposition within the establishment. Far from holding him back, these reactions cause him to be more and more explicit. Firstly he declares himself to be the source of the waters of life: 'Whoever is thirsty, should come to me and drink;' then the good shepherd: 'who gives his life for his sheep' and finally the light of the world: 'Whoever follows me will never walk in darkness.' And by way of explanation Saint John says: 'Jesus said this about the Spirit which those who believed in him were going to receive. At that time the Spirit had not yet been given, because Jesus had not been raised to glory' (*John* 7, 39).

The Passion and glorification

The controversy surrounding Jesus continues to grow. He gives sight to a man born blind: a miracle of some importance since Jesus brings into being something which has never existed. He raises Lazarus who has been buried for three days and declares: 'I am the Resurrection and the Life. Whoever believes in me, though he may die, yet shall he live.' Then, at a gathering in Bethany, he allows Lazarus's sister Mary to pour expensive perfume over his feet, justifying the gesture in terms of his imminent death. Finally he makes his triumphal entry into Jerusalem with the crowd shouting: 'Blessed is he who comes in the name of the Lord, the king of Israel.' This is recognition of Jesus, the Messiah.

But crowds can change from one moment to the next. The Pharisees and chief priests, jealous of Jesus's success, decide to have him killed. They use their authority, and no doubt a certain degree of intimidation, to turn the crowd against the Messiah. Jesus sees the way things are going and

---

The grain of wheat

'The hour has now come for the Son of Man to receive great glory. I am telling you the truth: a grain of wheat remains no more than a single grain unless it is dropped into the ground and dies. If it does die, then it produces many grains. Whoever loves his own life will lose it; whoever hates his own life in this world will keep it for life eternal. Whoever wants to serve me must follow me, so that my servant will be with me where I am. And my Father will honour anyone who serves me.' (*John* 12, 23–6)

announces that the time has come for the fulfilment of God's plan. Just as a grain of wheat thrown on the ground must die in order to produce much fruit, so it is with the Son of Man. When I am lifted up from the earth — and John explains that this is a reference to his suffering on the cross — I will draw all men to me.

Jesus and his own people

Jesus's last teachings before the Passion are directed to his disciples. After the washing of the feet, a sign of humility, and the institution of the Eucharist, the sacrament of Unity, the master makes a long speech. The theme of love is the first to be developed. It is clear that John wishes to root the love men have for each other in their sharing of a divine life in Christ. Let us not forget that this teaching comes after the Last Supper where the Apostles have eaten the bread which was Jesus himself.

Next comes the message of consolation: Jesus promises to return, he proclaims the coming of the Holy Spirit and lastly he confirms the Father will take special care of them during the time of separation. It is an evening of farewells but at the same time it

Thomas's doubts

'One of the twelve disciples, Thomas (called the Twin), was not with them when Jesus came. So the other disciples told him, "We have seen the Lord!" Thomas said to them, "Unless I see the scars of the nails in his hands and put my finger on those scars and my hand in his side, I will not believe." A week later the disciples were together again indoors and Thomas was with them. The doors were locked but Jesus came and stood among them and said, "Peace be with you." Then he said to Thomas, "Put your finger here, and look at my hands; then stretch out your hand and put it in my side. Stop your doubting and believe!" Thomas answered him, "My Lord and my God!"' (John 20, 24–8)

is a kind of consecration of the disciples. From this time onwards they are brought, through Jesus, into a close relationship with the Father, and are also assured of the help of the Holy Spirit. This change in the relationship is the inevitable consequence of the Passion and glorification of the Son of God made man.

Finally Jesus ends with a speech about Unity, a unity anchored in him: 'I am the vine and you are the branches.' That is to say that the Son of God and the disciples live the same life, that they have their breath in him, that they are only complete in union with him. What is described is a collective entity, the Church, the continuation of the Messiah beyond death, the 'total Christ' as Saint Augustine would call it later. Having understood this we can appreciate something of the great emotion in Jesus's final prayer addressed to his Father: 'I pray that they may all be one, Father. May they be in us just as you are in me and I am in you' (John 17, 21).

The Resurrection

John's narrative concerning the Christ's Passion is sobre in the extreme. It is marked by a great serenity and the use of certain symbols. Thus the water and blood which flow from the Saviour's pierced heart recall baptism and the Eucharist, important sacraments of the Church; the dividing up of the clothes is directly referred to in the Scriptures and there is no doubt that the seamless robe is intended to represent the unity of the disciples.

As for the Resurrection, John records the evidence for it: the empty tomb, the Lord's appearance to the Apostles with his wounded hands and side, the doubts of Saint Thomas; he also shows that this marks the beginning of the Church with the sending of the Holy Spirit, the power to forgive, and the miraculous fishing catch — a graphic illustration of the future task of the Apostles throughout the world. And the text ends by saying that the disciple testified to these facts and we know that what he said is true.

Acts of the Apostles
The early church

The spread of the Christian message

'You will be my witness in Jerusalem, and in all Judaea and Samaria, and to the ends of the earth' (Acts 1, 8).

The *Acts of the Apostles* is the second of Saint Luke's books, the first being the third Gospel. In it the author continues his account of the beginnings of the Church, echoing the final episodes of the first book at the beginning of the second: the appearances of the risen Christ, his last instructions and the Ascension. The two books must have become separated when the four Gospels were gathered together.

The early community

The day after the Ascension the disciples were all together, bound as they were by common memories, the presence of the risen Christ and the task he had given them. They chose Matthias to replace Judas, the betrayer, received the Holy Spirit in the form of a strong wind, and began to preach in all the languages of those who crowded round to watch this strange event. It was Peter who spoke in the name of God and the book of *Acts* is, certainly for the first part, the story of Peter.

The first conversions occurred immediately; Luke records almost 3000 baptisms on the day of Pentecost, when the Holy Spirit came. So the first Christian community of any size was formed: they all paid close attention to the Apostles' teaching, were faithful in fellowship and the breaking of bread and prayer. They held everything they had in common, sold their belongings and everyone shared in the proceeds according to their needs: pure communism! They were all of a single mind and their simple lifestyle found favour with the people.

The new converts continued to go to the Temple. There was no break with the established religion. Peter and John themselves still went to the Temple. One day, showing an assurance which he had not had in Jesus's time, Peter cured a man who had been crippled from birth and gave the crowd, who had gathered round to see this miracle, a colourful address on the role of the risen Christ as Messiah. Then the priests and the captain of the Temple guard came along: they seized the Apostles and brought them before the Sanhedrin, the Jewish Council.

This arrest did nothing to lessen Peter's zeal and he continued to proclaim his faith before the hierarchy of official Judaism and to invite people to change their ways. The people were very impressed by the miracles

Ananias and Sapphira

'But there was a man named Ananias, who with his wife, Sapphira, sold some property that belonged to them. But with his wife's agreement he kept part of the money for himself and handed the rest over to the Apostles. Peter said to him, "Ananias, why did you let Satan take control of you and make you lie to the Holy Spirit by keeping part of the money you received for the property? Before you sold the property it beloned to you; and after you sold it the money was yours. Why, then, did you decide to do such a thing? You have not lied to men, you have lied to God." As soon as Ananias heard this he fell down dead; and all who heard about it were terrified.' (*Acts* 5, 1–6)

performed in Jesus's name and the chief priests hesitated to condemn him. So they whipped him and then let him go. Gamaliel, one of the doctors of the Law involved, accounted for this attitude, saying: 'If what he is doing is of human origin it will fail, it it comes from God we will not be able to destroy it' (*Acts* 5, 38–9).

The first missions

The community grew quickly and the daily running of the group began to be a problem for the Apostles, taking up too much of their time. So it was decided to give a few of the disciples responsibility for practical matters, and they were called deacons. Seven of the most dedicated men, who were faithful in prayer and study of the word, were chosen, and the Apostles laid hands on them.

Stephen was a passionately keen young convert. Since being named as a deacon there had been no holding him. He performed great wonders and seized every opportunity to speak of his faith. Since those who opposed him were no match for him in wisdom and could not compete with the inspiration Stephen received from the Spirit, they hatched a plot and took him before the high priest. But even in this appearance in front of the high priest Stephen did not relent. He began to recall all the treachery in Israel's past, ending with his own judges who had crucified the Messiah. The longer he went on, the angrier his listeners became and he was seized, dragged outside, and stoned to death.

Among Stephen's torturers was one Saul. As a Pharisee, and son of a Pharisee, he had been brought up steeped in Jewish culture and was a fervent defender of the Law. Stephen's words exasperated him and he became the Christians' most zealous persecutor. As the community spread Saul extended his violence against them throughout the land. But one day on the road to Damascus he was struck down as if by lightning, the Lord called him, he joined the Christians and became the most illustrious of the Apostles, surpassing even Peter in fulfilling his mission.

While persecution and famine continued to ravage those in Jerusalem, the communities of believers spread along the coastal area of Palestine reaching Caesarea and Antioch. Help came from everywhere to aid those in distress. Peter travelled round the region preaching the word and in Caesarea he baptized the centurion Cornelius and his family, who were pagans. This immediately posed the problem of whether or not those converted from paganism should be subject to the obligations of the Jewish Law.

This was the purpose of what is called the Council of Jerusalem, presided over by James who was head of the local Church. Opinion was in fact divided. Luke does not record disagreement between Peter and Paul, the new name given to Saul — a disagreement the latter was to refer to in his Letter to the Galatians — he simply states that the final agreement was contained in a letter delivered to Paul and Barnabus for the outlying Churches.

Paul's missionary journeys

If the early part of this book is Peter's tale, the later sections are the tale of Paul. He is seen visiting in turn Troas, Philippi in Macedonia, Amphipolis, Thessalonica, Athens, Corinth, and Ephesus. Everywhere he went he preached the Good News, first in the synagogues to the Jews, then to the Gentiles. Often his words provoked riots: the

The conversion of Paul

'As Saul was coming near the city of Damascus, suddenly a light from the sky flashed round him. He fell to the ground and heard a voice saying to him, "Saul, Saul! Why do you persecute me?" "Who are you Lord?" he asked. "I am Jesus whom you persecute", the voice said. "But get up and go into the city, where you will be told what you must do." The men who were travelling with Paul had stopped, not saying a word; they heard the voice but could not see anyone. Saul got up from the ground and opened his eyes, but could not see a thing. So they took him by the hand and led him into Damascus. For three days he was not able to see, and during that time he did not eat or drink anything.' (*Acts* 9, 3–9)

role of Jesus as Messiah, the bodily resurrection, even the miracles performed in the Lord's name were ill-received. In Philippi, Corinth, and later in Jerusalem he was arrested and tried. Yet everywhere he went he set up churches which he returned to again and again in order to strengthen their faith.

Faced with the suffering of the Christians in Jerusalem, Paul organized a great collection to help them. This also gave him an opportunity to strengthen the links between the communities he had set up across Asia Minor and the Mother Church. So he set out once more for the land of Jesus accompanied by the delegates from his churches. Luke, who was certainly on the journey with them, gives us an account of their progress, the various ports of call, events along the way, and meetings with the faithful.

Imprisonment

The arrival in Jerusalem was not as might have been expected. The Christian community received him gladly, though they did ask for an explanation of his past deeds, but the Jews lost no time in stirring up a riot when Paul visited the Temple. The town was in uproar. Paul was dragged before the tribune, the Roman commander. Paul addressed the crowd, but to no avail. He was forced to take advantage of his status as a Roman citizen in order to escape a flogging. However, he remained in prison.

Before the Sanhedrin, the Jewish Council, he used all his cunning. As a Pharisee himself he was aware of the different beliefs held by the Sadducees and the Pharisees regarding resurrection and the existence of angels, and he skillfully manoeuvered them into a position where they disagreed amongst themselves so that no decision could be taken against him.

However, the anger continued to mount and some of the Jews vowed that they would neither eat nor drink until Paul had been killed. But this plot was discovered and the tribune, who wanted to be rid of this troublesome prisoner, sent him to Felix, the provincial governor, based in Caesarea.

Paul's captivity in Caesarea lasted for years. Felix was in a rather awkward position and let things drag on. His successor, Festus, was no better. For all that he questioned the apostle, improved his conditions, and had him appear before King Agrippa, he still hesitated to take a decision and prevaricated until Paul finally appealed to Caesar. His Roman citizenship entitled him to insist on being judged by the emperor himself. And so the journey to Rome was arranged.

Hurricanes, tempest, and shipwreck did nothing to ease their passage. The centurion acting as escort was helpful and authorized Paul to visit his colleagues at the various stops along the way. So the transfer of a prisoner in fact became a missionary journey. He spent three months in Malta, where he healed many people and received numerous gifts; at Puteoli he stayed for a week with a group of Christians; finally in Rome he immediately made contact with the Jews there and told them of the Good News. Luke ends his account by lamenting the Jews' lack of belief. According to the author Paul enjoyed this freedom to preach the kingdom of God for two more years.

Pharisees and Sadducees

'When Paul saw that some of the group were Sadducees and the others were Pharisees, he called out in the Council, "Fellow Israelites! I am a Pharisee, the son of Pharisees. I am on trial here because of the hope I have that the dead will rise to life!" As soon as he said this, the Pharisees and Sadducees started to quarrel and the group was divided. For the Sadducees say that people will not rise from death and that there are no angels or spirits; the Pharisees believe in all three. The shouting became louder, and some of the teachers of the Law who belonged to the party of the Pharisees stood up and protested strongly: "We cannot find anything wrong with this man. Perhaps a spirit or an angel really did speak to him!" The argument became more and more violent.' (Acts 23, 6–10)

Paul's Letter to the Romans

A letter to the heart of paganism

Justification by faith

Faith in Christ as offered first to the Jews and then to the pagans is the basis of salvation.

Having completed his missionary work in the eastern part of the Mediterranean area Paul wished to travel west, to Spain in particular, going by way of Rome. This letter was written by Paul to prepare the way for his visit to the community in Rome which had already been established by another missionary. This group was made up in the main of Christians from a pagan background along with a minority of converted Jews (Judaeo-Christians). The apostle uses this letter to set out the doctrine of his message at length. It was written at the beginning of AD 58, probably during a journey to Corinth.

The heathens

'Because those people refuse to keep in mind the true knowledge about God, he has given them over to corrupted minds, so that they do the things that they should not do. They are filled with all kinds of wickedness, evil, greed, and vice; they are full of jealousy, murder, fighting, deceit, and malice. They gossip and speak evil of one another; they are hateful to God, insolent, proud, and boastful; they think of more ways to do evil; they disobey their parents; they have no conscience; they do not keep their promises, and they show no kindness or pity for others. They know that God's law says that people who live in this way deserve death. Yet not only do they continue to do these very things, but they even approve of others who do them'. (*Romans* 2, 28–32)

The sin of men

Paul says that pagans arouse God's anger because they are capable of knowing the true God: for what has been invisible since the creation of the world is revealed through its works and its power to all who can perceive it. The pagans could and should have honoured him but they did not. Instead of giving glory to God they have preferred images of mortal men or birds, animals or reptiles, in short they have worshipped idols. This was not ignorance but wilful perversion. So God has left them to their desires and shameful passions and they have sunk into a life of envy, murder, dispute, treachery, spitefulness etc. What a terrible indictment!

The Jews hardly fare any better. Yes, they have the Law; they are proud of it and believe that it makes them superior to all others, called to be a guide for humankind. But instead of being useful to God, they use God; instead of working for God's glory, they work towards their own; instead of leading men to acceptance of the Law, they lead them to destruction. This is a perversion of God's revelation, a perversion of Abraham's mission which was intended to bring divine blessing to all nations; it is a perversion of the Law itself which is broken by the very ones to whom it was given. The importance of the Jews must be acknowledged, however, for it was to them that God's wisdom was entrusted; they are God's chosen ones and it is to them that the promises were made. The Jews are not better than the pagans, but they have the Law which 'makes man know that he has sinned' (*Romans* 3, 20).

Faith

All men have sinned and are deprived of God's glory, but through the redemption achieved in Christ Jesus, those who believe are justified. If we were saved by virtue of obedience to the Law, salvation would be something we earned, a kind of reward; we could pride ourselves on it because it would have been achieved by our own efforts: this was the thinking behind the conceited Judaism of the Pharisees of the time, which was so often condemned by Jesus. But this is to mistake the nature of salvation; it is a free gift from God, accepted in faith.

Paul returns to this subject taking the example of Abraham. This father of the Jewish nation was, in the first place, a believer: when God told him to go into another country he believed in God and went without hesitation; when he told him that he would have a son despite his and his wife Sarah's advanced age, he believed him. 'Abraham believed God and because of his faith God accepted him as righteous' (*Genesis* 15, 6 and *Romans* 4, 3). Abraham is accepted as the father of the Jewish nation but he is also, because of the faith that he showed, the father of all believers. He was a believer even before circumcision was given as the sign of belonging to the Jewish race and to him it was simply the mark of his faith. Abraham is the father of the circumcised and the uncircumcised, of the Jew and pagan alike.

Christians are not justified through any observaton of the Law. It was while they were still dominated by sin — pagans through their refusal to see God mani-

festedin his works, Jews through their breaking of the Law — that Christ gave his life for them. How much more will he save them now that they are free from their faults. As sinners, he died for them, and reconciled to God they received salvation through him. All glory based on man is destroyed, but now, through Christ, a much greater glory is given to men, participation in the glory of God.

Salvation

Paul draws a parallel between Adam and Christ. Their humanity is the link between them but is expressed in the disobedience of the one and the obedience of the other: Adam is the cause of death, Jesus is the cause of life, both have, by a single act, caused men to follow them. And 'the Law' says Paul, at the risk of shocking 'was introduced in order to increase wrongdoing'. It served to reveal sin and it provoked anger. But Christ came and 'where sin increased, God's grace increased much more' (*Romans* 5, 20).

Christ did, in effect, take on the nature of humanity and in so doing took on himself the sin of the world. He suffered death but conquered it through the resurrection. This is a new creation, a new inheritance for men, a new order of life which is entered upon through baptism in the death of Christ: it is no longer a regime of Law, but one of Grace; it is no longer a matter of obligations imposed from outside, but of communion with the Son of God.

Life in the Spirit

Communion with the Son of God is possible through the Spirit which 'lives in us', says Paul. This has nothing to do with being a slave to the Law, since this obedience to God stems from the depths of the heart. 'The Spirit makes you God's children, and by the Spirit's power we cry out to God, "Father, my Father!" God's Spirit joins himself to our spirits to declare that we are God's children' (*Romans* 8, 15-16). We are now dealing with a totally different relationship. Now there is no longer fear or servility, but the love of God.

What better way to end such a statement

The internal conflict

'I do not understand what I do; for I don't do what I would like to do, but instead I do what I hate. Since what I do is what I don't want to do, this shows that I agree that the Law is right. So I am not really the one who does this thing; rather it is the sin that lives in me. I know that good does not live in me — that is, in my human nature. For even though the desire to do good is in me, I am not able to do it. I don't do the good I want to do; instead I do the evil that I do not want to do. If I do what I don't want to do this means that I am no longer the one who does it; instead it is the sin that lives in me.'
(*Romans* 7, 15–20)

of doctrine than with a message of hope founded on the relationship offered to us by God and secured for us by Christ: that which a father has with his children and children with their father? This is a tremendous privilege measured in terms of the death and resurrection of Jesus, the supreme act of love. The promise is secure, founded as it is on the power of the omnipotent God and the depth of feeling he has shown for humankind. When compared to grace like this, what are our trials and tribulations, our anxieties, persecutions, hunger, nakedness, troubles of whatever kind? There is nothing that can take away what God has done.

The mystery of Israel

But what of Israel? A chosen people on whom God bestowed 'sonship, promises, glory, ancestry, laws, and true worship' (*Romans* 9, 4–5). Paul, the former scourge of these heretical Christians, knows what he is talking about here. Would God break his promises? Would he forget to be faithful? Would he be unjust?

There is a mystery here which Paul has to acknowledge but he uses the opportunity to affirm his faith. It is true that 'a small remnant' exists and that the community in Rome, to whom he is speaking is made up partly of Judaeo-Christians: it is also true that Christianity was born out of Judaism and that Christians can call themselves descendants of Abraham by faith. But the ultimate truth is that God's mystery is unfathomable. 'God is not like men, who lie; he is not a human, who changes his mind' (*Numbers* 23, 19).

Israel's rejection has been salvation for the pagans. The hardening of the Jews against the Gospel message shattered the old notion of the people of God and the Apostles turned to the pagan world. This is a historical fact seen on the day of Pentecost and Paul declares it to be part of God's plan. God knows how to bring good out of evil and from Israel's sin comes the beneficial extension of his Good News to all men.

But Paul's faith takes him much further. They have stumbled, but not fallen beyond all hope of rescue. Their situation, though it may last a long time, is not irretrievable. God keeps his promises: 'There is a secret truth, my brothers, which I want you to know. [...] The stubbornness of the people of Israel is not permanent, but will last only until the complete number of Gentiles comes to God. And this is how all Israel will be saved, as the scripture says' (*Romans* 11, 25–6). Paul is in no doubt that the Old and New Covenants will be fulfilled because they both come from God.

Advice

Paul ends his letter with some words of advice: he commands humility and charity, love for enemies, obedience to state authorities, caring for the weak and seeking unity among themselves. The children of God are children of light, they 'are clothed in the Lord Jesus Christ' to think like him, feel like him, and act like him. 'For the moment when we will be saved is closer now than it was when we first believed. The night is nearly over, day is almost here. Let us stop doing the things that belong to the dark' (*Romans* 13, 11).

The remnant

'Did God reject his own people? Certainly not! I myself am an Israelite, a descendant of Abraham, a member of the tribe of Benjamin. God has not rejected his people, whom he chose from the beginning. You know what the scripture says in the passage where Elijah pleads with God against Israel: "Lord, they have killed your prophets and torn down your altars; I am the only one left and they are trying to kill me." What answer did God give him? "I have kept for myself 7000 men who have not worshipped the false god Baal." It is the same way now; there is a small number left of those whom God has chosen because of his grace. His choice is based on his grace, not on what they have done. For if God's choice were based on what people do, then his grace would not be real grace.' (*Romans* 11, 1–6)

Paul's Letters to the Corinthians

The Gospel meets Greek culture

Christian wisdom

Paul addresses himself to a community well known for its tendency towards excitement, debauchery, and all forms of excess.

The old city of Corinth, rebuilt by Caesar, had a reputation for wealth and immorality: there was a saying, 'to go Corinthian' which meant 'to sink into debauchery'. Its inhabitants numbered around half a million. In reality it was a world of stark contrasts where the passionate freedom of the Greeks lived cheek by jowl with the narrow-mindedness of the Jewish ghetto, where enthusiasm for all sorts of new ideas co-existed with the most intolerant feelings of prejudice and philosophical seriousness with unrestrained outbursts of passion. It

Christian wisdom

'God purposely chose what the world considers nonsense in order to shame the wise, and he chose what the world considers weak in order to shame the powerful. He chose what the world looks down on and despises, and thinks is nothing, in order to destroy what the world thinks is important. This means that no one can boast in God's presence. But God has brought you into union with Christ Jesus, and God has made Christ to be our wisdom. By him we are put right with God; we become God's holy people and are set free. So then, as the scripture says, "Whoever wants to boast must boast of what the Lord has done."' (*I Corinthians* 1, 27–31)

was also a world made all the more confusing by virtue of the fact that the population was constantly changing.

Paul had lived there for a year and a half, had founded a solid community and succeeded throughout his stay in maintaining its morals at an acceptable standard. But four years had now elapsed. Greek laxness, the taste of freedom, intellectualism, and the prevailing atmosphere of self had bred divisions, sects, and scandals within this Christian circle. On his return from Corinth Apollos had warned the apostle of the danger and Paul had already written asking the faithful to shun all blasphemers, drunkards, and immoral characters.

It is the second and third letters which have come down to us. In them Paul sets out the information he has received: 'For some people from Chloe's family have told me quite plainly, my brothers, that there are quarrels among you ...' (*1 Corinthians* 1, 11). Some were calling themselves followers of Paul, others followers of Apollos and others followers of Peter. Paul has to remind them that it is Christ and he alone who was crucified for us and that this truth is no subject for petty squabbling.

True wisdom

Christians have no right to make distinctions between preachers of the Gospel, for all are committed to the same task, each one according to his own ability and without dependence on clever use of words. And what better place to proclaim this than here in this important centre of Greek thought where there were countless schools and academies. The world's wisdom is built entirely on human values: intelligence, intellect, debate, artistic and technical achievement. Its ideal is to have man as the ultimate standard against which everything is measured, 'mortal man', Jesus said to Saint Peter (*Matthew* 16, 17). This kind of wisdom is contrary to the Christian faith.

Paul is quick to associate the Jewish concept of wisdom with the wisdom of the Greek world. During his missionary journeys he had seen the Jews listening to him attentively as he spoke of Abraham, Moses, and the Law of the Prophets, but as soon as he came to Jesus, the Passion, and the Cross he saw them withdraw, turn against him, and persecute him. The Jews have their particular wisdom too: they seek to hold on to the promises made exclusively to their people, they ask for signs, they look for miracles, miracles which will confirm their supremacy over other races. This wisdom too is contrary to the Christian faith.

Christian wisdom is just as incompatible with the Greeks' notion of wisdom as it is with that of the Jews. It despises intellectual subtleties, linguistic cleverness and ingenious methods. It depends on God who supplies power in weakness, riches in poverty, and glory in humility. The fact is that neither Jew nor Greek can accept such a doctrine because it goes against human reactions and reasoning power. What God in fact wants is for us to rely on him for everything so that 'Whoever wants to boast must boast of what the Lord has done' (*1 Corinthians* 1, 31).

Christian maturity

The Corinthians, to whom Paul was writing, were Christians, believers at any rate, and, for the most part at least, very attached to their faith. They were, however, easily influenced by what went on around them, forgetful of the Spirit within them and refusing to let themselves be guided by it. Paul, who had given them milk to drink instead of solid food for which they were not ready, knew this and there was ample proof of it in the stories of division, discord, and jealousy which filtered through to him: these feelings went completely against the whole spirit of unity.

To live fully as a child of God it is essential to allow for the guidance of the Spirit. In this way one becomes 'mature' as Paul says (*1 Corinthians* 2, 6), spiritual, not rich in

brilliant theories, great powers of inspiration or exceptional deeds, but rich in love. And Paul, after giving practical advice about the specific cases reported to him: incest, recourse to pagan authorities, fornication, marriage, and virginity, the conduct of women in Church meetings etc, sings a hymn in praise of love.

This hymn to love is certainly one of the high points of the whole New Testament. In it Paul reaches the sublime, in describing the unique, impenetrable mystery which is, for the apostle, the inner life of God. His description is so intense that it departs from the human realm to touch on the very sight of God, a vision both real in the here and now, and inspired by the eternal and the world that is to come. There is no doubt that Paul, in this piece of exultation provided the Corinthians with an example of a man in whom God's spirit lived.

This, however, is only the 'least of all the apostles' (*1 Corinthians* 15, 9), yet he preached what they had all believed, the knowledge that Christ had risen from the dead. Paul was horrified therefore to see that some were denying the Resurrection. In ending his letter he reaffirms the witness of the Church. Certainly the Resurrection was difficult to understand, philosophically,

---

The hymn to love

'I may be able to speak the languages of men and even of angels, but if I have no love, my speech is no more than a noisy gong or a clanging bell. I may have the gift of inspired preaching; I may have all knowledge and understand all secrets; I may have all the faith I need to move mountains — but if I have no love I am nothing. I may give away everything I have, and even give up my body to be burnt — but if I have no love, this does me no good. Love is patient and kind; it is not jealous or conceited or proud; love is not ill-mannered or selfish or irritable; love does not keep a record of wrongs; love is not happy with evil, but is happy with the truth. Love never gives up; and its faith, hope, and patience never fail. Love is eternal. There are inspired messages, but they are temporary; there are gifts of speaking in strange tongues, but they will cease; there is knowledge, but it will pass ...'
(*I Corinthians* 13, 1–8)

scientifically, intellectually, especially for the Greeks of that time. Nevertheless, it remains at the heart of the Christian message. 'The first Adam, made of earth, came from the earth; the second Adam came from heaven' (*1 Corinthians* 15, 47).

The Apostle

Paul had many difficulties with the Corinthians. In the letter which we call the *Second Letter to the Corinthians* we see him defending himself against unjustified attacks. His character and methods have been called into question; his intentions doubted; even his status as an apostle has been challenged. Does he lecture and accuse his attackers? No, that is not his way. He simply presents the testimony of his conscience and in this way describes his own idea of apostleship.

The apostle does not speak by his own authority, he speaks in Christ, called by God to be a minister of a new covenant; his only recommendation is that of the Christians who live by the Spirit and not according to the Letter of the Law: 'for the written law brings death, but the Spirit gives life' (*II Corinthians* 3, 6); finally he is destined for an eternal glory, for, if the ministry of the written Law carried out by Moses — a ministry of death according to Paul — was surrounded by a glory so great that the Hebrews could not look at it, how great will be the glory surrounding a spiritual ministry.

But now this great mission is beset by human frailty: 'Yet we who have this spiritual treasure are like common clay pots, in order to show that the supreme power belongs to God, not to us' (*II Corinthians* 4, 7). Paul lives like this from day to day: he is burdened with many troubles, but never crushed; he is persecuted, but never abandoned; he is hurt but never destroyed. He suffers a thousand deaths and so carries in his body the death of Christ. Such are the weaknesses in the apostle's ministry.

Strength and weakness, victory and defeat, life and death. The apostle's life holds the same paradoxes as did the life of Jesus: 'For even though it was in weakness that he was put to death on the cross, it is by God's power that he lives' (*II Corinthians* 13, 4).

So the apostle glories in his weakness which is the instrument of divine power. 'My power is strongest when you are weak' (*II Corinthians* 12, 9). His strength does not come from the flesh, but from God and is given to him in order to build up the faithful in the truth.

Paul ends his letter in praise of himself, not that he wishes to whitewash his character — he has spoken too much about his own weakness — but because the attacks aimed at him were damaging to the apostle of Christ. This passage is marked by an unparalleled strength and liveliness. He wishes to demonstrate his steadfastness in testing times, the purity of his intentions, his forbearance and generosity towards others, such are the fruits of the Holy Spirit in his apostles. Carried away by his feelings, he casts up to his detractors the revelations and visions he has had, and the testimony of his life: and there is plenty there in human terms to boast of. But Paul boasts only of this weaknesses (*II Corinthians* 12, 5).

Paul's defence

'Are they Hebrews? So am I. Are they Israelites? So am I. Are they Abraham's descendants? So am I. Are they Christ's servants? I sound like a madman — but I am a better servant than they are! I have worked much harder, I have been in prison more times, I have been whipped much more, and I have been near death more often. Five times I was given the 39 lashes by the Jews; three times I was whipped by the Romans; and once I was stoned. I have been in three shipwrecks and once I spent 24 hours in the water. In my many travels I have been in danger from floods and from robbers, in danger from fellow Jews and from Gentiles; there have been dangers in the cities, dangers in the wilds, dangers on the high seas, and dangers from false friends. There has been work and toil; often I have gone without sleep; I have been hungry and thirsty; I have often been without enough food, shelter or clothing. And not to mention other things, every day I am under the pressure of my concern for all the churches.' (*II Corinthians* 11, 22–8)

Paul's Letter to the Galatians

Meeting unorthodox doctrines

The call to Christian freedom

Paul vigorously defends his right to be called an apostle and delivers a swingeing indictment of false gospels.

The Galatians were the inhabitants of an area colonized by the Romans in Asia Minor. Paul would most probably have founded the community there during a short visit with Barnabas. There was a significant number of Jews in the community which would explain its unusual loyalty to Jewish traditions and the Law. Paul sees this as a misunderstanding of the New Covenant. It will not do! The Galatians reject Paul. Isn't he a rather late arrival among the Apostles? Isn't it a fact that he never saw Jesus during his life on earth? To be precise, isn't his Gospel second hand?

Paul's defence

From the outset the tone of the letter is firm and direct. The first words are not of grace or thanks but are a forthright affirmation of the status of the author, 'whose call to be an apostle did not come from men or by means of man, but from Jesus Christ and God the Father, who raised him from death' (*Galatians* 1, 1). This direct approach serves to underline Paul's authority whilst at the same time seizing the attention of those to whom he is writing.

Nor does Paul leave it at that. His vocation has been called into question and in response he gives a detailed account of how he was called by God: his past as a devoted Jew, his unrelenting persecution of God's Church and the damage he did to

its cause and then the revelation he received from the one who had chosen him in his mother's womb. Paul's sudden and inexplicable change of heart on the Damascus road was not simply a conversion experience but an exceptional instance of divine intervention, clear evidence that his mission came directly from God. So he 'did not go to anyone for advice', nor did he go to Jerusalem to see those who were Apostles before him, but simply went out to preach to the Gentiles.

It was not until three years later that Paul paid a visit to Peter, spending two weeks with him and meeting James, but none of the other Apostles. Afterwards he travelled to Syria and Cilicia. Paul was not known to those in the Mother Church at Jerusalem. They only knew what was said about his conversion, from persecutor to apostle and praised God for the miracle of it.

It was another 14 years before he returned to Jerusalem following a revelation: as ever, his direction is from God. Barnabas and Titus went with him, giving the appearance

The rebuke

'I am surprised at you! In no time at all you are deserting the one who called you by the grace of Christ and are accepting another gospel. Actually, there is no "other gospel", but I say this because there are some people who are upsetting you and trying to change the gospel of Christ. But even if we or an angel from heaven should preach to you a gospel that is different from the one we preached to you, may he be condemned to hell! We have said it before, and now I say it again: if anyone preaches to you a gospel that is different from the one you accepted, may he be condemned to hell.' (*Galatians* 1, 6–9)

of an official delegation and Paul, anxious to secure the unity of all the Churches, explained to the leaders the Gospel he was preaching. Not that there were any differences of doctrine between them, but the phenomenal spread of Christianity throughout the Gentile world had led to different attitudes being held depending on the preacher, the place or the believers themselves. Some clarification was badly needed.

Paul's Gospel

Paul's experience was quite unique: he had not known Christ on earth, his vocation was miraculous, and his mission was first and foremost to the Gentiles. Add to this his past experience as a teacher of the Law and we have the breeding ground from which God developed the Pauline doctrine: The Gospel of Paul. This is not intended to refer to the whole of Paul's teaching, much of which was in complete agreement with Peter's, but to those themes stemming from his own special revelation of Jesus Christ which are fundamental to his preaching.

For Paul, grace, the free gift from God, is the alpha and omega of the work of salvation. To give another principle of justice, the Law for example, or circumcision — is to reduce Jesus to a secondary role, to give

The disagreement with Peter

'But when Peter came to Antioch, I opposed him in public, because he was clearly wrong. Before some men who had been sent by James arrived there, Peter had been eating with the Gentile brothers. But after these men arrived, he drew back and would not eat with the Gentiles, because he was afraid of those who were in favour of circumcising them. The other Jewish brothers also started acting like cowards along with Peter; and even Barnabas was swept along by their cowardly action. When I saw that they were not walking a straight path in line with the truth of the gospel, I said to Peter in front of them all: "You are a Jew, yet you have been living like a Gentile, not like a Jew. How, then, can you try to force Gentiles to live like Jews?"' (*Galatians* 2, 11–14)

subordinate status to his death and resurrection, perhaps even to doubt its effectiveness. Paul stands for the break with the requirement of Jewishness, the independence of Christianity, and freedom from constraints.

Peter and the community in Jerusalem were operating under different circumstances. The Jewish religion imperceptibly imposed its customs, traditions, and requirements. The external social pressures extended their influence to the heart of the Christian community. They were afraid of scandal and did not wish to cause offence. Deep down, however, they were of the same mind: proof of this lies in the fact that they did not insist on circumcision for Paul's Greek companion, Titus.

At the Jerusalem assembly, agreement was reached between Paul and the other Apostles who found no fault with his Gospel. Furthermore, the leaders of the Church declared that God had in fact designated specific tasks for each of them: Paul was to preach the word to the uncircumcised and Peter to the circumcised; God, who had made Peter the Apostle of the circumcised had also, and with the same authority, made Paul the Apostle of the uncircumcised. They gladly shook hands on this agreement.

However, the agreement did not immediately have the expected effect. Peter paid a visit to the Christians at Antioch and among these converted Gentiles he dispensed with the Jewish dietary laws and lived as they did. But before long some people of Jewish origin arrived, members of James's group of believers who were strongly attached to their Jewish customs; Peter immediately withdrew from the original group and resumed all the Jewish practices. Paul was upset by this and reacted strongly.

Faith and Law

So much for the facts. Let us now turn to the arguments. Paul is a man of logic: he develops, explains, demonstrates. First of all he addresses himself to the converted Gentiles and reminds them of their first contacts with the faith, the vivid description of Christ which he gave them, the receiving of the

Spirit, the miracles, the healings, the inspiration, the enthusiasm everyone had for the cause, the persecutions. Then he asks them: 'Did you know the Law of Moses at that time?' Of course not. Isn't it obvious therefore that this Law is not necessary for salvation?

It is clear that to link observation of the Jewish Law with faith is to take a step backwards and question whether we are in fact entering the Messianic era. Paul says 'To show that you are his sons, God sent the Spirit of his Son into our hearts, the Spirit who cries out, "Father, my Father". So then you are no longer a slave but a son' (*Galatians* 4, 6). Slavery is the condition of those who are under the Law, liberty belongs to those who are sons.

Hagar and Sarah

Paul then turns his attention to the Christians of Jewish background and finds in the Law, namely the Revelation or Old Testament, an argument against the Law, that is the ritual regulations of Judaism. The word 'Law' stands for these two separate things and it was quite common to interchange them. But, for Paul and the Christians it was clear that the Word of God would stand forever whereas Jewish legalism had been abolished by Christ.

Abraham had two sons, first Ishmael, by his slave Hagar, and then Isaac, by his wife Sarah. Thus one was the son of a slavewoman and the other the son of a freewoman. The one represents the Old Covenant made by Moses, a regime of slavery, the other represents the New Covenant in Jesus, a regime of freedom. The parallel does not stop there. In *Genesis*, Ishmael, the slavewoman's son, persecutes Isaac, the freewoman's son, to the point where Abraham has to send away the slave and her son: 'the son of the slavewoman will not have a part of the father's property along with the son of the freewoman' (*Galatians* 4, 30 and *Genesis* 20, 10).

So the situation in which Paul and the Galatians found themselves echoed in a mysterious way that story recorded in the first pages of the Bible. This interpretation of Paul's had the great advantage of using both allegory, which was a common device among the rabbis and therefore familiar to the apostle, and a rereading of the Bible in the light of Christ as practised by the Christians. An effective argument indeed.

Christian freedom

Christians are therefore the sons of the freewoman. It is freedom which makes the Christian. This is why 'neither circumcision nor the lack of it makes any difference at all' (*Galatians* 5, 6), neither the submission of the slave, nor observing the Law to the last detail; 'you were called to be free', Paul says, 'stand then as free people and do not allow yourselves to become slaves again.' But liberty is not licence, for the Spirit lives in the Christian and is opposed to the flesh as the flesh is opposed to the Spirit.

At the end Paul stresses the need for charity. 'For the whole Law is summed up in one commandment: 'Love your neighbour as you love yourself' (*Galatians* 5, 14). Love is not in reality some rule which is imposed from outside, it is not a law in the normal sense of the word, but a force, an internal energy springing from the Spirit which lives in the Christian. In this way freedom and love are united.

The teaching of the Law

'But before the time for faith came, the Law kept us locked up as prisoners until this coming faith should be revealed. And so the Law was in charge of us until Christ came, in order that we might then be put right with God through faith. Now that the time for faith is here, the Law is no longer in charge of us. It is through faith that all of you are God's sons in union with Christ Jesus. You were baptized into union with Christ, and now you are clothed, so to speak, with the life of Christ himself. So there is no difference between Jews and Gentiles, between slaves and freemen, between men and women; you are all one in union with Christ Jesus.' (*Galatians* 3, 23–8)

Paul's Letter to the Ephesians

A letter to Christians

Contemplation of the mystery of the Church

God's plan, fixed for all eternity and obscured for centuries, is accomplished by Jesus and lived out by the Church.

Despite its name, the *Letter to the Ephesians* does not appear to have been addressed solely to the Ephesians, but to all the Churches of Asia Minor; it is in the nature of an encyclical or circular letter. It is not so much a letter, dealing with current situations, as a theological essay, or rather an admiring meditation. In it Paul reveals the essential elements of his thought and meditates on the greatness of the mystery of his experiences. It was probably written during his captivity in Rome between the years 61 and 63.

The revelation of the mystery

The *Letter to the Ephesians* resembles a liturgy with blessing, thanksgiving, address, prayers

etc. After the customary greeting comes a hymn of praise outlining God's plan for the world: the predestination or destiny of Christians for eternity, the redemption in the blood of Christ, the revelation of his mystery, the bringing together of everything in heaven and on earth under Christ, and the sanctification of all in the Holy Spirit. There is a recurring refrain 'Let us praise God's glory' which is reminiscent of the responses of the people during services.

The thanksgiving follows, giving thanks for the faith and love of Christians, the people to whom Paul was writing. Then comes the prayer asking God to give them a spirit of wisdom and insight. The act and its understanding, are two aspects which the apostle is constantly comparing: both have their origin in God; both are the legacy of the saints; both are greater than can be imagined, not only now, but in the time to come; both are concerned with the person of Christ, who is risen from the dead and seated on the right hand of the Father in Heaven, the one who rules over all. The mystery and its revelation are like two aspects of the same reality.

Redemption

How terrible things were for the pagan before Christ came! He was in the power of the prince of this world and lived according to his carnal desires (the flesh and blood Matthew speaks of, which is a world limited in space and time). He followed his own wishes and unworthy thoughts. But God loved us. We were dead, he brought us back to life, and raised us to sit with Christ in heaven. This salvation is not our doing, it does not come through our words, God made us as we are and had already prepared the good deeds which we were to perform.

Before Christ, people were divided into

Predestination

'Let us give thanks to the God and Father of our Lord Jesus Christ! For in our union with Christ he has blessed us by giving us every spriritual blessing in the heavenly world. Even before the world was made, God had already chosen us to be his through our union with Christ, so that we would be holy and without fault before him. Because of his love, God had already decided that through Jesus Christ he would make us his sons — this was his pleasure and purpose. Let us praise God for his glorious grace, for the free gift he gave us in his dear Son!'
(*Ephesians* 1, 3–6)

two distinct groups: the Greeks and the Jews. The Law was an impenetrable barrier: the Jew was proud, he was aware of possessing certain promises, of having been chosen from the masses to be the élite of humankind; he looked down on other people, distrusted and shunned them for fear of contaminating himself. The Greek, on the other hand, had nothing but contempt for any kind of constraint, challenged what he couldn't understand and labelled as barbarian anything that was foreign to him. There was no contact between these two groups because they had become separated by a fierce hatred which was reinforced in each generation: the discrimination reached right to the Temple at Jerusalem where the Gentiles were forbidden to enter on pain of death.

With Jesus, the barrier came down, the Law no longer ruled. He destroyed hate, he reunited those who were separated, reconciled them in a new man and made from them a single body: 'So Christ came and preached the Good News of peace to all — to you Gentiles who were far away from God and to the Jews who were near to him' (*Ephesians* 2, 17). For he gave life to both in the same Spirit and gave everyone access to the Father. Paul compares the new humanity to a building: Christ is its cornerstone; the Apostles and the Prophets are the foundation. It is a holy temple, God's dwelling place.

The Church

Paul is proud of having had the mystery of God revealed to him. The men of the past did not have it and those to whom he went, the Christians of Asia had their knowledge of it through him, Paul. He is the master of the Word. The honour of preaching the unfathomable riches of Christ's love to the Gentiles has been given to him.

It is for this reason that he is now a prisoner. But testing is a part of God's plan so there is no point in getting upset about it. The apostle's only prayer is one which complements his mission perfectly, namely that Christ might live in their heart, making them realize the greatness of God's love.

Each person has a God-given role to play: some are apostles, others prophets, others evangelists, others pastors and teachers. All God's people are thus prepared for the work of building up the body of Christ into a perfect unity. They are to grow continually in the knowledge of God's son and of faith so that they mature into a body with the risen Christ as its head and with the limbs joined to him by every joint and nerve, and by the various functions which each part performs in building up the whole body.

The Church is a living thing, it lives the life of Christ himself and this same life flows through all its members. In John's Gospel Jesus had spoken of the vine and its branches. Here Paul is exploring the same theme. Perhaps this gives an even clearer illustration of the diversity among the members of the Church, the differences that are apparent between them without breaking the powerful link which unites them, since that is the same power which raised Jesus from the dead and now continues to work through the mystical body of Christ.

The new life

Paul continues his letter in giving some advice for living. This inclusion in the mystical body of Christ makes certain demands. The apostle takes the very biblical image of

---

Greeks and Jews

'You Gentiles by birth — called "the uncircumcised" by the Jews, who call themselves "the circumcised" (which refers to what is done to the body) — remember what you were in the past. At that time you were apart from Christ. You were foreigners and did not belong to God's chosen people. You had no part in the covenants, which were based on God's promises to his people, and you lived in this world without hope and without God. But now, in union with Christ Jesus, you who used to be far away have been brought near by the death of Christ ... So then you Gentiles are not foreigners or strangers any longer; you are now fellow citizens with God's people and members of the family of God.' (*Ephesians* 2, 11–13 and 19)

clothing: take off the old man and put on the new. To the Hebrew mind this would not signify simply a superficial external change, but a profound transformation of character: it is to go from the first creation to a new creation 'which is created in God's likeness and reveals itself in the true life which is upright and holy' (*Ephesians* 4, 24), and Paul's instructions are clear and unequivocal: put away all bitterness, rage, anger, offensiveness, and insult etc, be kind and loving towards others, and forgive them as God has forgiven you: 'Since you are God's dear children, you must try to be like him' (*Ephesians* 5, 1).

These are hard demands which would be unthinkable without the help of the Church and the Son of God. Paul makes the comparison with a marriage: 'A husband has authority over his wife just as Christ has authority over the Church' (*Ephesians* 5, 23). Christ now holds the position held by God in the Old Testament where Israel was referred to as the unfaithful wife of Jahweh. He has shown his love for the Church by his death, he makes its members holy and pure

---

The Church, the bride of Christ

'Husbands love your wives just as Christ loved the Church and gave his life for it. He did this to dedicate the Church to God by his word, after making it clean by washing it in water, in order to present the Church to himself in all its beauty — pure and faultless without spot or wrinkle or any other imperfection. Men ought to love their wives just as they love their own bodies. A man who loves his wife loves himself. No one ever hates his own body. Instead he feeds it and takes care of it, just as Christ does the Church; for we are members of his body.' (*Ephesians* 5, 25–30)

---

by baptism and wants it to be glorious and without blemish. In order to emphasize this intimate union, the apostle turns to the passage in Genesis recalling the words: 'the two will become one flesh' (*Genesis* 2, 24 and *Ephesians* 5, 31).

The spiritual battle

This wonderful vision of the Christian's situation does not mean that he can rest on his laurels and take life as it comes. Quite the opposite. Jesus has triumphed, but his victory is not total. The powers of Darkness — Paul says: the principalities, powers and authorities of this world, the forces of evil — will try to reclaim what they have lost. The Christian life is a battle.

Once again Paul employs a biblical image to demonstrate the harshness of the struggle: the Christian must put on the armour of God: he must wear truth like a belt, righteousness as a breastplate, and take as his shoes the readiness to announce the Gospel, with faith as a shield, salvation as a helmet and the Spirit as a sword. As we have seen, all the weapons used in this fight are spiritual ones, for the Christian does not rely on his own strength but on God's power.

So the warrior, armed to the teeth in this way, is simply an instrument. The *Letter to the Ephesians* does not contradict the *Letter to the Corinthians* in which Paul takes a pride in his weakness which enables God's power to be revealed. But this reference to the fighter lends greater force to his final injunction: 'Pray on every occasion as the Spirit leads.' And Paul reminds them of the necessity for prayer on his behalf to enable him to fulfil his work as an apostle and have the boldness to continue his mission despite his imprisonment.

Paul's Letter to the Philippians

A letter to very dear friends

A discourse on the nature and character of Christ

A letter from prison which is marked by great serenity, bearing witness to an exceptional faith.

Paul had a great affection for the Philippians. Philippi had been founded by Philip, the father of Alexander. It was colonized by the Romans in 42 BC and was the first city Paul visited in Europe. The Christian community he founded there was made up almost entirely of former pagans and was very lively. The group often met in the home of Lydia, a seller of purple. Paul was regularly in touch with her and received great financial support for his work from her.

At that time Paul was in prison in Rome but enjoyed a certain amount of freedom. He had had a visit from a Philippian friend, Epaphroditus, who had brought him an important gift. The apostle was moved by this proof of affection. On his part, the visitor was in a position to relate a number

---

To die or to live

'For what is life? To me, it is Christ. Death then will bring more. But if by continuing to live I can do more worthwhile work, then I am not sure which I should choose. I am pulled in two directions. I want very much to leave this life and be with Christ, which is a far better thing; but for your sake it is much more important that I remain alive. I am sure of this, and so I know that I will stay. I will stay on with you all, to add to your progress and joy in the faith, so that when I am with you again, you will have even more reason to be proud of me in your life in union with Christ Jesus.'
(*Philippians* 1, 21–6)

---

of good things. The community at Philippi was growing in faith and love, and was eagerly undertaking the struggle for the Gospel. There were some disputes among the women and the arrival of some Judaeo-Christian agitators had caused a few problems, but nothing serious.

Epaphroditus stayed with Paul for some time. After a short while, not being used to the hurly burly of city life he contracted a fever, became ill, and seemed near to death. Paul was beside him, tending to his needs and praying for his recovery. It was therefore with great joy that he saw his friend restored to health. Two years passed and when Epaphroditus took leave of Paul to return to Philippi, Paul gave him a letter expressing his affection and spiritual joy at the thought of this model community from which he wanted to lift the few remaining shadows.

The prisoner

Isn't it amazing to see this prisoner rejoicing in his chains because they embolden his fellow apostles to speak out even more strongly in proclaiming the Word of God? For Paul only one thing really matters: the Gospel. His mission is important, not his personal fate. As long as the Gospel is not imprisoned — and how could it be? — he is filled with joy.

Even if some of his colleagues act out of envy, jealousy or pride, even if some profit by his absence from the public scene by taking his place and making a name for themselves, even if some of them imagine that in so doing they make his imprisonment worse, he is happy. There are still those who preach Christ sincerely and what does it matter after all: 'I am happy about it, so long as Christ is preached in every way possible, whether from wrong or right motives.' (*Philippians* 1, 18)

Moreover, from the depths of his cell Paul poses a fundamental question: whether to live or to die. To die is to be instantly and for ever with Christ. There can be no doubt that this is the most precious thing a Christian can aspire to. To live is to continue his work as an apostle, ensuring the spread of the Good News and strengthening his brothers in faith and love. Paul does not hesitate for long: it is more important for you that I live. 'So I will stay on with you all.'

In the same breath, as if his decision requires some immediate application, he gives some very simple and practical advice: whether he is with them or not he will hear news of them and hopes this will help them to stand firm, to face their adversaries unafraid, and to accept suffering, for that too is a privilege from God. All Christians are united in the common fight.

Humility and glory

The exhortation ends with an invitation to humility. The reference to welcoming suffering leads into this quite naturally, but here humility is not a simple acceptance of what one is — or at least that is not what is intended — it is the recognition that others are superior to oneself, it is putting oneself at the service of others, it is in fact to have the same motivation as Jesus.

The Messiah's humility

He always had the nature of God, but he did not think that by force he should try to become equal with God. Instead of this, of his own free will he gave up all he had, and took the nature of a servant. He became like man and appeared in human likeness. He was humble and walked the path of obedience all the way to death — his death on the cross. For this reason God raised him to the highest place above and gave him the name that is greater than any other name. And so, in honour of the name of Jesus, all beings in heaven, on earth, and in the world below will fall on their knees, and all will openly proclaim that Jesus Christ is Lord, to the glory of God the Father.' (*Philippians* 2, 6–11)

This conclusion gives rise to one of the finest hymns of Christian doctrine in the New Testament: it is vigourously expressed in rhythmic style and is packed with meaning. There seems to be a break in Paul's letter here as if he were inserting a passage which he had taken particular pains with or one which he had used before, possibly in another letter or in religious ceremonies. This hymn is a summary of Christ's entire theology, the heart of Christianity.

The relationship between humility and glory is the fundamental theme of this song, a song which has echoes of that of Isaiah's suffering servant (*Isaiah* 53, 4–12). Perhaps Paul took his inspiration from there. He would certainly have been familiar with it, and by the similarities in style and thought he demonstrates the continuity between the Old and New Testaments, between the promises and their fulfilment. Christ is the Messiah that was promised.

The three verses each mark a stage in the unfolding of Jesus's incarnation. Firstly there is the antithesis of the Son of God being born in the flesh. He who had equality with God, who had an absolute natural right to the privileges of divinity: majesty, glory, and power in the universe, refused the way of honour and intimacy with God, and chose that of humility, taking human form. Divine form is contrasted with human form, eternity with time, and glory with humility. Jesus chooses humility.

The second verse further develops the idea of humility. Jesus, who now has the appearance of a man and is regarded as a man makes himself the least of men: he does not command, he obeys and this obedience is pushed to extremes, since it goes as far as death, a death which in itself is extreme, being that most shameful of deaths, death on the cross.

The third verse conveys the reverse of that antithesis used in the first verse. In a sense we are taken back to the beginning, the action begins and ends with the eternal God. But there is one major difference: the final glory of the Son of God is not quite the same as at the beginning, it is due to his humility, his taking of the servant's role and his death. There is an exact correspondence between his humility in the human realm and his glory in the divine realm.

True Christians

After speaking as poet and theologian, Paul returns to the role of friend and pastor at the end of his letter. He praises the Philippians for their faith and love, encourages them to grow in the Christian life, and goes back over the disagreements that have arisen in the community. Then he gives free rein to his enthusiasm and returns to a theme which is close to his heart: that of faith and the Law, a theme which might be called Paul's Gospel.

'Watch out for those who do evil things, those dogs, those men who insist on cutting the body' (*Philippians* 3, 2). He discusses at some length the circumcision of the flesh and that of the spirit. It is true, as he says, that he has nothing to envy in those who live by the Law. He has, in that respect, accumulated every honoured qualification and he recites them all including his role as persecutor of the Church. Is there any Jew more Jewish than he?

But in Paul's case there has been a break, a conversion, the discovery of a whole new scale of values. He has suddenly lost interest in the very things which were formerly of greatest importance to him and the thing which he despised has become central to his life. There is no longer any question of believing in justice through the Law. From the moment of his conversion, the whole structure of his former life: circumcision, Israel, the tribe of Benjamin, and Pharisaism, falls apart.

From now on the greatest blessing in life is to know Christ, share his sufferings and experience the power of his resurrection. When we understand the significance of the Hebrew word for 'to know', namely to have intimate experience of the other person, we realize that Paul is implying a very strong sense of unity with Christ which amounts almost to assimilation, being absorbed into him. This new Paul has certainly come a long way since his days as scourge of the Church!

But the road to be travelled is a long one. Knowledge of Christ grows deeper each day. Paul himself confesses that he has not reached the goal, he is not perfect, but he is pressing on. 'Let us go forward', he says to his friends, 'Let us go forward according to the same rules we have followed until now' (*Philippians* 3, 16). There is no question of looking backwards or of stopping. Then, as if to strengthen their commitment, Paul looks to the future where, beyond the trials of this world, he sees the Lord Jesus coming from heaven, 'to change our weak mortal bodies and make them like his own glorious body'. This is assimilation again, but this time it is assimilation into his resurrection.

Paul's defence

'If anyone thinks he can trust in external ceremonies, I have even more reason to feel that way. I was circumcised when I was a week old, I am an Israelite by birth, of the tribe of Benjamin, a pure-blooded Hebrew. As far as keeping the Jewish Law is concerned, I was a Pharisee, and I was so zealous that I persecuted the Church. As far as a person can be righteous by obeying the Law, I was without fault. But all those things that I might count as profit I now reckon as loss for Christ's sake. Not only those things; I reckon everything as complete loss for the sake of what is so much more valuable, the knowledge of Christ Jesus my Lord. For his sake I have thrown everything away; I consider it all as mere refuse, so that I may gain Christ.' (*Philippians* 3, 4–8)

Paul's Letter to the Colossians

Letter to a Church in crisis

Christ as the absolute authority in the Church

A warning against 'the worthless deceit of human wisdom which comes from the teachings handed down by men and from the ruling spirits of the universe'.

Colossae is a town in Phrygia which Paul never visited. It was evangelized by one of Paul's disciples, Epaphras, who founded a lively Christian community there in Paul's name and in close consultation with him. Paul therefore felt as responsible for this church as he did for all the others in Asia Minor and intervened as soon as any conflict or crisis arose.

Phrygia is a rather turbulent area: storms often gather there, there are frequent earth tremors, the ground is riddled with craters and faults from which sulphurous gases escape. For the people living there then, the world was, as Thales said 'infested with demons'. It seemed to them that they were witnesses to the eternal struggle between the spirits of the air and the underworld, and there was even a place near Hierapolis which was reputed to be the gate of hell. Rumours went so far as to detail the proliferation of the earth's demons, the multitude of thrones, principalities, forces and powers of the sky, and the profusion of evil spirits in the air. An entire world of magical inhabitants.

This apparently primitive mentality had nevertheless profoundly influenced the people and in order to draw together, at least superficially, the crude traditional beliefs and the more considered doctrines, a kind of syncretism, or mixture of religions, was created which was able to accommodate Jewish aspirations, elements of Greek philosophy, bits of the orphic mysteries, and even the religious doctrines from Zoroastrianism, a Persian religion based on the opposition of good and evil. The intermediate beings, angels or spirits figure prominently in all this and it was even claimed that one of them had presented the Law to Moses and that Christ himself was in fact a mediating angel.

The *Letter to the Colossians* does not give a detailed account of the particular heresy which was sweeping Phrygia at the time. After all, Paul is writing to the group of Christians on the spot who would have known all about it, but the warning note he sounds gives him the chance to go deeper into certain aspects of his theology and to present it afresh. There are no virulent condemnations or harsh words in this letter. He has confidence in the reliability of these Christians and only wants to alert them to the danger.

Thanksgiving

We always give thanks to God, the Father of our Lord Jesus Christ, when we pray for you. For we have heard of your faith in Christ Jesus and of your love for all God's people. When the true message, the Good News, first came to you, you heard about the hope it offers. So your faith and love are based on what you hope for, which is kept safe for you in heaven. The gospel keeps bringing blessings and is spreading throughout the world, just as it has among you ever since the day you first heard about the grace of God and came to know it as it really is. You learnt of God's grace from Epaphras, our dear fellow-servant, who is Christ's faithful worker on our behalf. He has told us of the love that the Spirit has given you.' (*Colossians* 1, 3–8)

Knowledge of the mystery

Strangely, in the jumble of theories, dogmas, and beliefs fashionable in Phrygia at that time, 'knowledge', wisdom — but what kind of knowledge? What sort of wisdom? — was not only held to be of greatest importance, but was even supposed to bring salvation as if by magic: knowledge had in fact become a magic word, just like gnosis, meaning 'mystical insight', did in later years. Paul does not set out to challenge this whole notion, isn't Christianity itself a revelation of knowledge? But he does aim to get rid of the fanciful elements in it, separate it from its dubious esoteric aspects, and make it focus once more on the Christian mystery.

But where others spoke of purely intellectual speculation, Paul is talking about effective knowledge. He sees that the word of truth, the Good News 'keeps bringing blessings and is spreading throughout the world'. This means that it changes whoever receives it, inspiring them with a powerful energy, making them produce 'all kinds of good deeds', and giving them absolute steadfastness and endurance. With joy Paul gives thanks to the Father who has given the Colossians a share in this knowledge through the ministry of his dear companion Epaphras.

Christ's work

The Christian mystery is the work of Christ and on this theme Paul composes another of those Christological hymns (hymns on the theme of Christ's character), for which he has a talent. The style changes, the rhythm becomes regular, more and more use is made of parallels and repetitions. What we have here is a poem in two parts: the first part exalts Christ's work in Creation and the second his work in Redemption. This is a summary of the whole message, a charter for the Christian community.

This is a very skilful hymn which, in its first part uses terms which are well suited to the context of those times: the invisible God, things visible and invisible etc, as if the apostle was deliberately drawing on the fashionable speculations of the day to produce a new format for the orthodox doctrine. But the supreme importance of Christ is in no way sacrificed. On the contrary, his claims here are among the most audacious that he has ever made. 'God created the whole universe through him and for him.'

So, using very concise phrases, Paul declares Jesus's equality with the invisible God, his existence before all creation, and his decisive and necessary intervention in the life of humankind, and the make-up of the world on earth and in heaven. Christ is placed on the one hand at the most spiritual philosophical level, and on the other at the very realistic level of *Genesis*. Here Paul is the worthy representative of both Greek thought and Jewish tradition.

Contrasted with the idea of creation is the idea of salvation expressed in the second section. The first-born before all creation is also the first-born of the dead: this is a strange phrase, dictated by the format of the poem, meaning that he is the first of the risen. The antithesis between the two ideas is underlined by a parallel construction and the use of similar terms, even at the risk of startling the reader. But it is indeed a question of a new creation which concerns the things of earth and the things of heaven. Jesus was the cause of the first creation and

Primacy of Christ

'Christ is the visible likeness of the invisible God. He is the first-born Son, superior to all created things. For through him God created everything in heaven and on earth, the seen and the unseen things, including spiritual powers, lords, rulers, and authorities. God created the whole universe through him and for him. Christ existed before all things and in union with him all things have their proper place. He is the head of his body, the Church, he is the source of the body's life. He is the first-born Son, who was raised from the death, in order that he alone might have the first place in all things. For it was by God's own decision that the Son has in himself the full nature of God. Through the Son, then, God decided to bring the whole universe back to himself. God made peace through his Son's death on the cross and so brought back to himself all things, both on earth and in heaven.' (*Colossians* 1, 15–20)

he is the cause of the second; he brings back everything to himself in the second as in the first.

Between the two passages is this small phrase which, because of its situation in the poem, takes on a particular resonance: 'He is the head of the body of the Church.' This typical Pauline theme of the Church as the body of Christ is very strongly associated here with the redemptive and saving work of the second creation, since even before going on to glorify this work, Paul makes a natural link between it and the Church.

The service of the mystery

This link is certainly one which particularly motivates Paul. He is a missionary before he is a theologian. In all his letters, and particularly in this *Letter to the Colossians*, it appears that his knowledge of the mystery is neither bookish nor speculative and that before speaking it, he lives it. Each new expression of the mystery of Christ leads to a new expression of Paul's own vocation, mission, and life, as if the one was primary by its importance and the other primary in his experience.

Thus he is led to give the Colossians one of the most beautiful phrases expressing the Christian life: 'by means of my physical sufferings I am helping to complete what

---

Paul's ministry

'And now I am happy about my sufferings for you, for by means of my physical sufferings I am helping to complete what still remains of Christ's sufferings on behalf of his body, the Church. And I have been made a servant of the Church by God who gave me this task to perform for your God. It is the task of proclaiming his message, which is the secret he hid through all past ages from all humankind, but has now revealed to his people. God's plan is to make known his secret to his people, this rich and glorious secret which he has for all peoples. And the secret is that Christ is in you, which means that you will share in the glory of God.' (*Colossians* 1, 24–7)

---

still remains of Christ's sufferings on behalf of his body, the Church' (*Colossians* 1, 24). Paul sees communion with Christ even in his sufferings as a prisoner, and at the same time he is aware of being within the Church. This is so true that he feels the same energy at work in Christ, in himself, and in the Church.

His experience leads him on to the experience of those to whom he is writing. Granted, he is not with them in the flesh; he has never even visited them, but he knows them and is present among them in spirit: like him they have been buried with Christ in baptism; like him they have been raised with Christ, they are alive again, pardoned, freed from sin and death. Together he and they are part of the mystical body of Christ.

The new life

This transformation has important consequences. The chief concerns are no longer things of the flesh, but only things of the spirit. For, in Paul's eyes, there are two levels of thought. Problems of food, drink, holy days, and the Sabbath, these belong to thoughts of the flesh. So too do rituals, rules, and the worship of angels; they are 'things which become useless once they are used', they are 'man-made rules and teachings'.

The Christian looks to the things of heaven, where Christ is to be found. Paul then explains this idea: the Christian rejects injustice, greed, violence, vengeance, hate, and selfishness in all its forms, things which subordinate everything, even God to the power of the self, and he seeks justice, gentleness, forgiveness, and love, things which make the self subordinate to others and to God. 'And to all these qualities, add love which binds all things together in perfect unity' (*Colossians* 3, 14).

Paul ends his letter with some simple practical pieces of advice, his news, and good wishes: 'At the same time pray also for us, so that God will give us a good opportunity to preach his message about the secret of Christ. For that is why I am now in prison. Pray then, that I may speak, as I should, in such a way as to make it clear' (*Colossians* 4, 3).

Paul's Letters to the Thessalonians

Letters to a young community

The Day of the Lord

Writing to young Christians who are feverishly awaiting the end of the world, Paul talks of the forerunners and the suddenness of the Day of the Lord.

During one of his first journeys, Paul was called by a vision to go and preach in Macedonia. He went without delay to Thessalonica, the capital of that Roman province, and began to preach Christ in the town's synagogue and public places. The Greeks flocked to hear him, but the Jews, jealous of his success among the Gentiles, at first showed indifference, then distrust, and finally a hostility which became more and more overt, forcing Paul to go away. His first letter to the Thessalonians was written from Corinth c. AD 51–2.

Paul would be well aware of the situation facing this new community: on one side the temptations of the pagan world; on the other the hostility of the Jewish world which was stirring up opposition to them. He sent his friend Timothy to them and he returned with the reassuring news that these Christians were holding firm to the faith. They were, however, involved in some lively debates: they remembered that Paul had proclaimed the return of Christ, an event they were now anxiously anticipating, wondering what would become of those who would die before it happened. Paul felt obliged to try and clarify these problems in order to bring peace to the community.

This letter is full of the kind of affection a father or mother has for their children. The sudden separation before he was able to get the community fully established, the danger confronting them which also prevented his visiting them, and perhaps a deep sense of harmony with them made Paul feel especially fond of this particular community. Over and over again he says that he is thinking of them, that he is praying for them, that he is filled with joy because he knows the fervour of their faith, the effectiveness of their love, and the strength of their hope.

Joy is a word which appears often in this letter. Paul brought the Gospel message to the Thessalonians, he also brought them joy, a joy which they demonstrate despite their sufferings and difficulties, something they share with the churches in Judaea, the martyrs of today, and the prophets of the past who were all persecuted, it is a joy which bears witness to the authenticity of their faith. It says in the book of *Acts*: 'As the Apostles left the Council, they were happy because God had considered them worthy

---

The dead

'Our brothers, we want you to know the truth about those who have died, so that you will not be sad, as are those who have no hope. We believe that Jesus died and rose again, and so we believe that God will take back with Jesus those who have died believing in him. What we are teaching you now is the Lord's teaching; we who are alive on the day the Lord comes will not go ahead of those who have died. There will be the shout of command, the archangel's voice, the sound of God's trumpet, and the Lord himself will come down from heaven. Those who have died believing in Christ will rise to life first; then we who are living at that time will be gathered up along with them in the clouds to meet the Lord in the air. And so we will always be with the Lord.' (*I Thessalonians* 4, 13–17)

---

to suffer disgrace for the sake of Jesus' (*Acts* 5, 41). Such joy can only come from the knowledge of Christ's Passion, the certainty of the resurrection and the hope of his return to be with his own.

... And the dead?

Although Paul's short stay at Thessalonica had enabled him to pass on the basics of Christianity it had not allowed him the chance to tackle every question. There was quite a lot to be getting on with: they were to turn away from idols, acknowledge the one true God, live in a manner worthy of his kingdom and his glory. For these new young converts the most important question was the return of Christ: they spoke about it, rejoiced in it, considered the triumph of it, and lived for it. Their whole community was pervaded with the sense of expectation of this future; the coming of the Lord was what bound them together, what formed the basis of their love, and what inspired their celebrations.

They were understandably distressed when death struck in their ranks. They had not thought that some of them might die before Christ's return, so imminent did that event seem to them. Then, this community which was dear to them, which represented for them the country of their faith, which seemed to be the sign of the presence of the Holy Spirit, suddenly found that part of itself was missing: there were brothers who were now absent and no longer shared in the discussions, the love or the communion. What was to become of them when Christ returned? This was the problem Timothy reported to Paul.

The apostle feels duty-bound to reply. Firstly he insists on the holiness of the life required of God's people, a holiness of life which he knows exists in Thessalonica. However, he rests this exhortation on the uncertainty of the moment: 'The Day of the Lord will come as a thief comes at night.' But at once he says: 'you are not in the darkness, you are children of the light, so the day will not surprise you like a thief.' Then comes the order: 'do not be asleep like the others, but stay awake and sober.' The two ideas Paul wants to get over to these converts are the security of a perfect life and

the uncertainty of the particular moment. By bringing these two ideas together Paul is able to emphasize the necessity for vigilance without rebuking them for any lack of it.

Having given this advice Paul tries to satisfy his correspondents' curiosity. His description certainly has an imaginative, almost childlike quality with its trumpet of God and voice of the archangel, which could be distracting. But the essential point of what he is saying is obviously to guarantee that those who will witness paradise in their lifetime will not have any advantage over those who have died, and to emphasize that the important thing is to be reunited with Christ. And in replying to the Thessalonians' questions Paul confirms that: the entire group will take part in the joy of Christ's triumph. The apostle calls the dead 'those who have fallen asleep in Christ' and those who have died in union with Jesus remain in union with him beyond death and into paradise.

No doubt this reply of Paul's would leave several grey areas in the minds of the curious. It cannot be otherwise, for in speaking about eschatology, the things concerning the end of the world, it is difficult to find words in our vocabulary, or indeed ideas in our minds which give adequate expression to this subject. Paul himself uses a literary style which is apocalyptic, where symbols, signs, and prophecies are mingled together to present a theological assertion, namely the resurrection of the body.

The Lord's coming

A few months after this letter, the community in Thessalonica was again showing signs of nervousness and tension. The persecution was continuing, rumours abounded, and bogus letters from Paul were circulating. 'The Day of the Lord is at hand' was the story going around and certain idle people seized on this as justification for their laziness. They walked the streets, faces haunted by the prospect of the end of the world and preferred begging to their daily work, living as parasites and spreading trouble in the community.

Paul's *Second Letter to the Thessalonians* uses a firmer tone than the first. The apostle is somewhat irritated by all this upheaval: 'I beg you, my brothers, not to be so easily confused in your thinking or upset by the claim that the Day of the Lord has come. Perhaps it is thought that we said this while prophesying or preaching, or that we wrote it in a letter. Do not let anyone deceive you in any way' (*II Thessalonians* 2, 2–3).

Yes, the Lord will come again. And on this point Paul launches into a very mysterious passage. In order to describe the events surrounding the end of the world, he turns once again to the apocalyptic style, but this time, even more than in his first letter, he uncovers 'hidden things', which are like a new revelation. There, he said that the Day of the Lord will come like a thief; here he points out the harbingers which will announce his arrival.

Several times Paul refers to the appeal he has already made to the Thessalonians. So this passage is all the more obscure for us. But we discover that the last days are to be marked by great trials for the faith: the great apostasy, or denial of the faith; in which the wicked one will be revealed, the son of perdition, the enemy, who will seek to be worshipped like a god and will be under Satan's control; we also discover that this wickedness cannot show itself for the moment because there is some obstacle standing in the way. And what is this obstacle? Perhaps the Thessalonians knew the answer to that, but we remain in the dark.

Paul ends his instructions by returning to the reality of daily life. He alludes to those who, under the pretext of awaiting the Lord's coming, neglect their duty to work and, taking himself as an example, Paul reminds the Thessalonians that he was never a burden to anyone, that he worked day and night, that he did not beg for the food he ate. Then comes the order, brief and to the point: 'Whoever refuses to work is not allowed to eat' (*II Thessalonians* 3, 10).

The two *Letters to the Thessalonians*, written in the years 51–2, even before the Synoptic Gospels, are chronologically the first texts of the New Testament. It is curious to note that they outline an apocalypse, a final disclosure of hidden things, which will be so magnificently developed in the last book of the New Testament, the *Revelation of John*, as if the whole of the Christian message were focused on the end of the world.

The Day of the Lord

'For the day will not come until the final Rebellion takes place and the Wicked One appears, who is destined for hell. He will oppose every so-called god or object of worship and will put himself above them all. He will even go in and sit down in God's Temple and claim to be God. Don't you remember? I told you all this while I was with you. Yet there is something that keeps this from happening now, and you know what it is. At the proper time, then, the Wicked One will appear. The Mysterious Wickedness is already at work, but what is going to happen will not happen until the one who holds it back is taken out of the way. Then the Wicked One will be revealed, but when the Lord Jesus comes, he will kill him with the breath from his mouth and destroy him with his dazzling presence.'

(*II Thessalonians* 2, 3–8)

A friendly community

'Now Timothy has come back, and he has brought us the welcome news about your faith and love. He has told us that you always think well of us and that you want to see us just as much as we want to see you. So, in all our trouble and suffering, we have been encouraged about you, brothers. It was your faith that encouraged us, because now we really live if you stand firm in your life in union with the Lord. Now we can give thanks to our God for you. We thank him for the joy we have in his presence because of you. Day and night we ask him with all our heart to let us see you personally and supply what is needed in your faith.' (*I Thessalonians* 3, 6–10)

Paul's Letters to Timothy

Letters to a leader of the Church

Moral exhortations

Paul lays the responsibilities of Church leadership before his faithful companion.

Timothy was a reserved and timid young man when Paul noticed him in Lystra during one of his journeys. As the son of a Jewess converted to Christianity and a pagan Greek he was brought up to know the Holy Scriptures. He was circumcised so as not to upset the Jews and attached himself to the apostle who always referred to him as his 'dear and loyal son in the Lord', his brother or his fellow-worker. The apostle and his disciple remained on the best of terms throughout their lives.

At the time of writing the first letter, Paul was leaving for Macedonia and charged Timothy with ensuring the smooth running of the community at Ephesus. There are no great theological insights in this text; the master is simply giving his disciple some practical advice concerning prayer services, the conduct of women, the role of church leaders and helpers, the place of widows, elders, and slaves. The letters to Timothy are of a pastoral nature, like letters of guidance from a minister to one of his flock.

God's plan

The minister must keep watch over the purity of the doctrine and so Paul warns his friend against those preachers who teach false theories, recount legends and are fond of long lists of ancestors (*I Timothy* 1, 3-4). The peoples of Asia Minor are known for their appetite for those discussions which would later be called 'Byzantine', meaning artificial and of little interest. It is safe to assume that this build-up of speculation was troubling the people, for Paul is very strict about this matter.

Women

'I also want the women to be modest and sensible about their clothes and to dress properly; not with fancy hair styles or with gold ornaments or pearls or expensive dresses, but with good deeds, as is proper for women who claim to be religious. Women should learn in silence and all humility. I do not allow them to teach or to have authority over men; they must keep quiet. For Adam was created first, and then Eve. And it was not Adam who was deceived; it was the woman who was deceived and broke God's law. But a woman will be saved through having children, if she perseveres in faith and love and holiness with modesty.
(*I Timothy* 2, 9-15)

False teachers

'I want you to stay in Ephesus ... Some people there are teaching false doctrines and you must order them to stop. Tell them to give up those legends and those long lists of ancestors, which only produce arguments; they do not serve God's plan, which is known by faith. The purpose of this order is to arouse the love that comes from a pure heart, a clear conscience and a genuine faith. Some people have turned away from these and have lost their way in foolish discussions. They want to be teachers of God's Law, but they do not understand their own words or the matters about which they speak with so much confidence.' (*I Timothy* 1, 3-7)

No sterile arguments, no foolish quibbling, no made-up stories. God's plan is simple and effective: it cannot be truly followed by means of convoluted thinking, judicial subtleties or complicated practices, but by a simple act of faith which is available to every sincere person. This is very characteristic of Paul, destroyer of a Law he had venerated and promoter of a faith without flaw.

In each of his letters he recalls his miraculous conversion because he sees in that a striking sign of the free nature of God's gift. He, Paul, had nothing in his favour; he was a blasphemer, a persecutor, and critic of the Gospel. And this is not a case of empty words, but of a confirmed fact beyond all doubt: 'Christ Jesus came into the world to save sinners. I am the worst of them' (*I Timothy* 1, 15).

The universal prayer

Next, Paul reminds Timothy, as head of the community, what Christian meetings should be like. Prayer is central, but prayer for all people without exception. As grace is a free gift, every person can receive it. It is through prayer that we can achieve some measure of that universalism, or belief in the ultimate salvation of all which Paul discovered in his vocation and was already present in Christ's last words to the Twelve: 'Go then to all peoples everywhere and make them my disciples' (*Matthew* 28, 19).

There is a certain tension in this standpoint. The persecutions, slow progress in evangelism, and all kinds of difficulties on the one side and the warmth of a group of brothers, the mutual help of Christians for one another and unity in the faith on the other, might incline people to keep their prayers for those who are close to them. In a way Paul does this when he asks first that the Church will have 'a quiet and peaceful life with all reverence towards God and with proper conduct' (*I Timothy* 2, 2).

However, the principle of universalism is never absent and is clearly and repeatedly affirmed. It is a pressing invitation to be united to the will of God through prayer and action. Paul was the ideal person to remind the Church of this for he had been called to evangelize those who were not of the chosen race and to loosen the ties which bound early Christianity too closely to Judaism, a role which sometimes provoked a strong reaction. The fact remains that this insistance on the universalism of prayer must have been useful for a community faced with so many obstacles.

The passage concerning women is curious. Perhaps Paul, who had remained celibate, was rather wary of them at that time. He always makes them inferior to men: they must dress modestly, without ostentation, no jewels or elaborate hair styles. They are to remain silent during the meetings and must submit to men. The apostle's reason for this is quite simply that women were second in the Creation and first in sin.

'But a woman will be saved through having children.' It seems that, according to Paul, a woman's primary vocation is to bear and rear children. Perhaps these words have to be seen in the context of where and when they were written. There were in Ephesus, in fact, devout groups and meetings where 'wise' and religious ladies took the leading role. They were flattered at being in the forefront of things like this, and were secretly vain and proud as a result. Paul has therefore asked Timothy to remind them of their rightful place. This letter is not a statement of beliefs but a pastoral letter which deals with specific problems.

The passage dedicated to widows has to be looked at in the same way. Perhaps he

---

Advice to the missionary

'I solemnly urge you to preach the message, to insist upon proclaiming it (whether the time is right or not), to convince, reproach, and encourage, as you teach with all patience. The time will come when people will not listen to sound doctrine, but will follow their own desires and will collect for themselves more and more teachers who will tell them what they are itching to hear. They will turn away from listening to the truth and give their attention to legends. But you must keep control of yourself in all circumstances; endure suffering, do the work of a preacher of the Good News and perform your whole duty as a servant of God.' (*II Timothy* 4, 2–5)

had had some unfortunate experiences on his travels with young widows on the look-out for a new husband, for he is quite harsh towards them too. Those who think only of pleasure, although still living are really dead. The real widows are those who remain quite alone, putting their trust in God and dedicating their days and nights to prayers and requests for his help. Moreover, in order to be included among the widows, a woman must be at least 60 years old and have been married only once.

These are the pieces of advice given by an older man to the head of a community: Paul also lists for him the duties of elders, priests, deacons, slaves, and rich people. He reminds him where his authority comes from, namely his profession of faith. In a second letter to Timothy written from prison Paul is more precise, and speaks of his ordination and the sufferings endured by him and his disciple for the sake of the Gospel.

To suffer for the Gospel

This second Letter is more poignant than the first. Paul senses that his end is near. He wants to leave his dear disciple some sort of spiritual testimony. He is suffering: he suffers in the flesh, and also in his heart. He would love to have Timothy near him, the friend with whom he has so much in common: a Jewish education, a conversion experience, and above all 15 years of working together for God. One of them is powerful, enterprising, and bold, the other is timid, reserved, and gentle. No doubt they complemented each other wonderfully over many years. But, at the moment of his going, the apostle experiences the need to call his disciple to be brave and vigilant.

Suffering is the condition of glory, and Paul chooses three parables to illustrate the fight for truth: first there is that of the soldier who, in wartime, does not get mixed up in the affairs of civilian life or trouble himself with the glory in which he shares, but concentrates entirely on the action; then there is the athlete who must give his all to the race and abide by the rules if he is to win the crown he deserves; finally we have the farmer who has all the hard work of sowing and must then wait for the plants to grow and bear fruit before being the first to receive his share of the harvest.

This is how it is for the Christian too and that is why Paul is imprisoned like a criminal. But God's Word is not in chains and we know that: 'If we have died with him we shall also live with him. If we continue to endure we shall also rule with him. If we deny him, he also will deny us' (*II Timothy* 2, 11–12).

Paul paints a gloomy picture of the last days: false teachers will keep repeating their evil message, but Timothy is to remain faithful in proclaiming the word of truth; men will be selfish, stupid, boastful, proud, slanderous, and will rebel against their parents etc, but Timothy is to hold fast to what he has been taught and firmly believes. The man of God will find himself fully qualified and equipped for every good deed.

Paul says that his time is almost at an end. He has fought the good fight, run a good race, and kept the faith. A crown of righteousness has been prepared for him.

Paul's Letter to Titus

Letter to a young Church

The pastor

How to lead God's people to a better Christian life by the choice of responsible leaders and the good organization of the community.

Titus was a very close colleague of Paul's. He was a Greek who had converted to Christianity but had never been circumcised. He was, in fact, mentioned in this regard at the Council of Jerusalem. His greatest claim to glory in the apostle's eyes was his action in the community of Corinth, which was in turmoil after the visit of some false teachers: after Timothy had tried and failed, Titus succeeded in calming everyone and as Paul was very grateful, he gave Titus the job of organizing the young community in Crete about which he had grave misgivings: after all wasn't it said that the Cretans were 'always liars, wicked beasts, and lazy gluttons?' (*Titus* 1, 12).

Such a community surely needed to be kept on a tight rein. Paul therefore asked Titus to name some elders of irreproachable character, give them specific areas of responsibility and so establish an institution with varius different aspects. This marks the end of the travelling missionary Church. Paul always continued to feel responsible for the communities he founded and took care to set up a structure of authority which would reflect its permanence and stability.

A sound faith

'For there are many', says Paul, 'who rebel and deceive others with their nonsense, especially converts from Judaism. It is

necessary to stop their talk' (*Titus* 1, 10). So Paul advises Titus to take a firm line with these false prophets who are only interested in making money out of it. He is the one charged with keeping the faithful to a doctrine which is sound and rejecting anything which does not agree with it. Everything is pure to those who are pure but to the defiled everything is defiled.

Then comes a list of the duties belonging to each category of the faithful: the old men should be sober, sensible, and self-controlled ... older women should behave as those who live a holy life ... the younger women should be reserved and pure, and good housewives who submit to their husbands ... the young men should be self-controlled in everything ... slaves should submit to their masters ... so that the enemy will have nothing bad to say about us.

The Christian is awaiting the coming of our great God who has purified us so that we might become his people, zealous for what is right. Once we were foolish, rebellious, and lost people but now we have been given new life by the water of baptism and by the Holy Spirit and have been justified by the grace of Christ which makes us fit for eternal life.

The recruitment of elders

'An elder must be blameless; he must have only one wife, and his children must be believers and not have the reputation of being wild or disobedient. For, since a church leader is in charge of God's work, he should be blameless. He must not be arrogant or quick-tempered, or a drunkard or violent or greedy for money. He must be self-controlled, upright, holy and disciplined. He must hold firmly to the message which can be trusted and which agrees with the doctrine. In this way he will be able to encourage others with the true teaching and also to show the error of those who are opposed to it.' (*Titus* 1, 6–9)

Paul's Letter to Philemon

Letter to an owner

Freedom in Christ

There is no longer Jew nor Greek, slave nor freeman, man nor woman; we are all one in Christ.

Philemon was not simply a believer but an influential member of the community at Colossae. As a rich man he was able to accommodate Christian meetings in his house quite easily. Paul knew him well, and his wife Apphia, whom he calls his sister, and their son Archippus, whom he calls his fellow-soldier: it is thought that Archippus was the one who led the worship there. Paul knew that he could count on these Christians whose generosity he had already experienced.

In some slave market or other Philemon had bought an alert and intelligent young man as a slave. He called him Onesimus, which means useful. Now this slave Onesimus turned out to be lazy and dishonest. Philemon could not allow that and often took him to task. The relationship between master and slave soon deteriorated to the point where Onesimus decided to run away.

He finally ended up in Rome, the big city and haunt of dubious characters. But once there he found himself with no means of supporting himself; he was a vagrant and as a runaway slave he was also an outlaw, practically driven to theft and crime. Perhaps he remembered the apostle that he must have met in his master's house? Perhaps he had been struck by his kind and accepting manner? What we know for certain is that, finding himself in trouble and knowing that Paul was in Rome, he went to his door asking for help and was converted.

Brotherhood

The *Letter to Philemon* is the note Paul sent to the master asking him to receive his slave as a brother since they were both now members of the same community. No doubt Onesimus would have strong misgivings about his return. The fate of a runaway slave was covered in law. He was branded on the forehead with the letter F (*Fugitivus*) and, if he had stolen anything, the master could give him a beating to the point where death might well follow.

Paul begins with a fond recollection of Philemon's faith and love, then he puts his request with the utmost warmth and delicacy. He asks, rather than commands.

In doing this Paul does not condemn slavery although he wishes for, and indeed suggests, the freeing of Onesimus. The Christian is, in effect, no one's slave, he is a brother and because of these fraternal links, submission no longer has the same meaning.

The request

'So I make a request to you on behalf of Onesimus, who is my own son in Christ; for while in prison I have become his spiritual father. At one time he was of no use to you, but now he is useful both to you and to me. I am sending him back to you now, and with him goes my heart. I would like to keep him here with me, while I am in prison for the gospel's sake, so that he could help me in your place. However, I do not want to force you to help me; rather I would like you to do it of your own free will. So I will not do anything unless you agree. It may be that Onesimus was away from you for a short time so that you might have him back for all time. And now he is not just a slave; he is a dear brother in Christ.' (*Philemon* 10–16)

The Letter to the Hebrews

A letter to the Judaeo-Christians

The priesthood of Christ

Jesus, Son of God, high priest of heaven, last messenger from God among men, is made perfect by his obedience in suffering.

It is certain that the *Letter to the Hebrews* was not written by Paul. The vocabulary, style, and subjects tackled differ greatly from the Pauline Epistles. However, it does have something in common with those written by Paul. It can be said to tie in with a Greek culture which was widespread in the Jewish Diaspora, the scattered Jewish communities beyond Palestine, and this would explain both the importance of the quotations from the Old Testament and a format which is usually associated with philosophy.

The high priest of God

The whole of the letter is centred on the Son of God. The opening words speak of the greatness of the incarnate Jesus, seated at God's right hand. He is greater than the angels and the author goes on to quote a number of biblical passages which tell, on the one hand, of his eternal glory and his identity through the ages, and, on the other hand, of the subordinate and serving role of the angels. So, if the message brought by the angels proved to be true and every act of transgression was to be punished, how much greater will be the truth of the message preached by the Lord.

It was not because God wanted Jesus to be placed a little lower than the angels for a while that he did not establish his domination over all things. The angels' position did not alter. It was rather he who took the nature of a man, becoming our brother, like us in every way, sharing our flesh and

blood, and accepting suffering and death in order that we might be freed from the power of death, and in so doing he became a merciful and faithful high priest on our behalf before God.

Jesus is greater than Moses: both were faithful in their work but Jesus was greater than Moses in that he was like the son of a house whereas Moses was like the servant. Moses was a highly significant figure for the Jews: he was the founder of the religion, the intermediary between God and man, he had spoken in the name of the Almighty and had led the people to the Promised Land, the land of rest. Yet they did not listen to him, they disobeyed and caused the great rebellion against God in the desert. God, however, kept his promise and by allowing men to be joined to Christ by faith he has given them God's rest, that is the peace which withstands all testing. We are to see to it that we do not copy the unbelief of the Ancients.

Christ is the great high priest. The priest was one chosen from among men to plead

The greatness of God's son

'In the past, God spoke to our ancestors many times and in many ways through the prophets, but in these last days he has spoken to us through his Son. He is the one through whom God created the universe, the one whom God has chose to possess all things and the end. He reflects the brightness of God's glory and is the exact likeness of God's own being, sustaining the universe with his powerful word. After achieving forgiveness for the sins of humankind, he sat down in heaven at the right-hand side of God, the Supreme Power. The Son was made greater than the angels, just as the name that God gave him is greater than theirs.' (*Hebrews* 1, 1–4)

for them before God. Christ is the ultimate example of this, because, by his incarnation he took on himself human weakness, he suffered and when faced with death cried out to God in prayer, but he was obedient; and also because he was the Son, he had been called by God to the task and had been made perfect by his exemplary life on earth.

So God keeps the promises made to Abraham long ago. There is continuity in his action. The priesthood of Christ is like that of Melchisedek, a comparison which would be very meaningful to the Hebrews. Melchisedek was a priest in the time of Abraham, that is at the very beginning of the story of salvation, a priest of God most high and king of peace. It was said that he was 'without father, without mother, without ancestors, whose days have no beginning and whose life has no end.' So, like the Son, he is a priest forever.

The author uses Melchisedek, this fleeting image from the Old Testament, to show that there can be, and is a priesthood greater than that of the Levites and Aaron on which rested the Law given to the people. And, if there is change in the priesthood there is change in the Law. Therefore 'The old rule is set aside because it was weak and useless. For the Law of Moses could not make anything perfect. And now a better hope has been provided through which we come near to God' (*Hebrews* 7, 18–19), a covenant of which Jesus is the guarantee. In the Old Covenant there were many priests because they could not escape death; in the New Covenant, the high priest lasts forever, the priesthood remains with him and the salvation he procures is absolute.

Christ's sacrifice

'Every Jewish priest performs his services every day and offers the same sacrifices many times; but these sacrifices can never take away sins. Christ, however, offered one sacrifice for sins, an offering that is effective for ever, and then he sat down at the right hand side of God. There he now waits until God puts his enemies as a footstool under his feet. With one sacrifice, then, he has made perfect for ever those who are purified from sin.' (*Hebrews* 10, 11–14)

The new sanctuary

The Old Covenant had its sanctuary, its place of worship: it consisted of tents which were erected and equipped; there would be the lampstand, tables, bread, and the Ark of the Covenant, completely covered in gold as well as the cherubim, Aaron's stick and the tablets of the Law, so many objects made by the hands of men. The gifts and sacrifices which were offered there did not have the power to make the worshipper perfect in his heart and so he had to make a new offering each day, each year. The gifts and sacrifices were no doubt representations of heavenly realities, but they were also illustrations from the present.

Christ's Temple is greater and more perfect, it is not a man-made place, it is Christ himself who is the spotless victim, not any imperfect symbol; he offered himself once for all, at the end of the age, and not many times; he poured out, not the blood of goats or bulls, but his own blood; by his sacrifice he abolished sin completely for many, and we will see him a second time when he brings salvation to those who await him.

The author goes on to ask his readers to persevere in trust; for the one who has made the promise is faithful; to be unfailing in love: for he has cleansed their hearts of all stains and washed their bodies in pure water; and to be faithful in meetings with other Christians: for the Day of the Lord is coming. 'For just a little while longer and he who is coming will come; he will not delay' (*Hebrews* 10, 31).

Faith

The author speaks at some length about faith. He recalls the long story of salvation, mentioning in a few sentences the great forefathers who marked it with their blind trust in God: Abel, Enoch, Noah, Isaac, Jacob, Joseph, Moses etc. They all received promises which they did not live to see fulfilled, but they had faith in the one who had given his word and they became examples to everyone.

Sometimes they found themselves in situations which could not be understood in human terms and they still kept faith; there was Sarah who was promised a child when she had already reached old age; there was Abraham to whom God had promised many descendants through his son Isaac, and yet the same God demanded that he sacrifice Isaac while he was still a child. Abraham went along with it although it made no sense at all, for he was sure that the Almighty could never break his word, and indeed he did not.

All the other similar instances cannot be listed here. They all believed in things they could not see and they all stood firm. Despite their faith, 'they did not receive what God had promised, because God had decided on an even better plan for us. His purpose was that only in company with us would they be made perfect' (*Hebrews* 11, 40).

The faith of the ancestors

'To have faith is to be sure of the things we hope for, to be certain of the things we cannot see. It was by their faith that people of ancient times won God's approval. It is by faith that we understand that the universe was created by God's word, so that what can be seen was made out of what cannot be seen. It was faith that made Abel offer to God a better sacrifice than Cain's. Through his faith he won God's approval as a righteous man, because God himself approved of his gifts. By means of his faith Abel still speaks, even though he is dead. It was faith that kept Enoch from dying. Instead, he was taken up to God and nobody could find him, because God had taken him up. The scripture says that before Enoch was taken up he had pleased God. No one can please God without faith, for whoever comes to God must have faith that God exists and that he rewards those who seek him.' (*Hebrews* 11, 1–6)

Whatever trials we may face are minimal when compared to their testimonies and that of God's son. We should understand that sometimes God corrects us as a father corrects his children. We would not really be his children if he did not correct us, and his purpose is to make us fit to share in his holiness. At the time a punishment does not seem like an occasion for rejoicing but later on it brings its own reward of peaceful and righteous life. In this way our faith tells us to 'Lift up your tired hands then, and strengthen your trembling knees!'

For those who do not believe, things are very different. We should not forget Esau who sold his birthright for 'a mess of potage', a single meal. Later all his tears and pleadings were in vain, it was never restored to him: he was rejected. This is what it will be like for those shameless irreverent people who can spoil everything they touch.

The Old Covenant received by Moses on Sinai was a tangible reality: the fire, the darkness, the storm, the trumpet blasts, and the sound of a voice must have been a terrifying experience. But it was an earthly message. The New Covenant was made in the city of the living God, in the heavenly Jerusalem, amidst hosts of angels, in a joyful gathering of God's first-born sons whose names are written in heaven. 'Be careful then and do not refuse to hear him who speaks from heaven to establish an unshakeable kingdom and truths which will remain.'

The Letter ends with some advice: be charitable, especially towards strangers and those in prison; respect fidelity in marriage; do not be obsessed with money; obey the leaders of the community and above all, despite all opposition, follow Christ to the point of death and the permanent city of heaven. In a way this is a summary of the general moral doctrine of the Letter.

The Letter of James

The letter written by Jesus's brother

Faith informed by love

The letter in which true religion is said to be not only a matter of faith, but also one of action.

It is not known who wrote this letter. It is traditionally attributed to James, the Lord's brother. The authority with which he speaks, the atmosphere in which he lives, and the subjects treated do seem to indicate that it comes from this same James who, as head of the Christian community in Jerusalem, had so much influence during the time of the Apostles that Paul himself reported back to him and who, quite naturally, presided over the first council of the Church. This letter would have been written c. 57–62.

The author is clearly of Jewish origin: the style and vocabulary bear traces of Semitism; his turn of mind, way of speaking about down-to-earth things, and his references to Abraham as father, to the twelve tribes and to the Law all link him with ancient Judaism. But he is also a Christian, as evidenced by the ideas expressed, the favour shown to the poor, the forgiveness of sins, the view of the last days etc.

Respect for the poor

'Suppose a rich man wearing a gold ring and fine clothes comes to your meeting, and a poor man in ragged clothes also comes. If you show more respect to the well-dressed man and say to him, "Have this best seat here", but say to the poor man, "Stand over there, or sit here on the floor by my feet", then you are guilty of creating distinctions among yourselves and of making judgments based on evil motives.' (*James* 2, 2–4)

The *Letter of James* is simply a long moral discourse similar to the learned books and kinds of sermons used in the synagogues. But it can also be compared in some ways with the writings of the moral teachers in paganism: dialogues, questions and objections, interruptions, lists of commands, personifications, images, and antitheses. This should not really surprise us for we do not know how much influence the philosophical form of argument had over the Judaeo-Hellenistic (Greek influenced) and Judaeo-Christian cultures.

Poverty

It is known that the early preaching of the church appealed particularly to the poor and disadvantaged, and no doubt many of them saw conversion as a means of improving their lot. This hope would be fostered by the feelings of solidarity, the company of some of the rich converts and the joyful atmosphere of the Christian communities. But nothing was changed: the rich were still rich and poor were still poor. The former continued to flaunt their wealth and arrogance; the latter still found it hard to make ends meet. So perhaps from time to time complaints were voiced.

The Letter responds with a line straight from the Gospel: 'Blessed are the poor'. Those who suffer testing times should rejoice. God has chosen the poor in the world's terms to be rich in faith and to possess the kingdom. And the humble too are promised exaltation, they will have the crown of life, they will have their inheritance.

By contrast, he has no words harsh enough to condemn the rich man: he is the one who oppresses the poor, despises them, and hauls them up before the courts; he is the one who speaks ill in the good Name of Yahweh, given for their protection, but he will pass away like the flower if a wild plant withers in the burning sun and loses all its beauty. In the eyes of faith, riches are an obstacle, a humiliation, in reality an actual burden, and can keep somebody from the kingdom of God.

But we should not believe that the difficulties of the poor, which are real evils, are God's responsibility, on the simple pretext that everything comes from him and nothing happens without his agreement. God has no dealings with evil and he tempts no one. The temptation comes from the covetousness of each person which traps and ruins him. Man alone is responsible for his own sin and all that comes from God is good, particularly the Word of the Gospel.

Faith and works

James is not Paul. Whereas Paul emphasized justification by faith, in the *Letter to the Galatians* amongst others, James emphasizes that faith must be active. To put it bluntly we have: on the one hand faith without works; on the other hand faith and works. Some people will see in this a contradiction between the two apostles, others will simply find the two ideas complementary. Certainly there are opposing tendencies in these two positions but these probably stem from the different groups to whom the letters were addressed, the times at which they were written and the circumstances which led to their being sent.

James begins by speaking of how the Word is received: 'Whoever listens to the word but does not put it into practice is like a man who looks in a mirror and sees himself as he is. He takes a good look at himself then goes away and at once forgets what he looks like' (*James* 1, 23–4). This is how it is with religious devotion, it is not enough to say: 'Lord, Lord', Jesus warned, and James goes on to say, 'One must also take care of orphans and widows in their suffering, and keep oneself from being corrupted by the world.'

Then the author becomes more direct: 'My brothers, what good is it for someone to say that he has faith if his actions do not prove it?' Faith alone, without love is dead, the faith which saves is that which is accompanied by good works. In order to underline the meaning of this, James takes the example of Abraham, the very example used in Paul's *Letter to the Romans* (*Romans* 4, 3), which demonstrates that there is harmony between their two positions. Paul emphasizes the faith of Abraham, whilst James emphasizes the act which his faith makes him perform, and he can say: 'How was our ancestor Abraham put right with God? It was through his *actions* when he offered his son Isaac on the altar. Can't you see? His faith and his actions worked together; his faith was made perfect through his actions … it is by his actions that a person is put right with God, and not by his faith alone' (*James* 2, 21–4).

So, in the space of a few lines James is saying: 'Faith without actions is dead,' and also: 'Abraham believed God, and because of his faith God accepted him as righteous.' Giving expression to thoughts which are subtle is fraught with difficulties! This could be why he goes on to criticize uncontrolled

---

Faith

'Suppose there are brothers or sisters who need clothes and don't have enough to eat. What good is there in your saying to them, "God bless you! Keep warm and eat well!" — if you don't give them the necessities of life? So it is with faith: if it is alone and includes no actions, then it is dead.' (*James* 2, 15–17)

Language

'If a person never makes a mistake in what he says, he is perfect and is also able to control his whole being. We put a bit into the mouth of a horse to make it obey us, and we are able to make it go where we want. Or think of a ship, big as it is and driven by such strong winds, it can be steered by a very small rudder, and it goes wherever the pilot wants it to go. So it is with the tongue: small as it is, it can boast about great things. Just think how large a forest can be set on fire by a tiny flame! And the tongue is like a fire. It is a world of wrong, occupying its place in our bodies and spreading evil through our whole being …' (*James* 3, 2–6)

use of the tongue. At that time there was a great liking among the Jews for long and rather obscure discourses about doctrine. The Christians had fallen into the same habit and were setting themselves up as masters of doctrinal thought. James also asks them to exercise control over the tongue, 'a scourge which never rests'.

True and false wisdom

For James, true wisdom is not expressed in quarrels, jealousy, boasting, confusion, and lies; it is good conduct and acts of kindness. This is how he distinguishes between false and true wisdom: the first is of this world, unspiritual and demonic; the second comes from above and is pure, peaceful, gentle, and friendly, full of compassion without prejudice or hypocrisy. The first is man's speech and by its nature is tainted with evil; the second is good works which cannot lie.

All sorts of quarrels are to be opposed. If there are fights among you they stem from your desire for wordly things and your lack of desire for God. A person cannot be both the world's friend and God's friend. A choice must be made. 'Submit to God. Resist the devil and he will run away from you. Come near to God and he will come near to you.' That is true wisdom.

James continues his letter with renewed warnings to the rich: 'Weep and wail over the miseries that are coming upon you! Your riches have rotted away and your clothes have been eaten by moths. Your gold and silver are covered with rust and this rust will be a witness against you.' This speech develops into a very blunt denunciation of the rich as if he were trying to make a response in the strongest, clearest, and most radical terms, to those complaints from the poor which were referred to at the beginning of the Letter.

So, the whole discourse is placed between the complaints of the poor, who ought not to complain because they have the right to God's blessings, and the misfortunes of the rich, who ought to be complaining because they are excluded from the kingdom of God. Heaven help the community which brings the two together! The only guideline for judgment is the exercise of charity, nothing else.

The final exhortations are all focused on prayer during the wait for the Lord's coming: 'Is anyone among you in trouble? He should pray. Is anyone happy? He should sing praises.' Then, turning to those who are ill, the author advises calling the priests to their bedside, where they should pray over them, and rub olive oil over them in the name of the Lord. Then the patients will be saved and their sins will be forgiven. Throughout the centuries the Church has observed the rite of extreme unction or anointing of the dying and the anointing of the sick as duties first laid down in this passage.

The Letters of Peter

Letters from the leader of Christianity

The duties of the Christian life

Christian salvation is the source of courage and hope.

In his work as an apostle and leader of the Church, Peter devoted himself to supporting the communities in the north of Asia Minor who had been subject to a sudden wave of violent persecution. This is the object of his first letter. Throughout history its authenticity has never been in doubt, even though it was written in Greek, for the apostle did have a secretary by the name of Silas in his service, and despite the similarities between this text and some of Paul's letters. The letter form is only used here at the beginning and end of the text and the style is rather more like that of a baptismal sermon: it can be regarded as the first encyclical or circular letter from a Pope to the Church. It would have been written in Rome c. 57–60.

Joy

'Tremble with joy' Peter says to the persecuted Christians, because the trials you are suffering show the true worth of your faith, just as gold is tested by fire. So when Christ is finally revealed your faith will be a cause for praise, glory, and honour. From the start the apostle takes a comprehensive view of things. He brings the whole of Christian life together in one sentence: sufferings are nothing, or rather they are a guarantee of blessing and glory.

Widening his scope still further, the apostle then evokes the history of salvation. In times gone by the prophets sought salvation, they proclaimed it and they expected it. They predicted Christ's sufferings and his glory. But they also understood that this message was not for them, but for you and it has now been brought to you by those who preached the Gospel to you. Even the angels envy you.

The call to holiness

Peter then turns to a whole series of moral exhortations. His method of presentation is almost always the same: first the rules of life, then the evidence of Scripture and finally an instructive element which is given particular emphasis. In this way he roots the moral attitude in the faith: he turns from what is seen as the social custom, and arrives at what is lived, the doctrine, which in a way is summed up in the baptismal regeneration which makes one a Christian.

First, be alert: take care not to live as you did before, when you were ignorant, not to live like your fathers who did not know the Good News. Now, you are sons of God so be

The new priesthood

'This stone is of great value for you that believe; but for those who do not believe: "The stone which the builders rejected as worthless turned out to be the most important of all." And another scripture says, "This is the stone that will make people stumble, the rock that will make them fall." They stumbled because they did not believe in the word; such was God's will for them. But you are a chosen race, the king's priests, the holy nation, God's own people, chosen to proclaim the wonderful acts of God who called you out of darkness into his own marvellous light. At one time you were not God's people, but now you are his people; at one time you did not know God's mercy, but now you have received his mercy.' (*I Peter* 2, 7–10)

obedient children. In reinforcing this instruction the apostle recalls that redemption comes through the blood of Christ, who was chosen for this before the creation of the world – an amazing fact – and was revealed in the last days for your sake – what a privilege! Surely that is enough to make you want to live the new life!

Next comes love: love each other like brothers, without failing for you have been born again. Underlying these words is clearly the idea of baptism. It must be remembered that Peter is speaking to committed Christians living through a time of persecution: so a few references are sufficient to give the reader a picture of the Christian mystery.

But he does insist on certain points: you have been born of an incorruptible seed, he says, wanting to stress that from now on everything is totally changed. 'The God of all grace, who calls you to share his eternal glory in union with Christ will himself perfect you' (*I Peter* 1, 10).

Some commentators have viewed the first part of the Letter as the unfolding of a liturgy or service form for baptism, beginning with a hymn expressing the Christian's joy and ending with a sermon setting forth the moral rules deriving from baptism. The evidence for this point of view is open to debate but this passage does show how much importance the apostle, leader of the Church, attached to baptism, the ritual by which the new convert joined the community and was also symbolically included in the death and resurrection of Christ, as he went down under water and rose again.

A hymn to the Church marks the concluding section of this passage. The word Church is never actually mentioned but there is no mistaking the meaning in the use of other expressions like 'cornerstone', 'spiritual temple', and 'people of God'. Peter says, 'You are the chosen race, the king's priests, the holy nation, God's own people.' So many terms which show the Church as a separate world which can bring down the unbeliever and save the faithful, who are referred to here as 'living stones'.

Civic and domestic duties

It is precisely because of this separate nature of the Church that a certain number of particular obligations are laid upon Christians. 'I appeal to you, friends, as strangers and refugees in this world', says Peter and he lists their various civic and domestic duties: the resisting of carnal desires, the submission of slaves to their masters and of everyone to the authorities, the obedience of wives to their husbands and the understanding of husbands for their wives, brotherly feelings, compassion, mercy, a spirit of humility towards others etc. 'For the Lord watches over the righteous and listens to their prayers' (*I Peter* 3, 12).

The author stresses the persecutions which the Christians suffer because of their new way of living: do nothing wrong which might justify these persecutions, renounce the sinful life, even if this leads to further trials, but follow Christ's example in accepting undeserved suffering, knowing that they are beneficial since baptism is involvement with Christ who 'was put to death physically but made alive spiritually'.

After an evocation of paradise and the last Judgment, Peter, speaking with the authority of one who has witnessed Christ's

---

Christians and pagans

'Since Christ suffered physically, you too must strengthen yourselves with the same way of thinking that he had; because whoever suffers physically is no longer involved with sin. From now on then you must live the rest of your earthly lives controlled by God's will and not by human desires. You have spent enough time in the past doing what the heathen likes to do. Your lives were spent in indecency, lust, drunkenness, orgies, drinking parties, and the disgusting worship of idols. And now the heathens are surprised when you do not join them in the same wild, reckless living, and so they insult you. But they will have to give an account of themselves to God, who is ready to judge the living and the dead. That is why the Good News was preached also to the dead, to those who had been judged in their physical existence as everyone is judged; it was preached to them so that in their spiritual existence they might live as God lives.' (*I Peter* 4, 1–6)

sufferings, gives some advice to the elders: 'Be shepherds of the flock that God gave you ... take care of it willingly as God wants you to, and not unwillingly.' Then, addressing himself to the younger men, he says 'You must submit to the older men.' He ends with a few words written no doubt in his own hand as was the custom. He acknowledges the help of Silas, his secretary, and sends the usual greetings.

Against false teachers

The second Letter does not seem to be from Peter, despite the fact that the author lays great stress on his being the chief of the Apostles. It is usually attributed to a Christian from a Greek background, though Jewish by descent, possibly one of Peter's followers but certainly someone intent on passing on Peter's teachings. The differences in style between this and the first letter make it clear that the author is not Peter's secretary, Silas. Whoever he may have been, after much hesitation, the Church finally accepted his letter into the canon of scripture as an inspired work.

The author of this second Letter distances himself from the text, adopting a more neutral and impersonal style. Christ is only presented here as an object of knowledge. There is none of the life, the emotional tension, or the wealth of teaching which abound in the first letter. The writer stands slightly apart from his text whilst occasionally employing neat little phrases which are particularly convincing.

After the usual greetings the text begins with exhortation: respond to God's goodness by living a virtuous life; to God's gifts by living a life of holiness. This is what is necessary for growth in the faith and entry into the eternal kingdom. This is no made-up story but is based on what the author has seen and preached, and what was proclaimed by the prophets.

Then follows a long passage condemning false teachers, especially those called apostates, who have betrayed their faith and those who set up harmful sects. Woe betide them, for their denial of Christ and return to an immoral life leads them into a state which is worse than ever. Yet they are successful, which is not really surprising:

they play on fleshly desires to tempt people, especially those who had only just escaped from a life spent in corruption, and who had little strength to resist. They are like wild animals destined to be destroyed.

But their punishment is coming, and soon. They are foolish to accuse the Lord of delaying the fulfilment of his promises. In his eyes a day is like a thousand years and a thousand years like one day: it is not for man to judge the ways of God. Yet God will be patient with all men for he does not want anyone to perish.

It is worth noting that this letter contains one of the rare mentions of angels which are referred to here as Glories. Writing in connection with punishment the writer speaks of two categories: those who retain a certain degree of strength and power and are faithful to the Lord, and those who have committed a mysterious sin, and will be cast into the realms of darkness until they are judged.

There is an obvious connection between this Letter and the *Letter of Jude*: identical facts and ideas, the same expressions and similar arguments. Yet there is in the *Letter of Jude*, none of the emphasis on the final coming of Jesus and its apparent delay which appears in this second *Letter of Peter*.

Call to holiness

'For this very reason do your best to add goodness to your faith: to your goodness add knowledge; to your knowledge add self-control; to your self-control add endurance; to your endurance add godliness; to your godliness add brotherly affection; and to your brotherly affection add love. These are the qualities you need, and if you have them in abundance, they will make you active and effective in your knowledge of our Lord Jesus Christ. But whoever does not have them is so short-sighted that he cannot see and has forgotten that he has been purified from his past sins. So then, my brothers, try even harder to make God's call and his choice of you a permanent experience; if you do so you will never abandon your faith.' (*II Peter* 1, 5-10)

The Letters of John

Letters from the Elder

God is love

We know that we have passed from death to life because we love our brothers.

The similarities in vocabulary, style, and theology between the fourth Gospel and the first *Letter of John* are so great that there can be no doubt that they are by the same author. Both have references to the contrast between light and darkness, life and death, truth and falsehood, children of God and children of the devil, followers of God and of the world. All these are themes strongly associated with John and they do not occur elsewhere in the New Testament with anything like the same frequency and emphasis.

The first *Letter of John* is not actually a letter in the strict sense of the word: there is no mention of who the letter is from or to whom it is addressed, no words of greeting at the beginning or the end. The writer seems to be so keen to get on with his subject that he tackles it right from the outset and never pauses for breath until the end. Nor is it a logically constructed lec-

The Commandments

'If we obey God's commands, then we are sure that we know him. If someone says that he knows him, but does not obey his commands, such a person is a liar and there is no truth in him. But whoever obeys his word is the one whose love for God has really been made perfect. This is how we can be sure that we are in union with God: whoever says that he remains in union with God should live just as Jesus Christ did.' (*I John* 2, 3–6)

ture: ideas are regularly repeated, the tone changes from the controversial to the encouraging, from the instructive to the meditative. The text which has come down to us could almost be taken for a collection of unrelated fragments.

There is no doubt that this gem of Scripture is difficult to read. John's manner is that of a contemplative person. His thought is expressed in cycles where the key words are constantly repeated, the main ideas recur and the major themes are explored in depth. The text is a whirlpool drawing us into the heart of the mystery, a symphony of variations attempting to give shape and expression to the same impenetrable truth. His language is more musical than logical.

The Letter begins with the same words as the fourth Gospel: 'In the beginning ...' and the writer states the aim of his letter. His declaration of the Gospel has three distinct stages: first of all, John has known God through knowing Christ, 'We have heard it and we have seen it with our eyes; yes we have seen it and our hands have touched it', which is to say that this was an understanding gained through the senses which opened the way for a spiritual understanding; then John bears witness to what he has seen and proclaims the eternal Life which was with the Father and was made known to us; and finally, Christians are in fellowship with this witness and are therefore in fellowship with the Father and his son Jesus Christ.

The Letter in fact uses the same format as the Gospel where the song at the beginning was a summary of the history of salvation. But this condensed statement is so loaded with meaning, it brings such consequences and opens such perspectives that it is the best introduction to the themes of the Gospel and the Letter. It is the essential heart of the message and the variations which follow are simply examples, analogies, parables or attempts to prove, explore and explain it whilst demonstrating the extent and importance of its implications.

The Christian experience

It is impossible to analyse a text which is so varied and condensed, but we can at least pick out the main ideas behind it. The first is the Christian's union with God, which is defined as a real and vital relationship: he is born of God, he knows him, he lives in him. This communion is a reciprocal indwelling: God is in him and he is in God. But, the very essence of what makes someone a Christian is, above all, the fact that he is born of God or generated by God and this generation is something which continues (*I John* 2, 29). This act of birth does not separate us from God, quite the reverse, God's action is continuous.

Of course this experience is difficult to clarify. There is a great danger of getting lost in complicated explanations. So John offers several criteria for arriving at a sure understanding. God is light which is absolutely pure, a light which cannot be marred by evil. And we must walk in the light, that is to say, we must be honest, pure, upright, and truthful. If we say we have no sins, we are in darkness. If we confess our sins, God is just and faithful to his promise to forgive them.

God is love (*I John* 4, 7–16) and this love is God's spirit in us, which goes on growing until it flows back to its source. 'Whoever does not love does not know God' and 'whoever lives in love lives in union with God and God lives in union with him'

(*I John* 4, 14). This is not a question of some external exercise but of a deep commitment. It springs from the deepest urges of the soul, finds its outward expression in faith and love, brings its own light and proclaims our knowledge of the God of love.

John lays particular stress on a third criterion: love God, not the world. There are not only the sons of God, there are also the sons of the devil; there is not simply faith and love, there is also hate and injustice, wealth and pride, the desires of the flesh and lusting after what the eye sees. The world is presented as a tempter. Thrust into the world as we are, we must resist its seductions because it will pass away and 'he who does the will of God lives for ever'.

Finally the same theme is echoed in the form of another injunction: fly from the Antichrist, or the enemies of Christ who strive to take his place. The enemies of Christ are those who are against Christ, who deny that he is the Son of God and also deny the Father. They have left the Church but they were not truly part of it. At the heart of their break with the Church was a lie, their own denial of God! This has simply proved that they had not received the Spirit's blessing and knowledge and faith. But John has confidence in those to whom he writes: 'you have had the Holy Spirit poured out on you'.

The end will come with the return of Christ. For the Christian experience stands between two revelations: the saving incarnation which made us children of God and the second coming which will make everything known. Therefore it holds two rather obscure ideas: the first concerns what we are, which we only know by faith; the sec-

Love

'Dear friends, let us love one another, because love comes from God. Whoever loves is a child of God and knows God. Whoever does not love does not know God, for God is love. And God showed his love for us by sending his only Son into the world, so that we might have life through him. This is what love is: it is not that we have loved God, but that he loved us and sent his Son to be the means by which our sins are forgiven.' (*I John* 4, 7–10)

The child of God

'We know that no child of God keeps on sinning, for the Son of God keeps him safe, and the Evil One cannot harm him. We know that we belong to God, even though the whole world is under the rule of the Evil One. We know that the Son of God has come and has given us understanding, so that we know the true God. We live in union with the true God — in union with his Son Jesus Christ. This is the true God, and this is eternal life.' (*I John* 5, 18–20)

ond concerns what we will be, which we only reach by hope. We are sons of God, but 'it is not yet clear what we shall become. But we know that when Christ appears we shall be like him, because we shall see him as he really is' (*I John* 3, 2).

So the first *Letter of John* is a rhythmic piece in which there is a constant ebb and flow of ideas from being chosen by God and being redeemed through the life of morality to the final revelation of the second coming. The whole work is characterized by a concern for precision and honesty which makes it one of the high points of Christian literature. In its style and theology this Letter is very close to the fourth Gospel. It must therefore have been written at approximately the same period, probably at the end of the first century.

Two notes on particular occasions

The second and third *Letters of John* are very different from the first. They are very short notes about particular matters addressed to one Church only and are presented as the work of someone called the Elder. This title probably has nothing to do with age, but suggests someone of undisputed authority; it is possible that we are dealing here with John the apostle.

The second Letter is a pastoral message addressed to the dear Lady and her children. It was thought that this referred to an important Christian woman. But in fact it is a reference to a Church, perhaps one of the communities in Asia Minor. This particular Church has been split by heretics, people who deviate from the true faith, in this case by denying that Jesus Christ was born in human form and 'have gone out all over the world', meaning that they have set themselves up as teachers of this false doctrine.

The author does not enter into controversy by debating the issue. He simply declares his confidence in the majority of the community who have remained loyal to the true faith. He rejoices in this and asks them to live in purity, showing love to one another and rejecting false teachers. This second Letter looks very much like a summary or a first draft of John's first Letter: it is written in the same spirit, with the same style.

The third Letter comes over as a piece of personal correspondence. It gives us a true-to-life sketch of the kind of thing that was happening in the Churches. The Elder is one of the people in charge: he sends out his representatives to spread the gospel, gather in funds, and encourage the local communities. But it turns out that some of these representatives have been badly received. So the Elder is writing here to Gaius, giving him great praise because he lives according to the truth and has proved generous. Demetrius is someone else who is singled out for praise. Diotrephes, by contrast, is rebuked for his ambition to be the leader, 'the terrible things he says about us and the lies he tells ... He will not receive the Christian brothers when they come.' The Elder closes the letter by announcing his intention to come and sort all these matters out in person.

The Letter of Jude

A letter from James's brother

Against false teachers

A warning against those heretics who lead corrupted lives and misrepresent the Good News.

The writer of the *Letter of Jude* claims to be the brother of James. Why does he not say that he is the Lord's brother, a rather more prestigious claim? He may have been an Apostle. Some conclude that the name Jude was simply a pseudonym. In any case, the Letter would have been written c. 70 AD. It shows a fairly good knowledge of the Scriptures, particularly the apocryphal Scriptures, those ancient religious writings not included in the Old Testament as we now know it; a knowledge which also reflects a deep understanding of Jewish tradition.

It is certain that, at the time at which Jude was writing, the ideas and practices he was attacking had not been eradicated from the Christian community. The false teachers were amongst the faithful, sharing in their meals and spreading their wrong ideas even there. Their gluttony, greed, and debauchery were shocking and people were outraged by their blasphemy against the angels, their denial of Christ, and their complaints against God himself. They were setting up false divisions among the Christians according to their own rules which were without foundation in the faith.

A strong condemnation

Was this a liberal interpretation of Paul's doctrine of freedom or a heresy influenced by Greek philosophy? Was it corrupt thinking brought about by loose morals, or was it the other way round? Jude does not go into these niceties, he refuses to give any details of the errors he is condemning; no doubt those to whom he was writing would know what he was referring to in this uncompromising denunciation.

His argument presents examples. Remember, says Jude, that the Lord rescued the people from the land of Egypt, but destroyed those who did not believe, that the angels who left their own realm now await the Day of Judgment in darkness, that Sodom and Gomorrah suffer the punishment of eternal fire for their immorality.

The second part of the Letter is an encouragement. Jude asks his readers not to be alarmed: the Apostles foretold that in the last days people would come to mock them, evil people who would cause divisions. The important thing is to stand firm in the sacred faith, to act out of love and to hope for eternal life through God's mercy. In the present situation his advice is to help those brothers who have doubts and to 'hate the very clothes, stained by their sinful lusts' of those who have fallen.

The depraved

'How terrible for them! They have followed the way that Cain took. For the sake of money they have given themselves over to the error that Balaam committed. They have rebelled as Korah rebelled, and like him they are destroyed. With their shameless carousing they are like dirty spots in your fellowship meals. They take care only of themselves. They are like crowds carried along by the wind, but bringing no rain. They are like trees that bear no fruit, even in autumn, trees that have been pulled up by the roots and are completely dead. They are like wild waves of the sea, with their shameful deeds showing up like foam. They are like wandering stars, for whom God has reserved a place for ever in the deepest darkness.' (*Jude* 11–13)

Revelation of John

The book of John the Prophet

The imminent approach of the end of time

In the midst of troubles comes the promise of a new world where every evil, including physical death, will have disappeared.

When the first waves of persecution were unleashed against the Christians by Nero and by Domitien they provoked a feeling of helplessness and confusion. How could it be that Christ, who had triumphed over death had not conquered the world? Wasn't everything supposed to have been completely transformed by the Resurrection and the pouring out of the Spirit? Why was there all this hatred and violence when Jesus had preached gentleness and love?

John the Prophet — who may have been the Apostle John, or one of his followers — is writing from the island of Patmos, to which he had retreated because of what was happening, to the seven Churches to boost their morale. He knows the Scriptures perfectly and can quote them by heart, like many of his Jewish contemporaries, and he

---

Greetings

'From John to the seven Churches in the province of Asia: Grace and peace be yours from God; who is, who was, and who is to come, and from the seven spirits in front of his throne, and from Jesus Christ the faithful witness, the first to be raised from death and who is also the ruler of the kings of the world. He loves us and by his death he has freed us from our sins and made us a kingdom of prests to serve his God and Father. To Jesus Christ be the glory and power for ever and ever.' (*Revelation* 1, 4–6)

---

draws on them for elements of the visions he is going to describe. He recalls the trials of Israel, past persecutions, and crises and places them in the context of God's plan, as did the prophets of those days. Just as Ezekiel and Daniel and other visionaries of the Hebrew people did before him he now presents his revelation of the present and the future.

Prophecy and revelation

John calls himself a prophet. In the history of Israel the prophet is called by God to remind the sinful people of their moral duties. He is a messenger from God, the interpreter of his Word. In order to do this, he is favoured with visions concerning future happenings and these are the signs which justify what he says. The prophet speaks of punishments or the prospects of reconciliation and revival. But the primary function of his mission is always moral: his interventions have an immediate practical purpose for the individual or the group.

In the list of gifts mentioned by Paul in the first *Letter to the Corinthians* prophecy comes in second place, straight after the gift of being an apostle. The prophets' mission is to explain the Scriptures and to show, in the light of the Holy Spirit, how the words of the forefathers apply to contemporary history, to proclaim the future as and when necessary and to set events in God's mysterious plan. Their aim is to encourage and comfort the faithful.

Revelation is also like this. Like prophecy, it is a particular gift; it manifests itself through extraordinary visions; and it looks to the future. But, whereas prophecy's main objective is moral rectitude with revelation of the future as a secondary aim, revelation is aimed directly at the mysteries of the future. It occurs most often in moments of crisis, when there is an urgent need to uphold the courage of the faithful by reminding them of the supernatural meaning behind what they are experiencing.

At the time of the Jews' exile to Babylon, the prophet Ezekiel began to sketch out this literary style which was widely used by Daniel and which was very successful in Jewish circles around the beginning of the Christian era. There are still many works of this type in existence: the book of Enoch, Jubilees, Assumption of Moses etc. They all foretold the last days, but only the *Revelation of John* has been accepted into the canon of the Scriptures.

The apocalyptic style

The central interest of the apocalypse, or final revelation, is the mystery of the invisible world: the beginning and the end, retribution and the beyond, God's plan and the future, so many concepts which go far beyond our capabilities of thought, judgment, and expression. The apocalypse is a revelation or unveiling ('apocalypse' means revelation). But, given what is to be revealed, a different approach is needed from what applies when dealing with the visible world.

Here the qualities of material things are used to suggest non-material things and abstract ideas. The text ought not, therefore, to be taken literally. What it means goes far beyond what it actually says. It is immediately apparent that the descriptions in it are confused, the visions described are fantastic and the phenomena which appear are incomprehensible. On first reading it seems inconsistent and pointless. But there is a historical code which is there to be cracked at a second reading. The *Revelation of John* was intended for people who knew the Old Testament through and through, and were also accustomed to the apocalyptic literature around at that time. They would be familiar with the symbolism attached to certain numbers and things, with the mysteries of the special language used and with the accepted relationships between expressions and ideas. The loss of this whole style of literature and the fact that this work of John's was itself excluded from the accepted canon of scriputre for some time no doubt makes it difficult for us today to grasp the full extent of its meaning.

A whole new vocabulary has to be learnt. Numbers, for example, are not given for their numerical value: seven signifies the whole and six, imperfection; twelve is the symbol of Israel; four, that of the created world; a thousand represents a very large number. The use of colours is no less significant: white represents victory, purity, and heavenly joy; red is for violence, wealth, and debauchery; black is for death; green for decay etc.

The Son of Man

I turned round to see who was talking to me, and I saw seven gold lamp stands, and among them there was what looked like a human being, wearing a robe that reached to his feet, and a gold belt round his chest. His hair was white as wool or as snow, and his eyes blazed like fire; his feet shone like brass that had been refined and polished, and his voice sounded like a roaring waterfall. He held seven stars in his right hand, and a sharp two-edged sword came out of his mouth. His face was as bright as the midday sun.' (*Revelation* 1, 12–16)

The Lamb

'Then I saw the Lamb standing in the centre of the throne, surrounded by the four living creatures and the elders. The Lamb appeared to have been killed. It had seven horns and seven eyes, which are the seven spirits of God that have been sent throughout the whole earth. The Lamb went and took the scroll from the right hand of the one who sits on the throne. As he did so the four living creatures and the 24 elders fell down before the Lamb. Each had a harp and gold bowls filled with incense, which are the prayer of God's people. They sang a new song: "You are worthy to take the scroll and break open its seals. For you were killed, and by your death you bought for God people from every tribe, language, nation, and race: you have made them a kingdom of priests to serve our God and they shall rule on earth."' (*Revelation* 5, 6–10)

By this method we have symbolic descriptions which are concrete in what they say and abstract in their meaning. The picture of the Son of Man (*Revelation* 1, 13–16) is an eloquent example: his long robe represents priestly dignity; his gold belt, royal power; his white hair, eternity; his shining eyes, divine knowledge; his brass feet, stability; finally his voice, which 'sounded like a roaring waterfall', strength.

The *Revelation of John* is made up of a number of separate pictures: each one is intended to represent one aspect of reality, create a particular atmosphere or suggest an impression. Any attempt to pigeonhole or make an intellectual system out of this text would be a betrayal of its deep significance. Symbolism is king here and its dazzling images remain rather enigmatic for today's reader.

The Letter to the seven Churches of Asia

The first part of *Revelation* has a rather different style. The visions in this part are less important. Christ's return and the last days are there but do not represent the main thrust of the message. What really count in this passage are the moral exhortations and the need to hold the faith in trust. More prophetic than apocalyptic, the letter to the seven Churches strives to re-awaken religious fervour by recalling the promised rewards: 'If you have ears, then listen to what the Spirit says to the church' (*Revelation* 2, 7).

This letter is also very well constructed: after the vision of the Son of Man, the writer addresses himself to each of the seven Churches represented by the seven lamp stands. He admires the constancy of the Church in Ephesus, but asks it to return to its former behaviour. To the Church in Smyrna he writes of sufferings to come and promises the crown of life. He warns the Church at Pergamum to fight against heresies. The Church at Thyatira is asked to drive out Jezebel, a false prophetess. The Church at Sardis is reproached for its conduct. He offers his protection to the Church at Philadelphia. The final message is for the Church in Laodicea, reproaching it for the lukewarm nature of its faith.

The seven seals

In the first vision the apostle sees God the Father seated on his throne, surrounded by the heavenly court. In his hand he is holding a book with seven seals. Only the lamb (Jesus Christ) can break the seals. When he breaks the first four seals, four horses appear; the first is white, the second red, the third black, the fourth greenish, symbols of war, hunger, suffering, and disease, the four main evils of humanity. At the opening of the fifth seal the martyrs ask to be avenged. At the opening of the sixth seal comes a great earthquake across the land. Finally, when the seventh seal was broken there is a great silence in heaven.

The seven trumpets

Then seven trumpets are placed in the hands of seven angels standing before God. When the first is blown hail and fire rain down on the earth and a third of the earth is destroyed. At the sound of the second trumpet a great fiery mountain is thrown into the sea and a third of the sea turned to blood. When the third trumpet sounds a star falls from the sky on to the rivers and springs, and a third of the water is turned bitter. When the fourth trumpet sounds a third of the sun and the moon and the stars go dark. When the fifth sounds locusts attack the people who do not have God's mark on their forehead. When the sixth sounds two hundred million mounted troups massacre a third of humankind.

Then comes a pause during which an angel comes down from heaven holding in his hands a small open book. He gives a great cry like the roar of a lion. Then the apostle is asked to eat the book. It tastes as sweet as honey in his mouth but fills his stomach with bitterness. The apostle then has to proclaim the message about many nations, races, languages, and kings, and then go and measure the Temple.

Two witnesses are sent to earth and they proclaim God's word for 1260 days. When they have finished this task the Beast comes up out of the abyss, fights them, and kills them. But three and a half days later God raises them to life to the great terror of those who were busy celebrating their death, and a voice calls them up to heaven. They go up just as a terrific earthquake shakes the earth.

Then the seventh angel blows his trumpet and, amidst thunder and lightning and voices, the time comes for the dead to be judged, for 'your servants, prophets and all who worship you' to be rewarded and for those who destroy the earth to be destroyed. This is the proclamation of the last Judgment.

The woman and the dragon

Now there appears a woman on the point of giving birth and a dragon waiting in front of her ready to pounce on the child that is to be born. The woman gives birth to a male child who is immediately taken up to be with God, and the woman flees to a shelter in the desert prepared for her by God. Michael and his angels come out of the temple to fight the dragon and throw it out of heaven down to the earth. So victory is achieved in heaven but that bodes ill for the earth and the sea because the dragon now dwells with you. The dragon is in fact still pursuing the woman.

Then an enormous beast rises up out of the sea. It has seven heads and ten horns

The Whore of Babylon

'I saw a woman sitting on a red beast that had names insulting God written all over it; the beast had seven heads and 10 horns. The woman was dressed in purple and scarlet, and covered with gold ornaments, precious stones, and pearls. In her hand she held a gold cup full of obscene and filthy things, the result of her immorality. On her forehead was written a name that has a secret meaning: "Great Babylon, the mother of all the prostitutes and perverts in the world." And I saw that the woman was drunk with the blood of God's people and the blood of those who were killed because they had been loyal to Jesus. When I saw her, I was completely amazed. "Why are you amazed?" the angel asked me. I will tell you the secret meaning of the woman and of the beast that carries her, the beast with seven heads and 10 horns.'
(*Revelation* 17, 3–7)

and on each horn is a crown. The dragon gives his power to the beast. The whole earth follows the beast and bows down before it. It begins to shout insults to God, it fights and conquers the righteous people. It gains power over every race. Another beast comes up out of the earth. Like some false prophet it had the people worship the first beast.

'This calls for wisdom', says *Revelation.* The number of the Beast is given as 666. There has been a lot of speculation about this number: the six is repeated three times, the day of Man's creation, an imperfect day compared with the seventh, the day of perfection. Some have also used methods of mystical interpretation on it, letting each number represent a letter thereby arriving at the words 'Nero-Caesar' in Hebrew letters, or the name of some other tyrant. So the number of the Beast continues to provoke a lively interest and gives rise to a number of interpretations.

During this time the Lamb and the virgins remain on Mount Zion. The angels proclaim the fall of Great Babylon (Rome) and the eternal punishment of the ungodly. Another vision superimposes itself on the last: seven angels receive bowls filled with the anger of God: they contain the plagues God is keeping for the last days of the world. The Beast reacts by spewing out three impure spirits like frogs who gather together the kings of the earth to do battle. But the seventh bowl contains a violent earthquake which splits the great city into three parts.

The Whore of Babylon

A new vision reveals the famous prostitute. She is seated on a scarlet beast covered with names insulting God. This time the apostle gives some explanation of his vision. The Beast was once alive but is no more and it is about to come up from the abyss but will go to its destruction. The seven heads are seven hills (Rome is a city built on seven hills): there are also the seven kings (no doubt the seven Roman Emperors, the sixth of whom, Nero, was then in power). They will do battle against the Lamb, but the Lamb will be victorious.

The text again proclaims the fall of

Babylon. The people of God are urged to flee because the city is to be consumed by fire and its suffering will be as great as its splendour once was. Then follow laments over the city: 'In just one hour you have been punished', and the songs of triumph in heaven: 'The Lord has taken possession of his kingdom.'

The thousand-year reign

A new vision tells of the two final battles: the first sees the King of kings, the Lord of lords, mounted on a white horse, against the Beast and the kings of the earth with all their armies. The beast is captured and, along with the false prophet, is thrown alive into the lake of fire. The birds eat their fill of their flesh.

This battle is followed by a 1000-year reign during which Satan is shackled whilst all those executed for bearing witness to Christ are raised; the others must wait for the second resurrection.

(This idea was taken literally by the

The new Jerusalem

'And I saw the Holy City, the new Jerusalem, coming down out of heaven from God, prepared and ready, like a bride dressed to meet her husband. I heard a loud voice speaking from the throne: "Now God's home is with mankind! He will live with them and they shall be his people. God himself will be with them, and he will be their God. He will wipe away all the tears from their eyes. There will be no more death, no more grief or crying or pain. The old things have disappeared." Then the one who sits on the throne said, "And now I make all things new!"' (*Revelation* 21, 2–5)

---

millenarians who believed in the return of Christ after 1000 years.)

But after 1000 years Satan is released and the fight is renewed in the four corners of the earth. Then a fire comes down from heaven and destroys all the enemies. The devil joins the Beast in the lake of sulphur, the book of life is opened and the judgment of the dead takes place.

The new Jerusalem

The final vision is of the heavenly Jerusalem, depicted as a young bride. It is God's dwelling place among men. This is where it is written that God makes everything new and it is important to remember, in this context, the many biblical references to Israel as an unfaithful wife. The contrast emphasizes the complete nature of the change. Perfect salvation has been achieved.

Then the account is taken up again with a second description of the new Jerusalem, which is more detailed and precise. The holy city shines with the Glory of God. Its 12 gates each bear the name of one of the 12 tribes of the children of Israel. On the 12 foundation stones are written the names of the twelve Apostles of the Lamb. It has no Temple, for the temple is the Lord and the Lamb. The city has no need of the sun's light because the Glory of God shines on it. The gates stay open all day and there is no night. The nations walk in its light and the kings of the earth bring their treasure to it. Finally, there will be no more cursing for the throne of God is set up in the city.

Church leaders have always seen in this description a picture of the Church triumphant, just as the seven Churches of Asia have been taken to represent the church militant, and the two witnesses the Church suffering.

Confucianism

It appears that China was already acquainted with the use of writing and the calendar as early as 2000 BC. Not that many documents from that time have come down to us, far from it. Changes of dynasty, internal wars, and all kinds of rebellions contributed to the loss, not only of the earliest writings, but also of less fragile documents like monuments and pottery etc.

The earliest official Chinese history appears in the 9th century bc in the form of annals consisting of a vast collection of government papers. Traces have been found, for example, of the *Ch'un-ch'iu* (Spring and Autumn Annals) which speaks of the principality of Lu (now Shantung) during the years 722–481 BC.

A famous thinker

K'ung Fu Tzu (Confucius), philosopher and thinker of the 5th century seems to have gathered together the most wide-ranging collection of texts with the intention of learning all that he could from the experiences of the past; this led to the establishment of six classic works: *I Ching, Shu Ching, Shih Ching, I Li, Li Chi,* 'Canon of rites', and *Yüe Ching,* 'Canon of music' (lost), to which he added *Ch'un-ch'iu* (Spring and Autumn Annals), chronicles concerning his province.

However, this collection of books, giving examples of how things were done in all the regions of the country, was not popular with Ch'in Shih Huang-ti, head of a small feudal state who, after much bloodshed, had succeeded in taking over all the kingdoms in 221 BC. Having become the first 'emperor', he set about changing the course of history: the land was divided into districts, the nobility abolished, the peasant families enlisted in the army etc.

The Confucian scholars could find no justification for this action in their books and said so. The minister Li Ssu advised that this opposition should be stamped out and all the harmful writings of Confucianism burnt, except for those dealing with medicine and agriculture and those in praise of the Ch'in dynasty. This led to one of the largest scale book burnings in history.

Ch'in Shih Huang-ti only lived for three more years after this act of censorship, his dynasty ended with him and was replaced by the Han dynasty. So the texts, which the scholars often knew by heart were more or less revived, their teaching was adopted officially and the schools began to teach the six canons.

The Shu Ching
The 'Book of historical documents'

The historical paper

The Shu Ching is the oldest and most important work for understanding the ancient traditions of the Chinese people.

From time immemorial Chinese society has tried to trace the causal links between the events of history. It has also sought to see a reflection of the present reality in ages past. History is therefore of prime importance to that society.

From the 8th century BC historiographers at the royal court were charged with recording any deeds and words worthy of note, meaning those in particular which showed signs of relating to future events. The Chinese would then find in these documents the ingredients of a moral code.

The *Shu Ching* is the oldest of these documents. It contains various speeches, decrees, and exhortations pronounced by rulers or officials: it takes us back to the time

of the famous sovereigns Yao, Shun, and Yü who lived some 20 centuries BC at the time of the first three dynasties Hsa, Shang, and Chou. K'ung Fu Tzu (Confucius) counted it as one of the six classics.

Like most of the ancient books, the *Shu Ching* disappeared at the time of the book burning of 213 BC. It was restored to us through Fou Cheng, an old man from Shantung, who was blind but was able, at the age of 90, to dictate what he had memorized: 29 of the 100 sections of the work were recovered in this way in 176 BC. Forty-four years later one of the princes of Lu wanted to rebuild K'ung Fu Tzu's house and several works written on bamboo were found within one of the thick walls; it turned out to be a copy of the *Shu Ching*.

In the first century BC, K'ong An-kuo, a descendant of K'ung Fu Tzu's family, set about deciphering the manuscript written in sigillary characters (a difficult form of script), with the help of Fou Cheng's 28 chapters and managed to produce 29 further parts. So we had two versions of the *Shu Ching*, then called *Shang Shu* (the Noble Book), that of Fou Cheng, called the *Chin Wen* ('New Text'), and that of K'ong An-kuo, called the *Ku Wen* ('Old Text').

But more misfortunes lay in store for the *Shang Shu* which was lost and reformed several times; it is generally admitted that the ancient part, the 'Old Text' is now simply made up of 11th-century forgeries. Yet it is this version which is in the canon of Scriptures and took the name of *Shu Ching* at the time of the southern Sungs (11th–12th centuries).

A holy history

The work is divided into four parts: the first, the *Yü Shu* or 'Book of Yü' deals with the three ancient Kings Yao, Shun, and Yü and covers the period from 2357 to 2206 BC. The second part, the *Hsia Shu* or 'Book of Hsia' speaks of Yū and the princes of the first dynasty (2205–1767 BC); it contains the *Yū Kong* or 'Yū's Tribute' which is a summary of the ancient geography of China and the account of the canal projects undertaken by Yū the great, and the *Hong Fan* or 'The Great Rule', held to be the oldest essay of Chinese philosophy.

The third book, the *Shang Shu* or 'Book of Shang' relates the events of the second dynasty (18th–11th century BC); finally the *Chou Shu* contains the documents relating to the third dynasty (11th–3rd century BC), including the *Lu Hsing*, a type of penal code dating from the beginning of the Chou period and explaining the penal laws of the prince of Lu.

The *Shu Ching* appears as a sacred history which glories in the fine deeds, eloquent words, and wise decisions of the great kings Yao, Shun, and Yū, of the minister Kao Yao, of Tang the Happy, founder of the second dynasty, of Wen, Wu, and the duke of Chou and which also condemns the behaviour and blackens the memory of the tyrants Chie and Shou Hsin who brought about the fall of the first two dynasties.

Moral rules

In the second chapter of the first book, the *Shu Ching* speaks about five rules (*wu tien, wu kiao*). They will be mentioned many times throughout the work, which goes so far as to credit them with divine origins. These five rules or five duties (*wu lun*) concern the mutual obligations between father and son, ruler and subject, husband and wife, old and young, and finally between friends.

This idea of relationships based on mutual obligations is one of the central principles of Confucianism. The prosperity and stability enjoyed by China over many centuries is attributed to this simple principle and every revelation and misfortune is seen as the result of one of these rules being broken. From these rules are derived the 10 virtues of justice (*Chi i*) which the *I Li* lists as follows: 'Paternal affection and filial compassion; the gentleness of elders towards those younger than themselves and

the respect of the young for their elders; the fairness of the husband and obedience of the wife; consideration in old people and submission in the young; kindness in rulers and loyalty in their subjects' (*I Li*).

The heavenly mandate

To a certain extent the legitimacy of the sovereign depends on these five rules. Yū the Great, for instance, the founder of the Hsia dynasty owed his celestial rank entirely to his extreme virtue. But there came a time when one of his successors, Chie, preferred the pleasures of his office to the responsibilities and so he lost his mandate and in 1400 BC heaven put him in the hands of Tang the Happy, founder of the second dynasty. In the same way, the infamous Shou Hsin was abandoned by heaven in 1122.

So it is virtue alone and therefore the imitation of the perfect rulers of old which bestows the right to assume power. Anyone wishing to seize power might claim the celestial mandate only if he fulfilled these conditions. The emperor is in fact the son of heaven, guarantor of the harmony between heaven and earth. 'From what I know of the heavenly path (T'ien tao)', said the Emperor Wen, 'calamities are the result of wrong actions and happiness comes from the pursuit of virtue. Every officer's faults must originate in myself. Officers responsible for secret missions transfer the disasters to their juniors: this all makes it clear that there is no virtue in me.' (Ssu-ma Ch'ien, *Shih Chi* (Historical essays) II, 473).

The Hong Fan

This concept is analysed in great detail in the *Hong Fan*, a theoretical treatise incorporated in the *Shu Ching*. It explores a general numerology which indicates relationships between space, time, tastes, virtues, and joys with a view to clarifying the organization of the universe:

1. water moistens, reaches the depths, and produces saltiness;
2. fire blazes, reaches upwards, and produces a bitter taste;
3. wood bends, curves, straightens up again, and produces acid;

4. metal is capable of being drawn out in many forms and produces pungency;
5. earth is a seed bed, fertile, harvested and produces sweetness.

Thus everything is arranged according to a system with five headings, a system which is in harmony with that of heaven.

The *ming tang* temple is the symbol of these relationships and is considered to represent the universe: its base is square because the earth is square, its roof is round because heaven is round. It is in this temple that the ruler exercises his political and cosmic function; by moving around there he enlivens space and fosters the unfolding of the seasons. There he publishes the decrees which harmonize men's tasks with the actions of heaven.

Importance of the Shu Ching

In the 2nd century BC, Tong Chung-shu said to the Emperor Wu: 'Everything which is not in the domain of the six classics should be discarded.' Without going quite as far as that, the ruler did have the classics taught in his schools. Studies of and commentaries on the *Shu Ching* proliferated throughout the time of the Han dynasty. In AD 175 the official text of it was engraved, using incised plates, on stone and put on display so that everyone could consult it and correct their own manuscripts according to this model.

The ups and downs of history and especially the introduction of Buddhism to China overshadowed the *Shu Ching*. But the first European missionaries discovered ideas similar to their own in it and their sympathetic attitude to this statement of belief led to the 'Conflict of Rites' which set the Jesuits against the Vatican from 1630 to 1742.

The good emperor

'On studying antiquity, we find that the Emperor Yao was humble, intelligent, accomplished, and thoughtful, naturally, without any effort. He was sincerely courteous and given to kindness. The influence of his qualities reached to the four corners of the empire and stretched from the earth to the sky. He was in a position to honour capable and virtuous men and, in that way, he extended his love to the nine classes of his relations who all became united. He ruled over and civilized peoples who all became brilliantly intelligent. He united and brought into harmony innumerable states and so the black haired people were transformed. Universal agreement has been the result of this.' (*Shu Ching* I, 1)

The bad princes

At that time, Hsi and Ho, giving themselves over to vice, trampled their duties underfoot; they threw themselves headlong into drunkenness. They went completely against the duties of their office and therefore forfeited their status. From the beginning they brought trouble to the heavenly pattern and totally rejected their proper function. On the first day of the last moon of autumn, the Ch'in (conjunction of the sun and the moon) was not in harmony with Fang (the Scorpio group of stars: no doubt it was an eclipse). Hsi and Ho were practically useless; they neither understood anything, nor learned anything. They no longer saw or cared about the heavenly signs and brought down on themselves the punishment meted out by the kings, our predecessors.' (*Shu Ching* II, 4)

The search for a successor

'Although he did have a son, the Emperor Yao asked his ministers to seek out a man capable of taking a share in the empire … They suggested Yü Tsu-ch'ou, his own son, whose wisdom was widely acclaimed. "You are mistaken", said the emperor, "Yü Tsu-ch'ou is not totally straightforward; he likes to argue: would such a man really be suitable? … Think about those who do not have a job and lead a private life." They all replied: "There is Shun who is unmarried and of lowly birth … Shun, although the son of a blind father who has neither talent nor wit, although born of a wicked mother who ill-treated him and although the brother of Hsiang who is full of pride, keeps the rules of filial obedience and lives in peace. He has managed, imperceptibly, to correct the faults of his family and prevent it from making any great mistakes." So the emperor gave him his two daughters in marriage to see how he behaved with them.' (*Shu Ching* I, 1)

The Shih Ching
The 'Book of Odes'

The feast songs

Rites, prayers, sayings, and games which are from the common basis of Chinese wisdom and are contained in the Shih Ching.

In ancient China at the great feasts of spring and autumn, boys and girls would dance and sing together in alternate verses. Men and nature would combine on the same project following the same rhythm of life and thus producing the same images. Everything would contribute to the work they all had in common.

These regular recurrences in trees, plants, rivers, and men draw out the same words, the same proverbs, the same poems, the same songs. These are poetic verses and calendar sayings. Each time, they are reinvented. Each year new creators improvise formulae whose effectiveness is assessed as it has been since the time of the forefathers and which harmonize wonderfully on that day.

This is how the ancient Chinese worked: finding the freshness of the present moment in ancient words; reviving the symbolic strength of traditional poetry, that strength which attracts, challenges, and compels. For them, songs and poems are not only signs, they are powerful rites and forms of fulfilment in themselves. Songs and poems are an integral part of the renewal of spring and the act of love.

None of these works is intent on finding original expressions or feelings, for their authors believe that the best way of giving power and conviction to their songs is to clothe them in traditional forms, to slip them into formulae which are well tried

and are held in considerable esteem. So a collection of themes relating to all times and places has existed since time immemorial.

The *Shih Ching* contains the most important part of this common fund of Chinese poetry. If tradition is to be believed, this selection is the work of K'ung Fu Tzu (Confucius) who, as is proper, could only retain those which were 'inspired by the purest wisdom' (*La Pensée chinoise* (Chinese Thought), Marcel Granet).

Kuo feng, ya and sung

The work is traditionally divided into three parts: the *kuo feng*, which are popular poems, the *ya* which are courtly poems, and finally the *sung* which are religious hymns which sing the praises of the first kings.

The *kuo feng* are in the main love songs, full of innocence and charm: there are accounts of meetings and separations, agreements and quarrels. Stereotyped descriptions, conventional emotions, the use of symmetry and parallelism have made these works into well-loved old songs which are easy to remember.

There is no doubt that these songs revealed a lot about the people's thinking

---

Song of love
'Boys come with girls to the orchids! The girls invite them — Shall we go down there? And the boys reply — We have been there already! — That is true, but let's go down again for, once over the Wei, there stretches a fine lawn. The boys and girls then play their games together; and then the girls receive a flower as a pledge! The ch'en and the Wei are swollen with clear waters! Many boys and girls are gathered together!' (*Shih Ching* I, 18)

---

and for that reason the king had a mind to collect them together in order to get a better understanding of his people, but certain critics are of the opinion that they must have undergone certain changes at the time of being written down, in order to make them intelligible throughout the kingdom.

It matters little whether they are the winners of poetry contests held to mark the great seasonal feasts or the work of scholars making use of the most standard rustic themes. They have retained a truly poetic freedom and naivety even if, here and there, some moral or political explanations have been added to alter their meaning.

The *ya* are courtly poems. The main themes of this text are accounts of historical facts, praise of notable princes, celebrations of a great city or simple hunting songs. Yet, some ministers or courtiers who were highly regarded at court were able to use them symbolically, without seeming to, as a means of reproaching the prince for some mistake, satirizing some of society's attitudes or giving expression to the complaints of the people.

Guests at a banquet would be divided up according to their princely family and then poetry competitions would be held in which one clan was set against another. One group would choose a poem relevant to the situation and the other would have to reply with an appropriate piece. It is said that these peaceful contests often ended in regular brawls.

But the fact remains that these songs have some real literary merit: they are down-to-earth, are based on believable circumstances and express sentiments of great truth. The rhymes are meticulously worked out, the expressions are very fully developed, and the verse form is quite regular.

The *sung* are religious hymns. These are beyond doubt the most ancient writings in this work. They date from the 10th century BC. Their form is therefore very primitive: no rhyme scheme, no verse form, a style totally without elaboration. What they convey is quite simply a very fervent religious feeling.

Most of them celebrate the first kings of the Chou dynasty, certain gods of nature, or quite simply God: God 'veiled in obscurity' they say (*Shih Ching* II, 4), as if recognizing the principle of one God. It seems that they were sung when sacrifices were offered to their ancestors. Some of them from the principality of Lu are later documents.

Influence

K'ung Fu Tzu's (Confucius's) early endorsement of the *Shu Ching* was certainly the start of its success and from then on the influence it had in scholarly circles in China was considerable. This work is the Confucianists' book of instructions and is part of the canon of Confucianist Scripture. It was condemned to be burned, like so many others, by Ch'in Shih Huang-ti. K'ung Fu Tzu would have said that a man who did not know the *Shih Ching* was like someone standing in front of a wall, with a limited outlook and no possibility of moving forward.

Offering prayer

'Here are our offerings: there are sheep, there are oxen; may they be acceptable to heaven! Let us take King Wen's ritual as our model, so that every day the whole empire will be guaranteed peace; the great King Wen has already accepted our offerings and tasted them. Let us fear the majesty of heaven night and day so that it will continue to look favourably on us.'
(*Shih Ching* III, 7)

The I Ching
The 'Book of Changes'

The reflection of the universe

As a method of interpreting the things of the universe from the infinitely great to the infinitely small, the I Ching is at the very heart of Chinese wisdom.

The *I Ching* is a collection of signs whose very basic meaning is 'yes', an unbroken line: ▄▄▄ and 'no', a broken line: ▄ ▄

Long, long ago these simple lines produced more complex combinations whose meaning was more mysterious: a second line was added, then a third. In this way eight different trigrams (three line figures) were obtained, which were supposed to represent every possible situation on earth and in heaven.

Later on the unbroken line would be called *yang* and the broken line *yin*, and the trigrams, most often doubled to form hexagrams (with six lines) show the constant transformation of yang into yin and vice versa, like the ongoing mixture of the masculine and feminine in everything that makes up the universe. Only the trigram with three unbroken lines, the symbol of heaven and the one with three broken lines, the symbol of earth are not themselves made up of a mixture.

The signs change from one form to another like the phenomena which can be observed in the universe:

after spring ☳ comes summer ☲
which is followed by autumn ☱
and by winter ☵ , and the cycle

begins again. The same signs call up realities of the same order: ☳ underlies both spring and morning, and summer and

winter; spring and autumn are directly opposed to each other. So an entire code

---

Method of consulting the oracle
1. Take 50 flower stems (or 50 sticks). Put one aside which will never be used again.
2. Divide the pile of sticks into two roughly equal parts.
3. Take one stick from the right pile and put it between the little finger and ring finger of the left hand.
4. Divide the left pile into groups of four sticks, the last group being made up of four, three, two or one stick.
5. Place this remainder between the ring finger and the middle finger of the left hand.
6. Do the same thing with the right pile and put this new remainder between the middle finger and the index finger of the left hand.

The total number of sticks kept is nine or five.

The same processes are followed two more times with those sticks which have not been retained the times before: the result is eight or four. In this way one arrives at a sum of three numbers.

The sum 5+4+4 is expressed as one positive moving line.

The sum 9+8+8 is expressed as one negative moving line.

The sums 9+8+4, 5+8+8, and 9+4+8 are expressed as one positive line at rest.

The sums 9+4+4, 5+4+8, and 5+8+4 are expressed as a negative line at rest.

(Of course these numbers can also be arrived at by spinning three coins.)

The same procedure will have to be gone through six times to produce the six lines of the revealing hexagram or hexagrams.

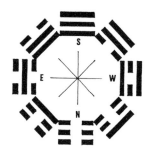

Fu Hsi's arrangement

by which the universe can be interpreted is established.

The traditional book

Traditionally, the invention of trigrams is attributed to the mythical ruler Fu Hsi, 'wise in the things of heaven as in the things of earth', one of the three 'Great Ones' who presided over China's golden age: a way of saying how very ancient and venerable they are. This legendary emperor is also credited with an arrangement of the eight trigrams in the form of a compass (Fu Hsi's arrangement), illustrating the various complementary and opposing relationships of the phenomena they represent: a kind of synthesis of the universe.

The collection of hexagrams we have today would have been the work of King Wen (c. 11th century BC), the founder of the Chou dynasty. We have another arrangement of the eight trigrams done by him (Wen's arrangement), which is not contrary to Fu Hsi's but complements it. But Wen had the particular idea of regrouping the trigrams in twos, thus forming 64 hexagrams: a kind of analytical view of the events of the universe.

This collection of hexagrams forms the central core of *I Ching*. 'All the rest', as Marcel Granet says, 'is merely comment, explanation or key to help in their decoding.' (*La Pensée chinoise* (Chinese Thought)). In fact, each of them is followed by a short assessment: it is said that King Wen wrote them while he was imprisoned in the jails of the tyrant Chou Hsin.

Wen's son, the duke of Chou also added his comments and it was in this state that this work called 'The Transformations of Chou' was used for a long time as a book of oracles.

K'ung Fu Tzu (Confucius) knew it well. He dedicated himself to the study of it and gave numerous interpretations of it: he is generally credited with the authorship of 'Commentary on the decisions' which follows the 64 hexagrams. But the *I Ching* has continued to show its vitality: it is certain that disciples of K'ung Fu Tzu produced the 'Commentary on the images' and others after them the 'Great Commentary', and yet others the 'Commentary on the words of the text', and that is only the tip of the iceberg! Together these writings form the 10 off-shoots or developments and have become an integral part of the *I Ching*.

The work is therefore the fruit of a long maturing process in Chinese thought; every philosophical or religious school of thought from K'ung Fu Tzu to Zu Lao Tzu has found the revelation of essential truths in the 64 hexagrams and used them as a framework for their teaching. The *I Ching* is the key which opens all doors.

A means of foretelling the future

The book contains a record of the changes in the world. It reveals all its possibilities: the 64 hexagrams take in the whole range of feasible arrangements. In six yin or yang lines all diversity is given expression: no two hexagrams are alike; it assumes movement: one single line changes one hexagram into the one most similar to it and the change from one to the other is contained in that similarity. For the main interest of

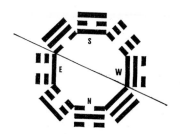

Wen's arrangement

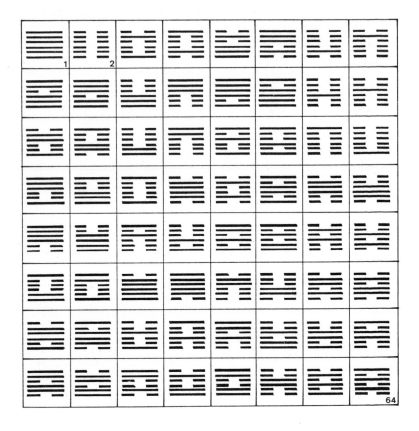

*The whole of **I Ching** is found in these 64 hexagrams — the rest is merely commentary — and there is no hexagram which is not included in the* I Ching. *So these symbols represent what has existed, exists now, and will exist, and they therefore contain, in some mysterious way, an exhaustive knowledge and a total power.*

the *I Ching* is not the essence of things — trigrams and hexagrams cannot go beyond a simple symbolism —, what the *I Ching* is concerned with is, as its name suggests, changes, mutations, and transformations, and there the signs used can be a revelation of what happens in the macrocosm, the universal scale, as well as in the microcosm or on the smaller scale.

It is also tempting to try and discover the seeds of future events and explanations of the past in the *I Ching*. The book was, without doubt, firstly an instrument of

divination, or means of foretelling the future: the handling of flower stems let us choose one or several hexagrams to read and the line which, in one or other of them, could be altered to make the change from yin to yang or vice versa. The change thus indicated gave rise to many interpretations.

A book of wisdom

No doubt the wisest of the Ancients soon realized that there was no point in expecting a precise, exact, and detailed description of each person's future from the *I Ching*. The book simply gives a general outline, a global view: it only deals in those trends and laws which are vital to the universe: from looking at a seed one can tell the type of tree that will grow from it, but one cannot predict how it will take root and grow, nor the shape its branches will take, far less the date when the woodcutter will come to fell it.

In the 11th century BC, King Wen and his son, the duke of Chou, made a book of wisdom out of the book of divination. The *I Ching*, in its wonderful judgment shows how things, events, and beings follow from each other, are linked to each other, and fit together: so it is able to guide human actions and be a catalogue of advice indicating the correct behaviour in each particular case. In this way man is involved in the shaping of his destiny.

Lao Tzu knew the work and was inspired by it, and K'ung Fu Tzu both meditated and commented on it at such length that it has become one of the great classics of Confucianism.

The *t'ai chi* is the idea underlying the whole book: the word means 'roof beam', precisely that which separates what is above and what is below, what is on the right, and

yin

yang

what is on the left, what is in the light and what is in the shade, in fact the yin and the yang. The roof beam is one line, but its very existence establishes duality.

There are three basic essentials to *I Ching* thought. The first holds that a constant harmony exists between heaven, earth, and man; what happens down here is merely the reflection of what is happening up there

and it is important to conform to this agreement. The second is the importance given to numerology: numbers help to penetrate the mysteries of the universe, they are the laws which cover everything, even if we do not fully understand them: the hexagrams are numerical symbols given geometrical formulae. 'The ancient Chinese avoided any distinction between arithmetic and geometry ... The disciplines of numbers, diagrams, government, and divination all merge together' (Marcel Granet). The third is the principle of order, an order in which everyone on earth and in heaven must find their own rightful place: a woman must not have a man's authority, nor subjects the same powers as their rulers; hence the importance of rituals (*li*), which represent the cosmic order of things transposed into human society.

The *I Ching* is a code book for interpreting the universe. Its method of analysis and exploration is so general that every school of thought can make use of it. The Chinese

Community with men

Concerning hexagram no. 13 Confucius says: 'Life leads the thoughtful man along a tortuous and varied path. Its course is often full of obstacles, then everything becomes smooth. Here, an eloquent thought pours forth easily in words. There, the heavy burden of knowledge must be locked in silence. However, when two beings are united in the intimacy of their hearts they can break through iron and bronze.' (*I Ching*)

Universal harmony

'As long as man grows close to heaven and to earth, he does not get into conflict with them. His wisdom embraces all things and his way governs the whole world. This is why he does not make any mistakes. He is active everywhere, but nowhere does he allow himself to be carried away. He finds his joy in heaven and knows his destiny. This is why he is free from cares. He is satisfied with his lot and genuine in his kindness. This is why he can love.' (Hsi Ts'en III, 3)

schools find support for their teachings in it, although they are all so different from each other: some see objective data in it, others rules of morality, and all have adopted it as a means of meditation.

Influence

The *I Ching* has enjoyed a degree of renown which has never faded throughout history: it escaped the burning of all books ordered by the Emperor Ch'in Shih Huang-ti and has been the object of an abundance of studies under the Chin dynasty (221–206 BC) and the Han dynasty (206 BC– AD 220). It was left to the great philosopher Wang Pi (226–249) to sort through this mass of documents and discover the essential wisdom of the *I Ching*. The first translation of the work into a European language dates from 1834; it was the work of Father Regis and appeared under the title *Antiquissimus Sinarum Liber* (The Most Ancient Book of the Chinese). Then came several translations including that into English by James Legge in 1882

and a French translation by P-L-F Philastre in 1885–93. Many others followed.

The greatness of the *I Ching*

'The Book of Changes is great and vast. Do you speak of what is far off? It knows no limits. Do you speak of what is close at hand? It is clear and precise. Do you speak of the space held between earth and heaven? It embraces everything.' (*The great commentary*, Hsi Ts'en, VI)

Numbers

'There are five heavenly numbers, there are also five earthly numbers. If they are shared out between five, each one finds its complement. The sum of the heavenly numbers is 25. The sum of the earthly numbers is 30. The total of all these heavenly and earthly numbers is 55. This is what perfects the changes and transformation and sets in motion the demons and the gods.' (Hsi Ts'en IX, 2)

Hinduism

There is no clean break between Vedism and Hinduism. It has been more of a slow evolution from the one to the other. No doubt the founding of Buddhism by Gautama and of Jainism by Haravira led to changes but never to rejection of the *Vedas*.

This is all the more true since the first fourteen *Upanishads*, which are related to Vedic literature, are already familiar with speculations about the *Atman*, the internal reality of the human being, and the *Brahman*, the Absolute, which mark the Vedanta or the end of the Veda, at the same time as the beginnings of the *bhakti*, devotion, of *yoga*, asceticism (self denial), and of the cult of Vishnu and Shiva which are the characteristics of Hinduism.

The fundamental texts

The reaction against detailed ritualism, intellectual mysticism, and the absolute power of the Brahmins, along with the popular desire for a personal relationship with the divinity, were certainly major factors in this evolution. So attention was focused on the more personalized Vedic gods, Vishnu and Rudra, soon likened to Shiva, probably a non-Aryan (not pure Hindu) tribal god, and the sacred literature faded from the liturgical code and theological development of the time: the *Mahabharata* and the *Ramayana* grew out of ballads relating the exploits of warriors, but they do carry within them the essence of Hinduism.

The *Vedas*, the *Brahmanas*, and the *Upanishads* remain the most sacred basis of the Indian religious literature. But since they are all but incomprehensible to the people, they are the preserve of the learned and those who have been initiated into their complexities, namely the Brahmins, who continue to study them and comment on them in the light of changes. On the other hand, the epics have been immensely successful and the ancient legends, the *Puranas*, bring new elements to popular religion.

There are in fact two large categories of texts in the sacred literature of India: the *sruti*, which means 'understanding' and the *smrti*, which means 'memory'. The first is made up essentially of the *Vedas*, the *Brahmanas*, and the *Upanishads*: it is the eternal truth understood by the Rsis. The *smrti*, whilst also sacred, is not on the same level: this is what is remembered and passed on from generation to generation: the *Mahabharata*, the *Ramayana*, the *Puranas*, and other Hindu writings.

The Upanishads

Didactic texts

The lessons of the master

The Upanishads present a spiritual doctrine, which is considered to be essential and is passed on from master to pupil.

The word *Upanishad* means 'the lesson': the term suggests a master teaching his followers as they sit at his feet. The *Upanishads* were written around the 6th century BC, at the time of Buddha. They are didactic essays, usually fairly short, which treat points of doctrine held to be fundamental.

The first *Upanishads* belong to Vedic literature; they mark the end of it, the Vedenta, and usher in the great variety of Hinduism.

The first Upanishads

The Veda *Upanishads* are prose texts, dialogues, and expositions with a logical bent. Here the emphasis is not so much on the narrative but on questioning, on a kind of fertile mixture of fables, enigmas, and didactic slogans with magical overtones. The reasoning is disjointed and full of digressions, puns, and evasions. In the midst of all this can be found wise sayings, poems, and parts of prayers.

So, like the *Brahmanas*, the *Upanishads* are a form of teaching reserved for a small number, yet they can be differentiated from each other by a kind of 'secularization' of themes. The ritual no longer has the importance which it had in the *Vedas*, nor is there the symbolic system of words nor the hidden meaning of melodies, nor any other intricate speculation. The *Upanishads* set out to offer explanations which are more intellectual than mystical: the problem to

be resolved is physiological and cosmological. They therefore extend their remit to include the notions of Atman, the soul of man, and Brahman, the universal soul pervading all things.

The Vedic *Upanishads* speak, for the first time in Indian thought, of reincarnation, *samsara*, which is dependent on our actions, Karma. This concept of life is one which was apparently shared by Buddhism and Jainism at that time. However, the *Upanishads* envisage a conclusion which is peculiar to them. Whilst the Buddhists aspire to extinction (nirvana), and the Jains to the liberation of the body, the *Upanishads* see the end of the samsara in terms of a union of each person's Atman with the universal Soul, the Brahman.

Absolute reality

The *Brhadaranyaka Upanishad* is one of the oldest and most important works, as notable for its size as for its thought. It introduces Yajnavalkya, one of the Satapatha Brahman

> **Reincarnation**
> 'All those who go away from this world arrive at the moon. It is thanks to their vital breath that the moon grows in the first half of the month; in the second half it makes them increase. For the moon is the door to the heavenly world. The man who meets her requirements is allowed to pass through, and the man who falls short she lets fall as rain after he has been turned into rain. So he is reborn here, as a worm or an insect, a fish or a bird, a tiger or a lion, a boar or a rhinoceros, a man or some other animal, in their respective places according to his actions, according to his knowledge.'
> (*Kausitaki Upanishad* 1, 2)

teachers who, through discussions with the other Brahmins reveals the identity of the human soul (Atman) and the cosmic Soul (Brahman), 'this thread by which this world and the other world and all things are linked together' (*Brhadaranyaka Upanishad* III, 7, 1).

The *Chandogya Upanishad* is almost as ancient and returns to theories about the Atman-Brahman relationship. Here the principal speakers are Uddalaka Arusi and his son Cvetaketu to whom he is teaching the idea of Brahman.

The devarsi or divine prophet, Narada, also appears here as a very wise Brahmin trying to find out about the Atman because he has heard it said that 'to know this is to cross the ocean of suffering' (*Chandogya Upanishad* VII). Samatkumara speaks to him, reasoning as follows: Is the Atman the Veda? 'It is all words and when we use words we have to be careful with their meaning. As for the one who takes words to define Brahman, he can say anything he likes, but only in words.' The same goes for speech, mind, knowledge, strength, memory, life. In conclusion he says: 'The Atman is below and above, in the west and in the east, in the south and in the north, it is everything that exists. He who sees things this way, thinks this way, understands in this way, who loves the Atman, who is in union with the Atman, who rejoices in the Atman, that person is the supreme teacher' (*Chandogya Upanishad* VII).

The Atman

Atman is the creator of the world the *Aitareya Upanishad* tells us: 'Atman was the only "it" in the beginning. Nothing else opened its eyes. He said: I want to send out worlds. He sent out worlds: heavenly waters, shafts of light, the land of the dead, cosmic waters. The heavenly waters are out there beyond the sky, the sky is what sustains them. The shafts of light are beyond the space between. The earth is the land of the dead, it is the earth which covers the waters' (*Aitareya Upanishad* 1, 1). The text ends by declaring that Atman is Brahman, and is Indra, and is Prajapati, and is all the gods and the five basic elements. What is expressed here, therefore, is a kind of pantheism, the idea

that God is in everything.

Next comes the *Kausitaki Upanishad*, which is made up of various pieces placed together but which holds throughout to the idea that Atman is the breath of life (*prana*). It begins to describe the path men follow after death, reincarnation for some, union with Brahman for others, then after outlining a few observations necessary for achieving certain desires, it changes into a hymn to the breath of life.

Brahman

The praise of Atman-Brahman continues in the *Kena Upanishad*. Brahman is 'different from the known and different from the unknown' and it has conquered the gods. But Indra 'is in some way beyond the other gods. For he has come closer to this Brahman. For he was the first to realize that it was Brahman' (*Kena Upanishad* IV, 3).

The *Taittiriya Upanishad* is also devoted entirely to the praise of Brahman. The exploration of the sense of bliss is found

---

The universe

'The universe is like a gigantic man and we may speak of his eye which is the sun, his breath which is the wind, of his limbs, his heart, and his thinking. Man is also the universe in miniature and we may speak of the sun which is his eye, the wind which is his breath. Plenitude or completeness is out there (*Brahman*): and plenitude is what is here (Atman). Plenitude is taken from plenitude: but although one draws plenitude from plenitude, plenitude remains.' (*Brhadaranyaka Upanishad* V, 1)

Brahman

'As a piece of salt thrown into water dissolves and there is no way of getting hold of it or of taking it out of the water, and yet there is still salt there, so it is with this great infinite Being, without limits, made of knowledge. Rising up from these elements, he is absorbed in them again, for there is no consciousness after death, I tell you. Thus spoke Yajnavalkya.'
(*Brhadaranyaka Upanishad* II, 4)

---

here: 'A hundred human blessings are as one single blessing of the gandharvas (genies). A hundred blessings of the divine gandharvas are a single blessing of the Fathers who have a long lasting world ... a hundred blessings of the gods are as a single blessing of Indra ... a hundred blessings of Prajapati (the creator god) are as a single blessing of Brahman and of the wise man instructed in the Vedas, free from desires' (*Taittiriya Upanishad* II). The *Isa Upanishad* is a very short poem which addresses the same theme once more.

The breath which gives life

With the other Vedic *Upanishads*, the links with the *Vedas* become increasingly loose. The *Katha* (or *Kathaka*) *Upanishad* recounts the adventures of Naciketas who is sent to the kingdom of Yama, the god of the Dead, because of his father's anger. But Yama is not there when the young Brahmin arrives and the hospitality rituals are not followed as they should be. So, to compensate for this mistake, Yama offers, on his return, to grant the young man three wishes. The first two, the soothing of his father's rage and the knowledge of celestial fire are granted easily.

But Yama begins to shy away from the third question: 'Does man continue to live after death?' Even the gods are a little uncertain on this issue. 'The way to the other world is not revealed to the thinking

---

Breath of life

'In truth, ether is an energy, and then come air, fire, water, earth, speech, the internal sense, hearing, and sight. Having presented the creature they keep it saying "It is we who support the body and keep it." The breath of life, the best of the energies says to them: "Make no mistake. It is I who, dividing myself into five, supports and maintains the body. They do not trust it. Gradually it pretends to leave the body through the top, for if it leaves all the others leave too and, when it comes back again, so do all the others ... So speech, internal sense, sight, and hearing sing the praises of the breath of life."' (*Prana Upanishad* II, 4)

---

of the immature man of confused mind, distracted by the folly of riches ...' (*Katha Upanishad* II, 6–7). Then Yama explains: to reach Brahman, free from all blemishes, one must receive that knowledge taught by death and the whole subject of yoga.

The breath, which plays the vital role in the techniques of yoga, comes to the forefront in the *Prana Upanishad*. Prajapati, the creator, first created a pair: abundance (*rayi*) and breath of life (*prana*). The first represents earthly goods, 'all that exists with or without form'; the breath of life is fire, the best of the energies.

For each function there is a corresponding breath: there is the descending breath which resides in the anus and genital organs; there is the ascending breath which is related to the eye, ear, mouth, and nose, and the equalizing breath controls the food taken, but also regulates our breathing in and out. There is also one additional breath, that which circulates in the body and in the cosmos.

Rudra-Shiva and Vishnu

The *Svetasvatara Upanishad* marks an important stage in the thinking of the text. It is in this particular book that the importance of yoga is stressed for the first time. 'Once the activity of yoga appeared, fivefold in its nature, born of earth, water, light, fire, and ether there was no longer any illness nor old age nor death for the one who had a body (filled) with the fire of yoga' (*Svetasvatara Upanishad* II, 12).

Quite naturally there gradually appears on the scene one Mahayogin, the teacher of yoga, who is actually Rudra. Later he will be considered as the creator, 'he who produced the cosmic golden egg' and described as Shiva, the kindly one. So the charge is made from Rudra (Vedic) to Shiva (Hindu). There is even a hint of the *Trimurti* (Shiva, Vishnu, Brahma) with the coming together of Vishnu and Brahman.

Despite this traditional group of three, the *Svetasvatara Upanishad* includes some very monotheistic claims: 'This one god, hidden in all beings. He is the internal Self, innate and omnipresent, of all beings, the overseer of every activity ...' (*Svetasvatara Upanishad* VI, 11).

The central point of the *Maitrayantya Upanishad* seems to be the substitution of internal sacrifice for the Vedic sacrifice of the Angihotra: 'Sacrifices are made with the help of formulae, plants, butter, meat, cakes, cooked rice etc which are poured into the fire; or again with the aid of food or drink that the fire did not consume, and are poured into the mouth to obtain the second form of Brahman-light and gain whole worlds of blessing and have eternal life' (*Maitrayantya Upanishad* II, 7).

This sacrifice has the same value as the external ritual: the god to whom it is addressed is Vishnu, the universal Brahman; the hearth in which the offering is burnt is the heart of the one making the sacrifice, the individual Atman; which is itself the food eaten by the individual, which is also Atman, three times a day in the morning, at noon, and in the evening. This is how one is instructed to perform this sacrifice.

This is one of internal dedication which is ideally achieved by total retreat from the world: 'We will make a vow to live in peace with all creatures, withdrawing into the forest and meditating there, ridding ourselves of all perception through the senses in order to see him in the intimacy of his innermost self' (*Maitrayantya Upanishad* 1, 7).

OM (AUM)

The *Mandukya Upanishad* is a long discussion of OM, the ancient Vedic mantra or chant intoned by all the faithful, morning and evening, at the beginning and end of ceremonies. It is the first word said by the creator and is the last word of creation. For OM is Brahman, it is the universe, it is consent. This mantra, which is recognized as such by all the great religions of India, signifies one's submission to *Dharma* or religious duties.

It is made up of three Sanskrit letters A, U, M and the commentator breaks it up into three parts: the first, A, corresponds to the state of wakefulness common to all beings; the second, U, to the state of light sleep; the third, M, to the state of deep sleep. This division into three parts is widely used in teaching. There is the common element, the element of light, and the element of knowledge, there is also being, consciousness, and bliss and at the end of the day there is Brahma, Vishnu, and Shiva, the Hindu Trimurti, the object of the *bhakti* or devotion.

The other Upanishads

The *Upanishads* kept on going as a literary form for 1000 years since they were being composed until the 16th century, sometimes using remnants of very ancient texts. There are usually reckoned to be 108 *Upanishads*, but there are probably many more. Certain sects of Vishnu, Shiva, yoga, and others have their own. So we find the *Yoga Upanishad*, the *Sannyasia Upanishad*, about the bhakti, the *Saiva Upanishad* from the name of a sect, and so on.

The most illustrious commentator of the *Upanishads*, although he has only written about nine of them, is Sankara, who lived at the end of the 8th century. His condemnations of the bloody sacrifices of the Brahmins and of Buddhist ideas are famous. His extremly rational mind is a great help in understanding such archaic subjects.

OM

'One says: OM! For that syllable is this entire universe, which to be precise means: "What was, is now and will be." Yes, the syllable OM is the entire universe; and this other thing which has gone away beyond the three temporal spaces is also the syllable OM. But here we have the universe, Brahman, and Atman.' (*Mandukya Upanishad* 1 and 2)

The Self

'Enveloped as it is in the five layers produced by its own power, the Self does not show itself, like water in a pond covered over with clumps of reeds. But when all the reeds are completely cleared away the clear water becomes visible to man, it quenches the agony of thirst and gives the highest degree of blesing.' (*Sankara Vivekacudamani* 149–150)

The Bhagavadgita
The 'Lord's Song'

The fifth Veda

This dialogue between Krishna and Arjuna, the Bhagavadgita lies at the heart of the Mahabharata and is the most important part of it.

The action takes place just as a war between cousins, the Mahabharata, is about to begin. Arjuna is troubled by questions of conscience: 'I can't stand still and my thoughts are in a whirl. What good is there in killing my own relatives in battle? Oh Krishna, I want neither victory, nor kingdom nor pleasure' (*Bhagavadgita* 1, 30–1).

Right through the 700 verses which make up the poem, Krishna, Arjuna's charioteer, who is also the incarnation of the god Vishnu replies to him: these thoughts lead neither to heaven nor to honour: heaven is within your grasp if you are killed in battle; earth will be yours to enjoy if you are victorious. No doubt these feelings you express do you credit but they stem from a misunderstanding of the order of things and could prove to be a weak point given the task that is before you.

'Man, once he is born, does not know how to die ... The soul is now seen to progress through the body's infancy, youth, and old age. It meditates on many things, on thought which may be virtuous or perverse, it accomplishes many deeds some of which may be glorious and others contemptible, some brilliant and others obscure, but the soul does not stop there, it clothes itself afterwards in other bodies which will live other lives. So the inevitable death of the present body, your enemies' as well as your own, cannot be a cause for sorrow.'

The liberating renunciation

Dharma (religious obligation), justifies the right, even the duty to act and to fight. The individual is placed in a religious and social context. He is a member of a caste or class, that of the Brahmins, that of the warriors or that of the vaisyas, the caste which was required to work in the fields; he is placed in a particular situation as regards the events and the people around him: these two factors are the only things to be considered in determining each person's individual *dharma* or religious law that he is to observe.

What counts is not in fact the aims or consequences of a particular action, but the action itself, the action as an element of the cosmic order. Some people do things to get such and such a result or to gain such and such a benefit or to acquire such and such an object: they are blind and ignorant. That is far from the attitude of a wise and assured man: he remains constant in pleasure and in pain; for him there is no desire, no happiness to be searched for, no objective to be reached. The source of action is

---

Reincarnation

'These bodies will come to an end; the spirit within them is eternal and indestructible. That is what we proclaim. That is the reason for fighting, son of Bharata. Just as a man who has taken off his old clothes puts on new ones, so the soul that dwells in man takes off the used body and travels on in other bodies which are new. The truth is that for everyone who is born, death is certain and reincarnation is certain for whoever dies; so, faced with something so totally unavoidable, there is no reason to feel compassion.' (*Bhagavadgita* II)

not outside the action, it is action in tune with *Dharma*.

The wise man is not bound by the material aspects of action, those aspects which reduce it to the level of the transient and the trivial; he is free from the concerns of the body and things that pass away. 'Our limited bodies come to an end, but the thing which possesses and uses the body is infinite, unlimited, eternal, and indestructible' (*Bhagavadgita* II, 1, 17).

Bhakti

This renunciation — this liberation from the twin opposites: cold/heat, pleasure/pain, wealth/poverty etc, this indifference, not only to the past, but also to the present and the future — does not banish the act, the way of the act is still one of the three ways to salvation, it is just as necessary as is the link between the soul and the material body.

The act without desire, however, is an approach to the second way, the way of knowledge, the intuitive rather than bookish grasp of absolute Reality, Brahman, and his link with his individual 'self'. This knowledge is gained through meditation, including yoga. It is therefore a question of a psycho-physiological discipline: its aim is to unify the senses, presenting the unity of one's being to oneself.

Bhakti is the third way, the highest and most effective way. It is a matter of man's fondness, devotion and love towards the divinity. 'Devote yourself entirely to Me', Krishna says to Arjuna. 'Consciously abandon all your duties and come to me, turn your thoughts willingly to yoga and let your heart and mind always be at one with me' (*Bhagavadgita* XVIII, 4, 57). Sri Aurobindo comments: 'Only one Master of our actions, one friend and lover of our soul, one inner spirit of our life, one Lord who dwells inside and outside our entire personal and impersonal being, and nature can deliver this intimate moving message to us.'

Monotheism?

This attitude of bhakti tends to personify the Absolute and make a person of God. Throughout the *Bhagavadgita* in fact, the character of Krishna, at first Arjuna's simple driver-bard-adviser, grows in importance. At the beginning he gives his thoughts, then he teaches doctrine and finally reveals himself as the incarnation of the god Vishnu, the sole object of the devotion that is bhakti.

So in the end Krishna takes his place as the supreme God and the appearances he has made in human form were simply to further the faithful man's personal relationships with his god. Furthermore, whatever god is adored, it is always to Krishna that hommage is paid, for the other gods are merely imperfect beings created by those who are still incapable of aspiring to the Absolute.

One God

'That which is in us is him and all that we experience outside ourselves is him. He is within and beyond, he is far and near, he moves and does not move, all at once. He perceives clearly what is beyond our understanding. He is one and indivisible, yet seems to have many forms and whatever he appears as seems to have a separate existence. Everything in eternity is born of him, is kept in his eternity and eternally returns to his unity.' (*Bhagavadgita* XIII, 16–17)

Devotion

Fill your thoughts with me, give me your love and adoration and your sacrifice, bow low before me and you will come to me. This is the promise I make to you, for you are dear to me.' (*Bhagavadgita* XVIII, 65)

Importance

The *Bhagavagita* is like the 'gospel' of Hinduism (Louis Renou). If the Mahabharata as a whole is considered to be *smrti*, tradition, the *Bhagavadgita* is *sruti*, revelation, along with the *Vedas* and the *Upanishads*. So the great sages of India have meditated on it, been inspired by it, and have published commentaries on it. Among the most ancient, mention should be made of Sankara and among the most modern there is Sri Aurobindo. Above all, the *Bhagavadgita* has nurtured the piety of the Indian people for 2000 years.

The Puranas
Ancient stories

A new expression of the Vedas

The Puranas are early epic legends linked with the sectarian divisions in Hinduism.

The *Puranas* probably originate far back in time. The last of the *Vedas*, the *Atharva Veda* speaks of them but we can only speculate about their imperfect form, their disjointed nature, their contradictions and imcompleteness. They are outlines which have been reworked, have suffered additions and deletions, and have been taken over by sectarian groups and used for their specific cult.

Was there perhaps one single primitive *Purana* of which those we have today might be fragments? No one can say for sure. Tradition attributes the compiling of them to Vyasa, the presumed author of the *Mahabharata*, doubtless with the intention of adding to his prestige. They are regarded as sacred works, though of less worth than the *Vedas*, which pertain to the higher castes. These, on the other hand, are intended for the lowest class and for women.

Each of the *Puranas* is supposed to follow a pattern composed of five parts. This is the same for all of them, but few follow it very closely, except perhaps for the *VishnuPurana*.

We have the pansalaksana which covers the initial creation of the world, the recreation of the world after each period of destruction (comparable to the Flood), the genealogy or line of descent of the gods and the Rsis, who with each creation, pass on the Veda to men, the ages of the world or cosmic periods and the geneaologies of the kings of both the sun line (the *Ramayana*) and the moon line (the *Mahabharata*).

The *Puranas* contain a little of everything: legends, stories of pilgrimages, descriptions of holy places, procedures for administering the State, moral principles, outlines of the penal system, taxation and commerce, and even summaries on the techniques of grammar, composition, the compiling of dictionaries, speech making, architecture, medicine etc. A kind of encyclopaedia of its time in fact, and one whose time is very difficult to fix with any precision: some suggest, probably wrongly, the 4th century BC: it is more likely that the compilation of the *Puranas* took place over a much longer time span.

The *smrti*

Tradition or *smrti*, as opposed to revelation or *sruti*, 'seen' by the Rsis, has simply been passed on by word of mouth from generation to generation. So its contents, form, and style have changed in the course of history. The great epics, the *Mahabharata* and the *Ramayana* are part of it, as are the *Puranas*. But the *smrti*, although inspired by the gods is also of human origin. Composed by holy men for the sole purpose of making the revelation relevant to the conditions of the age, it has produced a number of works. In response to the times, places, schools of thought, cults, sects, we have seen the Vedic *sutras* appear which discuss certain points of doctrine, the *tantra* within which a distinction is also made between the Vishnuite *samhitas* and the Shivaite *agamas*, and a number of more specialized religious and philosophical works.

Special mention must be made of the *Manusmrti* or 'Laws of Manu'. Manu, the first man and law-giver sets out in this book the laws and social customs, the rights and duties of governments, priests, spouses, masters, and servants, and the fiscal or taxation rules etc. This is a point by point examination of a complete framework for society.

The MahaPuranas

The 18 main *Puranas* are called *MahaPuranas* ('Great Puranas'). Like the *PadmaPuranas* they are divided into three groups: the Vishnuite *Puranas* connected with brilliant intelligence, one of Vishnu's qualities: the Shivaite *Puranas* connected with darkness and destruction, qualities associated with Shiva; and the Brahmanic *Puranas*, connected with activity, the attribute of Brahma.

This division is not very strict, however. For example, sections can be found in the *BrahmaPurana* which are dedicated entirely to the worship of Shiva, and the *BhagavataPurana*, which relates to Vishnu, by no means underestimates Brahma and Shiva. The series of Brahminic *Puranas* seems to be rather unnatural; despite these attempts at organization the whole work remains very disordered.

Brahma

The Vedic precedence of Brahma, personification of the Brahman, disappears: 'It is through my own will (says Shiva) that, becoming the god Brahma, whose existence depends on my existence, he has gained for ever my supreme divine power.' However, he remains the creator. 'All-knowing by my will, he is creator of the whole universe. Having become the god with four faces he brought about creation, he who was born of me' (*KurmaPurana, Isvaragita* VI, 12–15).

Brahma was born from the primitive egg where he remained for 1000 years, says the *MatsyaPurana*, then he broke it into two

Solidarity

'How is it, asks the king on a visit to the underworld, that I have the means to comfort them? What great and good act did I perform in the world of men which produces this rain that refreshes them? Tell me. Your body has been fed by the remains of the good with which you honoured fathers and gods, hosts, and servants; your soul was concerned for them. That is why this air circulating around your limbs gives comfort to sinners and they no longer suffer in torment.' (*MarkandeyaPurana*)

parts: he made one into the sky and the other into the earth, and placed the atmosphere between the two. In another version of the Creation recorded in the *PadmaPurana*, the *LingaPurana*, and the *VayuPurana* he took from his thigh demons which became the night, and he took from his mouth gods which became the day. Then, taking another imperfect form, men appeared. Finally, the *VishnuPurana* goes back to the old Vedic myth in which Brahma takes men of the different castes from parts of his own body.

Vishnu

As far as Vishnu is concerned the *Puranas* deal particularly with the avatars, the incarnations of the god among men. The list of these is long and varies from one document to another. The *BhagavataPurana* numbers 32 of them, from the tortoise and the boar to Rama and Krishna. Vishnu intervenes in this way because he is the saviour and protector of the world.

Ancient accounts are sometimes changed to enhance Vishnu's legend. So the little fish which warned Manu about the flood and led his boat to the high mountain when the rains came, becomes in the *MatsyaParana* (1, 1–2), a being of huge dimensions and an incarnation of the god.

The avatar of the tortoise is linked to the myth of the churning of the ocean. The gods searching for amrita, the drink of immorality, set out to churn up the ocean, using Mount Mandara, the axis of the world. Vishnu, taking the form of a giant tortoise, placed himself under the mountain so that it would not sink into subterranean regions.

The *VishnuPurana* gives a new version of the Flood to lead into the avatar of the boar. The Earth found herself 'hidden beneath the waters'. Seeing a boar plunge into the ocean she called out to him and asked him to save her. Then the boar who was none other than Vishnu reincarnated, lifted up the Earth with his great strength and then 'the waters fell down into the lower worlds with the noise of thunder through the holes his feet had made' (*VishnuPurana* 1, 4).

The *BhagavataPurana* in particular focuses on Krishna, doubtless because he is

*The **Puranas** are the first examples of the epic style which was to have great success with the Ramayana and the Mahabharata.*
Here Rama is leaving in his chariot to wage war on the demon Ravana who has raped his wife, Sita.
Shadows of the Karnatak (India).
Coll. of the Museum Kwok On, Paris.

the best illustration of the *bhakti*, the love and devotion owed to Vishnu. This avatar would later take on such significance that the name of Krishna would gradually take over from the name of Vishnu himself in certain sects and in certain areas and, in the 12th century would be the inspiration for one of the most beautiful poems in Sanskrit literature, the *Gitagovinda* of Jayadeva, called India's 'Song of songs'.

Kamsa was an illegal ruler who reigned over Mathura. An omen warned him that he would be killed by a child of his kinswoman Devaki. So he murdered all the children born to her. Krishna, the eighth child, was saved because he was exchanged for the daughter of Nanda the cowherd, who brought him up.

From a very early age Krishna revealed himself through his great powers. The story goes on at some length about his battles against demons. One day when the cowherds and their wives were preparing a sacrifice in honour of Indra, he intervened and told them to offer the sacrifice, not to the god, but to the mountain. Indra was infuriated and unleashed a terrific storm. But Krishna protected the cattle by uprooting Mount Govardhana and holding it at arms length above them.

Shiva

The lingam, a representation of the male sex organ, the phallus, is the most usual symbol for Shiva. One day when Brahma and Vishnu were arguing over the creation of the world, an immense lingam of fire came between them. Brahma took the form of a wild goose in order to discover the summit and Vishnu took the form of a boar to investigate its base. Both of them failed in their attempt. Humiliated, they bowed down before the object and Shiva appeared in his radiance and told them that they were both born of him. (*LingaPurana* XVII).

In the *ShivaPurana* the god finds himself responsible for the creation of woman. Brahma was concerned because the beings he created were not reproducing. Then an androgynous Shiva, one having both male and female characteristics, appeared.

The castes
'For the prosperity of the worlds he brought forth from his mouth, his arms, his thighs, and his feet the four castes: priests, warriors, merchants, and serfs. Having divided his body in two he became man for one half and woman for the other, and in this one the Lord gave birth to Viraj the Resplendent. But the one that this male Viraj brings forth, having stirred up his inner desire, is me, the creator of the whole world, oh best of the twice born.'
(*Manusmrti* 1, 31–3)

Brahma asked him to divide himself into two. So Devi-Shiva was revealed, his *sakti* (sakti is the life force of god), and from between its brows came forth a second sakti. The first one merged once again into Shiva's body.

Creation

'When Brahma created the world four classes of beings were born beginning with the gods and ending with inanimate beings, by way of men and animals. Then wishing to create this fourfold world of gods, demons, spirits, and men he fixed his own spirit in himself and a quantity of darkness took hold in his fixed spirit. So the demons were born from Prajapati's thigh in a spirit of creativity.' (*VishnuPurana* 1, 5, 27–9)

The abduction of Krishna

'One particular day, the innocent young Yashoda, having taken her son on her knee to caress him got the impression that the child had become as heavy as a mountain … Then Trinavarta, an Asura, appeared in the form of a tornado and took the child away … He strove to reach the sky as quickly as he could. The child was heavy and he felt like letting him go, but he could not, for the child, by some miracle remained unshakeably attached to his neck. Then with his breath cut off, the Asura fell with the child Krishna still attached to his neck. The terrible demon's bones were broken on the rocky ground.' (*BhagavataPurana* X, 7, 18–33)

Because the gods are afraid of Shiva's offspring, they always try to disrupt him in love. One day Agni, in the form of a parrot, intervenes: he goes so far as to carry off some of the god's seed. But when the other gods try to drink it they cannot stand it and vomit, forming a lake the colour of molten gold. Parvati goes to see this marvel, drinks some and produces a son, Skanda.

Ganesha is her second son. His birth is also rather curious. Parvati, in order to protect herself from her spouse's forays into her apartments creates a guard by using a little dust and some of her own flesh and from then on Shiva comes into conflict with this guard. One day, tired of war, the god decapitates the guard. This throws the goddess into a violent rage and she demands that her son be brought back to life or else she will destroy the whole world. Shiva agrees and orders that the head be cut off the first person he meets. So Ganesha receives the head of an elephant (*ShivaPurana, Rudrasamhita* IV, 13–19).

The UpaPuranas

Besides the 18 'Great Puranas' there are also the 'Little Puranas' or *UpaPuranas*. Tradition has it that there were also 18 of them, but in fact there are many more. They are less important in range, content, and popularity. They are also far more closely linked than the other Puranas with the sects which have claimed them for their own. To give one example, there is the *GaneshaPurana* whose aim is to elaborate on, and promote the cult and theology of the Ganesha worshippers.

The Ramayana

Rama's progress

The epic of a great king

A just king, defender of the Dharma, the divine law, and a loving and faithful queen are the main characters of the Ramayana.

At the time when the Mahabharata was taking its final shape, another epic, shorter and less prestigious perhaps, but better in its construction, with a more uniform style and altogether less daunting, began to emerge: the *Ramayana.* This too was born of a multitude of legends, sayings, and songs peddled around from village to village by minstrels. At the beginning of the first century a writer gathered them all together and made a poem.

Tradition credits Valmiki with compiling the poem but then goes so far as to claim

---

Rama and Sita

'You will see the bow, promised the king, and if Rama succeeds in bending it, he will have Sita, my daughter, the princess born from the earth ... Straight away the king gave the orders: five thousand well-built men strained to drag the eight-wheeled iron cart which contained the divine weapon. No one had ever been able to lift, let alone use, the colossal weapon. Try, commanded the devout king, and effortlessly Rama seized the bow and drew it. He bent it to such an extent that he broke it and the sound that the string made in breaking struck fear in everyone who witnessed it. My daughter, said the king, will be the prize won by your strength.' (*Ramayana* I)

---

that this man of low caste had 'seen' the Ramayana just like the Rsis who passed on the *Vedas* and in so doing it gives the poem in question very high status as a work of revelation, saying that it 'gives happiness, good fortune, and long life to those who listen to it and read it.'

The life of this Valmiki was also far from ordinary: abandoned at birth, he was brought up by a primitive tribe living in the forest and there learned to rob travellers. One day his victim was a wise old man and instead of robbing him he fell under his spell and decided to practise asceticism by remaining immobile. He stayed in position so long that ants (*valmika* in Sanskrit) built an ant hill all round him. He was finally set free by the same wise man and received the vision of the *Ramayana* as a reward from Brahma.

The story of Rama

Dasaratha, the old king of Ayodhya had no male child. During a sacrifice he received a liquid from Brahma which, when drunk by one of his wives, would enable her to conceive an incarnation of Vishnu. He gave half of it to Kausalya, his first wife, who gave birth to Rama; he gave half of what was left to Soumitra, his second wife, then half of what was then left to Kaikeyi, his third wife; finally, he came back to Soumitra to give her the last part. Kaikeyi gave birth to Bharata and Soumitra gave birth to Lakchmana and Catroughna. So the divine essence of Vishnu was shared very unequally between the four children.

When Rama reached marriageable age he entered a bow drawing contest and won the hand of Sita, the daughter of Janaka, king of Videha, a princess born of the earth, and Dasaratha set about giving her a share of the power. But Kaikeyi, who wanted to give advantage to her own son Bharata, had a secret weapon: she had secured some time before the promise of two favours from the king. She therefore asked for Rama to be banished for 14 years and for Bharata to be given his place. The king had no option but to comply; Rama had to submit and departed for the forest with Sita and Lakchmana, who was very fond of him.

On the death of his father, Bharata took power, but outraged by his mother's scheming, he refused the title of king. During this time Rama was waging all-out war on demons in the forest. One of them, Ravana, succeeded in carrying Sita off to the fortress of Lanka (Ceylon). He held her prisoner for a long time trying, without success, to seduce her.

The monkey race, deciding to help Rama, stormed the demon's palace and returned Sita to her husband. He was tormented by the doubts which had seized him with regard to her long stay in her captor's palace and he sent her away. But when the princess was subjected to trial by fire she was proved innocent and the couple, once more united, were welcomed back to Ayodhya to receive the crown.

Now, the people were not too happy about this, having their own doubts about the queen's innocence and they forced the king to abandon her in the forest where she was met by Valmiki himself and gave birth to two sons. Years later Rama found Sita again and asked her forgiveness, but she was swallowed up in the earth which bore her and Rama was taken up to heaven.

The story of Vishnu

The legend of Rama and his family is linked with another legend which is derived from it and is another distinguished version of its truth: the demon Ravana had once subjected himself to severe hardships in order to gain protection from Brahma against gods and all sorts of spirits. Only men had been left out of this arrangement, because he considered them to be so feeble. But now Ravana, drunk with power, was causing havoc throughout creation.

The gods met and complained to Brahma.

Then Vishnu, protector of the universe intervened: 'I will take human form and kill Ravana ... Eleven times one thousand years I will dwell among men and bring peace to the earth.' And he saw the offerings of Dasaratha, saw his virtues and settled upon him as the father.

Brahma did not stop at this. He made for Vishnu 'valiant comrades, fast as the wind, intelligent, courageous, and capable of wonderful deeds ... and the great monkeys make their appearance, those joyful forest animals who have the power to change their shape at will'. Among them was Hanoumat, son of the Wind whose body is made of diamond. The earth was overrun with this bold breed.

The monkeys however were primarily humble and devout creatures. They were fine examples of *bhakti*, love, denial, and self-sacrifice in devotion to god and his human manifestation.

Influence

Few works have enjoyed such fame and exercised such influence in the Far East. Translations or adaptations of it are found everywhere in that region. It has been an inexhaustible source of inspiration for the theatre, the novel, and for poetry. Even the literature of Buddhism and Jainism have been affected by this epic. The *Ramayana* has certainly been the most important factor in the spread of the cult of Rama: public recitals are known to have been given as far back as the second century and there are numerous temples dedicated to this particular divinity.

Sita and Ravana

'Come with me gentle lady, resist me no longer! Let us taste together the delights of living! What is the point of this sorrow? Is it not natural to want a share in the victory? It is I who am the victor! Why these hesitations? But Sita did not see him and did not hear him as she greived over the misfortune that had overtaken her. The demon savoured his handiwork with a cruel smile.' (*Ramayana* VI)

The Mahabharata
The great deed of the Bharatas

A survey of the Hindu legends

Myths, history, civil and religious laws: the Mahabharata bears witness to the sheer extent and fertile nature of the Indian genius.

The birth of epic poetry is much the same the world over: great feats performed by important figures are reported, altered, adapted, expanded, embellished, and immortalized by story-tellers, poets, and minstrels. The events of the *Mahabharata* were recited in this way and translated into the languages of the day; monologues and dialogues alternated as material from various sources was accommodated and absorbed into the work.

That the work has many different origins is proved by the diversity of language and style found within it, and the contradictions and disparities which are apparent in its

Vidura

'The princess like the god's daughter was horrified by the memory of the sight and smell of the great Rsi. So she did not obey her mother-in-law's command. She dressed up a beautiful slave girl in her own finery and sent her in her place to wait for Krsna Dvaipayana. When the Rsi arrived the slave presented herself to him. With his permission she sat by him paying him all the respect and honour due to him. Having spent some time with her in private enjoying the pleasures of the flesh, the great rsi, who led a life of strict austerity was well satisfied with this woman.'
(*Mahabharata* 49a, 106)

different parts. According to Indian tradition the person responsible for gathering the work together is one Vyasa, perhaps an incarnation of Vishnu. His disciple Vaicampayana is said to have recited it for the first time for the king Janamejaya who is mentioned in the last Vedic texts and, some hundred years later, Ugracravas is supposed to have recited it again for the Rsis assembled in the Naimisa woods. What could be more convincing in establishing the text's religious pedigree?

The *Mahabharata* is one of the longest and most famous poems in world literature. Its present form dates from between the 4th century BC and the 4th century AD. Made up as it is of separate pieces and fragments, of fables, parables, didactic essays, anecdotes, poetry, and prose it still has one main thread running through it: the tale of the long war between the Kauravas and the Pandavas.

The origin

This war was willed by the gods with the aim of easing the earth's over-population. So it was the sons of gods or incarnations of gods themselves who waged the war. At the outset, King Santanu has a son by the goddess Ganga: he is Devavrata or Bhisma, an incarnation of the god Dyu, the Sky. So that his father may take another wife and have more children, Bhisma makes a vow neither to rule nor to marry. In exchange for this Santanu gives him the right to die only when he wants to.

The two sons of the king's second marriage die without having children. So, in order to keep the succession within their own dynasty, the two widows have relations with an old ascetic, a religious man, who, though ugly and deformed, turns out to be the elder son of the queen mother. But the women do not care for this arrangement;

the first child, Dhrtarastra, is born blind because his mother closed her eyes during the act; the second, Pandu, is born white because his mother paled at the sight of the old man's ugliness. The third time, a servant girl takes the place of the queens and the bastard son born of this act is Vidura, the incarnation of the god Dharma.

Pandu, the second son, is the only one fit to rule. His reign is a golden age for the whole land. But one day, in the forest, he strikes down an antelope in the act of mating. This is the punishment which falls on him: 'When you are mad with desire and come to your beloved, you will leave this world for the world of the departed in the same circumstances.' Fortunately, the beautiful Kunti, a wife who is completely dedicated to her husband's welfare, has already been given a charm which allows her to have relations with any of the gods. By this means the Pandavas are born: Yuddhisthrira the just, son of Dharma; Bhima the impetuous, son of Vayu, god of the Wind; and Arjuna, the brilliant, son of Indra, the chief of the gods. The same charm allows the second wife, Madri to have two other sons by the Asvins.

The blind Dhrtarastra who was denied the throne by virtue of his disability, has many offspring: 100 sons, the eldest of whom, Duryodhana, is the incarnation of the powerful demon, Kali. He is jealous of his cousins and continually sets traps for them: poison, drowning, fire, he uses every means he can to diminish the power of the Pandavas, or get rid of them altogether.

However, they are saved by the far-sightedness of Vidura, their bastard uncle, who is always one step ahead of their enemy.

However, this lack of security obliges them to flee to the forest with their mother. This is a difficult situation but it does not prevent Arjuna from winning, by force of arms, the hand of the princess Draupadi, the incarnation of the goddess Sri. Happily he takes her, along with his brothers, to the family's hiding place. But Kunti, their mother, on hearing them and believing that they are bringing home booty cries out: 'Take equal shares in everything.' As the word of a mother is an irrevocable command, Draupadi becomes the wife of the five brothers and lives with each in turn for two days at a time.

Later, Dhrtarastra, who has inherited the kingdom from his brother Pandu, shares it between Yuddhisthrira and Duryodhana, who is still as jealous and evil as ever. He draws Yuddhisthrira into a game of cards (the love of gambling is his only fault) and Yuddhisthrira loses all his belongings, his kingdom, and even the wife of the five brothers and their mother. Dhrtarastra is indignant at this and organizes their return. However, more gambling leads to more losses. This time the Pandava are condemned to wander the forests for 12 years.

The war

Throughout this long period the Pandavas live as hunter princes who have withdrawn from normal life. They have a great many adventures, the most notable being Arjuna's five year stay in heaven with his father, Indra. They meet hermits who tell them marvellous tales: that of the birth of the Ganges which was at first a heavenly river by the name of Milky Way; that of the flood; the birth of Skanda, god of War; the loves of Savitri and of Satyavan; of Nala and of Damayanti; and the adventures of Rama and Sita which will be the subject of another epic. Then comes the 13th year, a critical year, since they must not be recognized. So they go to the court of Virata, king of the Matsias. There Yuddhisthrira becomes a Brahmin skilled at cards, Bhima, a first-rate

---

Kunti's spell

'It was Kunti's responsibility to receive and honour the Brahmins. This is how she had the opportunity of serving the terrible Brahmin Durvasas, who had taken the strictest vows and knew every detail of the Dharma. This great spiritual man was pleased with the young woman's dedicated attentions and, foreseeing the difficult times which lay ahead, he passed on to her a very powerful magic formula: whichever god that you call upon by using this formula, by him you will have a son.'
(*Mahabharata* 112, 1–9)

Yuddhisthrira, inheritor of the kingdom, has only one fault, a passion for gambling.
He will lose everything through it.
*The **Mahabharata**: produced by Peter Brook in Avignon, July 1985.*

chef, Arjuna a eunuch and teacher of dance, and Draupadi a hairdresser.

This whole period is merely a time of preparation for the war and the Pandava's dream of retaking the kingdom. Their chance comes when, after the death of his general, Virata finds himself attacked by the Trigartas and the Kauravas. He pursues the former with the help of four of the Pandavas and Arjuna is the only warrior left to defend the city against the Kauravas. He puts them to flight but cannot conceal his true identity: the ordeal is over.

Krishna, who now takes on a key role, is sent as an ambassador to Dhrtarastra to recover the kingdom. The Pandavas are reasonable about it, a few villages would satisfy them. But, though Dhrtarastra, Bhisma, and Vidura are happy to agree, Duryodhana is obstinately opposed to any settlement. War is inevitable. Bhisma, who recognizes the wrongs of Duryodhana, still take command of his troops, on condition that he does not have to kill any of his nephews, nor that strange character Sikhandin, the girl turned boy. On the Pandavas' side the commander in chief is Dhrstadyumma, the incarnation of Agni,

the god of Fire. Krishna is Arjuna's charioteer.

The account of the battle is given to the blind Dhrtarastra by Sanjaya, the friend of a powerful ascetic who has bestowed on him the gift of second sight: 'He will know everthing that happens and will describe the battle to you. Whether it is a question of

Yuddhisthrira's dog

'Yuddhisthrira says: "And let this dog who has always been so devoted to me come with me; I am not a harsh man." Indra: "Since you have achieved immortality and the joys of heaven today, leave your dog. There is no harshness in that."
Yuddhisthrira: "For a noble man any ignoble act is difficult. I would not wish to gain any good fortune at the cost of abandoning a devoted servant." Indra: "The world of the gods is no place for people to bring dogs, for they are fierce animals who run off with the sacrifices." Yuddhisthrira: "My resolve on this matter is unshakeable." Finally, Yuddhisthrira is admitted with his dog in the chariot of the gods.'
(*Mahabharata* 18)

things seen or unseen, by day or by night, Sanjaya will see everything, even into the minds of the opponents.' The philosophy of this epic is contained in the *Bhagavadgita* which records the conversation between Krishna and Arjuna.

Bhisma commands Duryodhana's army for the first 10 days without gaining the victory. Under instruction to bring the battle to a favourable conclusion, Bhisma, the invincible, the one who has the right to choose the hour of his death, tells the Pandavas how they can kill him: by hiding behind Sikhandin, the soldier who was born a woman and whom Bhisma has sworn not to attack.

The surprise attack

Commanders-in-chief follow one another, great duels take place, Duryodhana is struck down just when his lieutenants led by Asvatthamon, the incarnation of Rudra-Shiva, penetrate the Pandava camp in their absence with a great horde of monsters which massacre all the soldiers and destroy everything. Then they come to gladden Duryodhana's last moments with the account of their infamy.

It is then that a terrible battle takes place. Asvatthaman has gone into the forest, the Pandavas have caught up with him there. He launches a missile at them which is capable of destroying the world, Krishna prevents it from reaching its goal, but because it must find some target Asvatthaman directs it at the unborn children the Pandava women are carrying and will carry in their bodies. Krishna then condemns him to an exile of 3000 years.

The reconciliation

Despite this evil spell the Pandavas prevail. The Kauravas suffer heavy losses, they grieve for their dead, especially the wives. They had been the first to encourage the fighters, but now they hold their cruelty against them and weep bitterly. The survivors from both sides have to go to the banks of the Ganges for the funeral rites: this leads to the first meeting between them since the battle.

On his deathbed Bhisma makes a long speech full of anecdotes, and legal and moral sayings, pointing out the lessons of history and thereby brings about a general reconciliation. In the end Yuddhisthrira reigns in peace and justice, and holds the ritual of the horse sacrifice which brings the period of war to an end.

The main characters of the story then disappear one after the other, whether as the result of a forest fire or in a dispute where reeds turn into clubs or under a hail of arrows fired by a hunter. Yuddhisthrira hands over the crown to his great nephew Pariksi, who was born dead because of Asvatthaman's curse but brought back to life by Krishna, and ascends to heaven where he meets the gods incarnate and sons of gods who were his old companions.

A sacred book

The extraordinary events of this turbulent tale are contained in a religious epic. The Hindus do not make any clear distinction between the sacred and the ordinary, the divine and the human. Throughout the poem the notions of Dharma, the personal religious duties, of Karma, the force of past actions, of avatar, the incarnation of the gods, and of bhakti, devotion, play an essential role.

The *Harivamsa*, written in the 4th century is intended as a complement to this epic. It is composed of myths, legends and hymns in praise of Vishnu-Krishna, in the style of the *Puranas*.

The great dancer

'Arjuna says: "I sing, I dance, and I play musical instruments. I am a good dancer and a fine singer. So place me in the service of Uttara. I will be the princess's dancing teacher, O king. What would be the point of telling you how I came to be what I am? That would simply add to my sorrow. Know me, O king, as Brhannala, a son or daughter with neither father nor mother."' (*Mahabharata* 4, 7–12)

Islam

At the beginning of the 7th century, the population of Arabia was made up of nomadic herdsmen, farmers settled around the oases, and merchants based in the town. There were Jews and Christians scattered throughout the country but most of the inhabitants were polytheistic, worshipping many gods. Mecca, the capital, was the site of the Kaaba, built like a large stone cube and venerated as if it had fallen from the heavens.

Muhammad was born between 567 and 573 into the Hashemite tribe. Orphaned at an early age, he worked on the camel trains before marrying a rich young widow. He was an honest, straightforward character: he became known as Al-Amin, man of trust. At the age of 40 came the revelation which changed his life: a voice said to him: 'preach!' The message he was to preach was that there is but one God (Allah). He was listened to by slaves and freed men, by his customers and by rebel tribesmen, but in Mecca of all places he met strong resistance. For 10 years he was the focus of hostility from the merchants who saw in his preaching nothing less than the complete overthrow of the established order.

In the year 622, unable to take any more of this, the Prophet and a few companions took refuge in the northern oasis of Yathrib, later Medina. It was there that Muhammad found a group of followers with whom he made a covenant and this proved to be the starting point for the Muslim era. At Medina he founded a state on the agreement made between his companions from Mecca and their allies from Medina. The result was a religious community and an earthly city growing up at the same time. For 10 years he preached, parleyed, and fought his way towards uniting the neighbouring tribes. The Meccans were finally won over to his cause and he entered the city to deliver a memorable address. He died in Medina in 632. The Arabian peninsula had been converted.

He was succeeded, on his death, by his father-in-law followed by other caliphs. Islam's territorial expansion continued reaching Syria, Egypt, the Indus, and eventually Europe as far as Poitiers (732). At this time came the great schisms in Islam: the Shi'as are followers of Ali, son-in-law of the Prophet and one of the first caliphs; the Sunnis follow the orthodox tradition and the Kharidjites are the strictest of all. There have been divisions, victories, and defeats with Damascus, Ankara, Baghdad, and other cities each predominating in turn. Its long history spans many ups and downs in its fortunes but Islam had taken firm root and now numbers several hundred million followers throughout the world.

The Koran

The book of the believers

The unchanging criterion of orthodoxy

As the word of God the Koran embodies the same authority for every Muslim, whether Sunni or Shi'a and makes Islam 'the religion of the book'.

Muhammad could not write, which was not surprising for the time, so he told his listeners the words which had been revealed to him and scribes noted them all down in the rudimentary writing of that time in Arabia on 'pieces of leather, shards of pottery, palm leaves, and shoulder blades or ribs of camels' (*Le Coran* (The Koran) Blachère, Paris, 1947). There were some disciples who set themselves the task of memorizing their master's words and repeating them, thereby maintaining them in oral form. According to tradition there were six of these men who could recite the *Koran.*

When Muhammad died these men were the keepers of the sacred text and the supreme authority, but in 633 three of them were cut down in battle and silenced forever. A more secure solution evidently had to be found. The first caliph, Abu Bakr, charged the young Zaid ibn Thabit, who had been Muhammad's scribe, with collating the complete text. Other collations were made: notably one by Ali, the Prophet's son-in-law which is important to the Sunnis, one by Ubaiy and several others.

Uthman, the third caliph, wanted to put the whole thing into some kind of order. He commissioned four scribes, under the direction of Zaid ibn Thabit to establish a definitive body of writings. In it the suras (chapters) are arranged, not in chronological order, but in order of decreasing length,

each one beginning with the phrase: 'In the name of God the Compassionate, the Merciful.' After some controversy this version, usually called the Vulgate, was accepted by the whole Muslim world from India to the Maghreb.

The eternal book

In the eyes of the Muslims the *Koran* is an exceptional book, quite unique, owing nothing to man's earlier experiences, nor to any intellectual activity of the Prophet who passed it on, nor to the circumstances in which it was conveyed to humankind for it is simply a slavish copy, faithful in every detail, of a heavenly origin. Muhammad

The Hadith

Not all of Muhammad's words are found in the *Koran.* However, his companions were keen to hold on to all his acts and deeds, all his ideas and sayings. No doubt these were not all on the same level as his sacred utterances, no doubt there would be some human notions mingled with the divine inspiration, but the veneration in which the Prophet was held and the reliability of his interpretations gave them great authority. So, in the first century after the Hegira, (Muhammad's flight from Mecca to Medina in 622), what were called the Hadith were gathered together. There were several groupings of them, sometimes classified according to content or sometimes according to the route by which they were handed down. The Muslims recognize six Hadith collections, dating from the 9th and 10th centuries. They contain anthologies, proverbs, maxims, moral tales, formal prayers, and judicial decrees. They play an important role in the organization of the Muslim community.

was merely a messenger entrusted with recording the sacred material dictated to him by the angel Gabriel.

Islam does not dispute the earlier revelations (the Jewish *Torah* and the Gospels). Muslims too call themselves sons of Abraham. But whilst the prophets of the Old Testament are seen as spokesmen for God, the translators or interpreters of his thoughts, and whilst they were influenced by the conditions of life in their time, the prevailing attitudes of their society and their own personal experiences, Muhammad is simply the physical instrument by which the eternal *Koran* was conveyed to earth.

So we can understand the veneration that surrounds the *Koran*: yes, the message it brings is important for humanity; yes, it should be taken as a whole and not divided into sections with one sura being explained in terms of another; yes, it should be read and reread, learned by heart, and constantly repeated. And yet, as it is the work of God himself neither form nor content should be in any way altered and care should be taken over every letter that is uttered when reading from it. The greatest degree of purity is required in everything pertaining to it.

The child learns to read and think from it. The singing of its verses punctuates family and social events. Every prayer, ceremony, and gathering culminates in reciting part of it. It is the most highly regarded motif used in decoration of the splendid monuments of Muslim art, and it has given rise to the greatest masterpieces of calligraphy (decorative writing). Its miraculous nature and incomparable qualities are never doubted. As it is often said, Islam is founded on the *Koran* in the same way as Christianity is founded on Jesus.

The text

The *Koran* is the oldest piece of writing in the Arab tongue. Within the work those suras originating from Mecca can be distinguished from those coming from Medina: those in the first group, written in rhyming prose, are more halting and breathless in style; they express in short poetic phrases which are repeated like incantations, the few simple ideas which form the basis of Islam; the ones in the second group are longer, written in a gentler less rhythmic style, using well thought out, rather complex sentences sprinkled with evocative stories: they are mainly concerned with reprimands and instructions.

The *Koran* does not follow any obvious plan, there is no division according to themes and ideas, no rational organization of the chapters. The classification is quite arbitrary. This is no theological dissertation, it is a cry, a tirelessly repeated cry, filled with emotion, enthusiasm, and faith. Concepts mingle together, overlapping and running into each other to produce a majestic and evocative work of poetry.

A rhythm which rocks the soul, a soothing tone, and a constant harmony have made the *Koran* a model for all poetry. Incomparable and wonderful in itself, it has become the reference point for literary work and has imposed its language and standards of literary merit on the Muslim world from Europe to Asia.

The *Koran*
'The *Koran* was invented by none other than God, but it is the confirmation of what existed before it.' (*Koran* X, 37)

God
'Say: God is one God! God the unfathomable. He does not beget, he is not begotten. There is none equal to him!' (*Koran* CXII)

The Scriptures
After the prophets we sent Jesus, son of Mary, to confirm what was before him in the *Torah*. We gave him the Gospel which contains a way and a light in order to confirm what was before him in the *Torah*; a way and a warning meant for those who fear God. The people of the Gospel are to judge men according to what God has revealed there. We have revealed to you the Book and the Truth to confirm what existed of the Book before it, preserving it from any changes. (*Koran* V, 46–7)

The one God

No doubt originally proclaimed specifically against the polytheism (worship of many gods) of the Meccans, the idea of one God is the principal dogma of Islam and the thing which marks it out as being different. No other religion affirms this truth with such force. It appears in one form or another on every page of the *Koran*. God is one God, always, everywhere and without exception. It implores the people of the Book (Jews and Christians) to speak the truth about God: 'Believe in God and in his prophets. Do not speak of 'Three'; stop doing that, it will be better for you. God is one God! Glory to him' (*Koran* IV, 171).

God is transcendent, surpassing human knowledge. He is the master, he is the king; he knows everything: 'That which is in heaven and that which is on earth belongs to him, his knowledge extends to everything' (IV, 126). He can do everything: 'He created the heaven and the earth without being tired by creation, he can give life to the dead. In very truth he has power over all things' (XLVI, 33). He is self-sufficient (LXIV, 6). He lives on eternally (XX, 73).

God is inaccessible: one can know neither his nature, nor his intimate life. He is 'the one who remains hidden' (VI, 103), for the knowledge of man cannot reach him (XX, 110). He is the Living, the All-Powerful, the Invincible, the Most High, the Truth, the Genuine, the Light of the Heavens and of Earth. The names and qualities of God are innumerable. The text of the *Koran* gives a great many of them, tradition goes so far as to number 99. But the one which constantly recurs is the Merciful.

The Creator

'Is it not he who created the heavens and the earth and for your sake made water come down from heaven thanks to which we make our beautiful gardens grow, where you could not possibly make trees grow? Or is there some divinity besides God? — Is it not he who established the earth as a dwelling place; who made the rivers spring forth; who placed the mountains on the earth and a barrier between the two seas? Or is there some divinity besides God?' (*Koran* XXVII, 60–1).

God's action

There is no Creation story in the *Koran* as there is in the *Bible* but rather a clear and frank statement that God is the Creator: he created men, he created animals, plants, nature and he continues his creation in the birth of little children: 'We put what we wish int the womb for a certain time and then we have you come out as little children in order to achieve your maturity later' (XXII, 5).

And he signs an agreement with these men whom he creates, he makes a covenant: 'With the Prophets, with Noah, Abraham, Moses and Jesus, Son of Mary, we have made an eternal covenant, in order that God might ask the truthful ones for an account of their sincerity, but he has prepared a painful punishment for the unbelievers' (XXXIII, 7 and 8). God's mercy is shown in this way from the time of Adam's creation down through all the warnings of the prophets of Israel.

Muhammad is 'the seal of the prophets' (XXXIII, 40). He has been announced in the *Torah* and the *Gospel* 'Those who believe in him, those who support him, those who help him, those who follow the light which has come down with him: they are the ones who will be blessed. Oh you men, I have been sent to you all as the Prophet of the one to whom kingship in heaven and earth belongs. There is no other God but him. He is the one who has power over life and death' (VII, 157–8).

Submission to God

The word 'Islam' means submission: 'He who has submitted himself to God and does what is right will have his reward from the Lord' (II, 112). The Muslim must accept God as master and Lord: 'If you obey, God will give you a rich reward' (XLVIII, 16), and the Prophet states: 'I have come to you with a sign from your Lord; fear him and obey me' (III, 50).

Prayer is one of the believer's first obligations: 'Turn your face in the direction of the sacred Mosque: wherever you are, turn your face in its direction' (II, 144). It must be performed several times a day: 'Glorify God at the end of the day and when you wake up in the morning. Praise be to him in the heavens and

*The **Koran**, the uncreated book, led to Arab writing being given a kind of sacred status: its eloquence and the artists' talents have produced some fine calligraphy.*
Text of the *Koran.*
Musée Condé, Chantilly.

on earth, in the night and in the middle of the day' (XXX 17–18).

The second obligation unfailingly repeated like the first and often linked with it, is to give alms or charity, and to do it without hesitation: 'Give part of the wealth we have allowed you as alms before death strikes one of you and he finds himself saying: "My Lord, if only you would allow me a little more time, I would give alms and be a good person"' (LXIII, 10); to do it discreetly: 'He who gives out his money in order to be seen by men (...) is like a rock that is covered

with earth, a heavy rain will come and leave it exposed' (II, 264).

Ramadan, the month in which the *Koran* was revealed to men (II, 185) is the occasion for a particular demonstration of devotion; during this time Muslims fast until nightfall and, at night they 'eat and drink until a white thread can be distinguished from a black thread by the light of the dawn' (II, 187), then the fast begins again until the following night. The men and women who have submitted to God are the men and women who fast (XXXIII, 35).

The last duty, the pilgrimage to Mecca, to the temple once visited by Abraham, is also clearly laid down in the *Koran*: 'Clear signs are found in this place where Abraham stood. Whoever enters there is safe. It is incumbent upon all men who have the means to make a pilgrimage for God to this place' (III, 97).

The profession of faith, followed by these four obligations form what tradition has called the five pillars of Islam. But the *Koran* also contains a complete moral code, commandments comparable to those of Moses:

The faith of Abraham

So we showed Abraham the kingdom of the heavens and of the earth so that he might be in the number of those who firmly believe. When the night enveloped him he saw a star and said: "Here is my Lord." But when it disappeared he said: "I do not like things that disappear." When he saw the moon rising he said: "Here is my Lord." But when it disappeared he said: "If the Lord does not direct me I will be numbered amidst the lost." When he saw the sun rising he said: "Here is my Lord, the greatest of all." But when it disappeared he said: "I deny what you think of as God, I turn my face like a true believer towards the one who created the heavens and the earth. I am not one of the polytheists."' (*Koran* VI, 75–9)

Alms

'Those who give away their goods with the desire of pleasing God and strengthening their souls are like a garden planted on a hill, if a heavy rain falls on it, it will give twice as much fruit, and if there is no heavy rain, the dew will make up for it. God sees perfectly what you do.' (*Koran* II, 265)

it forbids crime (IV, 151), lies (XXII, 30), usury or money lending in order to make a profit (II, 275); it recommends politeness (XXIV, 17–28), kindness, particularly towards one's parents (II, 83); it sets out rules for marriage (IV, 22–4), for inheritance (II, 180–2); it orders one to fight in the defence and for the expansion of Islam (*Jihad*); finally it provides for certain punishments: the *lex talionis* applies, basically, an eye for an eye and a tooth for a tooth (II, 178), there are the 100 lashes for the adulterous couple (XXIV, 2), the cutting off of the hand for the thief (V, 38), and death for the infidel (IV, 89).

Paradise and hell

The life of the believer is a life of obedience. It is God who has decided, for all eternity, that such and such an act which he has ordained will be rewarded and some other act which he has forbidden will be punished, to the point where reward is purely a favour from God and punishment a consequence of disobedience. Having said that, the prophets, including Muhammad, the last of them, did come to warn of future events and proclaim the last judgment and the day of man's return to God.

There is to be a great catastrophe, the mountains will tremble, the earth will open and give up its dead, tongues of fire will cross the sky and Allah will bring the dead to life. The book of destiny will be opened to reveal the list of the just and that of the sinners. Unbelievers will go to the fiery depths of Gehenna (hell), they will be chained there, tortured, and showered with boiling water. The just will go to paradise where flow the 'rivers whose water is ever pure, rivers of milk whose taste never spoils, rivers of wine which is a delight to those who drink of it, rivers of purest honey' (XLVII, 15).

Jainism

The Jainist religion had already been established for a long time when Vardhamana Mahavira came into the world in the 6th century BC. He was simply the 24th of the Tirthankara, 'voyagers across the torrent of rebirths until they reach the other side'. Many others had gone before him, from Parsva who had lived three centuries earlier and Bhagavan Aristanemi who had already been in a state of nirvana for 84000 years, right back to Rsabha, the first of them all. Vardhamana Mahavira was not the founder, he was a reformer.

His parents Siddhartha and Trisala were pious Jains living in the flourishing city of Vaisali (near Patna). Mahavira was their second son. He married a young girl chosen by them whose name was Yasoda, and they had a daughter Anojja. When his parents died, his elder brother succeeded them and Mahavira became a Jainist monk. He applied himself to the rules required for entry into the monastic life. After the 13th month, following a long period of testing he got rid of his clothes, achieved the state of 'isolation-integration', and experienced omniscience (total knowledge) and complete separation from earthly ties. For the next 42 years he preached the message throughout the land and died at Pava, aged 72.

According to Mahavira, there is no God, the world and the universe have neither beginning nor end. Everything is governed by Karma, except for the soul which has been freed from the stream of rebirths. The first and most important of Jainist amendments is absolute respect for life, for everything has a soul, from the most highly evolved animals to plants, stones, and drops of water. So the Jainist monk sweeps the ground in front of him as he walks and wears cloth over his mouth for fear of swallowing some tiny insect. Deliverance only comes through deliverance from all karmic matter (deeds), that is the ending of all contact with the material.

Some of the Mahavira's disciples had memorized his teachings. At the end of the 4th century BC the members of the Jainist community decided to safeguard its content. They met at Paliputra in 312 BC and agreed on the text of the *Angas*. However, the texts were lost, and to make matters more difficult, the community split into two factions: on the one side, the *digambara* or 'sky clad' who lived naked; on the other, the *svetambara* or 'white clad'. It was these *svetambara* who established a new canon of Scriptures at the council of Valabhi in the 5th century AD.

The Angas

Points of doctrine

Detachment from the material world

Legends, numerology and cosmological data all have their part to play here in presenting the doctrine.

The *Angas* are 11 books which set out the main points of the Jainist doctrine and discipline for monks and lay people alike.

It is a fairly chaotic mixture of prose and poetry, presentations and illustrations, orthodox teaching and other viewpoints, but each passage, even those taken from the common fund of Indian culture at that time (such as the legends of Krishna, Draupadi, and other Hindu heroes) is evidently coloured by Jainist ideas.

The first anga, the *Acaranga* is essentially concerned with the behaviour of monks. It gives as an example the life of Mahavira, who, as a monk wandering naked through the open countryside, subjected himself to the

The thought of renunciation

'For many years I enjoyed the position of an Indra: however, the taste for pleasure was not done away with. What use will a few drops of earthly water be for someone whose thirst was not quenched by the ocean of ambrosia (the food of the gods)? The taste for pleasure is increased by enjoyment, like the strength of a fire is when more fuel is added. No doubt pleasures are delightful at the time but the consequences are bad; for the sake of satisfying the desires of the senses one has to cover the ground of suffering (...) and travel from birth to birth going so far as to enter the kingdom of the beasts.' (quoted by H Zimmer in *The Philosophies of India*)

severest asceticism whilst maintaining a tranquil mind and total indifference to both pleasure and suffering.

Other tales are scattered throughout the collection of books: there is the story of the imperfect conversion of Kali who, feeling touched by a sermon by Parsva, the last but one Tirthankara, becomes a nun, dies and is reincarnated in the form of the goddess Kali (*Nayadhammakahao anga*), the story of Gayasukumala, son of Queen Devaki and brother of Krishna (*Upasakadasa anga*), the one about the eight kings ordained by Mahavira (*Sthana anga*), and the story of the pious Dhanya in which the effects of prolonged fasting on his emaciated body are described with something approaching delight (*Anuttara Aupapatika*).

The vows of Jainism

Explanations of the teachings are often given by Mahavira, in response to questions put by his young disciples. The fortunate young man to whom he addresses himself is Gautama Indrabhuti (*Vyakhyaprajnapti*). This dialogue is particularly informative with regard to the master's personality.

The five Great Vows are explained: not to destroy any living and feeling creature, not to lie, not to steal, not to give oneself over to sexual acts, not to be attached to material goods; and the other seven vows: namely those about only going in certain directions and for certain distances, about avoiding useless words and actions, avoiding thinking about unworthy things, limiting one's food intake and enjoyment each day, worshipping at fixed times, morning, noon, and night, fasting on certain days and showing charity every day (*Tattvarthadhigama Sutra*).

The monks devote themselves to a strict observation of these vows, while the lay people try to follow them on a minor scale.

The Upangas
Complementing the doctrine

Hell and paradise

Karma, asceticism, and non-violence leave a number of questions hanging in the air, and the Upangas give some kind of response.

The Upangas are considered to be sub-angas. They only give supplementary explanations. In fact they are constructed exactly like the *Angas* (see p121): sermons, conversations, and stories of all kinds remain the format, and the subjects tackled are the law, reincarnation, the counting of different creatures, astronomy, cosmology, and even geography.

Three quarters of the first upanga (*Aupapatika Sutra*), is taken up by a long sermon preached by Mahavira in the presence of King Kunika at Campa. The final quarter records a conversation between the prophet and Gautama on the condition of deliverance and the dwelling of the delivered souls in one of the 12 worlds of the gods.

Next comes a moving dialogue between the King Prasenajit and the monk Kesin which leads to the king's conversion (*Rajaprasniya*). This passage is followed by reflections (*Jivabhigama*) on the classification of different beings and the 148 types of Karma, divided into two main groups: the Karma which strikes, wounds, and kills, the *ghati-karman*, and the Karma which does not strike, the *aghati-karman*, among which are found anger, pride, treachery, greed, as well as idleness, pleasure, distress, fear, and disgust.

This kind of numerical list often appears in the other upangas as in many Jainist writings: So we have references to the 26 subjects of philosophy, the 22 attacks, the 10 aspects of monastic morality, the nine truths, the five methods of saving living beings etc.

Other works of the Jainist canon
Rituals, legends, and hymns are the main object of the 10 *Prakirnakas* which paint a picture of both fortunate and ill-fated moments, like the curious study of man's body based on the quantity of rice he can absorb during 100 years of life. The *Chedasutras* deal mainly with monastic life: they give their rules in detail, and outline the organization, the conditions of entry, the rituals, the punishments, and the means of atonement. Only one passage in the *Asaradasa*, called *Kalpasutra*, records the life of Mahavira and gives a list of his followers, the different schools, and their leaders. Finally, the last texts in the canon, the accepted body of literature, are the *Mulasutra*, which form a kind of anthology of all the other texts. Lessons of doctrine, tales of legends, prayers, and hymns are all to be found there in the form of a sermon.

Mahavira's reform
'According to Parsva, the Great Vows only number four, so why did Mahavira declare that there are five? — Parsva understood the spirit of his time and felt that the enumerating of four Great Vows was acceptable to his contemporaries. Mahavira added a fifth vow in order to make Jainist doctrine more acceptable to the people of his time. There is nothing essentially different in the teachings of the two Tirthankara.' (*Rajaprasniya*)

Judaism

Judaism: the religion of a people now scattered throughout the world and one which has nourished in its bosom another religion of universal salvation, Christianity. It could be said that both of them spring from the same soil and share, along with their common historical origins, an identical central dogma: the idea of one God. They also have some sacred texts in common: what the Jews call the written *Torah*, Christians call the Old Testament, the different shades of meaning conveyed by these terms being more a matter for specialist scholars than for the simple believer. The Jews are more closely identified with the oral *Torah* and the Christians with the New Testament, that is to say that in each case it is the other part of their Scriptures which is of greater importance.

In the beginning we have a people and in particular a law-giver, Moses. Later writings and tradition all attribute the essence, the core, and the founding of the religion to him. There is no reason for us to doubt what he actually wrote. In any case, he is considered to be the one to whom God speaks, the guardian of the covenant between Yahweh and the chosen people, and the real religious and social founder of the Jewish nation. The adventure had, however, begun long before: first there was the Creation, then the calling of Abraham, the trials and tribulations of the great father figures, the patriarchs, Isaac, Jacob, Joseph etc. But all of that was merely the backdrop to the essential act of the making of the covenant with Yahweh on Mount Sinai, and Moses is the reporter of all these facts.

Due to the force of events, the text of the *Torah* retains an incomparable authority, although it is clear that it has been reworked, adapted, and augmented many times. When it was rediscovered in Solomon's Temple by Josiah in the 7th century BC, it became the Law of the kingdom. When the Jews were carried off in captivity to Babylon and the Temple was destroyed, it became the only sacred object acknowledged by the people as a whole. When they were scattered throughout the world in the Diaspora it was their one link with their brothers, their race, and their God.

Alongside the texts reputed to be by Moses, there grew up a prophetic and historical body of literature. Kings, prophets, and scribes of very sort felt the need to set down in writing the events of the nation's life, the appeals God made and the tasks he set.

The chronicles of the kings of Judah and Israel, the warnings of the prophets and the traditions handed down constituted the *Torah* as put into practice in history. So the Jewish priests in exile gathered together, edited, and circulated these writings. The collected writings became a national treasure, regulating the nation's life, and from all this activity Judaism was to emerge. Three groups in particular have their own versions of the texts and their prophetic statements: the Jews remaining in Judaea, the exiles in Babylon, and the Samaritans, who make up an entirely separate grouping.

It was under the leadership of the priest Ezra and when the Persians had driven out the Assyrians that the *Pentateuch* appeared in what was to be more or less its final form. It was proclaimed in the reconstructed Temple at Jerusalem, probably in 398 BC. The second part, *Joshua, Samuel,* and *Kings* had been agreed round the end of the exile period as was the collection of prophetic sayings c. 330 BC. In the 3rd century BC Ptolemy II, king of Egypt, had 72 elders come from Palestine to make an official translation of the Law of Moses into Greek: this is the version called the Septuagint. Did they extend their work beyond the *Pentateuch?* Someone certainly did. It was not until the end of the first century AD that the rabbinical authorities (the Jewish religious authorities) catalogued most of their sacred writings.

Unlike the Christians, the Jews have no concept of a canon or agreed body of Scripture and discussions still go on amongst the rabbis as to whether or not such and such a book (not the *Pentateuch,* of course) 'soils or does not soil the hands' (*Mishna, Toharot* 11; *Yadaim* III, 5), meaning, is sacred or not. The later development of the oral *Torah,* the teaching passed on from generation to generation since the time of Moses, is even more vague in its notion of what might constitute the canon, all the more so since this teaching, also the Word of God despite being adapted to times and circumstances, has resulted in the huge and complex volumes called the *Talmud.* There are, in fact, two *Talmuds:* the Jerusalem which is thought to have been compiled around the year 400 and the Babylon which is a century younger and is the authoritative version.

At the time of the drafting of the *Talmuds,* Judaism developed its new structure: morning and afternoon prayers replaced the temple sacrifices; the profession of faith, the *shema,* was decided; it is made up of three passages from the *Torah: Deuteronomy* 6, 4–9; 11, 13–21 and *Numbers* 15, 37–41. 'Israel, remember this! The Lord — and the Lord alone — is our God.' The *Pentateuch* was read in the synagogues on the Sabbath; regular festivals became traditional; the rabbi assumed the central role in the community and the specific requirements like circumcision, the dietary laws, and the observation of the Sabbath became the link binding each individual to the people of God.

The Torah or the Pentateuch

The five books of the Law

The origins of the world and of the Hebrew people

The Torah, the most sacred book of the Jewish religion, is also part of the foundation of Christianity.

In the beginning — but just how far can one go back in time? — there were, in the families, tribes, or groups of tribes which made up the Hebrew people, some established rhythmic songs, customs, traditions, rites, incantations, and perhaps even legendary tales. These elements would be handed on from generation to generation deviating very little from the old ancestral form which gave them a sacred, indeed a sacrosanct, character.

The most ancient of these oral documents would be either the songs easily committed to memory:

'Lamech said to his wives:
"Adah and Zillah listen to me: I have killed a young man because he struck me.
If seven lives are taken to pay for killing Cain,
Seventy-seven will be taken if anyone kills me."'

(*Genesis* 4, 23–4)

The curse

'And he said to the woman: "I will increase your trouble in pregnancy and your pain in giving birth. In spite of this you will still have desire for your husband, yet you will be subject to him." And he said to the man: "You listened to your wife and ate the fruit which I told you not to eat. Because of what you have done the ground will be under a curse. You will have to work hard all your life to make it produce enough food for you."' (*Genesis* 3, 16–17)

or perhaps magic words supposedly possessing great power:

'Dan will be a snake at the side of the road,
A poisonous snake beside the path,
That strikes at the horse's heel,
So that the rider is thrown off backwards'

(*Genesis* 49, 17),

or again sayings or legal rules like the formula of the *lex talionis*: 'An eye for an eye, a tooth for a tooth' (*Leviticus* 24, 20), a formula often repeated in the *Torah*.

All these brief and concise expressions, however, are quickly followed by accounts full of imagery, which, though sparing in descriptive detail are meaningful in content. Take, for example, the story of the well at Beersheba, one of the only wells dug by Isaac without arousing the opposition of the neighbouring tribes, an obvious sign of Yahweh's protection: 'I am the God of your father, Abraham. Do not be afraid; I am with you' (*Genesis* 26, 23–5).

As soon as writing was invented one can see how these accounts would gradually be grouped together. Places, shrines or groups of people would give them a home, make them their own and enable them to be safeguarded and become widely known. Recognized groups of writings would be established according to their origins, their geographical roots or their themes: no doubt at the time of the Judges, distinction could be made between the epic tale of the patriarchs, that of the Exodus, and that of the wanderings in the wilderness.

During the time that the Hebrew people were a wandering race, with no established claims in the Promised Land and the kingdom of Israel not yet constituted, these literary elements maintained their slender influence in the local traditions. However, David and Solomon instituted a centralized monarchy, the professional scribes increased in importance and the writings which confirmed the structure of society and basis of the nation's life were regrouped. The *Torah* or Law of Israel took on a canonical value, that is to say, it became accepted as authoritative and unchangeable.

Usually authorship of the whole of the *Torah* is attributed to Moses, the founder of the nation. There is no doubt that he himself wrote the main part of the Decalogue (the Ten Commandments), and many laws of tribal and religious life. But it was the origin of the nation and its prophecy rather more than the historical truth that was sought after in the matter of authorship. Moses was the one God spoke to, he was the guarantee of the sacred nature of the text and therefore of the unity of the people of Israel. The *Torah* became te law of Moses.

The two original documents

However, it must be stated that, if this law is made unique by the honour in which Israel holds it, some of the elements in its make-up are familiar.

The *Yahweh story* has its own vocabulary: it always calls God Yahweh — hence its name — its descriptions are down-to-earth and spicy, its character sketches full of life. There is however a recognizable style, a literary character, an already developed doctrine, which certainly borrows something from Egyptian and Mesopotamian wisdom and definitely echoes themes which are already known.

It confirms the will of Yahweh to live with men and is not afraid to employ anthropomorphism, the idea of God as a human being, in that connection. We see God visiting Adam and Eve in the cool of the day and taking meals with Abraham or Moses. And yet he is transcendent, he speaks with authority, lays down rules and prohibitions, often connected with religious observance, and punishes very severely.

Yahweh is the national god who reveals himself to Abraham, delivers his people, makes a covenant with them, and promises that all the nations of the world will be saved through them. Yahweh holds the power over the earth and gives it to whom he wishes.

The Yahwist document is considered to be the oldest portion of those writings which make up the *Pentateuch*. It originates from Judah (the south of the country). It is usually dated in the reign of Solomon (10th century BC), but it seems to be a collection of numerous oral pieces which were known in the holy places.

The principal themes of the Law are also found in it. It certainly outlines the whole work: the Creation, the Flood, Abraham, Joseph, and the exploits of Moses. On the other hand there is no legislative text, with the exception of what is called the Yahweh Code (*Exodus* 34): 'I now make a covenant with the people of Israel ...' (34, 10).

The Elohist document has a less colourful style, without embellishment or vigour. It gets right down to basics and has a more legal tone. It also contains occasional archaic and regional expressions.

One of the features is that it calls God Elohim, the plural of El, a word used by the peoples of the Middle East to indicate God. It suggests that the Elohim of the Hebrews has become integrated with the other gods of the nations. But at the same time and perhaps because of that very thing, it stresses the Covenant, the contract agreed between Elohim and the Hebrew people, including obligations on both sides.

To compensate for this assimilation with the other gods it is at pains to avoid the anthropomorphisms characteristic of the Yahwist document. 'No one can see God without dying'. So God's appearances become dreams, angels are substituted for the divinity and all representation of Elohim is strictly forbidden.

Babel

'They said to one another: "Come on, let us make bricks and bake them hard." So they had bricks to build with and tar to hold them together. They said, "Now, let's build a city with a tower that reaches the sky, so that we can make a name for ourselves and not be scattered all over the earth." Then the Lord came down to see the city and the tower which those men had built ... and Yahweh said, "Let us go down and mix up their language so that they will not understand one another." So the Lord scattered them all over the earth and they stopped building the city.'
(*Genesis* 11, 3–8)

The Yahwist document is more concerned with religious observance and the Elohist document with moral matters. The latter even seems to distrust the idea of religious rites for fear of deviations being introduced. Its first objective is to point out the faults which should be avoided and the duties which should be fulfilled in respect of Elohim and in respect of one's neighbour. God is firstly the god of the Commandments, commandments which are constantly recalled by the prophets, who are of paramount importance in this text.

So it might well be that this document originated in the northern kingdom where there were a great many prophets. In fact, there is great concern over the theological construction: no Creation story, no Flood. The text begins with the deeds of Abraham. It is a sacred account, sober and profound, centred on the Covenant and the blessings bestowed by God. Joseph gives meaning to the events and Moses is forever struggling against the faithlessness of the people.

Although it is much later (8th century BC) and comes from another region of Israel (the north), the Elohist account is so interwoven with the Yahwist account that it is sometimes difficult to find an obvious distinction between the two. It also seems to be continued in certain passages of the books of *Joshua, Judges,* and *Samuel,* where the same notions of sin, penitence, and forgiveness are to be found.

The third document

Solomon's reign was spectacular. The king built towns, developed agriculture, and expanded trade. It was an era of prosperity which made possible the construction of the Temple of Jerusalem on Mount Moria, traditionally the site where Isaac was to be sacrificed. But the growth rate speeded up,

the burden of taxation increased and crisis loomed. It finally came with the death of the king, and the kingdom was divided: Israel in the north and Judah in the south.

When the northern kingdom was annexed by Assyria, Jerusalem took in her refugees and, as a mark of the new union between the north and south in allegiance to the one God, the Yahwist and Elohist traditions were brought together in a single work, which tried as far as possible to respect the beliefs of both.

Alongside this work of gathering things together, another task was being pursued, namely that of clarifying, emphasizing, and codifying the Law. This resulted in the book of *Deuteronomy.* It bears some relationship to the Elohist document, but gives primary importance to the actual code of Law which is interspersed with speeches or accounts which the author uses to illustrate various points. These texts were no doubt written against the background of the northern kingdom.

Deuteronomy warns against the attractions and temptations of the neighbouring pagan tribes and urges the people to be on guard against all forms of infiltration. It stresses that the Hebrew people were chosen by God and are therefore all brothers. It draws together the history of reforms imposed by different kings and the interventions made by the prophets. It is a plea on behalf of Israel's authentic traditions and the teaching of its men of wisdom.

The priestly document

A new event was to lead to a further revision of the *Torah.* After the fall of Jerusalem in 586 BC and the removal of a large number of Judaeans to captivity in Babylon, community life had to be organized. As the kings had already failed in this, the task now fell to the priests. The Hebrew people found themselves thrown back upon the fundamentals of their faith: the one blood, the one tradition, the one priesthood.

It was the Jerusalem clergy who undertook the revision of the text into a document which was more sober, systematic, and theological: the sacerdotal or priestly document. Its style is rather dry, its vocabulary technical and exact; it is in fact a

---

Blessing over Levi

'They obeyed your commands and were faithful to your covenant. They will teach your children to obey your Law; they will offer sacrifices on your altar. Lord, help their tribe to grow strong; be pleased with what they do. Crush all their enemies; let them never rise again.' (*Deuteronomy* 33, 9–11)

---

catechism, a tool for the teaching of the faith. Its main concern lies, not with the events of men's lives, but only with the interventions of God.

Where it says 'In the beginning, when God created the universe, the earth was formless and desolate. The raging ocean that covered everything was engulfed in total darkness, and the power of God was moving over the water' (*Genesis* 1, 1–2), the document said: 'When the Lord God made the universe, there were no plants on the earth and no seeds had sprouted, because he had not sent any rain and there was no one to cultivate the land' (*Genesis* 2, 4–5).

The text was to be revised again at the time of the return from captivity and the rebuilding of the Temple (beginning in AD 538). It would give great importance to the site of Jerusalem and the priests connected with it. The community is seen to be organized along hierarchical lines, with a high priest, priests, and Israelites. The codes of law are brought together and the Temple becomes the place where sacrifices are made in atonement for sins against the Covenant. The whole of *Leviticus* and two thirds of *Numbers* are attributed to the priestly document.

There were probably disputes between the Hebrews returning from Babylon and the Samaritans who had remained in the country over some of the customs included in these priestly collections. It was necessary, therefore, to establish the official legislation once and for all. This was the task of Ezra (beginning of the 4th century BC). From that time these five books were recognized by all the Jews as the canon of the Law, with any differences being limited to the area of interpretation of the text.

The promise of the return

'Then Jacob said to Joseph, "As you see, I am about to die, but God will be with you and will take you back to the land of your ancestors. It is to you and not to your brothers that I am giving Shechem, that fertile region which I took from the Amorites with my sword and my bow." Then Jacob called for his sons ...' (*Genesis* 48, 21–2)

Genesis

The Jews call it *Bereshit*, 'in the beginning', after the first words of the text. In fact, the book covers two areas of the history of the Hebrew people. The first part concerns the whole of humanity; it includes the accounts of Creation, the story of Adam and Eve, Paradise and the Fall, the confrontation between Cain and Abel, the descendants of Seth, the Flood, Noah, and the populating of the earth. The picture it paints is one of man's sinful nature and God's goodness which saves humankind at every turn by working with a tiny faithful remnant: Noah is the supreme example of this.

This idea is made clearer with the second part and the call of Abraham. The text emphasizes the attitude of the man who gives himself, bound hand and foot, to God (Abraham is ready to sacrifice Isaac, his son), but also the free and sovereign choice of the Almighty: he chooses Abraham, he chooses Isaac, Jacob, and Joseph. All these choices fly in the face of custom and tradition: Abraham is sent into an unknown land; Isaac and Jacob are preferred despite the rightful claims of their elders; Joseph is chosen after being sold to foreigners. Yet each of these turns out to be the saviour of his people.

The book ends with the death of Joseph and the prophecy of a return to the Promised Land. Genesis is the first basic text of the Hebrew people. It is the account of their prehistory and as such has been the subject of commentaries by the ancient Jews and the Fathers of the Church.

Exodus

The second book, the *Exodus*, which the Jews call *Weelleh Shemot*, contains the saga of Moses, the founder, not now of the Jewish people, but of the Jewish religion. There are two climactic events in the book: the escape from slavery in Egypt and the making of the Covenant on Mount Sinai. Joseph had been dead for a long time, his deeds forgotten and the Hebrews no longer regarded in Egypt as anything other than immigrants who were viewed with suspicion, misunderstood, and exploited. Once again God raises up a saviour.

Moses, the first true representative of Yahweh on earth, liberates the people from oppression, takes them across the Red Sea, leads them through the desert, feeds them, teaches them, pardons their lack of trust, their faithlessness, their blasphemy, and even their apostasy, their complete abandonment of the faith. But without any doubt the most outstanding event is the Covenant made with God on Sinai along with the revelation of the divine name, Yahweh, and the giving of the Ten Commandments, the Decalogue, by which the people of Israel became the chosen people.

Of all the books in the Bible, *Exodus* is the one which contains the greatest variety of literary styles: narratives, stories, poetry, genealogies, legal texts, religious rites, moral precepts. Everything pertaining to the organization of a Church is featured in it. *Exodus* marks the foundation of Jewish belief with the Covenant with Yahweh, it founds its religious observances with the account of the Passover ritual requirements, it founds its morality with the handing down of the Decalogue on Sinai, and it binds the nation of the faithful together in the trials of the Exodus, the escape from slavery in Egypt.

If *Exodus* has been the subject of fewer commentaries than has *Genesis*, the events which it records, which largely concern both Israel and Egypt, do occur in another version by the Egyptian priest and historian Manethan, who wrote in the 3rd century BC. In his account Moses appears as a man despised by the gods, an enemy of all religion.

Aaron's stick

The Lord said to Moses and Aaron, "If the king demands that you prove yourselves by performing a miracle, tell Aaron to take his stick and throw it down in front of the king and it will turn into a snake." So Moses and Aaron went to the king and did as the Lord had commanded. Aaron threw his stick down in front of the king and his officers, and it turned into a snake ... The king, however, remained stubborn and, just as the Lord had said, the king would not listen to Moses and Aaron. (*Exodus* 7, 8–13)

Leviticus

Leviticus is the third book of 'Moses'. The Jews call it *Wayyikera* after its first words. However, *Leviticus* is a good name for it since the tribe of Levi is the priestly tribe responsible for the religion, and the book brings together quite varied collections of ancient and more recent customs concerning worship, the priesthood, and the religious laws.

Interspersed throughout this rather wide-ranging collection of legal writings are minor narrative passages included solely in an attempt to give the origin of each particular law. The main concern of the authors is evidently to give precise and meticulous rules, to consider every situation and go into all the details.

This book can be divided into four basic parts. The first establishes the rules for sacrifices from the holocaust, in which the victim is entirely consumed, the oblation or offering of the produce of the soil, the sacrifice of communion, a kind of sacred banquet in which part of the victim is eaten by the faithful whilst the other is offered to God, the sacrifice for sin with a view to atoning for ritual faults, to the sacrifice of restoration in the case of a breach of justice towards God or man.

The second part sets out the rules of investiture for priests by recounting how Moses ordained Aaron and his sons, and how they took up their position in worship. Then comes the list of particular obligations concerning priests and the account of the punishment of Nadad and Abihu, those sons of Aaron who had neglected the sacred rituals.

The third part contains the law of purity. This law relates to animals and which of them one may or may not eat and touch, to illnesses and the rules to be followed if one suffers an attack and those to be followed with regard to others who may suffer from them, and finally, to sexual matters and the code of behaviour between people in that area.

The fourth part is the law of holiness. 'Be holy, because I, the Lord your God, am holy' (*Leviticus* 19, 2). In this text Yahweh gives Moses a group of laws which concern the people first of all and then the priests.

JUDAISM

Next, he gives instructions about the feast days, Passover, Pentecost, the day of Atonement, the feast of the Tabernacles, about the sabbatical year and the year of Jubilee.

Numbers

The book of *Numbers*, or *Bemiddebar* to the Jews, is so-called because its early pages include the census of 'the people of Israel by clans and families, listing the names of all the men 20 years old or older who are fit for military service' (*Numbers* 1, 2). It is important for the Hebrews to take this kind of census in the face of hard testing ahead. They are at the foot of Sinai and about to start on the long journey through the desert which will last for 35 years.

The account goes on to describe the preparations for the departure, the marching order of the tribes, the duties of the Levites, the moral laws, the laws for the celebration of Passover which must be observed during this difficult time, the manufacture of the silver trumpets which will be used to summon the community together, and the signals governing the movement of the people. Later comes the appearance of the cloud which guides the people and the fire of the Eternal One who shows his presence with them and punishes their sins.

Then there are the different stages of the desert journey, the complaints and revolts of the people, and the miracles of Yahweh which allow them to survive: water struck from a rock, food fallen down from heaven etc. When the king of Edom denies them

passage through his country the Hebrews go round it; on the other hand the king of Arad and the king of the Amorites attack them and become their sworn enemies. So eventually by means of treaties with some and victories over others the people of Israel approach Canaan, arriving on the eastern bank of the River Jordan.

The book ends with the division of Canaan among the different tribes of Israel and the naming of Joshua as their leader. A text in which narrative accounts and legal pronouncements are quite randomly mingled, *Numbers* is the story of the transformation of the people of Israel into a holy community: this gives it a theological character which has not been overlooked by Judaism nor by the Fathers of the Church.

Deuteronomy

Deuteronomy is the fifth book of the *Pentateuch*. The Jews call it *Elleh haddebarim* or simply *Debarim*. It is called *Deuteronomy*, 'second law' because, coming after numerous legal texts, it is generally looked on as a repetition of the Mosaic Law.

It is presented as a great farewell speech by Moses to his people: 'In this book are the words that Moses spoke to the people of Israel when they were in the wilderness east of the River Jordan … On the first day of the 11th month of the 40th year after they had left Egypt, Moses told the people everything the Lord had commanded him to tell them' (*Deuteronomy* 1, 1–3)

In the first part Moses recalls Yahweh's order to leave Horeb and the instructions he gave for the departure. Then he tells of the rebellion of the people at Kadesh and the vow of the Almighty: 'Not one of you from this evil generation will enter the fertile land that I promised to give your ancestors …' (*Deuteronomy* 1, 35).

Next he evokes the lands they have crossed, the countries they have conquered, the victories and defeats, and the constant support of Yahweh through times when they trusted him and times of betrayal. That is where the greatness of the divine choice is revealed: 'Because he loved your ancestors, he chose you, and by his great power, he himself brought you out of Egypt. As you advanced, he drove out nations greater and

The departure

'On the 20th day of the second month in the second year after the people left Egypt, the cloud over the tent of the Lord's presence lifted and the Israelites started on their journey out of the Sinai desert. The cloud came to rest in the wilderness of Paran. They began to march at the command of the Lord through Moses, and each time they moved, they were in the same order. Those under the banner of the division led by the tribe of Judah started out first, company by company, with Nahshon, son of Amminadab in command.'
(*Numbers* 10, 11–14)

130

more powerful than you, so that he might bring you in and give you their land, the land which still belongs to you. So remember today and never forget: the Lord is God in heaven and on earth. There is no other God. Obey all his laws that I have given you today and all will go well with you and your descendants. You will continue to live in the land which the Lord your God is giving you to be yours for ever' (*Deuteronomy* 4, 37–40).

Then the Ten Commandments of the Law are recalled and the *Shema*, the most important Jewish prayer: 'Israel remember this! The Lord — and the Lord alone — is our God. Love the Lord your God with all your heart, with all your soul and with all your strength …' (*Deuteronomy* 6, 4–6). Such has been the importance of this prayer for Jews throughout the ages, that it is the first thing they learn to say as children and the last word they utter before they die.

Deuteronomy emphasizes the idea of the one place for worship: 'Out of the territory of all your tribes the Lord will choose the one place where the people are to come into his presence and worship him' (*Deuteronomy* 12, 5). It condemns idolatory, invokes the benevolence of God and encourages respect for the Law. The book ends with the story of Moses.

The song of Moses

'Earth and sky hear my words, listen closely to what I say. My teaching will fall like drops of rain and form on the earth like dew. My words will fall like showers on young plants, like gentle rain on tender grass. I will praise the name of the Lord and his people will tell of his greatness. The Lord is your mighty defender, perfect and just in all his ways; your God is faithful and true; he does what is right and fair.
(*Deuteronomy* 32, 1–4)

The ninth day of the feast of the Tabernacles, the **Simchat Torah**, *is a day of great rejoicing: the scrolls of the* **Torah** *are carried in procession amidst singing and dancing.*
Scroll of the Torah *and its* **Tig** *(case).*
Musée de Cluny, Paris.

The Book of Joshua

The dividing up of the Promised Land

The deeds of Yahweh

How Yahweh fulfils his promise with the conquest of the Promised Land and its division between the sons of Israel.

The task of leading the Hebrews through the desert to the edge of the Promised Land had been entrusted to Moses (*Pentateuch*). Joshua, his disciple and successor, was entrusted with the task of directing the conquest and division of Palestine. As a responsible leader, Joshua wished to know more about the area and sent two spies out to Jericho. They were met by a Rahab, a prostitute who feared Yahweh, and she saved them from the wrath of the king, who was aware of their mission.

The crossing of the Jordan is described in terms of a religious ceremony in which Yahweh plays the leading role: the Ark of the Covenant was carried by the priests and when it arrived at the river the waters stopped flowing, allowing the procession to cross. So the Ark was carried like a means of

protection in the very place where the current was strongest while the people crossed in safety to the other side. The Ark was brought over and the Jordan began to flow once more. This account immediately calls to mind the crossing of the Red Sea under Moses (*Exodus* 14, 15); the Sinai Covenant still stands.

The hardest part is still to come: the conquest of the land. The *Book of Joshua* covers two remarkable victories in particular, one at Jericho and one at Ai. The first of these bears the mark of God's power: it is a holy war and is conducted by Yahweh; the conquest of the Promised Land is his business, it is he who makes a gift of it to his faithful people. The second victory, by contrast, is a close run thing: the Covenant is, in fact, a contract, and if one of the two partners — in this case the people of Israel — do not fulfil their obligations, they can expect nothing from the other, in this case Yahweh.

'I am putting into your hands Jericho, with its king ... You and your soldiers are to march round the city once a day for six days. Seven priests, each carrying a trumpet are to go in front of the Covenant Box. On the seventh day you and your soldiers are to march round the city seven times, while the priests blow the trumpets. Then they are to sound one long note. As soon as you hear it, all the men are to give a loud shout and the city walls will collapse: then the whole army will go straight into the city' (*Joshua* 6, 2–5). What was said was done and Jericho was doomed. Everything in the city was to be destroyed, apart from the gold and silver destined to fill Yahweh's treasury.

Unfortunately there was one Israelite who allowed himself to take something from the doomed city. Yahweh was enraged and withdrew his protection. Catastrophes followed immediately.

Spies were sent out by Joshua to

Gilgal

'There (at Gilgal), Joshua set up the 12 stones taken from the Jordan. He said to the people of Israel: "In the future, when your children ask you what these stones mean, you will tell them about the time when Israel crossed the Jordan on dry land. Tell them that the Lord your God dried up the water for you until you had crossed, just as he dried up the Red Sea for us. Because of this everyone on earth will know how great the Lord's power is, and you will honour the Lord your God for ever."'
(*Joshua* 4, 20–4)

---

reconnoitre the city of Ai, but they blundered badly. Three thousand men were not enough to take the city. They were comprehensively beaten. The people lost confidence and despair set in. In answer to Joshua's prayer Yahweh demanded that what was wrongfully taken be rooted out and the person responsible destroyed. So the guilty man was discovered and executed, thus assuring Israel's victory. 'I will give you victory over the king of Ai; his people, city, and land will be yours' (*Joshua* 8, 1).

So the struggle goes on: Israel's enemies form alliances, whilst the Gibeonites sign a peace treaty with Joshua, thereby avoiding extermination and instead obtaining his protection. Israel goes to the aid of these new allies and during a long battle, when the enemy are in flight, Joshua makes the sun stand still in the sky in order to complete his victory. So the five southern kings are defeated and their cities conquered. A vow of destruction is issued against the cities in the north and victory is total. Joshua has been faithful to his mission: he can point proudly to the list of vanquished kings.

The second part of the book of Joshua is descriptive, or one could say, geographical. The Hebrew leader travels the land that is henceforth his own. The Promised Land has become the acquired land, or rather the received land. The Covenant is fulfilled. It is now time for the division of the land between the tribes of Israel: to Ruben, Gad, and half the Manasseh tribe goes the region to the east of the Jordan; with other regions going to other tribes. Certain cities are set apart as cities of refuge, which are to be havens for those who accidentally kill another person, or as Levite cities, reserved for the priests.

An epic

The book of Joshua is such a fine sequel to *Deuteronomy* that one is tempted to include it in the *Pentateuch* (five books), thereby making it a *Hexateuch* (six books), and to consider it as an integral part of the Law of

Moses, the *Torah*. But it is certain that this is not a book written by Moses. Is Joshua the author as well as the hero of the story told here? We cannot be sure. The work might be a rewrite of ancient documents, local legends or epic stories linked to a particular holy place, rewritten perhaps by a single author, as the uniformity of style suggests, around the 8th century BC.

The story in its present form has all the characteristics of a national epic: a principal hero, the glorification of collective values, the presence of wonders, an extreme simplification of the action. No doubt, in reality, the conquest of Palestine must have taken years, or decades, if not centuries. Here the job is done in short order under the direction of one leader and accompanied by some extraordinary feats.

Joshua embodies the unity which God had introduced into Israel's heritage: even his name, Joshua, means 'Yahweh liberation'.

Archaeological research has led to the data in the book of Joshua being taken seriously. The excavations of Tell-es-Sultan correspond to the ancient Canaanite fortified city of Jericho which appears to have been destroyed by an earth tremor in the 14th century BC and those of Et-tell to the city of Ai. The epic has a basis in reality.

Joshua's testimony

'So be careful to obey and do everything that is written in the Law of Moses. Do not neglect any part of it, and then you will not associate with these peoples left among you or speak the names of their gods or use those names in taking vows. Instead be faithful to the Lord, as you have been until now. The Lord has driven great and powerful nations out as you advanced and no one has ever been able to stand against you. Any one of you can make 1000 men run away, because the Lord your God is fighting for you, just as he promised.'
(*Joshua* 23, 6–10)

The Book of Judges

From Joshua to Samuel

The Saviours

The era when the cycle of apostasy (denial of the faith), enemy invasion, repentance, conversion, deliverance, and prosperity were constantly repeated.

When Israel arrived in the Promised Land the outlook was not as rosy as might have been supposed from the account given in Joshua's 'epic'. The Hebrews were divided into tribes, clans, and families, each with their own territory. Theirs was a nomadic tradition with no political organization. 'There was no king in Israel at that time; everyone did just as he pleased' (*Judges* 17, 6). If the tribe of Judah helped the tribe of Simeon to establish their boundaries, it was simply with a view to having them do the same for them (*Judges* 1, 3). What was happening was separation of the individual tribes, rather than their unification.

The Canaanite towns had not all been destroyed, not by a long way. There were even some, like Shechem, which were very prosperous. The Canaanites were a well organized people, under the leadership of kings. They were well established in the area and had cultivated the land. Their religion celebrated fertility and fruitfulness, and suited their settled existence. Baal and Asherah granted them many benefits.

As far as the Israelites were concerned, worship of Yahweh was the only unifying factor in the nation's life. The only place where sacrifices were made was at Shiloh where the Covenant Box (Ark) was, and the Hebrews went there three times a year for the great festivals. But generations came and went, and eventually there were none left who remembered all the great things God had done for his people. Some of the old inhabitants of the land had been allowed to live on amongst the tribes, and there had been intermarriage. These people had taught the Hebrews how to cultivate the land and gradually Yahweh, the God of bygone battles, was forgotten in favour of Baal, the god of the fertility they now enjoyed.

Then the Canaanites, who had succeeded in establishing the supremecy of their lifestyle, their customs, and their god, also wanted to impose their laws. They subjugated the Israelites, reducing them to slavery and even obliterating the name of the nation. In the depths of their misery the Israelites realized their sins. They remembered the God of Israel, the god of wars and victory. They cried out to him in remorse and asked for his help.

The judges

God raised up a saviour from the ranks of Israel who was called a judge. He did not dispense justice or govern, nor did he exercise power permanently. His authority was

---

Ehud's cruelty

'With his left hand Ehud took the sword from his right side and plunged it into the king's belly. The whole sword went in, handle and all, and the fat covered it up. Ehud did not pull it out of the king's belly and it stuck out behind, between his legs. Then Ehud went outside, closed the doors behind him, locked them, and left. The servants came and saw that the doors were locked, but they thought that the king was inside, relieving himself.' (*Judges* 3, 21–4)

---

limited to a place and a time, and related only to the daring of his tactics, the exceptional might of his arm, and the extent of his exploits. Often only one act was required of him but this was enough to crush the enemy, restore pride to the people, reconstitute the nation of Israel, and revive their faith in Yahweh.

Ehud, the left-handed man, arriving to pay tribute to the king of Moab, manages to get himself left alone with him and stabs the king to death. 'That day the Israelites defeated Moab and there was peace in the land for 80 years' (*Judges* 3, 30). Later, Deborah, the prophetess, sends Barak to destroy Sisera's army on Mount Tabor. But it is another woman, Jael, who meets the fleeing Sisera and puts him in the ground, quite literally, by driving a tent peg through his head while he is asleep. Deborah sings God's praises and 'there was peace in the land for 40 years' (*Judges* 5, 31).

When we come to Gideon we see that faith is not as great as it was. The judge now asks for signs from the angel who has come from Yahweh to show him what he must do. Gideon has already gathered a huge army around him with a view to destroying the Midianites. But the Yahweh of the armies does not need so many men and crushes the enemy with only 300 warriors. War is no longer fought by cunning, but by reliance on the power of the God of the armies.

God works more subtly in the case of Jephthah. This brave soldier is a prostitute's son who is, at first, despised, rejected, and driven away by his half-brothers who later come looking for him to lead the Israelite army. Jephthah is a godly man who takes his responsibilities seriously and surrounds himself with the protection of Yahweh. He even makes a vow that, if he is victorious, he will sacrifice the first person who comes to meet him. This person turns out to be his only daughter, still a virgin, but he carries out his vow as his dedication to God demands.

The case of Samson is different again. Before he was born he was pledged by his parents to be a Nazarite, a person who shows devotion to God by avoiding strong drink and never cutting their hair, and he is blessed with incredible physical strength. His only weakness, but a considerable one, is women. Married for the first time to a Philistine girl who has caught his fancy, he then falls madly in love with another, Delilah, and can refuse her nothing. This is his undoing. Three times she asks the secret of his strength, and three times he lies to her, but the fourth time he confesses that his strength lies in his hair. Delilah cuts his hair while he is sleeping and delivers him to the Philistines. Samson will wait until his hair grows again before avenging himself, destroying the temple of his enemies and dying in the rubble.

The *Book of Judges* lists 15 judges: it is a gallery of scenes, portraits, and anecdotes, all very loosely linked. Whether it is in fact one single work could be open to doubt, but the general outline is still respected in each story and Israel plunges deeper and deeper into trouble: apostasy, denial of the faith, becomes more frequent, oppression more severe, and the periods of prosperity much shorter. Might the compiler of these accounts have been Samuel, who was to institute the monarch in the 11th century BC? This is an attractive possibility since it would provide arguments for the new ordering of society.

However, this fragmentary and anecdotal account should not be treated as history, in the modern sense of the word. The aims of the writers vary greatly; glorification of women, extraordinary feats, explanations for certain rituals etc.

Delilah's treachery

'Delilah lulled Samson to sleep in her lap and then called a man who cut off Samson's seven locks of hair. Then she began to torment him for he had lost his strength. Then she shouted, "Samson, the Philistines are coming!" He woke up and thought "I'll get loose and go free as always." He did not know that the Lord had left him. The Philistines captured him and put his eyes out. They took him to Gaza, chained him in bronze chains, and put him to work grinding at the mill in prison.'
(*Judges* 16, 19–21)

The Book of Ruth

The foreign woman

A story setting a good example

An example of virtue and compassion in an age of harshness and among an idolatrous people.

In the Middle East of thousands of years ago great famines were not unusual occurrences. Often, the solution was to go to other countries in search of what was needed: thus the patriarch Jacob went into Egypt, the prophet Eli to Sarepta etc. It was the same for Elimelech of Bethlehem who fled to the land of Moab with his wife Naomi and his two sons Mahlon and Chilion.

Their exile lasted a long time and the two sons found wives in their adopted country: one married Orpah, the other Ruth, they were both Moabite girls. Then the menfolk died, first Elimelech, then Mahlon and Chilion. Naomi found herself alone with her two daughters-in-law. Knowing that the famine in her own country was now over and wishing to return there, Naomi suggested to Orpah and Ruth that, in the circumstances, it would be best for each to

go back home to their mother's house.

Orpha did not need much persuasion but Ruth would not hear of leaving her mother-in-law and went with her to Bethlehem, arriving at the beginning of the harvest. Ruth went to glean wheat and barley in the fields belonging to Boaz, a rich relation of Elimelech. She was following the harvesters when the landowner himself arrived and asked who this young woman was. Knowing the story of the Moabite woman and her kindness to her mother-in-law, he instructed them to take care of her.

But Ruth took matters further. Emboldened by the man's good treatment of her and encouraged by Naomi, she went and lay down at his feet and asked him to follow the custom whereby the relative of a dead man was allowed to marry his widow in order to give him descendants. He was not the closest male relative, but the man who gave up his claim before the town elders at the town gates, making everything official.

Boaz married Ruth, the Moabite woman, and they had a son, Obed, who was to be the father of Jesse, whose son David would be the greatest of Israel's kings. So it is true that the royal line had among its ancestors a foreign woman, but one who was compassionate and devoted to her new country.

Ruth's decision

'Don't ask me to leave you! Let me go with you. Wherever you go, I will go; wherever you live, I will live. Your people will be my people and your God will be my God. Wherever you die, I will die, and that is where I will be buried. May the Lord's worst punishment come upon me if I let anything but death separate me from you.' (*Ruth* 1, 16–17)

The Book of Ruth

Written by an anonymous author after the exile, but relating deeds set in the tumultuous era of the judges, the *Book of Ruth* is a moving and calm tale, more serene than the *Song of Songs*: maternal instinct is personified in the character of Naomi, tenderness in that of Ruth and generosity in that of Boaz.

The Books of Samuel

From the last Judge to King David

The institution of the monarchy

Yahweh chooses a king to govern his people and fulfil his promises.

Living alongside the old inhabitants of the Promised Land proved to be a difficult experience for the Hebrews. Every so often the judges, acting in the name of Yahweh, would re-establish Israel's supremacy, but time and again the situation would break down. It became increasingly apparent that the people needed one permanent leader, a king like other nations had. Samuel, the last of the judges, was to be the means by which God set up the monarchy.

Samuel

A miraculous birth to a sterile woman, a vow taken by his mother, a pious childhood under the care of the priest Eli in the sanctuary at Shilo, and a special call from God all mark Samuel out as a dedicated man, a man of God. He is not a wartime commander like the other judges, he is Yahweh's representative among men, the guide and prophet whose words are listened to and followed.

The Philistines had got hold of the Covenant Box but found that it brought them nothing but trouble and so they soon sent it back. The Hebrews took it into safe keeping but there was great alarm and when they assembled at Samuel's call and learned that the enemy was massing against them; they cried for help. The prophet offered a sacrifice while the fighting was going on and God gave the victory to his people.

'Samuel ruled Israel as long as he lived' (*I Samuel* 7, 15). When he grew old he made his sons judges. They did not follow his example, however, and the leaders of the people came and asked Samuel to give them a king. So the prophet warned them what it would be like to have a king: he will take your sons and make them work for him, he will take your daughters, he will take a tenth of all that you have and you will complain bitterly because of the king. But the people refused to listen to Samuel and God told him to satisfy their demands.

Saul

Saul was a member of the tribe of Benjamin. He was 'a handsome man in the prime of life. He was a head taller than anyone else in Israel and also more handsome' (*I Samuel* 9, 2). He came to see the 'seer' or holy man to ask the way and Samuel, on God's instructions, anointed him as ruler. He was then chosen, through a process of elimination, by all the people gathered together and finally, after a victory over the Philistines was proclaimed king.

The call of God

'The Lord called Samuel. He answered, "Yes sir!" and ran to Eli and said, "You called me and here I am." But Eli answered, "I didn't call you; go back to bed." So Samuel went back to bed. The Lord called Samuel again. The boy did not know that it was the Lord, because the Lord have never spoken to him before. So he got up, went to Eli, and said, "You called me and here I am." But Eli answered, "My son, I didn't call you; go back to bed." The Lord called Samuel a third time; he got up, went to Eli, and said, "You called me and here I am." Then Eli realized it was the Lord who was calling the boy, so he said to him, "Go back to bed; and if he calls again, say: Speak Lord, your servant is listening."' (*I Samuel* 3, 4–9)

Saul was firstly a military leader. There was no central organization, nor anywhere that could properly be called the capital city. He was surrounded, in the main, by people from his own tribe of Benjamin, but was prepared to seek help from the other tribes, even looking beyond the Jordan. Israel was a theocratic society, one under God's rule. The king was subject to the orders of God, as interpreted by his prophet. Now Saul sometimes looked for compromises, he was afraid of the people, and he took possession of some plunder which had been pledged to destruction. As a result of this he was rejected and it was Samuel who made the declaration: 'Because you rejected the Lord's command, he has rejected you as king' (*I Samuel* 15, 23).

David

As Saul's successor, Yahweh chose Jesse's youngest son, David, 'a handsome, healthy young man, and his eyes sparkled'. Saul, who knew nothing of this, sent for David to play the harp for him and became very fond of him. David became the king's squire. But, when the giant Philistine warrior, Goliath, with his bronze and leather armour came and taunted Yahweh's troops, demanding single combat, it was David who came forward, though still a child, and let fly with a stone from his sling which hit Goliath right on the forehead and killed him.

This marked the beginning of Saul's great jealousy of David. On several occasions he raised his spear against his squire, but David was always able to avoid it. David now had his own command and led his men from victory to victory. He also won the friendship of Saul's son Jonathan, but so great was the king's animosity towards him that he was forced to flee to the south of the country with his followers and seek refuge among the Philistines. Meanwhile Saul and Jonathan continued the fighting, going from one defeat to another and were finally killed. David's grief is expressed in a song full of emotion: 'Women of Israel, mourn

for Saul! He clothed you in rich scarlet dresses and adorned you with jewels and gold. The brave soldiers have fallen, they were killed in battle. Jonathan has died in the hills. I grieve for you my brother Jonathan; how dear you were to me' (*II Samuel* 1, 17–27).

David's kingship

At Hebron, David was made king of Judah, whilst Ishbosheth was made king of Israel. The two sides began a battle to the death but Ishbosheth and his general, Abner, were killed and the northern tribes swore allegiance to David, who became the sole king of Israel. This was the beginning of a splendid reign marked by the taking of Jerusalem, the transfer of the Covenant Box, the Ark, to the new capital, and Nathan's prophecy that the dynasty would last for ever.

David's monarchy was not without its darker side. The king was sensual and cruel, although he did not act from motives of self interest and quickly repented of his crimes. There was, however, a strong rivalry between his sons: Amnon, the eldest, was killed after raping his half sister Tamar and the murderer, Absalom, having been allowed back at court, organized a rebellion which forced David to flee and then took possession of the royal harem. In the end the king prevailed and Solomon, the product of an adulterous union was named as successor.

The text

This is one of the finest examples of sacred literature. The author, who was formerly thought to be Samuel himself, brings the stories dramatically to life, the portraits are well drawn and the details well chosen. He seems to have had access to contemporary documents about these events and to have used the oral traditions which had come down to him. This explains the occasional contradictions and repetitions, and the overall unity of the work is not undermined.

The Books of Kings

From Solomon to the captivity

The fall of the monarchy

The taste for wealth, luxury, and ambition among kings gains the upper hand over their faithfulness to Yahweh.

The succession to the throne of Israel after David's death was a matter of some difficulty. His eldest son Adonijah plotted to have himself accepted by the influential members of the court, even before the king's death. But Nathan, the prophet, and Bathsheba intervened, and Solomon received his father's inheritance and punished Adonijah.

The judgment of Solomon

'One day two prostitutes came and presented themselves before King Solomon. One of them said, "Your majesty, this woman and I live in the same house, and I gave birth to a baby boy at home while she was there. Two days after my child was born, she also gave birth to a baby boy. Only the two of us were there in the house — no one else was present. Then one night she accidentally rolled over on her baby and smothered it. She got up during the night, took my son from my side while I was asleep, and carried him to her bed; then she put the dead child in my bed ..." But the other woman said, "No! The living child is mine, and the dead one is yours!" ... Then King Solomon said, ..."Cut the living child in two and give each woman half of it." The real mother, her heart full of love for her son said to the king, "Please, your majesty, don't kill the child! Give it to her!" ... Then the king said "Don't kill the child! Give it to the first woman — she is its real mother." (*I Kings* 3, 16–28)

Solomon

After his enthronement the king went to Gibeon to make a sacrifice there and, in a dream, he saw Yahweh who said to him: 'Because you have asked for the wisdom to rule justly, instead of long life for yourself or riches or the death of your enemies, I will do what you have asked. I will give you more wisdom and understanding than anyone has ever had before or will ever have again. I will also give you what you have not asked for; all your life you will have wealth and honour, more than that of any other king' (*I Kings* 3, 11–13).

Solomon returned to Jerusalem and showed his wisdom in the way he governed: he used a bluff to discover the true mother of a child claimed by two women; he organized the kingdom into regions with a governor in each one and, above all, he uttered maxims, proverbs, and parables which earned him a worldwide reputation for wisdom. 'Kings all over the world heard of his wisdom and sent people to listen to him' (*I Kings* 4, 34).

During his reign there was a great building programme. The king had cedars and junipers brought from Lebanon, he had enormous blocks of stone quarried and large quantities of bronze cast in order to build the Temple at Jerusalem. He brought the Covenant Box there and held a splendid feast to mark the opening of the Temple. He also built palaces and walls, and his wealth dazzled the nations. It even dazzled the Queen of Sheba and also increased trade with foreign countries.

But 'Solomon loved many foreign women. Besides the daughter of the king of Egypt he married Hittite women and women from Moab, Ammon, Edom (...) even though the Lord had told the Israelites not to intermarry with these people' (*I Kings* 11,

1). When Solomon was old his women imposed their gods on him and he was no longer entirely faithful to Yahweh, who then provoked Jeroboam to act against Solomon. He was in charge of the forced labour gangs from the northern tribes who were severely oppressed by Jerusalem whilst Judah was exempt from this work. Jeroboam stirred up a revolt amongst them, which Solomon was unable to put down.

Partition

When Solomon died the people of Judah readily accepted his son, Rehoboam, but the north demanded a lightening of their load and the break became inevitable. Jeroboam was proclaimed king of Israel and Rehoboam king of Judah. Political separation soon brought in its wake religious division. The northern tribes established places of worship replacing the Temple at Jerusalem, then they began to portray Yahweh in the form of a bull like the Canaanite god, Baal. There were now two nations: Israel and Judah.

Elijah

The prophet Elijah dogged the footsteps of Ahab, king of the northern tribes. He spoke out against the sins of Israel, foretold a three year drought, and when this happened he went to Phoenicia, where he was received by a poor widow. He performed a miracle to ensure that she had food and even brought her son back to life. Later he went to see Ahab who had been searching

Elijah is taken up to heaven

'Elijah said to Elisha: "Tell me what you want me to do for you before I am taken away?" "Let me receive the share of your power that will make me your successor", Elisha answered. "That is a difficult request to grant", Elijah replied. "But you will receive it if you see me as I am being taken away from you; if you don't see, you won't receive it." They kept talking as they walked on; then suddenly a chariot of fire pulled by horses of fire came between them, and Elijah was taken up to heaven by a whirlwind. Elisha saw it.' (*II Kings* 2, 9–12)

for him since the disaster had struck.

Then there unfolds the great test on Mount Carmel. It was a question of proving who was the true God, Yahweh or Baal. Elijah stood alone against 450 priests of Baal who, despite their shouts, their prayers and their pleas could not bring fire to the wood of the sacrifice. The prophet of Israel managed it without difficulty, achieving at a stroke both the end of the drought and the total defeat of his opponents, which sent Jezebel, Ahab's Phoenician wife, into such a rage that she forced Elijah to take flight.

His path took him to Mount Horeb where Moses had received the tablets of the Law. There he met Yahweh who came to him in the form of a light breeze and later he was to be lifted up to heaven in the presence of Elisha, his servant and his successor. He in turn would perform numerous miracles: raising from the dead, provision of food, aid to the poor. But, in addition, he would use his gifts of clairvoyance to reveal the enemy's plans to Israel's armies.

Josiah

Of all the rulers mentioned in the *Books of Kings* there are many who find favour with the author: for example Hezekiah, who began religious reforms, and Josiah. One of the major events of his reign was the rediscovery of the *Torah.* Josiah read it in public and, horrified at the breakdown of religious customs which there had been, he undertook certain reforms: the Temple was purefied, idols destroyed, their priests removed from office and a solemn celebration of the Passover was observed. But he was succeeded by Joahaz and Jehoiakim who 'sinned against the Lord'; the land was invaded by Nebuchadnezzar, king of Babylon, and the people were deported.

The author of this work often gives his sources: they are the annals of the kings of Judah or those of the kings of Israel. The dominant theme throughout is the downfall of the kings who commit Jeroboam's sin and worship Yahweh in the form of a bull, or Ahab's sin of following the religion of Baal. Yet the prophets, go on warning, threatening and speaking out in the name of Yahweh.

The Books of Chronicles

Happenings

The things left out

How history is rewritten to give praise to the great King David.

The *Books of Chronicles* are the books of the Bible which cover the longest period of history. They begin with Adam and go on to the edict of Cyrus and the return from captivity. Such a vast remit can only be covered by brief references to events. This is indeed what happens in the first part which goes from Adam to David and is made up almost entirely of genealogies or family trees.

This literary use of genealogy, very dear to the Hebrews, is not only the result of an historical curiosity, it is also an attempt to express solidarity between generations, to make past events come alive and to reveal the very heart of the people of Israel. Yahweh is the one who called Abraham, gave the Law, led the Jews in the desert, and conquered the Promised Land: he is the God of the Covenant. The children of Israel owe their existence to Abraham's obedience, the experiences of captivity, acceptance of the Covenant and faithfulness to the God who has revealed himself. The genealogy gives the details of what is meant by the phrase 'children of Israel', Israel being the name of Jacob, one of the forefathers.

The Midrash

The second part repeats the story which has already been written in the *Books of Samuel* and *Kings*. Often passages from them are quoted word for word. But it also has other sources: the 'annals of the kings of Israel', the 'annals of the kings of Israel and Judah', the actions of such and such a prophet and, also no doubt, oral traditions and reminis-

cences dating from the relevant period. All these documents are used very freely to support what the author is saying.

The chronicler uses a literary style called *midrash*. He feels no need to report the facts in any kind of detail as they happened in the past. He is not a historian, he is a theologian. His aim is a religious one: he wants to highlight what God has done. His study of the texts is coloured by the belief that they are still current, that they express the faith he holds today and demonstrate the indestructible union between Israel and the Word of God. So he plunders them shamelessly, omitting something here, adding something there, replacing paragraphs, and even using connections and illustrations entirely of his own creation. The main thing is to depart from the text and keep to the line that has been agreed on. This approach which has very distant origins in the Bible, was to become very widely used in Judaism.

So the *Books of Chronicles* speak only of the end of Saul's reign; they do not mention David's time in Hebron, nor his adultery with Bathsheba, nor the murder of Uriah, nor Amnon's assassination attempt, nor Absalom's revolt, nor the abandonment of

---

The consecration of David

'All the people of Israel went to David at Hebron and said to him, "We are your own flesh and blood. In the past, even when Saul was still our king, you led the people of Israel in battle, and the Lord your God promised you that you would lead his people and be their ruler." So all the leaders of Israel came to King David at Hebron. He made a sacred alliance with them, they annointed him, and he became the king of Israel, just as the Lord had promised through Samuel.' (*I Chronicles* 11, 1–3)

Saul's sons to the Gibeonites, nor the bloody dramas of the king's old age, nor Adonijah's attempt to take the throne, nor even the consecration of Solomon, the adultress's son. Most of these facts do nothing to enhance the glory of the founder of the dynasty and so, understandably, the author makes no mention of them.

By contrast, great attention is paid to the taking of Jerusalem, the transporting there of the Covenant Box, the description of the Temple, and the duties of the Levites. There is an exhaustive list of David's early followers, and he is given the key role in the project of rebuilding the Temple, in the organization of the worship, in the advice which he pours out to his successor and to the people, and it is very noticeable that the breakaway kings of Israel are completely ignored in order to concentrate exclusively on the kings of Judah, descendants of David, especially the reformers Hezekiah and Josiah.

No attempt is being made here to give an exhaustive account of the differences be-

---

Josiah

'Josiah was eight years old when he became king of Judah, and he ruled in Jerusalem for 31 years. He did what was pleasing to the Lord; he followed the example of his ancestor King David, strictly obeying all the laws of God. In the eighth year that Josiah was king, while he was still very young, he began to worship the God of his ancestor King David. Four years later he began to destroy the pagan places of worship, the symbols of the goddess Asherah, and all the other idols. Under his direction his men smashed the altars where Baal was worshipped and tore down the incense altars near them. They ground to dust the images of Asherah and all the other idols and then scattered the dust on the graves of the people who had sacrificed to them.' (*II Chronicles* 34, 1–4)

---

tween the *Books of Samuel* and *Kings* and the *Books of Chronicles*, but these instances show clearly enough that in the *Chronicles* it is David and his descendants who are the centre of interest. The object of the work is obviously to restore the prestige of the house of David at the very time when reestablishment of the monarchy is out of the question, and thus to underline his eminently religious role.

For this writer, Jerusalem is not the capital of the kingdom, but the Holy City. The *Books of Samuel* and *Kings* recount the history of kings but the *Chronicles* speak of the Aaronite priesthood, of priests, Levites, cantors (temple singers), and musicians who play an important and acknowledged role in the reforms and the festivals. The work goes on at some length about their organization, their services, their rewards, their rights. It is easy to imagine that the author might be one of their number.

The philosophy of history which emerges from the *Chronicles* is ideal for the purposes of the work. At the price of some distortion of the facts reported in the other works, the good kings, those who reform religious life, condemn idolatry, and encourage worship in the Temple, enjoy the blessing of a happy reign. The bad kings however, those who worship in the high places, neglect the Law, and mingle with foreigners, suffer invasions, famines, and diseases. This is the principle of retribution on earth.

The books

Everything points to the *Books of Chronicles* having been written after the exile: their content, language, and thinking. Furthermore, the last paragraph of the books is repeated word for word near the beginning of the *Book of Ezra*, which suggests that they have the same author and that they were written in the 3rd century BC. The Hebrew Bible places the *Chronicles* after *Ezra*, though logically and chronologically it should be the other way round.

The Books of Ezra and Nehemiah

The restorers

The religious community

Ezra the scholar and Nehemiah the politician, conscientious and effective people, were the initiators in the restoration of Judaism.

Cyrus came to the throne in Persia in 559 BC. He quickly took control of the neighbouring tribes and conquered Babylon. In so doing he established the widest empire the world had ever seen at that time. But Cyrus was a generous victor, and, by means of his famous edict, he authorized the Jews deported by Nebuchadnezzar to return to their land. He also authorized the return of the sacred vessels stolen by the old king and the rebuilding of the Temple in Jerusalem.

The *Books of Ezra* and *Nehemiah*, which originally formed one single book, contain the account of these events. For the reconstitution of the Jewish people was to take a long time, beginning with Cyrus's edict. Fifty years had passed since the deportation. Some had escaped and stayed behind, others had made a career in the administrative machinery of the Babylonian state or had settled and become full citizens of their adopted country.

Ezra

The first return expedition was led by Zerubbabel. He began the rebuilding of the Temple on its site and managed to avoid the traps laid by the Samaritans, who did not look kindly on the rebirth of Jerusalem: they did their best to discourage the labourers and even appealed to Darius, who had succeeded Cyrus, to put an end to the work. Nothing came of this, however,

and the Temple was rebuilt and the Passover celebrated there in the year 515.

Ezra, a scholarly priest, who was well thought of at the court of Ataxerxes, led the second expedition. The king gave him all the help he needed: money, supplies, directions. The order went out to all the governors and officials to give Ezra all the help he needed. But Ezra was a godly man and, before setting out, he fasted and said prayers asking for the only protection that really mattered to him, that of his God.

As soon as he arrived at Jerusalem he performed a sacrifice of thanksgiving: the community was re-established. However, a problem soon arose, a serious problem with regard to the Law of Yahweh which says 'The land which you are entering is a land stained by the wrongdoings of the people of that land ... Therefore, do not give your daughters to their sons, nor take their daughters for your sons.' Now, there had been many mixed marriages amongst the exiles and so Ezra took a census, called the community together and persuaded the people to send back the foreign women and their children.

Cyrus's edict

'The Lord, the God of heaven, has made me ruler over the whole world and has given me the responsibility of building a Temple for him in Jerusalem in Judah. May God be with all of you who are his people. You are to go to Jerusalem and rebuild the Temple of the Lord, the God of Israel, the God who is worshipped in Jerusalem. If any of his people in exile need help to return, their neighbours are to give them this help. They are to provide them with silver and gold, supplies and pack animals, as well as offerings to present in the Temple of God in Jerusalem.' (*Ezra* 1, 2–4)

Nehemiah

Ezra was responsible for the rebuilding of the Temple and Nehemiah for the rebuilding of Jerusalem. He too came from Susa: he was a cupbearer to Ataxerxes when, eager for news of the Holy Land, he learned that the walls of Jerusalem were in a sorry state. He was told that they lay in ruins. He asked his master to let him go and rebuild them, and this request was granted. So he went to Jerusalem and began the work with the help of the community there. The hostility of the Samaritans, who had grave misgivings about the fortification of this place on their borders, was a constant threat. However, Nehemiah wisely organized a rota of guards to protect the work.

It was doubtless because of these organizational skills that Nehemiah was soon named governor of the land of Judah. He showed himself to be a good governor, thwarting those who accused him before Ataxerxes of seeking independence, courageously standing up to his enemies who wanted to make him lose face, seeing through the work he had undertaken and repopulating the deserted city.

Soon it was possible to celebrate the rebirth of Israel. 'By the seventh month the people of Israel were all settled in their towns … they all assembled in Jerusalem'. Ezra read from the book of the Law, and the priests and Levites explained the meaning of what Ezra was saying, so that everyone understood. The feast of shelters was celebrated when everyone built his temporary shelter and lived in it for seven days in memory of the Exodus, the great journey out of Egypt and slavery. The 24th day of the month was the day of a great ceremony in which the people expressed sorrow for their sins and, finally, everyone signed a written agreement to obey the commandments. One point is worth noting: there was never any question of re-establishing the dynasty of David.

The Books of Ezra

The facts and events recorded in the *Books of Ezra* and *Nehemiah* are difficult to place chronologically in terms of the other books; but the fact remains that certain historical data are indisputable. Ezra himself is honoured by the Jews as the reinventor of their religion. He is sometimes credited, not only with the book which bears his name, and the *Chronicles*, but also with rewriting all the sacred books which would have been lost at the time the Temple was destroyed. His mission marked the beginning of well-founded institutions in Judaism, the scribe became the person who read, explained, and commented on the Holy Scriptures, and the assemblies he called together were the forerunners of the Sanhedrin, the main religious authority of later years.

Such was Ezra's prestige among the Jews that many other books were also attributed to him: the one which is called the third *Ezra*, and which is the first in the Greek version of the *Septuagint*, while the one mentioned above is considered to be the second, covers the first expedition of Jews to Jerusalem under Zerubbabel. But there is also a fourth, a fifth, and a sixth *Ezra*; these are obscure writings, much later than the third century, with different origins and with some parts common to them all. None of these later texts is considered as part of their canon by either Jews or Christians.

Nehemiah's departure

'One day four months later, when Emperor Ataxerxes was dining, I took the wine to him. He had never seen me look sad before, so he asked, "Why are you looking so sad? You aren't ill, so it must by that you're unhappy." I was startled and answered, "May your majesty live for ever! How can I help looking sad when the city where my ancestors are buried is in ruins and its gates have been destroyed by fire?" The emperor asked, "What is it that you want?" I prayed to the God of heaven, and then I said to the emperor, "If your majesty is pleased with me and is willing to grant my request, let me go to the land of Judah, to the city where my ancestors are buried, so that I can rebuild the city." ' (*Nehemiah* 2, 1–5)

Tobit

The angel's friend

The way of goodness

The tale of Tobias and the angel Raphael shows the support and help guardian angels give.

The book of *Tobit* is a tale in the oriental style. Is it for this reason or because of the date it was written (certainly no earlier than the 2nd century AD), that it is considered by Christians to be apocryphal (of suspect authenticity) and is not included by Jews in their canon of Scriptures? The fact remains however that Catholics have always seen it as an integral part of their Bible.

Tobit was a member of the tribe of Naphtali. He was deported to Nineveh with his wife Anna and his son Tobias, but remained true to his faith despite the denial of those close to him and many misfortunes and trials. Ruined, blind, insulted even by his wife, he begged God to take him from this world.

Sarah was the daughter of Raguel, an inhabitant of Ectabana in Media. She had married seven times and was seven times a widow, the demon Asmodeus having killed her husbands one after the other 'before they were joined to her as true husbands'. She was mocked by her father's servants and finally begged God to come and take her.

Tobit sent his son to recover a large sum of money which he had deposited with Gabael in the heart of Media. Just as he was leaving Tobias fell in with an exceptional travelling companion in Raphael who gave his name as Azarias. So the three of them set out, Tobias, Raphael and his dog. On the first night Tobias went to wash his feet in the river and was almost bitten by a fish. Raphael told him to catch the fish and bring him the venom, the heart, and the liver: 'These are useful remedies', he said.

The travellers made a stop at Raguel's house and it transpired that he was a relative of Tobit. Tobias asked for Sarah's hand, but took the precaution of burning the heart and liver of the fish in the bed chamber, which put the demon Asmodeus to flight. So, while Raguel was in the act of pre-paring the tomb of the eighth husband, the newly-weds emerged very happily from the bridal chamber.

On his return to Nineveh, Tobias put some of the fish venom on his father's eyes, which restored his sight and so everything turned out well in the end. Raphael then told them who he was and how he had been with the father when he gave alms, when he buried the dead, when he prayed; he had been alongside the son on his journey, at his marriage and on his return, and then they each sang praises to God's glory.

The book of *Tobit* has a fluid style and is full of variety. The writing is lively, using simple and evocative words, and the characters are finely drawn. The story is peppered with pieces of advice and proverbs, which bring to mind the 'Story of Ahiqar', a Babylonian work which was very popular throughout the Middle East.

Raguel's precautions

'Raguel got up, called his servants and they came to help him dig a grave. He had thought: "Let's hope he doesn't die! We will be covered in ridicule and shame." Once the hole was dug he called his wife and said to her, "Why don't you send a servant girl to the chamber to see if Tobias is still alive? Because if he is dead we could bury him without anyone knowing anything about it." The servant was sent for, a lamp was lit, and the door was opened. The servant went in, found them both fast asleep and said in a low voice: "He is not dead, everything is all right." Raguel blessed the God of heaven.' (*Tobit* 8, 9–15)

Judith

The liberator of Bethulia

A clever woman

The schemes of ambitious men are thwarted by the audacity of a woman.

There is no doubt that Judith was something of a local heroine. There were feasts and songs in her honour. Processions were organized, dances devised, and a whole legend grew up around her. There was probably a writer around who had a talent for embellishing historical tales. There is no real need to fix this work precisely in terms of time or place; the town of Bethulia would be an imaginary place somewhere in the kingdom. So the book was written, but, because of the lack of any real historical foundation for the deeds it recounts, the Jews have never accepted it into their canon, nor have the Protestants, but Catholics do consider it to be inspired.

The classic example of a Jewish wife

The story is simple and wonderfully constructed. An enemy general was besieging the town: the battle was hard and the resistance fierce. But the blockade grew harder and harder to bear, supplies were running out, and hope faded. Vague notions of surrender began to surface and capitulation looked inevitable. Then Judith came on the scene. She was a young widow who was beautiful, intelligent, and godly. Since her husband's death she had lived quietly in mourning. "Give me five days", she said. Then, dressed in her most beautiful clothes, adorned with precious jewels, and perfumed with rare oils, she presented herself at the enemy camp and seduced their proud, boastful leader, Holofernes. While he was weak with desire, alcohol, and sleep she cut

off his head, and brought it back to the opposite camp. After this stunning feat the attackers were routed and victory went to the besieged.

This brief summary cannot do justice to the skill of the narrator, an artist who uses his talent to great effect. The first seven chapters are a slow geographical progression: Nebuchadnezzar's army sets out from Assyria to conquer the land, it advances like a steamroller, crushing everything in its path and arrives at the walls of Bethulia, defended by a small band of God's people. The noose tightens around it. It's only strength is faith in the commandments as embodied in Judith.

All the details of the subtle plans God has laid for the saving of his people are set out. A tragedy unfolds: the risks are great and the outcome is uncertain. The narrative exudes anguish and concern. But the virtuous Judith proves to be surprisingly cunning, she carries things off with a quiet assurance and victory is hers. An instrument in God's hands, she is also the perfect example of Jewish womanhood, confident, dedicated, daring, and mistress of herself.

Judith and Holofernes

'When it grew late, his officers made haste to leave. Bagoas closed the outer tent after ushering out those who were still with his master. They went to bed, tired out from excessive drinking and Judith was left alone in the tent with Holofernes who had collapsed on his bed after over-indulging in wine. Judith (...) went up to the bedpost by Holofernes's head and took down his scimitar, then, approaching the bed, she seized the man's hair and said, "Make me strong this day, God of Israel." She struck at his neck twice with all her strength and cut off his head.' (*Judith* 13, 1–10)

Esther

The queen of Susa

The Letter about the Purim

How rivalries among courtiers and plots in the harem bring victory to the Jews.

In the 5th century BC, Ahasuerus (Xerxes I) reigned in Susa. He had fought many battles, crossed numerous seas and conquered a vast empire. He was now living in his capital where he undertook great building programmes and enjoyed his wealth. One day he invited all the great men of the kingdom to a banquet in order to display the splendour of his power before them and, when he was drunk, he sent for Vashti, the queen, so that her beauty could also be admired. She refused. She was accused of disrespect for the king and banished from his sight.

But the king kept thinking about Vashti, and in order to help him forget her, all the young and beautiful virgins in the kingdom were called together. From among them Ahasuerus chose the new queen. It was Esther, an orphaned Jewess who had been brought up as his daughter by her uncle, Mordecai, who held an administrative position at the palace. When he took her as his wife the king did not enquire into her origins or her family.

Mordecai kept in touch with Esther, and when he learend that the eunuchs Bigthana and Teresh were plotting against the king, he let her know about it. The queen spoke to the king about it on Mordecai's behalf and, after an inquiry, the two plotters were hanged. This event, which was recorded in the chronicles of the kingdom stirred up great feelings of jealousy in the new prime minister, Haman, who was already very annoyed at Mordecai's refusal to bow down

before him. He therefore set his heart on the extermination of all the Jews in the kingdom and had this decision ratified by the king.

Situations reversed

The date of the massacre was fixed by drawing lots; it was to take place in the 12th month, which is called Adar. In the meantime the order was sent out to the governors of the various provinces. As soon as he heard about this, Mordecai tore his clothes and put on sackcloth and ashes, the Jews cried out in despair and Esther decided to risk everything by going to see the king without being sent for. This was violating an unchangeable law and could be punished by death.

The beauty of the queen was so great, however, that the king did not hold this against her. On the contrary, he offered her half of his kingdom. But Esther's request was more modest: she simply invited him

---

The queen

'Esther was admired by everyone who saw her. When her turn came she wore just what Hegai, the eunuch in charge of the harem, advised her to wear. So in Xerxes's seventh year as king, in the 10th month, the month of Tebeth, Esther was brought to Xerxes in the royal palace. The king liked her more than any of the other girls, and more than any of the others she won his favour and affection. He placed the royal crown on her head and made her queen in place of Vashti. Then the king gave a great banquet in Esther's honour and invited all his officials and administrators. He proclaimed a holiday for the whole empire and distributed gifts worthy of a king.'
(*Esther* 2, 15–18)

and his prime minister to attend a banquet at her house the next day. That evening Haman had a scaffold erected for Mordecai and made preparations for the extermination of the Jews.

The night before, the king had been unable to sleep and had been rereading the chronicles. He wondered how the man who had saved his throne had been rewarded. In the morning he said to his prime minister: 'There is someone I wish very much to honour. What should I do for this man?' Convinced that he was the man in question, Haman outlined a really triumphal procession through the town. He was then ordered to organize such a procession for Mordecai who had once uncovered a plot against the realm. His wife said, 'You are beginning to lose power to Mordecai. He is a Jew and you cannot overcome him. He will certainly defeat you' (*Esther* 6, 13).

At the queen's banquet Esther spoke out clearly. She asked for her life and the life of her people to be spared. She then revealed Haman's dark plot to have the Jews killed and to have the entire race annihilated. The king was so distressed that he went out into the garden. Haman threw himself down at Esther's feet to beg for mercy and was still there when the king returned. Thinking that Haman was attacking his wife, the king immediately sent Haman to the gallows he had built.

Now the situation was completely reversed: Mordecai was made prime minister. A new decree was sent out. It did not nullify

The words of Mordecai

'It is from God that all this has come! If I remember the dream I had on this subject, nothing has been left out, not the little spring that became a river, nor the light which shone, nor the sun, nor the abundance of the waters. Esther is that river, she who married the king and whom he made his queen. The two dragons are Haman and me. The peoples are those who got together to destroy the name of the Jews. My people are the people of Israel, those who cried to God and were saved. Yes, the Lord has saved his people, the Lord has rescued us from all these ills.' (*Esther* 10, 3a–3f)

the first — that would have exposed the king's fallibility—so the target was changed. Henceforth the exploiters became the exploited, the persecuted became the persecutors, those destined for execution became the executors, and a great massacre took place at the time which had originally been agreed for the move against the Jews.

The festival of Purim

Mordecai had these events written down and he told Jews from all the provinces of the kingdom to celebrate this day which had brought them victory. Ever since that time, devout Jews throughout the world have made this day an occasion of feasting and jubilation: the account of these events is read in the synagogues, Esther and Mordecai are honoured, and gifts are given to the poor.

The book

Esther's silence about her origins, Mordecai's arrogance, excessive vengeance, and the massacre all leave a harsh impression. Add to that the fact that the name of God is not mentioned at all in the Hebrew text and this begins to look like an unedifying example of two-way prejudice.

Fortunately there are some Greek language additions which bring the light of religious meaning to the text; prayers have been added and feelings explained. God has now become the main character. No doubt it could be argued that these values were there underlying the original text. Indications of this are perhaps seen in the fast which is ordered after Haman's decree, Mordecai's advice to Esther, and even the pride which the Jew shows. It is an improvement to have these elements brought out, at least that is what the Greek writer of the supplementary text must have thought.

As for the writer of the Hebrew text, very little is known about him: his style is clear, simple and lively; he knows all about the area in which the action takes place, the customs of the city of Susa, the historical figures of the time; he is able to describe the protocol, banquets, and festivities of the Persian court. Perhaps it is Mordecai himself who is said in the text to have recorded all these events (*Esther* 9, 20).

The Books of the Maccabees

The martyr brothers

The holy war

Faced with a dominant Greek culture, the Maccabees brothers establish Judaism.

The two *Books of the Maccabees* are very different from each other: the first is as political as the second is religious; the one records history, the other seeks to move and persuade; finally, the one is based essentially on the Law which gives Judaism its character, while the other centres its arguments on the worship offered to Yahweh at the Temple. However, the two books do, in part, tell the same story, one which goes from the reign of Antiochus IV (175–164 BC) to the death of Simon, the last of the brothers of Judas Maccabaeus.

The surname Maccabaeus, which means 'hammer', was first given to Judas, the eldest son of Mattathias, and then it was borne by each of his brothers as they succeeded him in the defence of Judaism. In the end it became the name by which all those martyred in the resistance against Hellenism (the domination of Greek culture) at that time were known.

First Book of the Maccabees

Mattathias, the head of the Asmonean dynasty, gave the signal for the resistance to Hellenism as personified by Alexander. It should be stated that Antiochus Epiphanes, Alexander's successor, had wasted no time: he had introduced Greek customs into the Holy City, he had pillaged the Temple, devastated the town, committed sacrilege in the holy place, and finally forbidden the practices of Jewish Law, circumcision, observance of the Sabbath, and all festivals.

Mattathias responded to this by killing a renegade Jew on the altar. That was the start of the revolt and, when some faithful Jews allowed themselves to be killed on the Sabbath out of respect for the Law, it was decided that from then on that would not happen again and literal observation of the Law must come after the lives of those who observe it. Mattathias died, leaving Judas as his successor.

Judas was a war leader: he knew how to train troops, galvanize them into action and lead them to victory. He beat the Syrian armies, which opened the gates of Jerusalem for him, he purified the Temple and re-established worship. So wreathed in glory, he went from victory to victory, in Galilee, in Gilead, in Idumaea, and Philistia and to the furthest extent of the land to defend his persecuted compatriots. The reprisals were terrible, he died in a desperate battle at Elasa, but his great feats will always be commemorated in Jewish festivals.

Jonathan was a diplomat. With him there were no battle lines, no dazzling victories, but rather effective and timely skirmishes, and particularly diplomatic successes on a large scale. He profited from the rivalry between Demetrius and Alexander Balas,

---

In praise of Simon

'He brought supplies to the cities and fortified them so well that his fame spread to the ends of the earth. He brought peace to the land and Israel knew great rejoicing. Each man sat under his vine or his fig tree and there was no one to trouble him. Whoever fought him in the land disappeared and in those days kings were defeated. He strengthened all the lowly people, and put down the evil and ungodly. He observed the Law, worshipped at the Temple and enriched it with numerous vessels.' (*I Maccabees* 14, 10–15)

each seeking to be made the supreme authority. When Demetrius prevailed, his brother Simon was declared strategist in the neighbouring province. So Judas's brothers became officers of Epiphanes's successors. He took advantage of this in order to strengthen Jewish power by ringing the whole country with fortified places. However, this skilful diplomat was trapped by the ambitious Trypho, who put him to death.

Simon was a statesman. He consolidated the situation left by his brothers, drove Trypho out of the country, re-established links with Demetrius II, secured the surrender of the last pockets of resistance to Jewish sovereignty, and had himself recognized as ethnarque, or leader, of the Jews. He improved the links with Rome, Sparta, and Antioch and is considered to be the great liberator. The praises heaped on him have a messianic quality, treating him as saviour sent from God. He lived long enough to see evidence of the early successes of his son John, before dying during a banquet at the hands of a traitorous assassin.

The first *Book of the Maccabees* employs a sober, straightforward style. Only the speeches and prayers show the enthusiasm of the heroes who fought for the observance of the Law, imposing it by force if necessary. The victory of Judaism is the supreme aim and the only glory worth having is to die fighting, weapons in hand, for that cause.

Second Book of the Maccabees

The Second *Book of the Maccabees* has a totally different style. From the outset, the author makes it clear that he is simply translating and summarizing a work by a certain Jason of Cyrene with the aim of encouraging the people to celebrate the dedication of the Temple in a manner worthy of the memory of those who gave their lives for this cause.

The Temple was holy and inviolable, and governed by a high priest as pious as Onias, and when Heliodorus was going to desecrate it, angels appeared to demonstrate the sacred character of the place and punish the ungodly man. But a great many intrigues grew up around the supreme pontificat or authority and those in responsible positions began to think only of themselves and so the Temple was violated, Hellenization was introduced into the holy of holies and a new wave of persecution broke out. The author mentions the martyrs: Eleazar, the seven brothers, and others.

God's anger changed to mercy. Judas Maccabaeus, with his robust intervention, drove out the pagans, punished the violators of the Temple and returned it to its former purity. Then he carried on the fight on all fronts. Liberty of worship was proclaimed everywhere, and the rebellions of Alcimus, who wanted to seize the supreme pontificate for himself, and the blasphemies of Nicanor, head of the royal armies, mattered little. Judas was there to fight them and kill them. Every year there is a festival in memory of these victories.

This book is a plea on behalf of the defence. The style is rather grand and mannered. It is striking in its aggression, its violent expressions, and exaggeration of the facts. It is the work of a believer: God controls the world, nothing escapes him, miracles and the resurrection of the dead are his doing; there is nothing God cannot do in the cause of justice.

The martyrdom of the seven brothers

'When the first one had died in this way, the second was brought for execution. After stripping the skin from his head, hair and all, they asked him: "Will you eat pork before your body is tortured limb by limb?" He replied in the language of his fathers, "No." That is why he too was subjected to the tortures in his turn. With his last breath he said: "Villain that you are, you deny us this present life, but the king of the world will make us rise to an eternal life, we who die for his laws."' (*II Maccabees 7*, 7–9)

Job

The suffering of a just man

The mystery of evil and suffering

A just man's unshakeable faithfulness to God despite suffering and misfortune.

Why do the just suffer and the evil prosper? That is a question which is asked in every age and which is more acutely felt where the moral code is well developed and exacting. At the time of the patriarchs the consequences of good and evil were seen collectively, and the liberation from Egypt, the return to the Promised Land and military success etc served to obscure the problem of rewards and punishments. But when, especially in the time of the prophets, the question of being punished for faults was considered, it was done on an individual basis and from an earthly standpoint and that is where the reality of everyday life seemed to contradict the law. A short story, the book of *Job* describes the contradictions the just man encounters in life.

Being put to the test

Job was a good and happy man: he feared God and avoided evil. His family was thriving: he had seven sons and three daughters. His lands were flourishing: he had 7000 sheep, 3000 camels, and 500 pairs of oxen. He was an important figure in the Eastern world.

In heaven God was proud of Job's faithfulness and said so. Satan scoffed: 'Rest assured, it is not for nothing. It is easy to be faithful when one is rich and happy.' God took up the challenge and authorized Satan to attack Job, first of all in the matter of his goods and his family, then in his body and his bones. So with one blow after an-

other the poor man lost his animals, his servants, his sons, and his daughters, then a malignant ulcer developed on his body, covering him from head to toe. He sat among the ashes and said 'When God sends us something good, we welcome it. How can we complain when he sends us trouble?' (*Job* 2, 10).

The friends

Three friends, who heard about his distress, decided to go and comfort him. They sat down on the ground near to him and stayed for seven days and seven nights without saying anything. When Job cried out, Eliphaz of Teman, the oldest, and perhaps the wisest of them replied. He did not want to offend Job and hedged round things very carefully, making use of a furtive revelation to remind him of the teaching: 'Good is rewarded and evil is punished', and advised Job to ask for pardon and God would heal his wounds. In the face of such gentle reproaches Job remained calm and asked for one thing only, that his innocence should not be in any doubt.

Job's complaint

'Month after month I have nothing to live for; night after night brings me grief. When I lie down to sleep the hours drag; I toss all night and long for dawn. My body is full of worms; it is covered with scabs; pus runs out of my sores. My days pass without hope, pass faster than a weaver's shuttle. Remember, O God, my life is only a breath; my happiness has already ended. You see me now, but never again. If you look for me, I'll be gone. Like a cloud that fades and is gone, a man dies and never returns.' (*Job* 7, 3–9)

Bildad of Shuah was a strict master. He spoke like a teacher, with well constructed arguments and points to illustrate them. So, dispensing with the precautions thought necessary by Eliphaz of Teman, he went right to the point: 'No, God does not reject a righteous man' and if he has rejected you, he has his reasons. He added, 'It is one of history's abiding truths.' Faced with such a thinly veiled accusation Job reacted. He knew that his conscience was clear, and stressed that fact while not denying this particular doctrine. Who was right?

These conversations shocked young Zophar. It all seemed very clear to him: God was wise and just, he would not send misfortune on the just. Job has sinned since he was in such trouble, he should return to righteousness and then things would go well for him once more. That was going too far. Job could not bear the rigidity of this inexperienced young man. He spoke about how he understood things to be. He knew very well that evil people were often happy and good people unhappy: that was obvious to all. He could conclude from that that there was no justice, but he did not take that view, and so sustained by his unshakeable faith, he appealed to God for justice.

Eliphaz took this as a show of pride, Bildad as obstinacy, and Zophar found it insulting. Job no longer replied except in a tone of irony. The insults did not affect him. He was not discouraged by the fact

> ## Words of Yahweh
>
> 'Who are you to question my wisdom with your ignorant empty words? Stand up now like a man and answer the questions I ask you. Were you there when I made the world? If you know so much, tell me about it. Who decided how large it would be? Who stretched the measuring line over it? Do you know all the answers? What holds up the pillars that support the earth? Who laid the corner stone of the world? In the dawn of the day the stars sang together, and the heavenly beings shouted for joy. Who closed the gates to hold back the sea when it burst from the womb of the earth?' (*Job* 38, 2–8)

that God was taking a long time to dispense his justice. A newcomer to the debate, Elihu stressed the educational value of suffering. God tested men like gold in the fire. Misfortune was intended to cleanse man, lest unalloyed happiness be tainted with pride. Job was no longer listening to these speeches which explained nothing. He turned all his attention to God and made his case before him alone.

Yahweh's response

God spoke at last, but he spoke as a god, out of the centre of the storm, proclaiming the power that was his alone, and the wonders he had performed: the creation of the world, the life of nature and the history of humankind, the glory exhibited in his appearances to men. He said to Job 'Have you ever in all your life commanded a day to dawn?' Then he concluded: 'Job, you challenged Almighty God; will you give up now or will you answer?' — 'I spoke foolishly' Job admitted.

Yahweh went on to say: 'Answer my questions, are you trying to prove that I am unjust — to put me in the wrong and yourself in the right?' Skilfully employing an irony close to sarcasm, he suggested that he overturn his judgment, take over the running of the world, make his voice heard, bring down the proud, and crush the wicked. Job's reply was 'I talked about things I did not understand ... I am so ashamed of all I have said and repent in dust and ashes' (*Job* 42, 3–6). Finally, Yahweh made Job prosperous and happy again.

The book of Job

The book of *Job* was written by an anonymous Israelite poet around the 5th century BC, no doubt based on an Edomite model. Didactic in tone, it marks one stage in the development of the doctrine of retribution: for him suffering is not necessarily a punishment for sin. God is not an automatic dispenser of sanctions and in the end the good man's devotion to his faith is not motivated by self-interest nor dependent on the promise of rewards.

The Psalms

The religious songs of Israel

Praise

Prayers springing from the religious spirit of the people and gradually inserted into the official liturgy.

One particular literary genre has emerged from the depths of the Hebrew people's history: the psalms. They originated in the religious devotion of the people, spread throughout the tribes and have gradually taken their place in the official liturgy. For a long time they had a very fluid existence, following events as they unfolded, adapting to the developing institutions and changing religious concepts. They were overlaid by new ideas, and restructured according to the fashions of the day. Style and content were transformed by new methods of thought: spontaneous, sensitive, and sometimes passionate in the time of the prophets; high-flown, solemn, and impersonal with the establishment of the monarchy; systemized and ritualized with the Judaism of the rabbis.

The psalms therefore developed by stages and they retained traces of their constant adaptation to circumstances. But gradually the circumstances which originally inspired them became blurred with the passage of time and lost their significance. Eventually the community found itself in possession of an official body of prayers which no one had the authority to alter, either by additions or deletions: the psalter, the Book of Psalms, was born.

The *Psalms* should be looked at as a whole, for as such they can be seen to embody the formation, the survival, and the fruition of the life of Israel. They have

nurtured its thought, fed its acts, and sustained its feelings, carrying within them the past, present, and future. Each individual psalm may lose something of its identity through being viewed this way, but will gain a better sense of the historical context out of which it was born. No doubt it marks a point in time and a particular context, and expresses a particular view of things, but, more importantly, it is also part of a greater line of development and a more complex whole.

The psalter as it has come down to us must have been the more or less official collection of religious songs used in Jerusalem at the time of the second Temple in the 6th century BC: there are clear references to pilgrimages (*Psalm* 122), processions (*Psalm* 132), prostrations (*Psalm* 95), rituals, supplications, and prayers of every kind. From that time until the present day, the *Psalms* have been the main framework for the religious observances of both Judaism and Christianity.

A poetic form

The psalm is a poem. Its rhythm, its tones and occasionally its rhymes distinguish it

---

Prayer of the persecuted

'Oppose those who oppose me Lord and fight those who fight against me.' Take your shield and armour, and come to my rescue. Lift up your spear and your axe against those who pursue me. Promise that you will save me. May those who try to kill me be defeated and disgraced! May those who plot against me be turned back and confused. May they be like straw blown by the wind as the angel of the Lord pursues them. May their path be dark and slippery while the angel of the Lord strikes them down.' (*Psalm* 35, 1–6)

---

from ordinary language. It has been polished like a diamond, worked on by generations of worshippers who have expressed within it their conflicts, hopes, and feelings. The psalm is like a treasure house into which the nation gathers all that it holds most dear for safekeeping.

A number of literary devices are used in the *Psalms*: the acrostic in *Psalm* 19 where each verse begins with a different letter of the Hebrew alphabet; the repetition of a sentence, phrase or word in the body of a poem; the refrain or regular appearance of one, two or three verses; the inclusion or repetition of the same expressions at the beginning and end of a section; the use of parallel words or ideas; the division into stanzas etc.

The psalms often appear with musical footnotes. The very word psalm means 'tune played on a stringed instrument'; and there were specialized artists in Israel: the *Book of Chronicles* speaks of the sons of Asaph, Heman, and Yedutum as cantors (singers who lead public worship), and describes their calling as being as honourable as that of the prophets.

Literary styles

The canonical book of the *Psalms* consists of 150 items. They are grouped in five sections of unequal size and have two systems of numbering, one according to the

---

The work performed by Yahweh

'When the people of Israel left Egypt, when Jacob's descendants left that foreign land, Judah became the Lord's holy people, Israel became his own possession. The Red Sea looked and ran away; the River Jordan stopped flowing. The mountains skipped like goats; the hills jumped about like lambs. What happened, Sea, to make you run away? And you, O Jordan, why did you stop flowing? You mountains, why did you skip like goats? You hills, why did you jump about like lambs? Tremble, earth, at the Lord's coming, at the presence of God of Jacob, who changes rocks into pools of water and solid cliffs into springs.' (*Psalm* 114, 1–8)

Jewish tradition and the other, which is the one used here, according to the Christian tradition which follows the order of the Greek version of the Septuagint. The unity of the sections and sometimes even of the psalms themselves are often arbitrary: for example, the lines of *Psalm* 19 do not all have the same rhythm. It is possible, however, to group them according to their different styles.

The hymns express praise. They are characterized by a detached tone. Here there is no plea and no soul searching, everything is directed towards Yahweh and his glory. They speak of God the creator, the protector of the weak. After an invitation to praise Yahweh, the text develops the reasons for this praise and then ends with a brief conclusion which is a blessing, a vow or a prayer.

A distinction can be made between the cosmic and the historical hymns. The first of these are addressed to God the creator and master of heaven and earth: the themes evoked are the beauty of nature, its organization and fruitfulness. The finest example is found, without doubt in *Psalm* 104. The historical hymns celebrate God in the story of Israel. They recount his mighty deeds on behalf of his chosen people, or of men in general. Sometimes they give long descriptions of historical events in mainly narrative passages, as in *Psalms* 105 and 106.

The supplications, or lamentations as they are sometimes called, are appeals to God to favour those who call upon him. They may be collective, or individual, but even in the case of individual appeals, they can be taken as representing a collective supplicant, namely the people of Israel. Their construction is similar to that of the hymns with an introduction, a development, and a conclusion, but the matters for praise are replaced by a description of the ills of the supplicant. The aim is obviously to get Yahweh to intervene on their behalf and he is asked very directly to: 'Rouse yourself ... come to our aid' (*Psalm* 44, 23 and 26).

Within the group of psalms called supplications is a sub-group of penitential psalms. Some of these, like the *De Profundis* (*Psalm* 130) and the *Misere* (*Psalm* 51) have had a particular resonance throughout history, because of their frequent use in the liturgy.

These psalms are appeals for divine mercy and are very movingly inspired. They emphasize the sin committed and the pardon sought, imploring the help of the Almighty: 'Create a pure heart in me, O God, and put a new and loyal spirit in me'; certain of being heard, they promise thankfulness.

The psalms of thanksgiving make up another section. Some concern the whole community expressing gratitude after a victory, some express the individual thanks and praise of an unfortunate person who has been saved from disaster or a sinner who has been forgiven. In these psalms there is a good deal of narrative writing. There is an account of the misfortunes that have befallen the author and a description of how God acts to save him.

Finally there are the royal psalms which were written for ceremonies such as enthronements and anniversaries. Although more worldly they are barely distinguishable from the others, both types being sung by the same singers, at court as well as in the sanctuary. Mention is sometimes made of the psalms of David, or to David (addressed to David). This is of little importance, this David is much more the bearer of their messianic hopes than their actual historical leader.

Apart from these large groupings we have

In praise of the good person

'Happy is the person who honours the Lord, who takes pleasure in obeying his commands. The good man's children will be powerful in the land; his descendants will be blessed. His family will be wealthy and rich, and he will be properous for ever.' (*Psalm* 112, 1–3)

mentioned, there are also psalms which are didactic, philosophical, prophetic, or relate to the final struggle between good and evil etc. There are other biblical passages which should be associated with the psalter, such as the son of Moses (*Exodus* 15), the song of Anne (*I Samuel* 2), the song of Hezekiah (*Isaiah* 38, 10–20), the hymns of *Isaiah* (24–7), the song of Habakkuk (*Habakkuk* 3), the hymn of the three young men (*David* 3, 52–8), the psalms of *Ecclesiastes* (3, 1–8), and certain of Jeremiah's 'Lamentations': all these concern the experience of a dialogue with God.

The Psalms of Solomon

The second book of *Psalms* is wrongly attributed to King Solomon, but perhaps might there not have been another Solomon who could have been the author of this book? It is usually dated during the time of Pompey, and the invader described in the text seems to correspond quite well with what we know about this Roman consul from the historian, Plutarch. It has actually been claimed that Plutarch's writings are the best commentary on these psalms. The book probably originates from within the Pharisee or Essene culture — an opinion based on the doctrine expressed in it: belief in the Resurrection (*Psalms* 3) — it states that the righteous will rise to eternal life while sinners will be destroyed for all time — and faith in the wise and just Messiah descended from David who will triumph over the unjust princes (*Psalm* 18, 24), purify Israel and destroy the nations with a word from his mouth: and ideal king. This concept seems to lie halfway between that of the Old Testament and that of the superterrestrial Messiah.

The Book of Proverbs

Thoughts on everyday life

The art of proper behaviour

The prehistory of our attitudes and approaches to things, men, and societies, revealed through sayings, maxims, and observations.

Surely there can be no social grouping which has not served as a vehicle for all kinds of maxims, sayings, adages, and proverbs. Israel was no exception and indeed the whole of the Middle East was known for this kind of wisdom. That, at least, was the opinion of the Greeks who came to seek wise men. This kind of literature is found in Egypt, in the advice prepared for Ka-Gemni, son of a vizier of King Ouni (3rd millenium BC), for Meri-Ka-Re, son of Kheti, ruler of Herakleopolis (c. 2000 BC), for Sesostris, son of Amen-em-hat I (c. 2000 BC) etc. There are other examples from Mesopotamia, Sumer, and Assyria. Excavations at Ras-Shamra, in Syria, have even revealed the name of a Phoenician sage, Danel.

It is a short step from there to the conclusion, which many have unhesitatingly drawn, that a number of schools of learning existed in the Mediterranean area. Egyptian scribes were well known and certain passages in *Proverbs* are called the words of Agur, the words of Lemuel, and especially the words of Solomon. For wisdom is seen as a particularly royal attribute. David's son, who marks the high point of the kingdom was evidently well provided with it: 'He composed 3000 proverbs ... he spoke of plants ... animals, birds, reptiles, and fish. Kings all over the world heard of his wisdom and sent people to listen to him' (*I Kings* 4, 32–4).

The *Book of Proverbs* actually covers several centuries of the nation's life in its period of conception. It is the product of a slow process of maturing, during which a number of observations, comparisons, and reflections came together: expressions were formulated, clarified, and refined; some were dropped, while others, through repetition and through being seen to reflect reality, gained strength and established themselves as essential items in the work. This long process of ripening must have remained oral in form during the whole of the nation's nomadic and semi-nomadic periods, with the collection of proverbs being put in written form only with the establishment of the monarchy.

The structure of the book

Although these proverbs said to be by Solomon constitute the basis of the work, both in terms of quantity and of history, it still cannot be said to have a well defined structure or any real uniformity of style. Instead it consists of a collection of small essays of wisdom, in amongst which numerous sayings and proverbs are scattered, without any clear objective. There are different types of proverbs: instructions, alphabetical

---

Comparisons

A Babylonian saying states: 'Do not act badly towards someone who has a dispute with you; pay back anyone who has done you wrong with goodness; treat your enemy justly.' (*Babylonian Wisdom Literature*, M G Lambert, Oxford, 1960)

The *Proverbs* say: 'If you repay good with evil, you will never get evil out of your house.' (17, 13)

---

poems, maxims, descriptions, portraits, tales etc.

Perhaps the underlying unity of the work can be seen in their expression of faith in Yahweh. In fact, without departing from a universal wisdom which was probably common to the whole of the Middle East, it gives its own thinking and the two versions of the one theme can often be found side by side. So we have 'Better to eat vegetables with people you love than to eat the finest meat where there is hate' (*Proverbs* 15, 17), which in the Israelite sage's version becomes 'Better to be poor and fear the Lord than to be rich and in trouble' (*Proverbs* 15, 16).

Sometimes indeed, wisdom (presumably human) is compared with the religion of Yahweh: so that 'The teachings of the wise are a fountain of life; they will help you escape when your life is in danger' (*Proverbs* 13, 14) becomes for our writer 'Do you want to avoid death? Reverence for the Lord is a fountain of life' (*Proverbs* 14, 27). This rewriting of maxims and perhaps even the reworking of certain ideas does seem rather odd in a book whose aim is to celebrate wisdom.

Advice

Wisdom is in fact the main subject. Advice comes thick and fast: observe the Law, be neither greedy nor overindulgent, be just and fair, do not trust liars, be faithful in friendship, practise charity and the forgiveness of wrongs, do not renounce a woman for her youth and do not approach foreign women, be firm with servants but do not leave them in need; finally, do not trust in promises and fear God.

The lazy man

'Lazy people should learn a lesson from the way ants live. They have no leader, chief or ruler, but they store up their food during the summer, getting ready for winter. How long is the lazy man going to lie in bed? When is he ever going to get up? "I'll just take a short nap", he says, "I'll fold my hands and rest a while." But while he sleeps poverty will attack him like an armed robber.'
(*Proverbs* 6, 6–11)

The speech often takes on an antithetical form, a style of writing which contrasts a series of opposites: good men observe the Law, do not fear for their safety and enjoy great happiness, for they will have power, whereas evil men are unscrupulous, opposed to religion, agitators or criminals, and will be defeated; wise men are intelligent, learned, and full of good sense, their fathers are proud of them and they are a credit to society, whereas fools are crazy, they are scoffers, who lead debauched and worthless lives; the rich are men whose paths are devious and whose methods are shameful, their appetites are insatiable, they are dazzled by their desires and oppress others, whereas the poor are virtuous and reserved.

Lady Wisdom

The antithesis continues with the personification of wisdom and folly. The first brings assurance of power to the king, consideration to the servant, wealth to the worker, and honour to the humble. In contrast, the second brings insecurity, lying and vanity, it leads to distractions, disputes, anger and fighting, it produces nothing but misfortune.

But the *Book of Proverbs* goes much further. Wisdom has a house with seven pillars and servants to command. She has authority over the city and speaks in her own name. She appears as a mother who welcomes her children, she is sister, confidante, wife, most dearly beloved. She is God's eldest daughter and was there when God 'set the sky in place', when 'he ordered the seas to rise no further than he said', when he laid the foundations of the earth. She was at his side 'like an architect' (*Proverbs* 8, 27–31).

The goddess Maat in Egyptian theology seems to play more or less the same role. As daughter to Ra she has existed since the dawn of the universe, attending to the balance of everything and the harmonious relationships between creatures; she authenticates the actions of authority and ensures that individual lives progress well. She is justice and truth and the standard against which all behaviour is measured. The Egyptian Maat is the Israelite Wisdom, the one difference being that the latter has never been deified.

Nevertheless, it is described as a woman, with all that the words imply in terms of cleverness, gentleness, and tenderness, and the relationship between man and wisdom is treated as an amorous, not to say passionate, union: 'So be happy with your wife and find your joy with the girl you married — pretty and graceful as a deer. Let her charms keep you happy; let her surround you with her love' (*Proverbs* 4, 18–19).

The capable wife

The book ends with a portrait of the ideal wife (often called the strong woman of the Gospel), and through her, of a good middle class family, the husband is well thought of, he sits at the city gate with the elders; the children respect their mother and do not go around with gangs of hooligans; their domestic affairs are well run and the home is well cared for. This happy situation is due to the active, hard-working wife.

Is this a picture of wisdom personified or the description of a woman in love with wisdom? We cannot know for sure, but the fact remains that this is an instance where the praises of a woman are sung, a rare thing in that area and at that time, where man was the usual point of reference, for it was to him that everything was addressed and on him that everything depended.

The woman is rich in resources. She faces up to work and excites the admiration of men. She is a housewife without equal. She is virtuous, generous, and full of common sense: she has all the skills and know-how that she needs. She is a good mother, she is active and a good manager; she is gentle with the children and firm with the servants. Lastly, and this is the supreme compliment, her husband gives her credit for all that she does, proclaiming her virtues at the city gate.

The strong woman

'How hard it is to find a capable wife! She is worth far more than jewels! Her husband puts his confidence in her and he will never be poor. As long as she lives, she does him good and never harm. She keeps herself busy making wool and linen cloth. She brings home food from out of the way places as merchant ships do. She gets up before daylight to prepare food for her family and to tell her servant girls what to do. She looks at land and buys it and with money she has earned and plants a vineyard. She is a hard worker, strong and industrious. She knows the value of everything she makes ...'
(*Proverbs* 31, 10–18)

Influence

It is through the *Proverbs* in particular that Solomon, the king who had knowledge, who knew how to act with skill and cunning, and who had profited from the joys of life, became the symbol of wisdom. Although not much commented on by the Fathers of the Church, in the Middle Ages the book became an essential reference work for rabbinical schools, for mystical gnostic sects, and even for certain Muslim movements. A number of authors, particularly Spaniards, tried to write in the same literary style: we have the proverbs of Rabbi Sem Tob, in the 14th century, and the marquis of Santillana made a breviary, a religious book, from them for the Crown prince in 1437.

Ecclesiastes

Qoheleth, the preacher

The master of wisdom

*Is life worth the trouble
of living it?*

The *Book of Ecclesiastes* seems a little out of place in the Old Testament; it contains an invitation to earthly pleasures and a certain epicurism or over-indulgence of the flesh which is not at all the kind of attitude we expect from the Bible. Job had shown that the important thing was not based on what one experienced but on how one came through a sea of troubles. But what attitude should one take when things are going well?

After Job on his dung hill comes Solomon in his golden palace. For literary tradition insits that these are the words of Solomon, wisest of the wise, although the ideas contained in the book have obvious connections with the books of wisdom from Assyria and Babylon (*Dialogue of the master and servant*) and those from Egypt (*Song of the blind harpist*), and with the thinking of Greek authors (Theognis of Megara, Heraclitus, and Epicurus): all works of the Hellenist period around the 3rd century BC, long after Solomon's time.

According to the book, the great king has tried everything: he explored wisdom and knowledge, stupidity and folly, he tried pleasure, laughter, and drunkenness, he built palaces, planted vines, gardens, and orchards, and amassed silver and gold. He denied himself none of life's pleasures and cried out: 'It was like chasing the wind — of no use at all' (*Ecclesiastes* 2, 11).

When he speaks of wealth, he describes the lure of money, the desire it awakens, the appearance of scroungers, the sleepless nights and endless worries of the man of property.

The author's attitude is extremely pessimistic and he declares: 'So life came to mean nothing to me, because everything in it had brought me nothing but trouble' (*Ecclesiastes* 2, 17). However, he immediately adds a slight but significant shift of emphasis which is also characteristic of the work: 'The best thing a man can do is to eat and drink, and enjoy what he has earned' (*Ecclesiastes* 2, 24). Everything comes from God and it would be an insult to him to refuse what he has given, for he gives to whom he pleases and takes away from whom he chooses: the only happiness for man is to rejoice in his works.

The book has a few key ideas which are seen throughout: firstly to keep oneself from all forms of excess, in knowledge, pleasure, work, riches, and even in wisdom: 'So don't be too good or too wise' (*Ecclesiastes* 7, 16).

The second main idea is that God is in charge of events. Enjoyment of the good things of this life must not exclude reverence and the fear of God: 'If you obey God everything will be all right, but it will not go well for the wicked' (*Ecclesiastes* 8, 12).

> **Time**
> 'Everything that happens in this world happens at the time God chooses. He sets the time for birth and the time for death, the time for planting and the time for pulling up, the time for killing and the time for healing, the time for tearing down and the time for building. He sets the time for sorrow and the time for joy, the time for mourning and the time for dancing, the time for making love and the time for not making love, the time for kissing and the time for not kissing. He sets the time for finding and the time for losing, the time for saving and the time for throwing away, the time for tearing and the time for mending, the time for silence and the time for talk. He sets the time for love and the time for hate, the time for war and the time for peace.'
> (*Ecclesiastes* 3, 1–8)

The Song of Songs

Shir Ha-Shirim

A love song

A hymn of God's love for his people and the people's love for their God.

Around the 4th and 5th centuries BC, the Hebrews, returning from the exile in Babylon were living under the supremacy of the Achaeminid Persians. They cherished the memory of the great era of King David and King Solomon when their nation had dominated the whole of the Near East. They rebuilt the Temple, the centre of their religious life and symbol of their unity, and gave the land a period of great material prosperity. This was a peaceful time, during which the Jewish religion established its permanent institutions: the Hebrews absorbed the many experiences of their turbulent past. Their slavery in Egypt, their deportation to Babylon, their disagreements, their battles, the appeals of the prophets, and the betrayals of every kind were sharp and constant memories, but these experiences had given them a certain maturity and they were now ready for a new beginning.

The wedding 'weeks'

There is no doubt at all that the general attitude would favour feasting and emotional gatherings. This was also the way things were done in the surrounding countries. The wedding 'weeks', which are still traditional in Syria today, were the common practice. For a week, a fortnight or even three weeks, the betrothed couple, acting separately, would each invite their friends to joyful lively gatherings. The patriarch Jacob did the same thing when he

married Rachel (*Genesis* 29, 27), 'for this was a custom among the young men' (*Judges* 14, 10).

There would be a lot of singing, from popular songs, which could sometimes be a little rude, to the tenderest of poems; there was a huge range of this type of literature. The Syrian wassf (*wassf* means 'description') provides us with one example. The particular feature of these love songs was to link nature with the happiness of the lovers: the description of the young people's charms was compared to the beauty of the plants and the future fruitfulness of the union to the fertility of the soil.

These love songs were real marriage blessings which sometimes aspired to the religious level. They included incantations, spells, and love potions. Some of the Egyptian songs described all the stages of passion: love sickness, fondness, the strength of affection, happiness, jealousy, and even anger. The work of the gods was seen in this development of the emotions.

Egyptian love song

'To go away to the fields is delightful for he who is loved. The voice of the teal protests at having been taken by the lure, I cannot free myself from your love which has captured me.' (*Love Songs of ancient Egypt*, S Schott)

'The great entertainer'

A woman was the author of the love songs in the Chester Beatty I papyrus which came from Thebes and is now in the British Museum. It was also a woman who directed the dramatic productions shown on the bas-relief of El-Armana. It seems that women often played a key role in these sorts of festivities.

Standing as it did at the crossroads of the Eastern nations, Israel was familiar with these wedding songs. *Psalm* 45 celebrates the wedding of a king and a princess: 'You are the most handsome of men; you are an eloquent speaker. God has always blessed you' (v2). The *Song of Songs* is written in the same vein.

Solomon's 'Album of songs'

Solomon had a great reputation for wisdom and this work has also been attributed to him. However, there are some scholars who see this simply as a collection of poems on love and marriage gathered from various sources. But whether it is divided into five, six or seven songs (someone has even found it to contain 23), the whole thing is inspired by one single intention: the celebration by the lovers of each other, their physical charms, their mutual love, and their touching encounter.

The text is poetic: each word, each expression, each verse, echoes like a melody. The young girl's words are like a musical theme, soft like a whispered desire, then becoming more definite, they finally assert themselves quite openly like a soaring violin note. Those of her young man are more strident, they do not hesitate and proclaim the power of love loud and clear, like a trumpet call. Finally, the choirs attracted by this idyll are bewitched by the couple's harmony: they provide the orchestral backing.

The unfolding of the *Song of Songs* can be summarized as follows (*La Bible de Jérusalem* (The Bible of Jerusalem), A Robet, Paris, 1955): the first poem expresses the wonder the couple feel, each for the other; it is like a thunderbolt. But, 'Promise me, women of Jerusalem, that you will not interupt our love' (2, 7). The second describes how they sought each other: 'I was looking for him but couldn't find him' (3, 1). The third is the man's cry from the heart; he uses all his seductive skills and proclaims his love passionately: 'How beautiful you are, my love; how perfect you are' (4, 7). The fourth is the woman's sorrowful wait, a mixture of hesitation and the expression of her very intense feelings: 'I am weak from passion' (5, 8). The fifth brings the long awaited

meeting and each of the two lovers praises the beauty of the other: 'How pretty you are, how beautiful; how complete the delights of your love' (7, 6).

Several short poems or one long one? In the end it doesn't really matter. However, the man is sometimes seen as a shepherd, sometimes as a king (Solomon). If we are dealing here with different poems there is no problem: the name of the beloved changes from one song to another and that is all. On the other hand, if we are dealing with one poem, either it is a poem in the pastoral style where the king is symbolically depicted as a shepherd and his beloved as a shepherdess, or it is a story with three characters in which the love of the shepherd comes up against the king's attempts at seduction (*Le Cantique des cantiques* (The Song of Songs), G Pouget and J Guitton, Paris, 1934).

A drama

We are at the theatre. All the dramatic elements are there: dialogues, discussions, lyrical songs. The action is based on a case of conscience, a vital question, the choice of a marriage partner. It is simple and progresses easily, from the initial situation where the two men, the king, and the shepherd have equal chances, to the final outcome where the woman chooses happiness and fidelity.

A shepherd or Solomon himself?

'Tell me, my love, where will you lead your flock to graze? Where will they rest from the noonday sun? Why should I need to look for you among the flocks of the other shepherds? Don't you know the place, loveliest of women? Go and follow the flock and find pasture for your goats.' (1, 7–8)

The Sulamite

The Sulamite is the name given to the beloved woman by King Solomon: it is a title which could be seen as a compliment, but perhaps not. It would mean that she had been pacified with reference to Solomon, whose history and reign are traditionally linked with peace.

162

At the beginning the young woman is in the king's harem singing about her love. The king enters and makes advances to her. The Sulamite (as the young woman is called) dare not tell him that she loves another and she replies to all the king's declarations of love by affirming her love for her 'well-beloved', without making it clear who he is. He then appears and sees her alone in the confines of the harem. She tells him of her love in a song but she is worried and begs him to leave. The stage is set for the drama.

In the second act the daughters of Jerusalem, other ladies of the harem, arrive. The Sulamite pretends she has been dreaming. In order to convince her of his love, the king displays all his power and wealth. The daughters of Jerusalem exclaim in admiration: 'come and see King Solomon. He is wearing the crown that his mother placed on his head on his wedding day, on the day of his gladness and joy' (3, 11). The king renews his vows of love.

The shepherd has seen everything. In the third act he takes advantage of his rival's departure and, fearing that the king may have touched the woman's heart, he makes his most passionate declaration 'The look in your eyes, my sweetheart and bride ... has stolen my heart' (4, 9). The Sulamite is moved and she confirms her love openly. The women of Jerusalem want to know who inspires a love like this.

The king returns. His demands are more pressing and his promises more specific: 'She is her mother's only daughter, her mother's favourite child. All women look at her and praise her; queens and concubines

sing her praises' (6, 9). But the Sulamite is unmoved: 'I belong to my lover and he desires me' (7, 11).

Finally, we have the dénouement: the king releases the girl, not without some jealousy and regret, and the young lovers are reunited: 'Close your heart to every love but mine; hold no one in your arms but me. Love is as powerful as death' (8, 6).

A sacred book

Can a book celebrating human love in such a sensual style be included in the canon of Scripture? The Jews considered this question at the end of the first century AD. The rabbi Akiba ben Joseph (50–132) answered by saying 'No one in Israel has denied that the *Song* is a divine book; for it was a precious day when the *Song of Songs* was given to Israel (by God). All the books of Scripture are holy, but the *Song* is sacrosanct, sacred in the highest degree' (*Dictionnaire de spiritualité* (Dictionary of spirituality), Paris, 1932).

This traditional Jewish interpretation did not deter the Christian theologian Théodore de Mopsueste (350–428) from seeing in it simply the evocation of Solomon's marriage to the Pharaoh's daughter. Others regard it merely as the idyllic tale of a shepherd and his shepherdess or even as a satire on what went on at the king's court, a woman of the harem resisting the attentions of the sovereign. Théodore de Mopsueste's ideas were declared 'abominable to Christian ears' at the 5th ecumenical Council of Constantinople in 553.

The literal meaning

The text is therefore something other than a simple account of Solomon's love life or the love affair between a shepherd and a shepherdess. Is it not also a moral tale illustrating the duty to be faithful and the indissoluble nature of marriage: the young people are in this case linked together by their vow and withstand temptation as represented by the king. This view of the *Song* is rather deceptive. It seems to twist the meaning of the text which makes no mention of duty, it does not correspond to its flight of lyrical fancy and obscures the deep

---

The women of Jerusalem

They are the voice of the chorus in theatrical productions. They are generally considered to be either the women of the harem or symbols of the nations. In any case, theirs is merely a background role, they help us to see what is happening in the hearts of the main characters and give the Sulamite the opportunity to talk. Perhaps their words betray signs of the eternal curiosity of women and just a touch of jealousy. They represent good sense and are astounded that a shepherd could be preferred to a king.

'*How beautiful are your feet ... The curve of your thighs is like the work of an artist ... A sheaf of wheat is there surrounded by lilies. Your breasts are like twin deer, like two gazelles. Your neck is like a tower of ivory ... How pretty you are, how beautiful; how complete the delights of your love ...*'
(Song of Songs 7, 2–6)
Auguste Rodin: The Eternal Idol; plaster, 1890. Musée Rodin, Paris.

meaning of the work. This is what tradition teaches. Théodore's theories were condemned because they limited the understanding of the text to its literal meaning: the literal meaning is the one immediately understood in the phrases and descriptions, the natural and grammatical sense, the first sense of the word given in the dictionary. It is not the only interpretation a text may have.

The *Song of Songs* is a religious book and, like all religious books, it aims to uncover higher truths from simple, natural realities: the way is therefore open for various interpretations.

Interpretations

Judaism makes a parable of the *Song of Songs*: the young girl represents Israel, the beloved represents Yahweh. The poem expresses the strength of the bond of affection which unites the people with their God

The hymn to love
'Your lips cover me with kisses; your love is better than wine. There is a fragrance about you; the sound of your name recalls it. No woman could help loving you. Take me with you.' (1, 2–4)

and it includes references to the temptations, infidelities, and struggles which have punctuated the history of the chosen people. Its message is clear however: the tie which binds Yahweh to his people is as strong as love and that which binds the people to their God blossoms into love. The *Song* reveals the principle and the purpose of Yahweh's Covenant with Israel, the heart of Israel's religion. (*La Cantique d'après la tradition juive* (The Song according to Jewish tradition), E Vulliaud, Paris, 1925).

Christianity does the same thing. Only the terms of the parable are changed: the beloved is no longer simply Yahweh, but Jesus, the Son of God (is there really such a difference?), and the young girl is no longer simply Israel, but the whole Church. The *Song* expresses the nature of the relationship between God and man: it is neither indifference nor fear, but love and human love is the most vivid example we have of this love of God.

The passionate tones of the Sulamite lend themselves to a more personal interpretation. The Christian himself may make her words his own and experience an intensity of feeling towards the Lord which compares to that which she has for her beloved. he poem does bring love for God into sharp focus, drawing out its outward signs, and the things which hinder or enhance its growth. In his *Spiritual Song* St John of the Cross uses expressions which are very similar to the sacred text: "Where did you hide yourself, O beloved, and why did you leave me groaning? ... I came calling after you, and you had gone'.

Finally, who among all the believers had had a deeper relationship with Jesus than Mary, his mother? Mary is mother and in Christian mysticism she is also wife, and the simplicity of her love finds one of its expressions here. There are many interpretations along these lines. Denys le Chartreux (died 1471) gives a very full account of them in his *Enarratio in Canticum Cantorum Salomonis.*

Influence

There is no way of knowing exactly what influence the *Song of Songs* has had historically. It is one of the finest monuments to emerge from the Judaeo-Christian tradition and expresses the heart of its thinking. It is like a carefully preserved jewel, desired by all the believers and worthy only of the most mystical who know how to use it properly.

The missal and breviary (books of services used in the Catholic Church) often quote passages from the Song, applying them particularly to the Holy Virgin and the holy women.

The love of Israel and of Yahweh

'In the Ancient East the wife called the husband her baal. Basically she was simply a slave with privileges, the one the master had freely chosen to take out of servitude. And the sign of marriage was the ring, which recalled the tie with which a slave was bound. With the exodus from Egypt it was indeed a marriage covenant which was sealed between Yahweh and his people.' (*Le Cantique des cantiques* (The Song of Songs), G Pouget and J Guitton, Paris, 1934)

The Book of Wisdom

The Wisdom of Solomon

A new form of humanism

Where wisdom differentiates between the good and the evil both during their life and also in death.

The *Book of Wisdom*, also called the Wisdom of Solomon, has little to do with Israel's most glorious king. His name simply gives more authority to the work. It certainly appears to have been written in the century before Christ by an intellectual Jew who was keenly interested in Hellenism: it has the rigid structure, the methods of presentation and some of the ideas of Greek culture. It remains in the general orbit of the Old Testament. If we add that it was written in Greek, it will be understood that it is considered to be apocryphal by Jews and by Protestants.

The righteous and the ungodly

The Greek influence is noticeable right from the beginning of the text. The first part of the book takes the form of a diatribe, a debate between two factions. Two positions are stated and compared: on the one hand the opinions, life, and fate of the ungodly; and on the other hand, those of the righteous. The first say: life is short, in due course our names will be forgotten, there will be no one to set us free from hell: they enjoy their possessions, make use of other creatures and get drunk on fine wines: they summon death by gesture and by voice, waste away their lives and know nothing of God's mystery. The others believe in the rewards of a pure spirit; they are put to the test and found worthy of God; in the end they have eternal life. The apparent sterility

of the pure spirit is worth more than the legacy of the ungodly.

The book is addressed to young students living in the Jewish community in Alexandria who will one day be called to leadership roles in the community. Certain aspects of Greek philosophy such as Epicureanism, which held that physical and mental happiness should be the main aim in life, and stoicism, which is the endurance of hardship and pain without complaint, are examined and criticized. The writer's aim is to confirm his readers in their faith, to help them to see the positive side of their situation and to prepare them for their responsibilities. Solomon, the wisest and most brilliant of the kings of Israel, is therefore a good choice as presenter of the arguments.

In praise of Wisdom

The great king speaks in the second part of the book, talking to a gathering of kings as if he were the mentor of all the heads of state in the universe. He recounts his own experiences: he is simply a man like any other. Wisdom is, however, a gift which he

---

The discovery of Wisdom

'Wisdom is brilliant, she never fades. By those who love her, she is readily seen, by those who seek her she is readily found. She anticipates those who desire her by making herself known first. Whoever gets up early to seek her will have no trouble but will find her sitting at the door. Meditating on her is understanding in its perfect form and anyone keeping away for her will soon be free from care. For she herself searches everywhere for those who are worthy of her, benevolently appearing to them on their ways, anticipating their every thought.' *Wisdom* 6, 12–16)

---

received from God following a prayer, a gift he preferred to power, wealth, health, and beauty. It is worth more than all these other benefits because it can be used to gain them. It is an inexhaustible treasure for men and anyone who possesses it wins God's friendship.

Wisdom is understanding: it is a unity and yet has many facets, it is impassive yet penetrating, flexible yet firm. It teaches prudence and temperance, justice and courage. It knows past, present, and future, can decode puzzles and enigmas, and explain signs and wonders. It is a course of advice in times of good fortune and consolation in times of distress. It is a breath of divine power, a glimpse of God's glory, a reflection of his light. It is a mirror of his actions, springing from him and sharing his knowledge.

Solomon therefore calls upon the God who, through his Wisdom made man, ordered the world in holiness and administered justice. Without wisdom a man does not amount to much for he is incomplete. Without it, it is impossible to be in control or to discover what is in the heavens. It is the Holy Spirit which leads people on earth to follow the right paths, teaching them about what pleases God and gives salvation.

Some Christians have found, in this song of praise to a personified wisdom, a description of the logos, the word, the second person of the Trinity, and others a description of the Holy Spirit, the third person. Saint John and Saint Paul were both to use a formula modelled on this text when speaking about the Spirit. But the author of the *Book of Wisdom* had no such clearly defined or Christian notions of theology.

The works of Wisdom

The end of the book looks back over the role of Wisdom in the history of the world. No actual names are mentioned, but, for anyone with a knowledge of *Genesis* and *Exodus* the references are obvious: Wisdom guided all the patriarchs from Adam to Joseph, it kept physical and spiritual dangers away from them, and saved the chosen people, but those who did not know how to receive it were eliminated without hesitation, people like Cain or the inhabitants of Sodom and Gomorrah.

Next comes a long passage dedicated to God's people, whose trials serve to caution and improve them, whereas the trials visited on the ungodly destroy them. Yet God is seen to be merciful, even to the pagans. Only idolaters are held totally responsible for their misfortunes and the text explains the origins of idols through the worship of images of loved ones who had died prematurely, then by that of princes brought closer in the form of carved images and finally by the worship of images without reference to reality. This is a folly so great that it loses men the blessing God gives to all his creatures.

A humanism

Although the *Book of Wisdom* does not mention any of the earlier books of the Old Testament, it does take its direction from them, alluding to the history of Salvation and exploring the options within that. Certain themes have already been investigated: retribution in the life to come, the persecution of the righteous, the passionate search for Wisdom. However, it also sounds a Hellenistic note: the development of idolatry calls to mind Dionysus, manna recalls ambrosia and the search for Wisdom echoes the cult of Isis, already inspired by the Egyptian goddess Maat. If we add a few ideas borrowed from Greek logic we arrive at a harmonious blend which some have been quick to call humanism.

The origins of idolatry

'A father, afflicted by untimely mourning has an image made of his child so soon carried off, and now pays divine honours to what yesterday was only a corpse, handing on mysteries and ceremonies to his people; time passes, the custom hardens and is observed as law. Rulers were the ones who ordered that statues should be worshipped: people who could not honour them in person, because they lived too far away, would have a portrait made of their distant countenance, to have an image that they could see of the king whom they honoured; meaning, by such zeal, to flatter the absent as if he were present.' (*Wisdom* 14, 15–18)

Ecclesiasticus

The wisdom of Sira's son

Initiation into wisdom

Ecclesiasticus is one of the best testimonies of Jewish doctrine dating from just before the time of the Maccabees.

It is possibly called *Ecclesiasticus* because of the attention paid to the reading of it by the Christian Church. But the Jews have never recognized it as part of their canon, due no doubt to its relatively late publication. The book is introduced by the grandson of the author Sira who translated it into Greek for the Jews in Alexandria c. 132 BC. So it would have been written some 60 years before while the chosen people were under the domination of the Seleucides.

Sira was a devout Jew, a wise man and a scribe. He had a comprehensive knowledge of the religious literature of his people, was inspired by it and has quoted complete sentences from it. Some believe him to be the author of most of the discussions and maxims contained in the book, while others limit his role to that of collecting and editing without attention to order, development, repetitiveness or even contradictions.

The just society

It is an introduction to the ways of wisdom. Everything comes under consideration: profession, family, vocation, poverty, old age, and death. Everything is taken into account: anger, foolishness, women, friends, the powerful, and the rulers. Everything is taught: courage, patience, trust, dedication, and mercy. The author teaches the importance of maintaining fairness in all dealings, using moderate language, and exercising self control at all times. This passage in praise of wisdom is the climax of the work.

There is nothing very new in this book in relation to the other books of the Old Testament. Sira is first and foremost a traditional teacher who is not familiar with the latest doctrinal developments. This means that for him, any retribution for actions is essentially earthly and, if death does have an element of repayment, it lies in the fact that, for the righteous, it is calm and puts an end to the most terrible sufferings, whereas, for the ungodly, death comes unexpectedly and puts an end to the pleasures they had thought of as eternal.

However, Sira's arguments concerning wisdom are worth noting. Wisdom is born of God and dwells with him for ever; it is eternal and existed before time; it is a revelation of divine action and is spread throughout creation. As for man, God passes it on to him and it brings him invaluable benefits: the fear of God, the joy of the heart, the assurance of long life, and a tranquil end.

> **Avarice**
>
> 'Wealth is not the right thing for the niggardly, and what use are possessions to the covetous? Whoever hoards by stinting himself is hoarding for others, and others will live sumptuously on his riches. If someone is mean to himself, whom does he benefit? He does not even enjoy what is his own. No one is meaner than the person who is mean to himself, this is how his wickedness repays him. If he does any good, he does it unintentionally, and in the end he himself reveals his wickedness. Wicked is the person who has an envious eye, averting his face and careless of others' lives. The eye of the grasping is not content with what he has, greed shrivels up the soul. The miser is grudging of bread, there is famine at his table.'
> (*Ecclesiasticus* 14, 3–10)

Isaiah

The prophet touched by divine fire

For a universal God

The conviction that a just king will emerge triumphant from the line of David, one whose race will reign forever.

Isaiah was born c. 765 BC into a great Jerusalem family. It is sometimes said that he was related to the king. He was married and had two children to whom he gave symbolic names like Shear Yashub, 'a remnant will come back'. He was a citizen of Jerusalem and loved his city, spending time with the leading statesmen to whom he gave advice.

The call

Isaiah saw Yahweh in all his splendour in the year of King Uzziah's death (740 BC): the Lord was seated on a raised throne

The 'Song of the vineyard'

'My friend had a vineyard on a very fertile hill. He dug the soil and cleared it of stones. He planted the finest vines. He built a tower to guard them, dug a pit for treading the grapes. He waited for the grapes to ripen but every grape was sour. So now my friend says, "You people who live in Jerusalem and Judah, judge between my vineyard and me. Is there anything I failed to do for it? ... This is what I am going to do to my vineyard; I will take away the hedge round it, break down the wall that protects it and let wild animals eat it and trample it down. I will let it be overgrown with weeds, I will not prune the vines or hoe the ground ..."' (*Isaiah* 5, 1–6)

surrounded by seraphims who covered their faces with wings before his majesty and kept calling to each other: 'Holy, Holy, Holy, the Lord Almighty is Holy. His glory fills the world' (*Isaiah* 6, 3). Isaiah was very frightened: how could he, a man of impure lips, be part of this celebration and see God whom even the angels dared not look in the face?

Yet, if Isaiah was indeed there, it must be for some good reason. A seraphim had approached him, with burning coals in his hand and had touched them to his mouth, saying: your guilt has been taken away. And then, as if he had seen none of this, the Lord spoke, he asked the company: who could he send to perform a task? Isaiah was now able to speak and he said: here I am, I can be your messanger.'

The hardening

The revelation given to Isaiah is that of a universal God: it is he who is at the origin of everything, he who rules the changes of history, he who is the world's hope and aim, his glory filling the whole of the earth. As supreme master, nothing escapes him, not the harshness of natural phenomena, nor the deeds of peoples, nor the trials of Israel.

The message entrusted to Isaiah is one of great severity. It is addressed to 'this' people, as God calls them with indifference, this people who were once called 'my' people. The message is clear: it is a summons with no frills to return to the requirements of the Law, the obligations relating to the Covenant and the necessary of moral purity: 'Stop all this evil that I see you doing. Yes, stop doing evil and learn to do right' (*Isaiah* 1, 16–17).

Yahweh is well aware that he will no more be listened to today than he was yesterday.

This time the message is delivered through Isaiah, not to convert Israel, but to harden her heart: 'No matter how much you listen, you will not understand. No matter how much you look, you will not know what is happening' (*Isaiah* 6, 9). The prophet's mission is to make this people hard of hearing and to cover their eyes. That is the punishment foreseen in God's plan, the condition for a ransom which will not by any means be a quick solution, but rather a recreation.

The Book of Emmanuel

A new revelation, a new sign of God's faithfulness, the starting point for a new covenant, the *Book of Emmanuel* is all these things. It is when Ahaz refuses to ask the Lord for proof of his help that Isaiah declares: 'A young woman who is pregnant will have a son and will name him Emmanuel (God with us). By the time he is old enough to make his own decisions, people will be drinking milk and eating honey. Even before that time comes, the lands of those two kings who terrify you will be destroyed.'

Isaiah returns several times to the theme of this good news: 'The people who walked in darkness have seen a great light. (...) A child is born to us! A son is given to us! And he will be our ruler. He will be called "Wonderful Counsellor, Mighty God, Eternal Father, Prince of Peace"' (*Isaiah* 9, 2–6).

Later the prediction becomes more definite: 'Just as new branches sprout from a stump, so a new king will arise from among David's descendants (*Isaiah* 11, 1). In this, King David, son of Jesse, has the promise

---

The vengeance of the Lord

'The Lord has pronounced judgment on the kingdom of Israel, on the descendants of Jacob (...) The Lord has stirred up their enemies. Syria on the east and Philistia on the west have opened their mouths to devour Israel. Yet even so the Lord's anger is not ended; his hand is still stretched out to punish. The people of Israel have not repented; even though the Lord Almighty has punished them, they have not returned to him.' (*Isaiah* 9, 8–13)

---

confirmed which was made to him that he would reign forever, and it is quite an event because henceforth 'Wolves and sheep will live together in peace, and leopards will lie down with young goats. Calves and lion cubs will feed together, and little children will take care of them. Cows and bears will eat together, and their calves and cubs will lie down in peace. Lions will eat straw as cattle do ... On Zion, God's sacred hill, there will be nothing harmful or evil. The land will be full of the knowledge of the Lord' (*Isaiah* 11, 6–9).

A political prophet

However, such was not the case in Isaiah's time during the reigns of Jotham, Ahaz, and Hezekiah. The two small kingdoms of Israel and Judah were in the clutches of the neighbouring great empires. Four times the Assyrian armies threaten their borders. Judah looks for foreign allies but Isaiah disapproves of this political activity, and declares that he trusts only in the faith, saying that God is even using their enemies to punish the people for their sins.

When the kings of Israel and Syria unite against Assyria, Ahaz refuses to go with them. As a result he finds himself against them and war breaks out. 'Do not be afraid', says Isaiah, 'do not let your heart tremble before these two smouldering sticks' (*Isaiah* 7, 4). Despite this the king is indeed afraid and sends messengers laden with gifts to the king of Assyria in order to ask for his protection. Yes, Israel is conquered, but Judah becomes a vassal or dependent state of the conqueror.

When Hezekiah succeeds Ahaz, he immediately stirs up a revolt against the Assyrian protector, Isaiah laughs at this, but, when the king goes to seek help from the Pharaoh, he becomes angry: 'Those who go to Egypt for help are doomed! They are relying on Egypt's vast military strength — horses, chariots, and soldiers. But they do not rely on the Lord, the Holy God of Israel or ask him for help' (*Isaiah* 31, 1).

How can they have hope since they spend their time with scoundrels, greedy for profits and bribes, and think of nothing but buying 'more houses and fields to add to those you already have?' (*Isaiah* 5, 8). Isaiah is particularly scathing regarding the women whose only concern is their appearance and who spend their time making themselves up and putting on their finery.

'Second' Isaiah

Scholars are agreed that from chapter 40 onwards in the book of *Isaiah* we are dealing with a different author. The style is simpler, warmer, and more conciliatory. It is no longer the prophet of the 8th century, but perhaps one of his disciples. He is writing around the period 550–538 BC, that is after the Jews had been deported to Babylon, and before the victories of Cyrus which led to their return to the Promised Land.

So the Jews are in exile and the prophet begins each of his messages with the words: 'Comfort, comfort my people'. And, by way of comfort, the prophet describes the liberation from captivity and the rebuilding of the Temple as certainties. He celebrates them as a great victory.

And, moreover, it is not so much Israel's victory, as Yahweh's. He alone is the object of the prophecy, it is his reign that matters, his return to Jerusalem, and his glory: 'Prepare in the wilderness a road for the Lord. Clear the way in the desert for our God. Fill every valley, level every mountain' (*Isaiah* 40, 3–4).

The women of Jerusalem

'A day is coming when the Lord will take away from the women of Jerusalem everything they are so proud of — the ornaments they wear on their ankles, on their heads, on their necks, and on their wrists. He will take away their veils and their hats; the magic charms they wear on their arms and at their waists; the rings they wear on their fingers and in their noses; all their fine robes, gowns, cloaks, and purses; their revealing garments, their linen handkerchiefs, and the scarves and long veils they wear on their heads. Instead of using perfume they will stink; instead of fine belts they will wear course ropes; instead of having beautiful hair they will be bald; instead of fine clothes they will be dressed in rags; their beauty will be turned to shame.' (*Isaiah* 3, 18–24)

The prophet's words have a patriotic tone — Yahweh has not forgotten his people — but at the same time there is a strong element of total universalism. This is not the paradox it seems to be: Yahweh is the God of all peoples: 'There is no other God but me' (*Isaiah* 44, 6). In order to reveal himself he has chosen Israel: 'People of Israel, you are my witnesses' (*Isaiah* 43, 10), and his salvation is intended for all the nations: 'Listen to me, my people, listen to what I say. I give my teaching to the nations; my laws will bring them light' (*Isaiah* 51, 4).

Yahweh is already showing that he is totally in control of events: Cyrus will be his instrument in the liberation of the Hebrew people. Isaiah calls him Yahweh's shepherd, or again his beloved; he even goes so far as to say he is anointed (*Isaiah* 5, 1), as if he were acknowledging his royal status as being equal to that of David's dynasty. There is, however, no question of a reversal of roles. God controls all the peoples and gives each one its task. So, one by one, they each play the part which has been eternally assigned to them in God's plans.

The 'Song of the Servant'

The book contains within it a poem which appears in fragments throughout the work as if the author wanted to be constantly returning to certain ideas. It has been called the 'Song of the Servant'. The song conveys both a representation in a single individual of Israel's mission and a purification or spiritualization of that mission.

The servant is specifically set apart from the group destined for this task from his mother's womb: 'Before I was born, the Lord appointed me; he made me his servant to bring back his people, to bring back the scattered people of Israel' (*Isaiah* 49, 5); he has a mission to all men: 'I will make you a light to the nations — so that all the world may be saved' (*Isaiah* 49, 6); he is the glory of Yahweh: 'You are my servant, because of you people will praise me' (*Isaiah* 49, 3).

But, above all, while the people of Israel are deaf, sinful, and unfaithful, while they seek to return to their lands and subjugate the nations, the servant is operating on a completely different level. Power, wealth, success, and glory matter little to him. So, because he refuses to be a national hero, he is persecuted by his own countrymen and 'did not stop when they insulted me ... and spat in my face'; 'He is despised and rejected by men'.

The servant's mission is not of this world: 'I have a greater task for you my servant, not only will you restore to greatness the people of Israel' (*Isaiah* 49, 6); it is a spiritual task, consisting of spreading religious truth throughout the world and 'many nations will marvel at him and kings will be speechless with amazement' (*Isaiah* 52, 15). This attitude in fact goes against the tide, the sufferings of the servant are not negative 'they justify many', for 'he himself bears the punishment for their sins' and 'gives his life an atonement for many'.

Jesus Christ was to apply to himself (*Luke* 22, 37; *John* 1, 29) the image of the servant described in this song and this has given rise to talk of a 'fifth gospel' which seems to have been written in the shadow of the cross on Golgotha.

'Third' Isaiah

A third collection of writings in the same book, the third *Isaiah*, comes from a very different context. Around the 450s BC the Hebrew people returned to Palestine, there was no longer any external enemy to fear, but faithless Jews remained within the community itself. The prophet, or prophets — there has been some suggestion that more than one author is involved — sustains the righteous minority and speaks out against those who have opted for a semi-paganism.

This very division in the community brings a certain individualism in its wake. It is no longer a question of saving the people of God in its entirety, as a global entity, but of each man individually co-operating in his own salvation: 'He will punish his enemies, according to what they have done' (*Isaiah* 59, 18). For if you 'Remove the chains of oppression and the yoke of injustice, and let the oppressed go free, share your food with the hungry and open your homes to the homeless poor, (...) you will be like a garden that has plenty of water, like a spring of water that never runs dry! (*Isaiah* 58, 6–11).

Yahweh seems to favour the humble, strangers, eunuchs etc, who have been called 'Yahweh's poor'. He addresses himself to them, offers them his salvation, promises them glory. No doubt this is because these humble folk have no ties other than those which bind them to the Lord. They are consequently the example and fulfilment of real faith.

> **The prophet's mission**
> 'The sovereign Lord has filled me with his spirit. He has chosen me and sent me to bring good news to the poor, to heal the broken-hearted, to announce release to captives and freedom to those in prison. He has sent me to proclaim that the time has come when the Lord will save his people and defeat their enemies. He has sent me to comfort all who mourn, to give to those who mourn in Zion joy and gladness instead of grief, a song of praise instead of sorrow.' (*Isaiah* 61, 1–3)

Jeremiah
The man from Anathoth

The prophet of the heart

'I give you authority over nations and kingdoms to uproot and to pull down, to destroy and to overthrow, to build and to plant' (Jeremiah 1, 9–10).

Jeremiah was born c. 645 BC in Anathoth, some six kilometers from Jerusalem. The village was prosperous and lively: the prophet was to remember throughout his life the luxuriant gardens, the abundant harvests, the excellent wine, the animals, the feasting, the sound of tambourines, the celebrations, and weddings. Like Hosea, Jeremiah was a man of the countryside.

Anathoth was known as the village to which the priestly tribe of Abiathar withdrew after its disgrace. Solomon had, in fact, removed all the trappings of their office from them because they had taken the side of Adonias, the great king's rival.

Yahweh's strength

'Get ready, Jeremiah, go and tell them everything I command you to say. Do not be afraid of them now or I will make you even more afraid when you are with them. Listen, Jeremiah! Everyone in this land — the kings of Judah, the officials, the priests, and the people — will be against you. But today I am giving you the strength to resist them; you will be like a fortified city, an iron pillar and a bronze wall. They will not defeat you, for I will be with you to protect you. I, the Lord, have spoken.' (Jeremiah 1, 17–19)

But this banishment gave Abiathar the chance to see things differently: among other things he stressed the importance of the Ark or Covenant Box, the only sign of Yahweh's presence, disapproved of innovations brought in by the monarch and condemned pagan compromises. Anathoth became the symbol of a purer religion.

The call

At the time of Jeremiah, the situation had worsened once more: the Kings Manasseh (693–639 BC) and Amon (639–638 BC) had allowed things to deteriorate: the Temple seemed to be covered in idols, the high places used for rituals now covered the whole country and the people worshipped the hosts of heaven on every rooftop. The prophet regards this as the road to ruin.

God's call does not surprise him. He was accustomed to a certain closeness with Yahweh and experiences nothing of the 'fear and trembling' which had shaken Isaiah at the time of his call. On the other hand, he has even more doubts than his illustrious predecessor had about his abilities to perform his task: 'I don't know how to speak, I am too young' (Jeremiah 1, 6). So all he can do is put his trust in God who has destined him to take his place in the uninterrupted line of prophets reaching back to the origins of the nation.

'Scourge of Israel', as was said of Elijah (I Kings 18, 17), was what he was to be right from the start of his ministry. Even his own village of Anathoth holds his severity against him. The words he hurls at the people are harsh and unequivocal: prostitution, idolatry, immorality. They are linked to the most terrible threats: 'Your own evil will punish you' (Jeremiah 2, 19). Has he any lingering hope that a late conversion may yet prevent

Israel's ruin? Yes he has, for he adds: 'Unfaithful Israel, come back to me. I am merciful and will not be angry (...) only admit that you are guilty' (*Jeremiah* 3, 12–13).

The reform of 622 BC

King Josiah, coming to power after the assassination of his father, Amon, sets out to restore the union of the northern and southern kingdoms. In 621 BC the priest Heleias finds the text of *Deuteronomy*, the Law of Moses, in the Temple. This is an undreamt of chance for the young ruler — he is barely 25 years old — to restructure the nation. He solemnly proclaims the teachings of the *Torah* and embarks on a radical reform of the religious life of the country.

There is no doubt that Jeremiah, who is about the same age as the king, is overjoyed at these developments: the Temple is cleansed of all idol worship, the high places are destroyed, and the Passover is once more celebrated with reverence. He follows events closely, studies the text of the Law, even welcomes the reforms which are carried out, but does not show unbounded enthusiasm, as if he were aware that there could easily be a return to the past.

He quickly senses that, in fact, it is only the institutions which have been changed, that the reforms have been limited to the area of worship and that the attitude of the people has not changed at all. 'What do I care about the incense they bring me from Sheba, or the spices from a distant land? I will not accept their offerings or be pleased with their sacrifices' (*Jeremiah* 6, 20). Religion has become entirely a matter of form: they feel reassured because they have the Law, because they worship in the Temple, because they make sacrifices, but all of these are simply talismans, lucky charms, fetishes: the heart has not changed, the Law is not carried out, justice is not respected.

The sufferings

The Battle of Megiddo and the death of Josiah put an end to the reforms. The new king, Jehoiakim, is a puppet in the hands of his Egyptian masters who have placed him on the throne, but the worship practices of Josiah's time continue and are even strengthened. The Temple has now simply become a talisman which, in the eyes of the people, magically ensures protection and salvation.

Jeremiah reacts violently. He launches into a long denunciation of the Temple: 'And so what I did to Shiloh I will do to this Temple of mine, in which you trust. Here in this place which I gave to your ancestors and to you, I will do the same thing that I did to Shiloh' (*Jeremiah* 7, 14). The ruin of the Temple is predicted, as is the deportation and exile. Babylon is even indicated as the invader. There is nothing to be done about it, there is no appeal against this condemnation.

This outburst wins him no friends, the people turn against him, his family denies him, he is thrown out of the Temple, denounced, betrayed by his friends and to crown it all, he falls ill. And yet he loves this people, he wants to help them, to explain things to them, to convert them, he intercedes for them. But he finds that he is alone, abandoned by everyone except for his faithful secretary, Baruch, a feeble creature who is himself always in need of encouragement.

The hardest thing for the prophet to bear is the failure of his mission: 'What an unhappy man I am! Why did my mother bring me into the world? I have to quarrel and argue with everyone in the land. I have not lent any money or borrowed any; yet everyone curses me' (*Jeremiah* 15, 10). He begins to have doubts. Could Yahweh be

---

The speech in the Temple

'He told me to stand there (at the Temple gate) and announce what the Lord Almighty, the God of Israel, had to say to them: (...) Stop believing those deceitful words "We are safe! This is the Lord's Temple, this is the Lord's Temple, this is the Lord's Temple!" ... Look, you steal, murder, commit adultery, tell lies under oath, offer sacrifices to Baal, and worship gods that you had not known before. You do these things I hate, and then you come and stand in my presence, in my own Temple and say: "We are safe!" Do you think that my Temple is a hiding place for robbers? ... I, the Lord, have spoken.' (*Jeremiah* 7, 2–11)

making fun of him? God's reply comes firm and unmistakeable. The work of the upholder of the law must be carried out.

It is carried out to great effect. Jeremiah no longer fears being isolated among men, sure as he is of his intimacy with God and strengthened by constant dialogue with him. Against nationalist pressure and the prophets in favour at court, he advocates submission to Babylon which he considers to be an instrument of God's will. Against everyone else he advises the deported people to settle among their conquerors, cultivate the land, and take wives.

The New Covenant

Jeremiah's attitude is explained by the fact that he has internalized the relationship with God, in the first instance for himself — the cruel things which happened to him helped him to do this — but also for Israel. For him, religion is not so much a question of worship, temple, land or nation as one of feelings towards Yahweh, passionate obedience to his law, and love for him as a person. Until now Yahwism has been the religion of a people, a nation, but from now on he sees Yahweh as the God of a man's heart.

Basically it does not matter whether you are in one place or another, whether power is held by one party or another or by foreigners, whether one succeeds or fails, the important thing is to know Yahweh, to love him and to serve him. The Old Covenant made on Sinai between God and the people, by which he granted them his protection in exchange for their obedience has obviously been broken by virtue of the nation's sin. A New Covenant takes its place,

one which does not negate the first covenant but which gives it a deeper expression.

In order to be able to start from the beginning again, God wipes everything clean: he forgives our crimes and sins, pardons lapses and infidelities, he forgets weaknesses and wrongs. And yet he remembers that he has chosen Israel: 'I will give them a single purpose in life; to honour me for all time, for their own good and the good of their descendants' (*Jeremiah* 32, 39).

The New Covenant now makes each person individually responsible. Each person will have his own relationship with God and will no longer be able to rely on distinguished ancestry, membership of a chosen people or diligence in attending the Temple in order to set his mind at rest. For, 'when that time comes the people will no longer say, "the parents ate the sour grapes, but the children got the sour taste". Instead, whoever eats sour grapes will have his own teeth set on edge' (*Jeremiah* 31, 29–30).

Finally, the Law will no longer be only an object which is venerated, a subject for discussion among God-fearing people, a code of references to be consulted; it will no longer content itself with organizing the structures of institutions, ordering social relationships and regulating external attitudes. It will be internalized within each person establishing itself not by force or for reasons of self interest but from feelings of conviction, and will have its place in the heart of the individual: 'I will write it on their heart', says Yahweh.

The prophet's end

Jeremiah was no happier at the end of his life than he was at the beginning. Possessed by his divine inspiration which drives him to proclaim catastrophe after catastrophe and bring the wrath of the people down on him, weak and hesitant in daily life, not knowing where to go or what to do, he finds himself being swept along with migrant populations.

After the domination of Egypt, Judah has to suffer that of Babylon. Jeremiah still favours the way of submission. During the siege of Jerusalem he is considered to be a traitor, a 'collaborator'. He is put in prison and even thrown into a well of mud and left to die there. Help comes in the shape of

---

The New Covenant

'The New Covenant that I will make with the people of Israel will be this: I will put my law within them and write it on their hearts. I will be their God and they will be my people. None of them will have to teach his fellow-countryman to know the Lord, because all will know me, from the least to the greatest. I will forgive their sins and I will no longer remember their wrongs. I, the Lord, have spoken.' (*Jeremiah* 31, 33–4)

one of the palace eunuchs who pulls him out of this pit. When the city falls and the Temple is destroyed, Jeremiah is spared.

The influential Jews are deported but a group of the people remain in Judah gathered around Gedaliah whom the Babylonians have named as governor. Jeremiah is among them. However, this situation is quite unacceptable to some and in 587 BC Gedaliah is assassinated by Ishmael, a member of the royal family. Having been unable to trace the guilty party, the governor's officials are afraid of reprisals from Babylon and flee to Egypt. The prophet finds himself setting out on this new adventure.

He still has the living word: he proclaims the invasion of Egypt by Babylon, reproaches the refugees for their worship of foreign gods and the women for their offerings to the Queen of heaven. So his life ends with a prophecy of doom. One legend, recorded by Tertullian, claims that he was stoned to death by the people.

Influence

Jeremiah is included in the line of Israel's great prophets. He recalls themes already declared by his predecessors, the all-powerful nature of God, his hold on creation and history, his goodness, and the importance of morality in worship. Isaiah, Hosea, Amos, and the others had already helped to develop Israel's religious thinking.

But with Jeremiah an extremely important stage is reached. For until now salvation was only conceived of in terms of one distinct race, a narrow nationalism with a particular land and a form of worship kept exclusively for the Temple in Jerusalem. Now, however, it is dependent on one's knowledge of God, a personal dialogue with him, a selfless love for him.

This is the prophet's own experience, a mystical experience if anything, which in its expression broadens out to include the whole history of the Covenant. Most certainly the right words have not yet been found to convey this dramatic change, it is misunderstood and far from being a key issue among the Jews of the time, but the seed has been sown.

Jeremiah in the well

'Then the officials went to the king and said, "This man must be put to death. By talking like this he is making the soldiers in the city lose their courage, and he is doing the same thing to everyone else left in the city. He is not trying to help the people; he only wants to hurt them." King Zedekiah answered, "Very well then, do what you wish with him; I can't stop you." So they took me and let me down by ropes into the well, which was in the palace courtyard. There was no water in the well, only mud, and I sank down into it.' (*Jeremiah* 38, 4–6)

Lamentations
Public complaints

Israel's sadness

When calamities like the taking of Jerusalem and the exile struck with such force, the people turned to Yahweh.

In 587 BC Israel experienced the greatest catastrophe in her history: the sack of Jerusalem with the Temple and Covenant Box set on fire, the kingdom broken up and the Jews scattered or taken into exile. For years the survivors held services of worship on the site of the Temple. They sang of their grief and of hope for their nation. It was from this practice that the small book of five poems called *Lamentations* was put together by the people who had stayed behind.

There may have been some borrowing from the laments written by the prophet Jeremiah at the time of the death of the reforming king, Josiah, which occurred at the Battle of Megiddo in 609 BC and was remembered every year. There does seem to be some similarity in format with the communal laments used in Babylon in times of catastrophe and with the funeral dirges sung at burial ceremonies by the kind of professional mourners which exist in some countries.

A very structured style

These poems have a very structured format. Each one consists of as many verses as there are letters in the Hebrew alphabet, and apart from a few exceptions, the first letter of each verse follows the alphabetical order. Added to that there are particular words and phrases which recur, an expressive rhythm and the repetition of endings. All these features intensify the feeling of grief and anguish.

The first, second, and fourth of the five poems are funeral laments transformed into religious poems. The author deplores the misfortunes of Zion, personifying the holy city: 'All night long she cries; tears run down her cheeks. Of all her former friends not one is left to comfort her' (*Lamentations* 1, 2). Then Yahweh is mentioned, as sins are acknowledged before him and the cry goes up, 'Look, O Lord, at my agony!' (*Lamentations* 1, 20).

The third and fifth poems are community laments: the account of national misery is more detailed, the appeal to Yahweh is more collective in nature and there is deeper religious thought involved. Questions are posed: 'Why should we ever complain when we are punished for our sin?' (*Lamentations* 3, 39) — and the hope is expressed: 'The Lord is good to everyone who trusts in him (...) It is best for us to wait in patience — to wait for him to save us — and it is best for us to learn this patience in our youth' (*Lamentations* 3, 25–7).

Hope in Yahweh

'Nothing is left of all we were proud of. We sinned and now we are doomed. We are sick at our very hearts and can hardly see through our tears, because Mount Zion lies lonely and deserted, and wild jackals prowl through its ruins. But you, O Lord, are King for ever and will rule to the end of time. Why have you abandoned us so long? Will you ever remember us again? Bring us back to you, Lord! Bring us back! Restore our ancient glory. Or have you rejected us for ever? Is there no limit to your anger?'
(*Lamentations* 5, 16–22)

The Book of Baruch

A follower of Jeremiah

A composite work

This book attributed to Baruch is made up of elements of encouragement, prayer, wisdom, poetry, and prophecy.

The *Book of Baruch* is not part of the Hebrew Bible and is considered to be apocryphal by Protestants, but Catholics do include it in their canon. This situation is due to the fact no Hebrew or Aramaic version is known, that it is found, after Jeremiah, in the Greek translation of the *Septuagint* and that the Fathers of the Church often quoted it as an integral part of the book of *Jeremiah*.

It seems very unlikely that it was written by Jeremiah's secretary. The *Book of Baruch* is a composite work, originating no doubt from various different writings: it contains a penitential psalm expressing sorrow for sins, a hymn in praise of wisdom and a word of encouragement and consolation. It is made up of three distinct parts whose composition must have covered the period from the 3rd century BC to the 2nd century AD.

A masterpiece

The penitential psalm is a little masterpiece of literature: it returns again and again to the same themes, basing them on the Law and the Prophets, developing them through the history of Israel and exploring them in depth through faith in the Covenant, and gradually, rhythmically, it progresses from sin confessed, through the exile and the 'small remnant' to conversion or real change of heart. It is not at all concerned with the enemy. The prayer is very pure, a dialogue between God and Israel.

The hymn to Wisdom takes an original form here: no one can achieve it by his own means, neither the rich and powerful, nor those who speak in parables and seek after intelligence, nor those who cross the seas or climb to the heavens. Only he who created and governs the world possesses it and a long time ago he gave it to Jacob, his servant. It has appeared on earth, it has conversed with men, it is the Law.

The passage of consolation which closes the book exactly balances the penitential psalm which opens it. In a slow and rhythmic movement the line of thought goes from God's anger to his mercy. Jerusalem, poetically personified, weeps over the abduction or her children, recalls the pain she endured over their wilful disobedience, pleads with the Eternal on their behalf, calls upon her faith in him and shouts for joy to see them gathered from east and west.

The *Book of Baruch* is often followed by the letter of Jeremiah, which is certainly a separate work. Jeremiah writes to the exiles warning them against idols. Amidst colourful observations the leitmotiv, the main theme, returns with regularity: 'They are not gods, do not be afraid of them.'

Wisdom

'It is he who is our God, no other can compare with him. He has uncovered the whole way of knowledge and shown it to his servant Jacob, to Israel, his well-beloved; only then did she appear on earth and live among human beings. She is the book of God's commandments, the Law that stands for ever; those who keep her shall live, those who desert her shall die. Turn back, Jacob, seize her, in her radiance make your way to light: do not yield your glory to another, your privilege to a people not your own. Israel, blessed are we: what pleases God has been revealed to us.' (*Baruch* 3, 26; 4, 4)

Ezekiel

The prophet of the exile

The great visionary

The call

The collapse of Jewish nationalism and the destruction of the Temple made Ezekiel the key person in Judaism.

Jeremiah is the prophet of Jerusalem, Ezekiel the prophet of the exile: the one is as tortured, worried, and moving as the other is harsh, strict, and persistent. There is no doubt that the second had a great admiration for his elder, most of whose themes he takes up, commenting on them, exploring them further and adding to them. Yet he never speaks about him, and never quotes him: the prophet speaks nothing but the word of God.

Ezekiel is a rather strange character: he is both debator and dreamer, rational and passionate, brutal and sensitive, practical and ethical, meticulous and muddled, preacher and writer, prophet and priest. He seems to rise above history in his vision of events and yet he describes their details, unravels their complexities and predicts their tomorrows.

The book

'"Open your mouth and eat what I am going to give you." I saw a hand stretched out towards me and it was holding a scroll. The hand unrolled the scroll and I saw that there was writing on both sides — cries of grief were written there, and wails and groans. God said, "Mortal man, then go and speak to the people of Israel." So I opened my mouth and he gave me the scroll to eat. He said, "Mortal man, eat this scroll that I give you, fill your stomach with it." I ate it and it tasted as sweet as honey.' (*Ezekiel* 2, 8–3, 3)

Ezekiel would doubtless have been a priest in the Temple and was always to maintain a strong interest in worship and the practice of strict observance of all the rituals. Perhaps it was there that he acquired his horror of idolatry, disgust at sacrilege, and sense of Yahweh's majesty and what that required of him, all of which were features of his preaching in Jerusalem as well as in exile in Babylon.

It should be said that he was entrusted with his mission in a fantastic vision: the chariot of the Lord's glory was surrounded by extraordinary animals. Each one had four faces and four wings and the noise of the beating wings was saying: Blessed be the glory of Yahweh. God seemed to be in the middle of a fire, with burning coals, bright lights, and rainbows: God in his majesty, the Supremely Other; Ezekiel fell face downwards on the ground. From the time of his calling, the prophet becomes a writer. His world consists of an unlimited imagination, imposing, not to say overwhelming scenes, visions which are terrifying in their confusion, and striking allegories and symbols. When God appears he gives him his subject matter in a book in which are written 'cries of grief, wails, and groans' and the prophet has to eat it, feed on it, and fill himself so that he can take these words to the house of Israel. The divine revelation is so powerful that he spends seven days recovering from the experience. 'The power of the Lord came on me with great force' (*Ezekiel* 3, 14).

When he emerges from this daze his mission becomes clear: He has been made a watchman for the house of Israel, charged with warning the wicked to turn from their evil behaviour on pain of death and the just to be steadfast in their righteousness. The prophet is personally responsible for this mission, for if he did not give these warnings, he would die. So we can understand the passion he puts into his words, the anger he shows and the harshness of his judgments.

The trials of Jerusalem

So here we see him, soon after his call from God, proclaiming the siege of Jerusalem, and in order to make his message more vivid and easily understood he acts it out: 'Get a brick, put it in front of you and scratch lines on it to represent Jerusalem' (*Ezekiel* 4, 1), then the prophet plays out the attack on the city. There will be other symbolic mimes like this: one about food rationing; one where hair is cut and divided into three parts. A third is burnt, a third is chopped up with a sword, and a third thrown to the wind. Fire, sword, dispersion: three scourges which are coming to Israel.

The following year, in a vision, he sees all the abominations, all the things hateful to God, which are going on in Jerusalem: the idol that was an outrage to God standing at the gate of the Temple, 70 elders of Israel worshipping animals, women weeping over the god Tammuz, 25 men turning their backs on Yahweh and bowing down to the sun. 'Look how they insult me in the most offensive way possible', says Yahweh, 'Come here, you men who are going to punish the city. Bring your weapons with you' (*Ezekiel* 8, 7–9, 1).

The city is lost, God is going to leave it. The sentence is only slightly lessened by the fact that the righteous alone will be saved. They will be those marked with the *taw*—a cross—who moan and cry over the terrible things going on all around them. Ezekiel expands on the idea of personal responsibility: there are the righteous and the evil. If the evil persist in their evil ways they will die, if they change their ways, they will live. The same applies to the righteous: if they sin they will die, if they persevere in righteousness, they will live. There is no longer any question of paying for anyone else, be it father, son or nation, each one is now accountable for his own actions, no discussion.

The glory of the Lord leaves the city and stops at the mountain to the east of the city. Then a dreamlike vision follows which corresponds to the destruction of the city. Just before the fall of the kingdom, Ezekiel had thundered against King Zedekiah, who had broken with his overlord, and had then been struck completely dumb: he was bearing Israel's sins. It is the arrival of an escapee from Jerusalem in Babylon, where he now is, which gives him back his speech.

The resurrection

After the fall of Jerusalem Ezekiel becomes more caring. There is a surprising change of tone in his words due to the fact that from now on he is addressing only the exiled community. However, a number of passages are dedicated to pronouncements against the nations: Ammon, Moab, Edom, Philistia, Tyre, Egypt. The prophet tells Israel's enemies of the punishments they will receive.

The essential message, however, is that contained in the account of the vision of the dried bones. Ezekiel is taken to one of the many battlefields which were dotted around Israel at that time. The valley is covered with bones, the scattered remains of the dead. The prophet wanders about and the horror of the sight impresses itself upon him. 'Can these bones live?' asks the Lord. The bodies are reconstituted in two stages under the prophet's orders: first the bones join together and are covered with nerves, flesh, and skin, but there is no life in them. 'Prophesy', says Yahweh 'prophesy in the spirit'. Ezekiel orders the spirit to come and it comes: they come back to life and stand up, a huge army of men.

This is the resurrection of the people of Judah, but also that of those deported from the old northern kingdom; it is Israel as a

The New Covenant
'I will gather them out of the countries where I scattered them, and will give the land of Israel back to them. When they return they are to get rid of all the filthy, disgusting idols they find. I will give them a new heart and a new mind. I will take away their stubborn heart of stone and will give them an obedient heart. Then they will keep my laws and faithfully obey all my commands. They will be my people and I will be their God.' (*Ezekiel* 11, 17–20)

whole that is brought back to life. No longer will they be two nations, there will be no more division into two kingdoms, and 'my servant David will reign over them'.

Ezekiel's Torah

The prophet is almost 52 years old. For 11 years he keeps silent: this is not idleness but meditation, a long process of maturing. Ezekiel looks at all he has lived through: the Temple destroyed, the kingdom swept away, the Jews deported, exile. He remembers the promised resurrection, the reconstituted kingdom, unified and alone standing in David's line of descent. All these thoughts gradually give way to a great vision.

The prophet is transported to the site of Jerusalem. A man approaches him and tells him to pay close attention for he will have to remember all that is said in order to repeat it to the house of Israel. His guide is carrying a linen tape measure and a measuring rod, and he begins to measure the walls, the

---

The pieces of wood

'"Mortal man", he said, "take a wooden stick and write on it the words, 'The kingdom of Judah'. Then take another stick and write on it the words, 'The kingdom of Israel'. Then hold the two sticks end to end in your hand so that they look like one stick. When your people ask you to tell them what this means, tell them that I, the Sovereign Lord, am going to take the stick representing Israel and put it with the one that represents Judah. Out of the two I will make one stick and hold it in my hand."'
(*Ezekiel* 37, 15–19)

---

halls, the courtyards, and the gates of the Temple. This is not, in fact, the Temple of Solomon, which Ezekiel knew well, it is an ideal Temple for the new Israel.

The guide does not stop there, however, he goes on to speak about the details of the worship, the repopulation of Palestine, the sharing out of the land, the rights and duties of the ruler. It is a new *Torah* with all the details a law-maker can give. Furthermore, the prophet's style has changed. It is sharper and firmer. He goes straight to the essential point with no superfluous words.

Ezekiel's task is quite clear: to make the priest the living centre of the community and reduce the ruler to a subordinate role of a purely administrative nature. This is how the Temple of Jerusalem will rediscover its prestige.

Influence

In 'the avenue of unchanging giants of the human spirit', Victor Hugo placed Ezekiel alongside Homer and Aeschylus; a testimony to the prophet's influence. However, his new *Torah* did move away slightly from that of the *Pentateuch* attributed to Moses, and there were those who felt it should be omitted from the canon of the Scriptures. Some ingenuity in interpretation was necessary to avoid this.

To some people Ezekiel represents the classic prophet. His visionary gifts, his fantastic universe, and his unreal ideal make him a guide and there are some mystic movements in Judaism which follow him. He has also been a source of inspiration for writers treating the subject of the last days or the end of the world. The *Revelation of John* mentions him more than 50 times.

Daniel
The young nobleman in exile

The transcendence or supremacy of God

A visionary and interpreter of dreams, Daniel is the witness, in the time of the deportation, to God as the supreme saviour.

King Nebuchadnezzar had chosen a few of the young Jewish noblemen deported to Babylon to join his entourage at court. They were Daniel, Hananiah, Mishael, and Azariah, who were 'handsome, intelligent, well-trained, quick to learn, and free from any physical defects.' The king talked with them and found them to be 10 times better than all the magicians and sorcerers in the kingdom.

The huge statue

Nebuchadnezzar has a dream. He sends for his fortunetellers to interpret it, but in order to test them he does not tell them what he has dreamed but challenges them to discover it. None of them can do this and they are all condemned to death. Then Daniel intervenes. He prays to God to reveal to him the mystery of the king's vision and asks to appear in his presence. What the king saw in his dream was a huge statue; the head was of gold, the chest of silver, the hips of bronze, the legs of iron, and the feet partly of iron and partly of clay. A stone struck the feet, the iron and clay shattered, and the whole thing crumbled and was blown around like dust on the threshing floor in summer. As for the stone, it grew into a huge mountain filling the earth. This is what Daniel tells him.

He goes on to give an interpretation of the dream: the head of gold, is you; after

you will rise up another kingdom inferior to yours, and a third and a fourth; the feet of iron and clay are the symbol of a divided kingdom. There will come another kingdom which will never be destroyed. It will destroy and annihilate all the others. The dream is exact and the interpretation just as certain. Nebuchadnezzar bows low before Daniel.

The furnace

Daniel does not stay in favour for very long. The king, sure of his power, decides to erect an enormous gold statue in the plain of Dura and orders that, at the sound of his instruments, princes, governors, servants, and all peoples must bow down before it. Everyone does this except for the three young Jews at court. They are quickly denounced and ordered to obey; they refuse to worship the idol and are condemned to be burned alive in a blazing furnace. The torture is carried out and the furnace is so hot that it burns to death the servants who are stoking it and those who go near. All this time the young men are singing a hymn to Yahweh, thanking him for saving them from their enemies like this; their hair is not

---

The young men in the furnace

'Bless the Lord, faithful humble-hearted people, praise and glorify him for ever! Hananiah, Azariah, and Mishael, bless the Lord — praise and glorify him for ever! — For he has rescued us from the Underworld, he has saved us from the hand of Death, he has snatched us from the burning fiery furnace, he has drawn us from the heart of the flame! Give thanks to the Lord, for he is good, for his love is everlasting. Bless the Lord, the God of gods, all who fear him, give praise and thanks to him, for his love is everlasting!' (*Daniel* 3, 86–90).

---

burnt, their clothes show no change at all. The king is astounded at this phenomenon and has them brought out of the furnace. He orders that respect be shown to this God who gives such power to his followers.

The lions' den

Daniel's influence is great and continues to grow: he interprets Nebuchadnezzar's dream which foretells his period of madness and fall from power, he deciphers the message which appears in the middle of Belshazzar's feast, and proclaims the coming supremacy of the Medes and Persians. Darius, the new master of the land wishes to place him at the head of the kingdom for he clearly outclasses all the leaders and governors with his extraordinary mind. They, however, are filled with jealousy and seek to bring him down.

They quickly hit upon a foolproof plan to trap him and have the king pass a decree ordering that, for 30 days, all prayers must be addressed to the king and none other, God or man. Daniel, whose usual practice was to pray every day facing towards Jerusalem disobeys this rule and this is reported to the authorities. Darius has to comply with his own orders.

Belshazzar's banquet

'One night King Belshazzar invited 1000 noblemen to a great banquet, and they drank wine together. While they were drinking, Belshazzar gave orders to bring in the gold and silver cups which his father Nebuchadnezzar had carried off from the Temple in Jerusalem. The king sent for them so that he, his noblemen, his wives, and his concubines could drink out of them ... they all drank wine out of them and praised gods made of gold, silver, bronze, iron, wood, and stone. Suddenly a human hand appeared and began writing on the plaster wall of the palace, where the light from the lamps was shining most brightly. And the king saw the hand as it was writing. (MENE: God has measured your sovereignty and put an end to it. TEPEL: you have been weighed in the balance and found wanting. PARSIN: your kingdom has been divided, and given to the Persians.) He turned pale ...' (*Daniel* 5, 1–6)

It costs him dear, but Daniel is thrown into a pit of lions while Darius spends the night fasting and praying. In the morning he rushes to the place of punishment and calls 'Daniel ... Was the God you serve so loyally able to save you from the lions?' The prophet replies, 'God sent his angel to shut the mouths of the lions so they would not hurt me.' The king then pronounces the same punishment on those who had arranged this and declares his faith in Daniel's God.

The great visions

Daniel also has his own visions. Apocalyptic visions where the fantastic and the symbolic mingle together, where lions have eagles' wings, leopards have teeth of iron, and rams have four horns. The battles are bitter and decisive, the victories often short-lived and developments rapid. Each element in these fabulous pictures has a more or less mysterious significance. This is apocalyptic or revelation literature of the kind already employed by Ezekiel.

These visions, with their strong but mysterious assertions and their choice of certain subjects are a form of revelation but it is difficult for the human mind to understand the times in which they are set; they certainly refer to extraordinary events in times of great conflict, possibly even the end of the world. The apocalypse forces the mind to expand and, if it can accept the challenge, takes it far beyond the immediate world.

The interpretations given by Gabriel, Michael or any other angel do not go into all the details of the visions and indeed leave a rather bitter impression of confusion. If we understand the beasts to represent the kings who will rise up from the earth, and the fourth beast to signify a fourth kingdom different from the others, one which will trample them underfoot, and that the godly are to be delivered into that king's hands, then we have an idea of how the pattern of history will develop. Scholars have done their best to put actual names to the elements of the vision: they suggest the Babylonian Empire, the Empire of the Medes, that of the Persians and that of Alexander, with the final king being Antiochus Epiphanes (2nd century BC).

The main thing, however, is certainly the message of hope when the angel says: 'The power and greatness of all the kingdoms on earth will be given to the people of the Supreme God. Their royal power will never end' (*Daniel* 7, 27), or when the prophet sees the Son of Man coming from the clouds and approaching the Elder and all authority, honour, and power are given to him (*Daniel* 7, 13–14). Commentaries by the rabbis see 'the Son of Man' as someone who mysteriously transcends human nature; Jesus would later claim this title for himself; there is no doubt that these words in Daniel's text already convey the sense of Messiah.

The uncertainty and imprecise nature of prophecy occurs again in the vision of the 70 weeks which, in a complicated system of calculation outlines a succession of eras and events, and proclaims the coming of God's reign. The account then becomes less symbolic. We see the kings of the south and north clash, with the confrontation ending in a horrfying picture of a pagan image being set up in the Temple. There are to be wars, defeats, persecutions and victories one after the other — such is man's history.

Susanna

'Hardly were the maids gone than the two elders sprang up and rushed upon her. "Look", they said, "the garden door is shut, no one can see us. We want to have you, so give in and let us! Refuse and we shall both give evidence that a young man was with you and this was why you sent your maids away." Susanna sighed. "I am trapped", she said, "Whatever I do. If I agree, it means death for me; if I resist, I cannot get away from you. But I prefer to fall innocent into your power than to sin in the eyes of the Lord." She then cried out as loud as she could.' (*Daniel* 13, 19–24)

But the prophet is not a simple observer disillusioned by the constant round of the same old trials and tribulations: his mission is to proclaim eternal justice, which takes a new form at the end of this book. He uses the phrase 'At that time', to show that he is speaking about the end of the world. The persecutor will disappear, the righteous people will be saved and 'Many of those who have already died will live again; some will enjoy eternal life and some will suffer eternal disgrace' (*Daniel* 12, 2). Christians and many others take this to mean the resurrection of the dead.

The book

The author of the *Book of Daniel* has a good understanding of Chaldean society in the 6th century BC: the importance of magic, the education of young noblemen at court, the statues of rulers, the use of fire and lions as punishments. However, the work does seem to be made up of odd bits and pieces. So it is generally believed that it was written around the 2nd century BC and that sources in the oral tradition must have been used in its composition.

Moreover, the Greek version has important additions which are sometimes incorporated in the main text and sometimes added at the end. For instance, the episode about Susanna and the old men only exists in the Greek: Susanna was a very beautiful and God-fearing woman. Her husband was a rich and respected man who often received prominent Jews in his house. Two of these, old men who held the office of judge, were filled with desire for their hostess. They hid in the garden to watch for her and when she was alone they threw themselves on her. Susanna defended herself and so, in order to get revenge, they accused her of committing adultery in front of everyone. It was Daniel who managed to trap them in their lies by asking each one separately under which tree did they see Susanna and her lover. One said it was an acacia, the other an aspen.

Hosea
The tender-hearted prophet

The ridiculed husband

The prophet experiences in his private life a parallel with the relationship between Yahweh and his people.

Hosea is a prophet living at the same time as Amos, but unlike Amos he comes from the northern kingdom, he is not a solitary figure, but belongs to a group of prophets, and he has a long career stretching from the reign of Jeroboam II (783–743 BC) in Israel to the fall of Samaria, in 721 BC. He is well aware, therefore, of the troubles which followed Jeroboam's death: the political assassinations, the illegal seizing of power, the short-lived reigns, the payment of tribute to foreign nations, in short, total anarchy. This was an offence to Yahweh, the only true king and protector of the nation.

The constant tone of his words is one of rebuke and threat: rebukes against idolatry, injustice, immorality, adultery, lies, naked ambition, banditry, and wars setting brother against brother; and the threat of destruction of the kingdom, a threat which

Israel's crimes
'But as soon as they entered the land at Adam, they broke the covenant I had made with them. Gilead is a city full of evil men and murderers. The priests are like a gang of robbers who wait in ambush for a man. Even on the road to the holy place at Shechem they commit murder. And they do all this evil deliberately. I have seen a horrible thing in Israel; my people have defiled themselves by worshipping idols.'
(*Hosea* 6, 7–11)

he probably saw come to pass. But his message is double edged: there is compensation for the reprimand, the unshakeable love of God.

The hesed

Hosea sees this same situation being played out in his private life. His relationship with Gomer, his wife, is exactly the same as Yahweh's relationship with his people. On God's instructions he takes a wife, the daughter of Diblaim, who is a woman of loose morals and is soon unfaithful to him. He has three children by her. Inspired by God he names them Jezreel (the place where Jehu murdered his predecessor's children), Unloved, and Not-my-People. These names indicate the tensions which existed between Hosea and Gomer, and between Yahweh and his people.

Later we hear how he takes a fallen woman (is it the same one?) and makes her live a reclusive life in order to make her change her ways. This tragedy is described in simple language, the prophet does not go into great detail, but the message is clear: Yahweh's mystical bride, Israel, is unfaithful, God punishes her in no uncertain terms, but, driven by an unfailing love, he forgives her the moment she changes her ways. 'I will show love to those who were called "Unloved" and to those who were called "Not-my-People", I will say "You are my people" and they will answer "You are our God"' (*Hosea* 2, 23).

The main idea of the book is the word *hesed*. It signifies a love of and a dedication to God but not one without obligation. Religion is a matter of the heart and also one requiring fidelity. Hosea expresses himself in short, quick-fire sentences, almost falling over one another in an impetuous torrent of words fed both by anger and by love for his fellow men.

Joel

The son of Pethuel

The Day of the Lord

From today's catastrophe and the penitence it requires, to the judging of the nations and the salvation of Israel.

Joel lived c. 400 BC. He would know the prophets who had gone before him, would have absorbed their ideas and be of a mind to continue their work. Ezekiel in particular seems to be a strong influence on him. And yet, out of all the body of prophetic doctrine his small book contains only the theme of God's great mercy which can be gained through true repentance, and that of the future salvation of the people of Judah.

Perhaps he lived through a particularly devastating invasion of locusts. He certainly describes the horror of it with real feeling and an abundance of remarkable images: they are a consuming fire, the teeth of a lion, an army drawn up for battle, wave upon wave of rolling chariots; the enemy pounces on the city, launches itself at the walls, scales the houses, gets in through the windows; the countryside is ravaged too, vines are withered, fig trees destroyed, trees are dried up, seeds die, barns are devastated and granaries lie in ruins, the cattle bellow, and sheep cry out in distress.

Appeal to Yahweh

The prophet then sings a psalm of lament, calls for penitence and prayer, proclaims a fast, and convenes a special meeting for all the people in the land. For it must be remembered that Yahweh is kind and full of mercy, slow to anger and rich in grace. They must all say, 'Have pity on your people, Lord. Do not let other nations despise us and mock us by saying "Where is your God?"' (*Joel* 2, 17).

Yahweh does not delay his reply and so there follows a description of the land quite the opposite of that which began the book: corn and olive oil are in plentiful supply, the pastures are green again, trees bend under the weight of their fruit, the fields are full of wheat, the presses overflow with wine and the people are bursting with joy. Yahweh has been moved by jealousy for his land and has spared the people.

On the Day of the Lord, God will call the peoples of all the nations to come down to the valley of Judgment. Then the accusation will be heard: you have scattered my people throughout the nations, you have divided up my land, you have sold boys to pay for prostitutes, and sold girls to pay for wine, you have taken my silver and gold, you have taken away my treasures to your temples. Then comes the judgment: I will bring all the evil you have done on your own heads, Egypt will be devastated and Edom will become a desolate wasteland. At this time Israel will be restored: Yahweh will dwell in Zion.

Israel restored

'When that day comes, the mountains will run with new wine and the hills will flow with milk, and all the stream beds of Judah will run with water. A fountain will spring from Yahweh's Temple and water the gorge of the Acacias ... Judah will be inhabited for ever, and Jerusalem from generation to generation.' (*Joel* 4, 18–20)

Amos

The first of the minor prophets

Social justice

One of the humble shepherds of Judah speaks out against the wealth and moral decadence of the northern kingdom.

At the time of Jeroboam II's reign over Israel and Uzziah's over Judah, the land enjoyed peace and prosperity. Luxuries were the order of the day, debauchery was rife, and the poor became poorer. The worship of foreign gods took hold in the towns and the God of Israel was neglected, so Yahweh raised up a prophet.

Amos was a shepherd from Judah whom Yahweh would send into Israel. He was a rough-and-ready type, used to hard work in the fields, but nevertheless obedient to the Lord's command to prophesy against Israel and warn the people of the anger they had incurred through their degenerate ways.

Oracles of doom

The book begins with glimpses of universalism indicating that in the eyes of Amos, Yahweh was not nationally limited; a series of oracles are pronounced against neighbouring peoples before the focus is turned on Israel's punishment and the reasons why it was necessary. In various ways the people of Israel have transgressed, not least by worshipping in the temple of Bethel and Gilgal, oppressing the poor, and refusing to return to Yahweh in recognition of his merciful protection of his chosen peo-

ple, in the face of their enemies, severe famine and drought.

Amos thus portrays God as the Judge of the World who sees no ultimate distinction between the people's wrongs against their fellow men and their deliberate affronts to God's law; his forthcoming justice involves not only the destruction of Israel, but also his own refusal to respond to their inevitable cries for help: 'they shall run to and fro, to see the word of the Lord, but they shall not find it' (*Amos* 8, 12).

Several visions are declared, beginning with two of locusts and then fire eating up the land, but as a result of Amos's prayers against such total judgment, Yahweh concedes to hold back the doom. Visions of a plumb line and a fruit-basket follow with their warnings of impending destruction, the consequence of the Lord's determination to purge the land of evil — 'But let justice roll down like waters, and righteousness like an everflowing stream' (*Amos* 5, 24).

However the book does end on a more hopeful note, with the oracle of the rebuilding of the House of David, for which Amos's prophesy is later remembered (in *Acts* 15, 16): 'In that day I will raise up the booth of David that is fallen and repair its breaches, and raise up its ruins, and rebuild it as in the days of old' (*Amos* 9, 11).

The basket of fruits

'The Lord asked, "Amos, what do you see?" "A basket of ripe fruit", I answered. The Lord said to me, "The time is ripe for my people of Israel. I will not continue to overlook their offences."' (*Amos* 8, 1–3)

Obadiah

Yahweh's servant

The judgment against Edom

The one God, holy and just, is the one who breaks pride, exalts humility, and confounds that wisdom which is purely human.

Obadiah's prophecy concerning the destruction of Edom is the shortest book in the Old Testament. Its date may be referred to some time after Jerusalem's destruction by Nebuchadnezzar, king of Babylon, in 587 BC. The Edomites are denounced for their pride and especially for their lack of kindness towards Judah. The twin brothers Esau and Jacob were the ancestors of the nations Edom and Judah; even their mother was told by the Lord, that 'two nations are in your womb ... and the elder shall serve the younger' (*Genesis* 25, 23). Esau's subsequent failure to appreciate his privileged position of being born within the covenant later results in God's estimation of him: 'I have loved Jacob but I have hated Esau' (*Malachi* 1, 2–3), and God's promise to rebuild Judah but not Edom.

Just destruction

The first nine verses of Obadiah's prophecy depict a scene of destruction so thorough that nothing is left to plunder; every treasure is 'sought out' (it is always part of the judgment of God to bring to light things hidden in darkness), even the 'wise men' are destroyed and the 'mighty men' dismayed. The primordial reason for the prophet also recalls (in v 16) the way in which the Edomites caroused and drank in Jerusalem after the plunder of the city.

Obadiah's book conveys an overwhelming sense of God's power: he is Lord, Judge, King, Almighty, and the only true God. He decides a nation's prosperity, the success of its armies; and its ultimate glory. This nation that he wishes to see victorious can only be Israel, the chosen people. The judging of the nations is all part of God's plan for the history of the world, during which there will be one safe place, Mount Zion, where the survivors of Judah will congregate. Later Yahweh will reinstate them in the lands given them of old, to continue the chosen race.

Edom's sin

'Because you robbed and killed your brothers, the descendants of Jacob, you will be destroyed and dishonoured for ever. You stood aside on that day when enemies broke down their gates. You were as bad as those strangers who carried off Jerusalem's wealth and divided it among themselves.' (*Obadiah* 10–11)

Jonah

The man who converted Nineveh

A prophet in spite of himself

Fact or fiction, the story of Jonah is a colourful illustration of the call to the whole world to turn away from sin.

Jonah is a strange kind of prophet, one who thinks he can run away from the task Yahweh gives him, one who makes a prophecy which is not fulfilled and is grieved by the outcome of his mission. Nothing is known about him except for his resistance to God's will and his resistance to events as they unfold.

When the book was written it is certain that Nineveh was no longer in existence, crushed as it was by the Medes in 612 BC. But the town was remembered by the people of the area as an enormous city: 120 000 young children suggest more than a million inhabitants and three days' walking to cross it indicates a city of immense proportions, impossible for that time. Its memory has been kept alive as the supreme example of injustice, wickedness, and debauchery.

An impossible mission

It is to this daunting city that Jonah is sent. However, he avoids the situation by taking a boat at Joppa, destined for Tarshish in Spain. No doubt he was terrified by the impossibility of the task. But God unleashes a strong wind and violent storm at sea. The sailors are afraid and each one prays to his god while Jonah is sleeping soundly down in the hold. They wake him, and ask him to pray to his god too and they cast lots to see who is the cause of this disaster. The lot falls to Jonah and he tells them to throw him into the sea.

For three days Jonah remains in the stomach of an enormous fish, begging Yahweh to come to his aid and promising to be faithful to him. On the third day the fish spews him up on the beach and Jonah sets off for Nineveh. He goes through the city calling out: 'In 40 days everything will be destroyed.' The people of Nineveh then believe in God, fast, and dress in sackcloth. The king himself sits down among the ashes. God reconsiders the punishments he has threatened and does not carry them out. This upsets Jonah.

The *Book of Jonah* is a book with a strong message. Two ideas are highlighted in it: first, the universalism of the religion of Yahweh illustrated by the fact that there are examples here of worshippers of Yahweh, the sailors and the people of Nineveh, who prayed neither in the Temple nor at Jerusalem. The second idea which is positively asserted here, is the idea that prophecies of doom are simply threats applying in cases where there is no change of heart. Christians have seen Jonah's time in the fish as an image of Christ's descent into hell.

Nineveh repents

'The people of Nineveh believed God's message. So they decided that everyone should fast, and all the people, from the greatest to the least, put on sackcloth to show that they had repented. When the king of Nineveh heard about it, he got up from his throne, put on sackcloth and sat down in ashes. He sent out a proclamation to the people of Nineveh: "This is an order from the king and his officials: No one is to eat anything; all persons, cattle, and sheep are forbidden to eat or drink. All persons and animals must wear sackcloth. Everyone must pray earnestly to God, and must give up his wicked behaviour and his evil actions. Perhaps God will change his mind; perhaps he will stop being angry and we will not die."' (*Jonah* 3, 5–9)

Micah
The man from Moresheth

Judgment

Micah, the peasant from the village of Moresheth gives vent to his anger against the great city of Jerusalem.

In the village of Moresheth, during the reigns of Jotham (740–736 BC), Ahaz (736–716 BC), and Hezekiah (716–687 BC) we find a simple peasant, a hard worker, and a straight talker. He denounces the wealth and corruption of the great cities of Samaria and Jerusalem, the exploitation of the poor and simple by the ruling classes, and the seizure of lands by the hypocritical and the greedy.

His message is a cry from the heart and the prophet, in his simple faith, soon recognizes the sin against Yahweh: 'You eat my people up. You strip off their skin, break their bones, and chop them up like meat for the pot ...' (*Micah* 3, 3). He accuses the authorities of having built Zion with blood and Jerusalem on crime, with judges giving judgment for bribes, priests interpreting the law for pay, and prophets misleading the people for silver.

The catastrophe

Then comes the judgment which is terrible and inevitable. The prophet describes every phase of the disaster ahead. The ruin of Samaria: 'I will make Samaria a pile of ruins in the open country' (*Micah* 1, 6–7); the invasion of Judah: 'Now from the north their punishment approaches' (*Micah* 7, 4); the devastation of his own native land: 'You will sow, but not harvest the crop'

(*Micah* 6, 15); famine and defeat: 'I will destroy the cities in your land' (*Micah* 5, 11); and exile: 'now you will have to leave the city and live in the open country' (*Micah* 4, 10).

But the prophet's deep faith takes the form of an absolute trust in Yahweh: the promises of the Covenant will be fulfilled, he has no doubts about that. How then is Israel's sin and the punishment which goes along with that to be reconciled with the assurance of a promised salvation? Micah introduces the idea of the small remnant: it is not the whole of the nation now living which will see God's reign, but only those who survive the punishment and survive it because of their faith. Here is a fairly wild nationalistic dream being transformed into a moral concept.

Micah's style is fast-moving, lively, and passionate. He provokes his enemies, reads their thoughts, rebukes them sharply, and replies to them in detail. He deals in allusion, mystery, and enigma with little clear distinction between the prophet's words and the word of God. He plays word games making use of assonance and rhythm to engrave the key phrases of his speeches on the memories of those who hear him. Micah is an orator.

The small remnant

'"The time is coming", says the Lord, "when I will gather together the people I punished, those who have suffered in exile. They are crippled and far from home, but I will make a new beginning with those who are left, and they will become a great nation. I will rule over them on Mount Zion from that time on and for ever."' (*Micah* 4, 6–7)

Nahum

The consoler

The ruin of Nineveh

The prophet proclaims the end of earthly powers in the face of the reality of God's power.

In 653 BC, the Assyrian Empire, which had imposed its rule over the kingdom of Judah, suffers its first defeat: Egypt regains its independence. The following year Babylon revolts and new invaders threaten, the Medes, the Persians, the Scythians. This situation is a cause of rejoicing in Judah, all the more so since the reign of Josiah has encouraged a certain feeling of national independence, establishing itself in many areas of the northern kingdom.

The *Book of Nahum* is the Hebrews' cry of vengeance. The prophet expresses what they are feeling. It is the return of the god of Hosts who conquers Israel's enemies, crushing and annihilating them. Their only sin lies in opposing the chosen people, in being in the way, in proving to be an obstacle to God's plan. For this reason they are accused of every sin, of living on the profits of prostitution, of reducing nations to

slavery by their excesses, of enticing people astray through spells and through enchantment.

A nationalistic masterpiece

The *Book of Nahum* could be described as a magnificent poem of extreme nationalism: not a word about the sins of Israel, not a word about the mission Yahweh entrusted to the Assyrian and Egyptian armies, not even a word about the need for repentance or about conversion or faithfulness. This book does not seem to be a religious book. And yet the ruin of Nineveh as described here is not by way of a reward for Israel, nor of an act of vengeance on her part, but the punishment for idolatry, injustice, and violence.

The power of the universal God applies to all men. He uses nations, whichever ones they may be, and not just the chosen people, to implement his decisions. Here it is the Egyptians, the Medes, and the Persians who are his instruments in the punishment of the pride of the Assyrian; another time it will be another nation.

Both Judaism and Christianity have had no hesitation in claiming the *Book of Nahum* as one of the finest hymns to the glory of the one true God, master of all things, a statement of faith and hope going far beyond the event which originally inspired it. Through this, the prophet shows his fierce passion and joy, in the Lord's judgment. He brings all his artistic resources to bear: rhymes and rhythms which are striking and sympathetic to the emotions expressed, unexpected linguistic constructions; brilliant images and rare expressions which reinforce the point; short, vigorous sentences, unfailing zest and liveliness. All these make the *Book of Nahum* something of a masterpiece.

Threats against Nineveh

'Doomed is the lying murderous city, full of wealth to be looted and plundered! Listen, the crack of the whip, the rattle of the wheels, the gallop of horses, the jolting of chariots! Horsemen charge, swords flash, spears gleam! Corpses are piled high, dead bodies without number — men stumble over them! Nineveh the whore is being punished. Attractive and full of deadly charms, she enchanted nations and enslaved them.' (*Nahum* 3, 1–4)

Habakkuk

The prophet of the Temple

The lament of the chosen people

*The Book of Habakkuk: a dialogue,
a liturgy perhaps, but certainly an
exchange of some kind between God
and his followers.*

Habakkuk probably lived between the end
of Manasseh's reign (687–642 BC) and that
of Joachim (598 BC). Is he perhaps the son of
the Sunamite revived by Elisha as described
in the second book of *Kings* (4, 16)? Some
rabbis have made this claim. Whether or not
this is the case, he is a prophet, close to the
Temple restored and purified by Josiah, and
his book has been considered as a kind of
liturgical rite for the New Year festival.

It can, in fact, be seen as the people's
response, a kind of protest within the sanctuary, a lament in the face of Yahweh's silence
and the weight of overwhelming iniquity, in
the face of God's inactivity and the spread of
violence. It is a lament of grief, exasperation,
and heartfelt pleading: 'O Lord, how long
must I call for help before you listen?'
(*Habakkuk* 1, 2).

The cry of faith

God then speaks in response to the prayer,
the misery of the petitioner is met by the
power of the Lord which is exercised according to his will: 'I am going to do something
that you will not believe when you hear
about it' (*Habakkuk* 1, 5). Yahweh has raised
up the Chaldeans, a fierce and fiery people.
He has made them make a mockery of kings,
laugh at princes and show contempt for
fortresses. So God has willed this violence
himself. But then the tide turns, the Chaldean
takes pride in his own strength and must
therefore be punished.

The prophet speaks again, with more
pleading: 'You are my God, holy and eternal!' (*Habakkuk* 2, 12). In response to this
affirmation by faith God makes a very important declaration. It is to be written on
clay tablets for it is a prophecy for a particular time yet to come: 'those who are righteous will live because they are faithful to
God' (*Habakkuk* 2, 4).

Now the prophet has understood. After a
brief summary of all the evils from arrogance to unbridled greed, he launches into
a litany of curses, an unrelenting indictment
condemning the evil man who is unjust and
a criminal. But at no time is this evil character named. It is no longer the Chaldean, nor
the Egyptian, nor any other foreign power,
it is the man who is marked out by his own
sin. Evil brings misfortune and justice salvation. Although he cries out in distress,
Habakkuk is not sceptical. He expresses his
lack of understanding: how can God let this
happen? But he never doubts for a moment.
His God, unlike any other, has acted since
the earliest times, his reputation is known by
all, his power is formidable. He is the Holy
One, the Saviour.

The curses

'You take what isn't yours but you are
doomed! How long will you go on getting
rich by forcing your debtors to pay up? ...
You are doomed! You have made your
family rich with what you took by violence
and have tried to make your own house
safe from harm and danger ... You are
doomed! You founded a city on crime and
built it up on murder ... You are doomed!
In your fury you humiliated and disgraced
your neighbours; you made them stagger
as though they were drunk. You in turn
will be covered with shame instead of
honour.' (*Habakkuk* 2, 16–17)

JUDAISM

Zephaniah
The one whom Yahweh shelters

The Day of the Lord

*When divine justice will triumph
over man's iniquity and God will
settle his account.*

Zephaniah seems to have been of royal blood: most probably one of King Hezekiah's descendants. He lived in Jerusalem, understood the customs of the court and the upper classes, was familiar with different areas of the city, and noticed the corruption and idolatrous practices of the inhabitants. He lived during the reign of Josiah (640–609 BC), probably at the time that this king, whom Yahweh loved, undertook to reform the religious life of the kingdom.

This little book can be divided into three parts. The first consists of a threat: 'Dies irae, Dies illa', what a day of anger that will be. The Christian funeral service has taken up this idea of the Day of the Lord, meaning the Day of the Lord's judgment. Everything that lives will be subject to judgment, but especially Jerusalem, its rulers and noblemen who take divine warnings lightly. This

Call to conversion
'Shameless nation, come to your senses before you are driven away like chaff blown by the wind, before the burning anger of the Lord comes upon you, before the day when he shows his fury. Turn to the Lord all you humble people of the land, who obey his commands. Do what is right and humble yourselves before the Lord. Perhaps you will escape punishment on the day when the Lord shows his anger.'
(*Zephaniah* 2, 1–3)

Day of the Lord will bring a disastrous war, a total catastrophe, with frightful losses. Hence the call to conversion.

The second part is an exhortation and the prophet reinforces what he has to say by recalling Yahweh's vengeance on those nations which have martyred Israel: the Philistines, Moab, and Ammon, Ethiopia and Assyria, but, carried away by his vehemence, he goes on to rail against the rebellious and wicked Jerusalem: 'It has not listened to the Lord or accepted his discipline. It has not put its trust in the Lord or asked for his help' (*Zephaniah* 3, 2).

The promise of salvation

At last the promise of salvation comes: '"Just wait", the Lord says, "wait for the day when I rise …"' (*Zephaniah* 3, 8). The pagans will recognize and worship the one true God. The guilty ones will have been punished and the righteous rewarded. Jerusalem will be acknowledged by all as the source of true religious understanding. But 'I will leave there a humble and lowly people, who will come to me for help' (*Zephaniah* 3, 12).

The *Book of Zephaniah* must have been written all at once by an author who wanted to record the whole of the prophet's preaching. The whole thrust of the book turns on this notion of the Day of the Lord. The style is simple, serious, occasionally ornate but rarely given to poetic passages of the kind generally found in the writings of Israel's prophets. On the other hand, Zephaniah stands out because of his moving tone. He does not feel called to say anything new: Isaiah and Joel have already spoken about the Day of the Lord: Isaiah and Micah have spoken about the small remnant. But Zephaniah gives these themes more depth, bringing them dramatically to life.

Haggai

The restorer

Zeal for the house of God

When the Temple at Jerusalem is rebuilt, the people of God will be able to live again.

In 538 BC the Jews exiled in Babylon were authorized by Cyrus, king of the Persians, to return to their country. Those returning had listened to the teaching of Ezekiel, their religion had certainly been purified by the trials it had gone through, and their return to the Promised Land, received as a gift from God who keeps his promises, convinced them to rebuild the Temple of Jerusalem as soon as possible.

But things are very different now from the days of Solomon. The returning exiles are poor, they have a lot to do, building their houses, cultivating their land, getting rich. Many of them are quick to say: Ah, if only we had the great king's wealth! Even Solomon himself, with all his wealth and power, took seven years to build the Temple.

'Like a signet ring'

So God speaks through the prophet Haggai. We know nothing of him apart from the five speeches recorded in this book, but these speeches are very precisely dated: they were made between 29 August and 19 December of the second year of the reign of King Darius, Cyrus's successor.

No doubt work had already begun by that time on the foundations of the new Temple, but everyone was busy attending to their own business.

No one had noticed that the harvests were not so good. Haggai makes his point forcefully: if the land is not producing enough, it is because it is not the land of Israel, and it will not be the land of Israel until the Temple is rebuilt. He urges Zerubbabel, the governor, Joshua, the high priest, and all the people to go back to work on the Temple.

Prosperity will come as the Temple is rebuilt. It is very likely that, for the returning exiles, the rebuilding allowed them a glimpse of the messianic era, the time when a Saviour would appear. In his last speech Haggai makes Zerubbabel the chosen one: 'I shall take you … and make you like a signet ring. For I have chosen you' (*Haggai* 2, 23).

Whether on a tide of emotion or from a desire for purity, Haggai excludes the people already dwelling in the land from God's service. It is easy to imagine the returning exiles having many a brush with the existing population, inconveniencing them and perhaps even taking their lands. But they were not Jews, not pure Jews at least, and their impurity meant that they could not take part in the worship, as Haggai reminds them. More than any other figure, Haggai is concerned with the restoration of the temple and its worship. He urges the people of God to go back to the way things were, a state of affairs fundamentally based on faithfulness to the Covenant, worship in the rebuilt Temple and the dynasty of the house of David.

The reconstruction of the Temple

'You hoped for large harvests, but they turned out to be small. And when you brought the harvest home, I blew it away. Why did I do that? Because my Temple lies in ruins while every one of you is busy working on his own house. That is why there is no rain and nothing can grow. I have brought drought on the land — on its hills, cornfields, vineyards, and olive orchards — on every crop the ground produces, on men and animals, on everything you try to grow.' (*Haggai* 1, 9–11)

Zechariah

The prophet of the theocracy where the priests govern the nation

The hopes of the Jewish nation

Visions and oracles proclaim Israel's survival and ultimate triumph under the leadership of a descendant of David.

Zechariah was no doubt still a child when he returned from exile with his grandfather. He succeeded Haggai in the line of prophets and took up the themes developed by his predecessor. The subjects of his statements are the Temple, still not completed, the unrest in the land, and above all, the sin of the people. Yet in his prophecy there is no pessimism at all, no anger, no threats, but instead a great hope and an assurance of success.

Eight visions

His book begins with eight visions: the first is a vision of horsemen who go all round the earth and find it subdued and at rest. The angel asks Yahweh how much longer it will be before he shows mercy on Jerusalem, and God replies: 'I have a deep love and concern for Jerusalem, my holy city, and I am very angry with the nations that enjoy quiet and peace' (*Zechariah* 1, 14).

Then comes the vision of the horns and the blacksmiths, the horns representing the nations, and the blacksmiths with their hammers, those who have come to overthrow them; then the vision of the measurer, checking the dimensions of the new Jerusalem; then one of Joshua, the high priest, who takes off his dirty clothes and is dressed in fine new clothes; one of a lamp stand with the two olive trees beside it like God and his two 'anointed ones'; one of a

flying scroll which goes over the land bearing the curse which drives out thieves and liars; another of a woman who is shut up and carried off to a temple of idolatry; and finally the vision of the chariots bringing the spirit of Yahweh to the earth.

These visions are interspersed with appeals to those exiles remaining in Babylon to return, and encouragement to the exiles who have returned to live righteously. This first section ends with the words of Yahweh saying that he longs to return to Jerusalem and dwell there, in the 'faithful city' and 'Many peoples and powerful nations will come to Jerusalem to worship the Lord Almighty, and to pray for his blessing' (*Zechariah* 8, 22).

Most critics place the second part of the *Book of Zechariah* in the 2nd century BC, several centuries later. It is now no longer a question of rebuilding the Temple, no mention here of Joshua and Zerubbabel. The collapse of the Persian Empire has given new hope and the description of the final battle in the last days is made more vivid, despite numerous obscure references. How could it be any other way?

Salvation through the Messiah

'The Lord Almighty gave this message to Zechariah: I have longed to help Jerusalem because of my deep love for her people, a love which has made me angry with her enemies. I will return to Jerusalem, my holy city, and live there. It will be known as the faithful city and the hill of the Lord Almighty will be called the sacred hill. Once again old men and women, so old that they use a stick when they walk, will be sitting in the city squares. And the streets will again be full of boys and girls playing. ' (*Zechariah* 8, 1–5)

Malachi
The prophet of worship

The defender of God's rights

After the dedication of the new Temple and before Ezra's great reforms, an anonymous prophet urges the Jews to keep purity in worship.

Nothing is known about Malachi. This name means 'messenger' and has perhaps been used in the book of that name simply to show that this text is the record of a prophet speaking in God's name. The date of writing has been worked out from the following clues given in the text: it is obvious that the temple has been rebuilt and that Ezra has not yet launched his reform movement, since the author himself wishes to reform the worship. So the work is usually dated between 515 and 445 BC.

The Jews are depicted as disillusioned: as long as the Temple lay in ruins they could understand that there was no prosperity, since it was dependent on that duty being fulfilled. But now the sanctuary has been rebuilt, the priests perform their offices and the worship is conducted according to the old ways, and yet, contrary to what they might have expected, nothing has come their way, not prosperity, nor wealth, nor happiness. What good has religion done them?

The sun of justice

Yes, replies Yahweh — Here it is no longer the prophet who is speaking, but God himself — Look at the beasts you offer as sacrifices, they are all lame, sick or maimed. You wouldn't dare give them to the governor, nor to any of your friends. You promise me strong, proud male beasts and you offer me rubbish, you promise me a tenth of your income and give me pennies. How can I accept your offerings? Your altars are defiled, your gifts do not please me.

I had made a covenant with the tribe of Levi, the priestly tribe. For it is 'the duty of priests to teach the true knowledge of God. People should go to them to learn my will, because they are messengers of the Almighty', but you have wandered from this true path. Because of you, many have stumbled. You have broken your promise to the wife of your youth in favour of a young girl, with a foreign god. I hate this breaking of promises, says Yahweh.

But the Day of the Lord is coming. I will send my messenger and he will purify the sons of Levi and refine them in the fire like gold and silver, and they will bring the Lord the right kind of offerings. You will see the difference between the just and the unjust, between those who serve God and those who do not: the sun of justice will shine.

The triumph of the righteous

'"You have said terrible things about me", says the Lord. "But you ask, 'What have we said about you?' You have said, 'It's useless to serve God. What's the use of doing what he says or of trying to show the Lord Almighty that we are sorry for what we have done? As we see it, proud people are the ones who are happy. Evil men not only prosper, but they test God's patience with their evil deeds and get away with it.'"'

'Then the people who feared the Lord spoke to one another, and the Lord listened and heard what they said. In his presence, there was written down in a book a record of those who feared the Lord and respected him. "They will be my people" says the Lord Almighty. "On the day when I act they will be my very own."' (*Malachi* 3, 13–17)

The Talmud

The traditions of Judaism

The oral Torah

On Mount Sinai, in addition to the written Law, Moses received spoken instructions which have been passed on from generation to generation.

The destruction of the Temple in Jerusalem in AD 70 shattered the Jewish community once again. The rabbis felt a need to put all their traditions into some sort of order. So numerous scholarly groups in Judaea and Galilee set about the task of writing down the customs and interpreting Scripture in the light of the new situation. These commentaries on Scripture are important since they are more of an application of the written Law: they give us a practical Law, a living Law which is, in a way, better than the original. The rabbis called it the oral Law and attributed it, like the other Law, to the revelation given to Moses on Sinai.

Mishna and Guemara

So the rules, the *halakhot* (singular: *halakha*), were compiled. They are intended to legislate on every aspect of a Jew's life; there are no superfluous details, nothing is insignificant. The *halakha*, once defined, allows no breaking of its rule, except in a matter of life or death (save for three particular cases: idolatry, murder, and sexual depravity). No doubt the *halakha* finds its basis in Scripture (even after being formulated). This makes it different from the commentary: the *haggada* (plural: *haggadot*). This begins with

the text of the *Bible*, but interprets it very freely, embellishing the accounts given, adding folk tales and legends, turning odd words and phrases into pithy sayings or maxims. Its aim is not to give a set of rules but to be character forming and to maintain morale.

Taken together, the halakhot and haggadot, along with a number of *midrash* or free interpretations of the sacred text, form the *Mishna*. What it consists of is, in fact, a collection of oral traditions. Several rabbis were responsible for it, from Aquiba (died c. 135) to Juda Hanassi, who published it c. 200. A new stage was reached with the *Talmud*. Once the *Mishna* had been recognized as the supreme authority by the academics of Palestine and Babylonia, some extremly elaborate commentaries called *Guemara* ('finished off') were added, the *Mishna* and the *Guemara* together forming the *Talmud*: its style is complex, its thoughts confused, and its reasoning often strange. By seeking to record all the most contradictory opinions the authors of the Jerusalem *Talmud* produced a document that was far from simple. This is no doubt the reason why the Babylonian rabbis undertook to compile their own *Talmud* in which they do their best to explain the contradictions and give some answers.

Misogyny

'Why did God take Eve from Adam's side and not from any other part of his body? If he had taken her from the head she might have been proud; from the eye or ear, curious; from the mouth, talkative; from the hand, a thief; from the feet, a wanderer; he created her from his side so that she would be humble, and yet women still have all these faults.' (*Jerusalem Talmud*)

Mandaeanism

Between the Tigris and Euphrates, on the borders of Iran and Iraq, some small eccentric communities exist: they have the same beliefs, the same traditions, the same forms of worship, the same priesthood and the same Scriptures. Mandaeanism is a real religion. No one knows how the Mandaeans originated and, as far as they are concerned, it does not really matter. What they regard as important is the fact that their religion was founded by the world of Light, that it draws together the chosen people and that, from the very beginning to the end of time, those sent as saviours ensure an unbroken link with the Light.

The language of its sacred texts (eastern Aramaic), and certain of its themes and practices might suggest that this religion began in Palestine around the start of the Christian era. But this is not at all certain. However, its followers do stress their debt to John the Baptist, whom they set against Jesus, who is regarded as a deceiver and founder of one of the seven religions of hell. Comparisons could be made with certain Jewish sects, like the Essenes or with some heretical groups in early Christianity.

The sacred texts of the Mandaeans were written around the 8th century, probably under the influence of the hierarchy established by Islam between the religions of the Book and those which were purely human. There is no doubt, however, that these collected writings include older independent texts, hymns, legends, incantations, and magic spells which had been handed down from one generation to the next. From now on these would constitute the basis of their beliefs, traditions, and forms of worship.

The Mandaean suffers trouble and persecution because he knows that his body is both the object and the instrument of the hatred of the world of Darkness. He is an exile seeking salvation and a return to the world of Light by accepting the revealed truth, observing the commandments, receiving baptism in the living waters of a symbolic Jordan, and taking part in sacred meals with a blessing on the bread and wine mixed with water, the food of the heavenly beings.

Mandaeans take their name from Manda-d-Hiia, the Gnosis (Knowledge) of Life, personified here as an envoy of the Light who has received baptism from John. They are also called Nazarenes, a name which reveals their pre-Christian, Jewish origins. Finally, they are also called Sabenes, which means baptists.

The Ginza

The treasure

The Great Book

The collection of all the cosmological and religious beliefs of the Mandaeans is found in the Ginza, also called the Book of Adam.

An assorted collection of writings very different in origin and composition, the *Ginza* gathers together all the fundamental data of the sect. The first part, the *Ginza of the right* is made up of 18 chapters explaining, in a rather chaotic fashion, the myths on which the religion is founded and its conception of the universe; the second part, the *Ginza of the left*, is less important, dealing only with the soul's departure from this world of Darkness.

Dualism

The Mandaean religion is profoundly dualist, believing in the co-existence of two separate entities in the universe, like good and evil. So we have the higher world of Light and the lower world of Darkness. Even if creation is due to the devil Ptahill and is entirely evil, different texts cannot

---

The laments of the soul
'I suffer and am oppressed in this world, this world which is all night, full of twists and turns, all tied up in knots and sealed with seals, knots without number and seals beyond measure.' (*Ginza of the left*)

---

help but show that it has been achieved thanks to powers issuing from the 'Lord of greatness', but without his agreement. Whatever the mythological justification, the conflict is real, will last 480 000 years, and will see the devastating exploits of Death and the restorative actions of Life.

Man, who is at stake in this struggle, suffers moral failures, persecutions, and natural catastrophes but he just manages to come through it each time, thanks to the survival of one couple. He is tempted by the seven hellish religions founded at the instigation of the seven planetary powers: Zoroastrianism, Judaism, Christianity, Manichaeism, Islam, and two sects no longer known to us. But saviours are sent by the kingdom of the Light to strengthen the believers.

Three of these messengers in particular stand out. First Yohana, John the Baptist: persecuted from an early age by Jewish society, he is saved by divine powers and in his 22nd year goes to the banks of the Jordan and stays there for 42 years preaching and baptizing. He baptizes Jesus and also Manda-d-Hiia the second and most important messenger, a guide for the faithful who brings them the Truth, which is salvation. Finally the third messenger, Anosh Outhra, comes down from heaven to live among the Jews, he performs miracles, preaches the true doctrine, and convicts Jesus of lying. Then he goes back to heaven and returns in the form of a white eagle to punish Israel.

Apart from the *Ginza* there are other Mandaean sacred books: the *Book of John*, beginning as an appendix of the *Ginza*, recounts the same myths, and the *Qolasta* is a selection of songs and hymns for baptism and the ascension of the soul.

Manichaeism

In Persia, on 8 Nisan 527 in the Seleucid era, which would be 14 April 216, Mani or Manes was born. His mother was related to a princely family. His father, Patik, was a pious man, regularly attending the temple of Ctesiphon. One day, soon after the child's birth he hears mysterious voices urging him to abstain from alcohol, meat, and all sexual activity. So he goes away to Mesene in the south of Babylonia and joins the obscure Judaeo-Christian sect of the Elkesaites.

Manes is four years old when his father sends for him. This is where his education begins. He adopts certain Jewish traditions and observances, and obeys the commandments of Jesus: 'You were among us, like a betrothed girl, full of reserve' (*Greek Codex*, Ed. A Heinrichs). But gradually his critical mind awakens. He shows his disagreement and criticizes some of their practices: he does not, for example, see any advantage in baptism which seems to him to place value on a 'body of death' — something of which Saint Paul was always wishing to be free (*Romans* 7, 24).

At the age of 12 he receives an order from the Holy Spirit to leave the sect, then, when he is 24, the order comes to begin preaching his doctrine: the world's fundamental duality, spirit, and matter, light and darkness, and the continual conflict between these two principles. Proclaiming himself God's messenger of truth, he tries hard to make converts but the community authorities react against him, 'judge him and order him to leave'. So he goes away accompanied by his father and two disciples.

After a missionary journey to the north of India he returns home, meets the King Sapor who has just ascended the throne and obtains from him the right to preach his religion freely throughout the empire. He is highly regarded at court and divides his time between work on his writings, preaching in the land, sending out missionaries to East and West, and the setting up of his Church.

Sapor's death signals Manes's decline. After the short reign of Hormizd, Bahram I succeeds to the throne, the influence of the Zoroastrian clergy dominates and Manes's new religion is no longer the established religion. In the course of a journey he is taken *manu militari* (under armed escort) to Gundeshahpuhr and appears before the king himself. He is accused of heresy, condemned, spends 28 days chained up in a dungeon, and dies of exhaustion. His severed head is then displayed at the gate of the city.

The Manichaeist scriptures

The mysteries of the kingdom

Light and darkness

'Never have any books been written or revealed which can compare with those I have written' (Kephalaion 154).

According to Manes, the reasons for the failure of the religions of the Buddha, Zoroaster, and Jesus were due to the fact that none of these founders had written anything themselves. They had therefore allowed for the possibility of errors and distortions creeping in, and heresies taking root. Manes, however, was to put the basic themes of his teaching down in black and white himself. Unfortunately history has not treated his writings kindly and only a few examples of them have come down to us, while his Church, despite its promising beginnings throughout the world, barely survived into the 15th century.

However, Manes's intention was indeed to found a religion based on a body of canonical books which would be fixed for all time: scribes were instructed to copy them without any alterations because they were meant to contain a clear and precise account of the whole of revealed knowledge.

This body of literature, this canon, was composed of seven works attributed to Manes: the Living Gospel, the Treasure of Life, the Book of Mysteries (or Secrets), the Pragmateia, the Book of Giants, the Letters or Epistles, and the Book of Psalms or Prayers to which one would have to add a number of writings by disciples who were very close to the master. But since Manichaeism had succeeded in uniting all the emperors (Persian, Roman etc) and all the priesthoods (of Zoroastrianism, Catholicism, Islam etc) against it, those who preached it were persecuted and its books burned all over the world. Most of what is known about this literature comes to us from those who opposed it.

The Manichaeist myth

Manes's message is a gnosis, that is to say a fundamental knowlege which reveals to those initiated in its ways, and to them alone, the beginning, middle, and end of the human condition. It was easy for its opponents to attack this Truth using the principles of Reason, the requirements of Logic and the limitations of Reality. But

---

Manes is called

'When Manes had reached the end of his 24th year, At-Taum came to him and said: "The time has now come for you to reveal yourself and proclaim your message. Salvation be with you, Manes, from me and from the Lord who has sent me to you. He has chosen you for your message. For he has already designated you for calling men to your Truth. On his behalf, you will announce the joyful news of the truth and you will dedicate all your strength to that task."' (*Fihrist*)

The prophets

'Wisdom and good works have been handed down from one age to the next in perfect succession by the Prophets of God. At one time they were brought by the Prophet named the Buddha in the region of India, at another time by Zoroaster (Zarathustra) in the land of Persia, and in another time by Jesus in the West. After which the present revelation arrived and this prophecy is brought by me, Manes, God's true messenger in Babylonia.' (*Shapourakan* 1)

Among the 'elect' or 'perfect' members of
Manichaeism were the scribes whose task was
to pass on the Holy Scriptures without any
alteration whatsoever.

Manichaeist Manuscript of 8th or 9th century
from Chotscho (Central Asia).
Museum für Indische Kunst, Berlin.

they were on the wrong track, for this revelation is of an order which transcends the human mind.

Knowledge requires a lot of groundwork, it is transmitted by contact, by commitment to it and immersion in it. There is no need for discussion, reasoning or reflection. The doctrine only comes alive for those who humbly await it, who spend a long time contemplating it with admiration and are keen to absorb it every day. 'He who will listen to them (the words of salvation), who will first believe them and then preserve what they have put in the deepest part of himself, will never be subject to death, but, on the contrary, he will enjoy the eternal life of Glory. For the one who is initiated into the divine knowledge must certainly be held to be blessed.

The myth is well suited to this method of teaching: it belongs to the earliest times, not accessible by other methods; it has no time for the constraints of today's reality, but at the same time it does reveal some of its values or ambiguities; somehow or another it is able to reflect reality and transcends time while demonstrating the connections which do exist, at the deepest level, between past, present, and future.

The two kingdoms

In the beginning God and Matter (Satan) co-existed, each with its own kingdom, clearly separated. God's is the kingdom of Light, it extends northwards to infinity and everything there is peaceful, gentle, and pure. It is made up of five dwelling places: intelligence, reason, thought, reflection, and will. God the Father reigns over it all. The other kingdom is one of Darkness, it extends southwards to infinity, and everything there is disordered, foolish, and stinking. It is made up of five chasms: smoke, fog, consuming fire, air, and destructive wind. Satan reigns there.

The crisis occurs when the darkness tries to invade the kingdom of Light. The splendour of the kingdom of Light was, of course, bound to attract the greed of the other. But God, in his infinite knowledge has foreseen the danger. He decides to drive out evil himself and uses his own substance to produce the Mother of life from which primordial man emerges. This man goes down to the border but is thrown down into the infernal pit. So part of the substance of Light is now mixed up with and subject to the dark substance of Matter.

It does not end there. The two substances are incompatible, the demons are obliged to reject this light which they cannot bear and God stretches out his hand to primordial man. But the salvation is not complete; man has left something of his spirit in the realm of Darkness. Another rescue attempt is needed. In order to achieve this, the living Spirit (the creator) sets about arranging the world. It takes the skin of the hellish rulers to make the skies, their bones to make the mountains, and their flesh and excrement to make the earth.

A third envoy is needed to make the world into a machine for drawing in and absorbing the light which has been buried amid the darkness. In order to do this he sometimes appears in the sun as a virgin of light for the male demons, and sometimes he appears in masculine form for the females. In this way he stirs up their desire, makes some spend their seed from which light escapes and makes others spit out this light which they have devoured. But Matter is now afraid of losing all its treasure and therefore decides to concentrate most of it in two beings who will create Adam and Eve.

This explains the divine origin of man's soul, but since his flesh stilll retains its devilish lust he goes on mating, procreating, and therefore being a part of Matter. So the conflict continues. Other messengers will be sent. Manes recognizes the Buddha, Zoroaster, and Jesus as his precursors. But he himself is the Paraclete, the Holy Spirit promised by Christ: 'I will ask the Father and he will give you another Helper (Paraclete) who will stay with you for ever' (*John* 14, 16). 'The Spirit of Truth', says Manes, 'has been sent. He has come to you in this generation' (*Kephalaion* I, 14, 4–6).

The end of the conflict

This struggle between Light and Darkness, between Spirit and Matter will end when all the divine fragments still imprisoned in nature and in the body are set free, and are once more on the road to the kingdom of Light. So it is vital that the chosen ones do not allow evil to spread. The discipline imposed on them is very strict: they must avoid the sins likely to be committed by the mouth, the hand, and the body, which means, for instance, not consuming meat, blood or alcohol; respecting the light contained in all plants, that is to say not planting, growing or harvesting; and finally, they must not procreate. Fortunately there were, apart from those who perfected this code of life, a number of Hearers, as Manes's followers were called, who adopted a less strict form of asceticism and were able to meet the needs of the community.

Manichaeism has not survived as a Church, but the word has become the name commonly used to describe any philosophy in which Good and Evil are seen as two fundamentally co-eterna principles. Historically it has inspired a large number of heresies, one of its most notable descendants being Catharism, a sect which flourished in southern France and northern Italy.

The Church of Jesus

'After three days he (Jesus) was raised from the dead. He showed himself to his disciples. He endowed them with his strength and breathed his Holy Spirit into them before sending them out to preach his Greatness. He ascended into heaven once more. After Paul's time, despite the efforts of two righteous men (?), the Church of Jesus became corrupt. So the true Church which he had founded was also taken up to heaven. That which has remained on earth is not the Church of Jesus.' (*Kephalaion* I, 13, 16–35)

The Mormons

During the 18th century the Protestant Churches, particularly in the Anglo-Saxon countries, experienced religious revivals which overturned the existing customs and institutions: John Wesley and the Methodists, Jonathan Edwards and the Great Revival in America, and so on. At the beginning of the 19th century there was still a hunger, produced by this movement, for a purity of faith and life which was not being met by the great number of Churches, some of which were in constant conflict.

Joseph Smith, the prophet-founder of Mormonism had experienced this tension in his youth. He was born into a poor family in Vermont. His father was a labourer working on the land and doing other hard jobs for his neighbours. A move to northern New York State did not improve his financial situation. The father, mother, and children had a firm faith, read the *Bible*, went to the local churches, and attended evangelical meetings: each one was trying to work out his own way through the maze of institutions and traditions: it could be said that they were seekers after faith.

Joseph Smith had his first vision when he was not yet 15. When he spoke about it he was rejected, ridiculed, and even persecuted. And yet he was convinced that the Churches were going the wrong way, that they had become too humanized and were to some degree betraying the message they were charged with bringing to the world. In 1827 he had a vision in which a prophet led him to discover documents buried in the ground in the form of gold plates engraved with an ancient form of writing. Later, with God's help, he was to translate these plates into English and publish what is commonly known as the *Book of Mormon*.

This was to be the holy book of 'The Church of Jesus Christ of Latter-Day Saints', founded by Smith and five of his friends in a log cabin in New York State. They became preachers, propagandists, and missionaries. But there was plenty of opposition and persecution. Driven out of state after state they ended up in Utah which became the centre of their operation: there they drained and cultivated the land, making the area rich and prosperous. The largest community of Mormons is still based there but their Church has spread far beyond it, in America and as far as Europe.

The Book of Mormon

A testimony of Jesus Christ

The revelation made to Joseph Smith

Finding once more the fervour and values of early Christianity.

'There is a hidden book', says the prophet Moroni to Joseph Smith, 'written on plates of gold, giving the history of the ancient inhabitants of this continent (America) and details of where they came from.' He also says that the fullness of the eternal Gospel is contained in it, as it was given by the Saviour to these original inhabitants. These words were heard by the founder of the Mormons in 1823. A few years later, under the direction of this same prophet, Joseph Smith discovered the plates; they were buried in the ground on a hill in New York State (near Smith's home), in a stone box under a huge stone slab. This was the new revelation.

Descendants of Joseph

We knew from the Bible (*Genesis* 11) that Yahweh had scattered men 'over the entire face of the earth' to prevent them building the tower of Babel, but it was not known that the Jaredites had come directly from the tower to the New World and settled there. Nor was it known that, in the 6th century, a second group of the children of Israel, descendants of Joseph, had come from Jerusalem to America (*I Nephi* 18), whilst the Jaredite people had died out. These people were the ancestors of the American Indians and their history runs parallel to that of the Hebrew people in Israel; they have their prophets, kings, persecutions, and even their promised land.

The *Book of Mormon* records this history in the style of the *Old Testament*, but the prophecies proclaiming the coming of Jesus Christ are more detailed here. The terminology used is Christian in tone and the law of Moses as presented here is much more closely related to the law of the *New Testament*. All this begins to fall into place once it is known that Christ himself appeared to the chosen people of America after his resurrection: he appeared in the middle of a 'mighty and terrible tempest', while towns and villages 'were buried in the depths of the earth' and the earth 'rose up giving birth to great mountains'. 'I am Jesus, the Son of God', he said. (*3 Nephi* 9, 15)

Then Jesus recalled these words, spoken once before in Israel: 'I have other sheep who are not of this pasture; them also must I bring in.' Then he added: 'You have been separated from them because of their wickedness. You are my disciples, you are a light for this people which is a remnant of the house of Joseph.' He ordered them to baptize, to celebrate Communion and to preach.

The truth

'According to our records, and we know that our records are true; for it was a righteous man who kept these records; he performed many miracles in the name of Jesus; and there is no man who could perform miracles in Jesus's name if he were not entirely cleansed from his sin.' (*3 Nephi* 8, 1)

Rome

The Romans are said to have been the most religious people in the world. Religion in Rome takes on a character peculiar to that place. The Republic is a place which favours the spoken rather than the written word. The senate's laws, decrees and judgments come into existence by voting and by statement, that is to say by being read out by the appropriate authority. The priests are magistrates like many others, their particular responsibility being relations with the gods; they are answerable to the political authority and carry out their mission through their actions: prayers, sacrifices, soothsaying, finding their role through the decisions of the authorities and the functions which have been delegated to them.

There is neither revelation, nor books of reference. The gods are silent. They are neither benevolent nor malevolent so there is nothing one can do to gain their favour or divert their wrath. Yet the sense of the divine is required in certain public or private acts. It is therefore necessary to know when and under what circumstances it applies. This is the reason for augury, the observation of certain phenomena to foretell events.

So the formulae uttered by anyone addressing the gods — be they a priest, head of a family or an individual — were not so much prayers as incantations or magical invocations. These were very ancient words, no doubt originating with the 'fortune tellers', soothsayers or magicians who were asked to avert misfortune rather than simply to predict it. On no account must there by any alteration to the tone of voice, the order of words or the dance which occasionally accompanied these incantations. The meaning of these *carmina* was often lost, but that did not matter, they were effective in themselves. The most famous of these songs are those of the Arvales brothers and the Saliens.

However, the Etruscans, a neighbouring tribe who were often closely linked with the Romans, did have sacred books. According to tradition these contained the teaching of a child brought out of the earth and formed by the nymph Vegoia. The *libri fulgurales*, books on divination belonging to a people they must have driven out of their town, no longer had any authority under the Republic.

In fact it was a Roman king of Etruscan origin, Tarquin the Proud, who introduced the only sacred (?) texts which are truly Roman: the *Sibylline Books*. But the fate of these books was not that normally associated with sacred texts. Apparently, the Roman religion was unable to accomodate holy writ of any sort.

The Sibylline Books

The search for destiny

The corruption of the sacred book

How the authority of the state can undermine faith in books by constant exploitation and misuse of the contents.

The Sibyl comes from Ionia. A rival of the Pythia (prophetess) of Delphi in her powers of divination, she differs from her essentially in that she is an imaginary being: a woman, certainly, for her nature is more sensitive than a man's and therefore more able to enter into contact with the spirits, a 'virgin prophetess' as Pindarus says. The Sibyl does not seem to be bound by place and time, her prophecies have another dimension, as if her world goes far beyond and encompasses the human world.

No one has seen her, except perhaps for Heraclitus. She travels throughout the Mediterranean basin and many authors affirm her existence, including Euripides, Aristophanes, and Plato. She even seems to have multiple forms: there is the Sibyl of Erythrea, that of Marpessa, of Cumes, and of Samos etc.

Added to that there is language which is enigmatic, expressions which are rather obscure, and meanings which are uncertain. As a result the words of the Sibyl have acquired enormous prestige. We know that they were committed to paper, but nobody knows when, where or how.

Tradition has it that the king of Rome, Tarquin the Proud, bought a collection of oracles, called the *Sibylline Books* from an old woman, who may have been the Sibyl of Cumes. This was treasure beyond price, the destiny of Rome and the whole universe was written there: imagine the force of any decisions, decrees or laws stemming from the inspiration of Apollo himself. What legitimacy they would lend to those in power!

The ancient Romans were proud of their new possession. They placed it in a vault of the Capitol temple of Jupiter and entrusted it to the keeping of two special magistrates for whom this was their only task. Theirs was a very important function since the *Sibylline Books* were consulted, in the name of the state, in the event of any exceptional occurrences and guidance was sought as to the best course of action to take. In 367 BC a college of 10 members drawn half from the patricians (the ruling class) and half from the plebeians (the common people) was given the job of interpreting the texts.

When the *Sibylline Books* were destroyed during the burning of the Capitol in 83 BC, the senate, who had found them so useful in government, set up a special commission to go and look for the texts at their places of origin; Erythrea, Samos, Troy, any place where a Greek colony had settled. This resulted in a new version which, according to Varron, was a faithful reproduction of the original.

The prophetic virgin

'The sibyl who from her extraordinary mouth pours forth oracles without joy, ornament or perfume, may her voice echo them for 1000 years under the influence of god.' (Heraclitus according to Plutarch)

An oracle

'The man who escapes from one misfortune and who goes home proudly on his steed will soon fall into another. But even then the sibyl will reveal the remedy if you have confidence in her.' (*De divinatione*, Cicero II, 54)

The manipulation

At any rate it was worth more than was thought. The secrecy surrounding the *Sibylline Books* allowed things to get into a mess. It required real ingenuity to apply warnings which were obscure, impenetrable and, in a word, sibylline, to actual events of the time. The decemvirs, the college of 10, who later became the quindecemvirs (15), the various interpreters (the text was in Greek), and legal officials were not averse to introducing, under the pressure of events or from some authority, recommendations and ideas which had nothing to do with the original oracles.

The secrecy which was required by the sacred nature of the texts and was very convenient when it came to their manipulation, was difficult to maintain. The enlargement of the college of quindecemvirs and their assistants together with the necessary publication of the official interpretations soon became too much for such a contrived kind of mystery.

At the height of the troubles in 87 BC the senate decided, during a solemn sitting, to support its resolution by making the citizens aware of the Sibylline oracle which recommended driving out the dictator, Cinna. In 54 BC Cato used the authority of a specially commissioned oracle to try and put Ptolemy Auletes back on the throne of Egypt. Then the floodgates opened: there were soldiers relying on the books to challenge their superiors and plotters finding justification in it for their conspiracy against the state. The authority of the interpretations, if not the books themselves were greatly devalued as a result.

Cicero speaks about them in mocking tones: it is true that the use one wanted to put them to had little to do with the art of divination as it was practised among the Greeks: there it was the work of an independent personality, someone legendary, doubtful even, but nevertheless someone who created her own credibility; here in Rome it is the work of a tightly organized body of magistrates, subject to the official authorities, responsive to their demands in particular cases, and working for their interests. So despite the great skills of the manipulators the deception was denounced many times. The books survived, however, until AD 389, when they were burned on the orders of Emperor Theodosius.

The Christian sibyl

However, the Jews and the Christians have not always been so wary in their attitude to the books. The *Sibylline Books* were held in honour by the Fathers of the Church. Saint Justin, Clement of Alexandria, Athenagoras, and Theophilus used them in their opposition to the pagans; Lactantius found proofs of Christ's divinity in them and, at the Council of Nicea, the Emperor Constantine appealed to the authority of the Erythrean sibyl for definition of the dogma of the Trinity.

Saint Ambrose, on the other hand, expressed doubts, Origen and Irenaeus were sceptical, and Saint Augustine declared quite plainly that the sibylline prophecies which speak of the birth of Christ had been made up by the Christians themselves. The deception must have gone on for quite some time and 'Cumes may grieve for the end of its oracles' (Heraclitus).

Shinto

The origins of ancient Japanese religious beliefs and practices are lost in the mists of time. No one knows when belief in the many kami (spirits) began. But this kind of composite religion was flourishing when Buddhism arrived in Japan around the 6th century. The ancestral practices then took the name of *Shinto* and the two religions co-existed, borrowing certain ideas of worship and teaching from each other, opposing each other or coming together according to circumstances, with one sometimes having supremacy over the other.

There soon developed a movement in favour of a return to the roots of their Japanese nationalism or 'Nipponism'. This naturally based itself on the *Kojiki* which was compiled in 712 and gathered together the myths of Japan's origins. The fact that this work had been completed well after the adoption of Buddhism and that it had been written by fervent Buddhists steeped in Chinese culture, and finally that its aim had been more political than religious, namely, to legitimize the reigning dynasty, did nothing to prevent its being hailed as the 'Bible of Shinto'. All that remained to be done was for Shinto to be made the state religion; this step was taken in the 19th century.

But besides the state Shinto, which became moribund in 1946 when the emperor renounced his divine rights, there exists a popular Shinto with its own daily practices, traditions, and forms of worship, a Shinto of the temples which finds its expression through organized ceremonies in the thousands of village temples scattered throughout the land, and finally a Shinto of the sects which is more hierarchical in organization, more concerned with doctrine and sometimes more universalist in its approach.

Be that as it may, this religion has never been particularly strong on doctrine; this is why it can tolerate alliances with the imported religions, Buddhism, Confucianism, and even Christianity. The emphasis is put instead on participation in ceremonies which confirm membership of a community. Shinto rituals celebrate life, everyday life as well as the major events of life in that society.

Traces of the cult of the kami survive in the fashion for pilgrimages. Certain places and temples still attract immense crowds, and the sanctuary of Ise Jingu, dedicated to the Sun goddess, Amaterasu-o-mikami, the ancestor of the imperial family, is still considered to be the holiest place in the land.

The Kojiki

The book of ancient things

The origins of Japan

A book on which to found the structure of the state and establish the origin of imperial virtue.

In the 7th century, whilst China already had an important literary culture, the Japanese islands had produced nothing in that field. Legends were certainly passed on from generation to generation and village to village, but only by word of mouth and usually these traditions belonged to a particular clan who had created and sustained them: they were not national in scope.

In 682 the Emperor Temmu decided to rectify this state of affairs. He gave a man named Hieda no Are the task of engraving on his memory the noteworthy facts gathered from all over the country, correcting the errors and determining the truth. In fact, he asked him to establish the official truth about the clan of Yamoto, the emperor's clan.

Some 30 years later, the enterprise was brought to a successful conclusion thanks to an edict from the Empress Gemmyo who ordered the scholarly O no Yasumaro to take down Hieda no Are's dictation of the 'Notes on ancient things'. The work was completed in four months and O no Yasumaro presented the book called *Kojiki* to the empress in 712.

The *Kojiki* was the first book written in Japanese, although the Chinese form of writing was still being used. It contains the most ancient myths and traditions of the Japanese islands, but marshalled, reorganized and corrected in such a way as to meet the emperor's requirements. The work sets out to prove the legitimacy of the dynasty's divine right and the noblemen of other clans are given subordinate status when included in the genealogies: for example, 'Majesty — Young Bird — Courageous, Son of Majesty — Spirit-of-the-Ear-of-Rice, is the ancestor of the governors of the province of Izumo, the governors of the province of Musashi … etc' (*Kojiki* II).

The age of the divinities

At the beginning of the world, there are three heavenly divinities: Ama no minaka nushi, Takami-musuhi, and Kami-musuhi. These three have many children, including the creative duo, Izanaki and Izanami, a brother and sister who create the islands, the mountains, the rivers and innumerable kami. But while giving birth to the god of Fire, Izanami burns herself, is killed by the baby as it is born and must go to hell. In order to purify herself from all the stains she received in hell, she washes in a river. Then, from her left eye is born Ametarasu,

---

The *Nihongi*

A few years after the *Kojiki* collection another work was compiled called *Nihongi* or *Nihon shoki* (Chronicles of Japan). It records the same myths as the *Kojiki*. The only difference in the first books is that sometimes several versions of the same events are given, whereas later the *Nihongi* gives much more importance to relations with the continent. It does not hesitate to speak about Korea and their large neighbour, China. It was, in fact, by claiming the title of Emperor of the East that the Japanese gave themselves equal status with the emperors of China and were able to avoid becoming their vassals.

goddess of the Sun, from her right eye, Tsuki-yomi, god of the Moon, and from her nose, the wild Susanoo, god of the Sea.

Izanami divides the world between her three children; the heavenly Plain goes to Amaterasu; the realm of the Night goes to Tsuki-yami and the Plain of the sea goes to Susanoo, who refuses his share and wishes to join his mother in hell. The struggle for earthly power constitutes the main theme of the age of the divinities.

Ninigi is Amaterasu's grandson. He comes down to reign on earth and there he meets Konohananosa-kuyahime, the daughter of the Mountain god, who is as beautiful as trees in blossom. He asks for her hand in marriage and the Mountain god agrees. However, as well as sending this younger daughter he also sends his elder daughter, Iwanagahime, who looks like ancient rocks

and is very ugly. Ninigi cannot bear her ugliness and sends her back to her father. This is why the emperors have lives which are dazzling but are as short-lived as flowers. Iwanagahime would have guaranteed them eternal life.

The first book of the *Kojiki* records a number of similar episodes from different generations of gods who gradually take possession of the 'land of the eight great islands', which therefore becomes the land of the gods until the arrival of the first 'human' emperor, the half-legendary, Jimmu-tenno, who is tradionally believed to have lived in the 4th century BC.

The genealogies

The second and third books of the *Kojiki* consist of genealogies of the emperors. It was a period of history which guaranteed a kind of
eternity through the endless continuation of the dynastic line. However, the author does not miss the opportunity of describing a few moral episodes in the lives of the emperors and these tales appear as digressions from the main thrust of the work.

One example is the story of how the Emperor Nintoku received the title of wise emperor: having climbed up to a high place once when it was particularly cold, he noticed that there was no smoke rising from the houses. He concluded from this that the people were too poor to heat their homes and decided to end all taxation and all forced labour for three years.

These are vivid anecdotes, written in a lively style and they are occasionally accompanied by popular ballads, no doubt borrowed from traditional folklore, the same source which provided the main body of legends which forms the basis of the book. They give the whole thing an authentic flavour and help to root it firmly in the community.

The aim of the *Kojiki*

'The Emperor Temmu, lamenting the fact that the historical documents in the possession of the leading noble families contained numerous mistakes, wished to take the proper steps to ensure that the authentic traditions did not become forgotten. He therefore had these documents carefully examined and all the errors corrected. By chance there was a person in his own family called Hieda no Are who had great powers of memory and was in a position to repeat, without mistake, the contents of all the documents he had seen and never forget what he had heard.' (*Kojiki* preface)

Song for the country

'Yamoto, you are the most splendid of landscapes, mountain after mountain surrounds you like verdant hedges. Yamoto, how beautiful you are.' (*Kojiki*)

Sikhism

In 1469, some 60 kilometres from Lahore, Guru Nanak was born. He was of a noble family and until he was 27 he lived in the village of his birth and married there. He then had what legend calls a mystical encounter. After three days spent in silent retreat, he pronounced these words: 'There are no Hindus, there are no Muslims' and, feeling himself to be the bearer of a message of equality between all religions, love between all men, and faith in the one eternal, infinite God, who has no rival, is not limited by time, and can go anywhere, he set out on a long series of preaching tours across the whole of India, Iraq, and Arabia.

Guru Nanak had been commissioned by God to preach freedom from *samsara* (the endless cycle of rebirths) through loving devotion to God and the service of men. At the end of his life he settled in a village he had founded, called Kartapur and a community immediately grew up around him. His followers already regarded his words as divine revelation. As his successor as leader of the community he named Angad whom he regarded as an extension of himself and Angad later did the same. There were eventually 10 of these gurus who were as a single spirit in different bodies.

As the community grew in importance, each guru took steps to organize it: one set up areas of pastoral responsibility and districts for preachers, another determined the calendar of feast days and laid down the details of the ritual ceremonies of birth, marriage, and burial, a third built the Golden Temple at Amritsar and made it the most important centre of worship. The most decisive step taken was certainly the classification of the gurus' literary works. But relations with the political authorities grew acrimonious and the use of the sword became legal. The guru Gobind Singh (1666–1708) went further than this by creating the military order of the Khalsa, the Chosen of God.

It was this last guru who put an end to the personal succession of gurus by instituting the 'Sacred Book', the *Adi Granth,* to succeed him until the end of time. This book became the supreme authority and ultimate reference. The Sikh community is still very much alive. At one time it even set up its own state which was later swept aside by colonization. However, the community still takes an active interest in education and literature, plays a major role in the modern progress of society, and is not without success in the field of politics.

The Adi Granth

The book as teacher

The perpetual guru

Kept in the heart of the central sanctuary of the Golden Temple at Amritsar, the Adi Granth is the most important 'institution' in Sikhism.

When there is a teacher like Guru Nanak who, by his actions, exercises so great an influence over people and who draws such large crowds to hear his words, there will always be disciples ready to record what he says. From the early days of the Sikh community there were plenty of memorable texts from the founder. Then, as the 10 gurus succeeded one another, each one in the spirit of the first, the number of documents recording their declarations and prayers increased greatly. Thus there was a large amount of material to nurture the faith of the believers.

The fifth guru, Guru Arjun (1563–1606), decided to gather all these writings together into an official version which became the established canon of scripture. Later some poems by Guru Teg Bahadur (1621–75)

were added and the last teacher, Gobind Singh (1666–1708) included some of his own compositions before declaring the book to be holy, the last and definitive guru, sealing it and installing it in the centre of the Golden Temple, thereby consecrating it as the testimony of the Sikh religion.

Yet, it is somewhat astonishing to see that it contains, in addition to the words of the gurus, a large number of verses composed by famous holy men of India, Hindus, and Muslims alike. Arjun did not do this without reason: no doubt he wanted to emphasize that there was nothing sectarian about Nanak's message, that he had no prejudices. But he did not make a random choice: none of the verses in question lean towards idolatry, they are all monotheistic (holding to the idea of one God) and of great spirituality.

Guru Arjun's aim was to complete a huge summary of religion. So he included in the *Adi Granth* the eulogies of his predecessors performed by the poets who were attached to them. This is not a case of misplaced hagiography, the art of praising holy men, but a way of bringing into focus authentic and original doctrines. These songs of praise are written in rich and resonant language, they give their heroes the status of the Rsis, the authors of the *Veda*, and attempt to establish the teaching they laid down as real revelation.

The *Adi Granth* was therefore written by three groups of authors: first the gurus, then the holy men of India, and finally the poets or bards praising the founders. It is composed mainly of the major themes of the Sikh faith and of what might be called the applied faith, that is to say hymns and prayers, songs in praise of those who have made advances in the love of God, and especially those who have been bearers of the revelation.

Impurity

'Avarice is the impurity of the mind and falseness that of the tongue: looking enviously at the riches, the wife or the beauty of another is impurity of the eye; listening to scandal is impurity of the ear. Nanak, the soul of a man loaded with such impurity goes to the land of Yama.' (*Adi Granth, Asa ki Var*, sloka 18)

The Sikh faith

The first and most important declaration of faith is the belief in the one god and his infinity. He exists through himself alone, is limited by nothing, has never been made incarnate and cannot be represented by any image whatsoever. On the other hand, he is the only source of love and grace. At the time of Nanak, this faith was part of a mystical movement which, in the 15th and 16th centuries, was affecting Hindu society (the bhaktas) as well as the Muslim community (the soufis). This movement was opposed to the formalism and ritualism of official religion, and favoured personal experience. So it can be understood how the *Adi Granth* was able to include hymns by the leaders of this trend, no matter what their religion of origin.

Mukti is the supreme goal, that is freedom from samsara, the endless cycle of rebirths. The major obstacles to this is Haumai, which is egoism, the attitude of one who thinks of nothing but himself, his pleasure, his image, and who is therefore governed by the passions, sensuality, anger, greed, and pride. Without realizing it, this man is separating himself from his original source, God, whose spark still shines within him. Mukti, on the other hand, is achieved by getting rid of the ego and the ties which bind us to the world, and by concentrating the mind always on the divine name. The way to this freedom lies in the loving devotion which leads to complete union with God.

The hymns and prayers

The *Adi Granth* is also a book of prayers. One might think that it had been written along the lines of the *Rig Veda*. In fact, the hymns, long or short are ritually organized and appear in the order of the daily observances and the ceremonies of which they form part. They are accompanied by melodies, each of which has a particular meaning or relates to a particular response in the soul. There are tunes which can only be sung in the morning, others which can only be fully appreciated at midnight and so on.

The poems are grouped according to author, the first quite naturally being those of the gurus in chronological order, but also according to the musical key in which they should be sung. Not all the parts of the *Adi Granth* are acknowledged as being of equal value. It could be said that the third part was lacking in authenticity, that it had been added later, and some editions of the Sacred Book do not include it.

But any impartial study of the *Adi Granth* reveals its unquestionable religious importance and its devout spirit. It bears witness to social and religious conditions in the Punjab during the two centuries of its composition. It uses several dialects, but the language of Nanak is that of the early Punjabi poets and the other gurus each use the language spoken in their lifetimes.

Woman

'It is in a woman that man's body is formed, and it is of a woman that he is born, it is to a woman that he pledges his word, it is a woman who is his companion, with a woman that he shares his roof, and it is through her that his life is lived out. When a wife dies, one looks for another. Society can only exist through her since it is through her that kings are born. All creatures are born of the female of the species; without her none can exist. Nanak alone has no wife, he is the true Being. Every mouth which speaks his praise shines with perfect happiness, but only such faces, O Nanak, appear spotless at the true Court.'
(*Adi Granth, ki Var Mahala* I)

Taoism

Taoism is the product of a long ripening process in Chinese thought. Its origins are lost in the mists of time and its influence has continued to the present day. The first expressions of it are found in the *Tao Te Ching*, the *Chuang Tzu*, and the *Lieh Tzu* which date from the last centuries before Christ. They recommend an attitude which is 'self-effacing' or modest, and develop a philosophy in which the 'ineffable' or indescribable is of the highest importance. The essential idea of the religion, *tao*, is the idea of a first principle from which everything has to come and to which everything returns, 'the Absolutely Real': every contingency — and contingency must be taken in its widest sense — is simply a by-product, not only of no interest, but actually harmful because it distances one from the eternal *tao*.

So, for thousands of years, numerous wise men have lived out this doctrine, hermits hidden in the mountains, indifferent to events, to feelings, to other people, and to themselves. They taught the doctrine, made disciples, propagandists, and the movement grew, taking different forms.

There have been many Taoist sects. They are usually linked to what is called religious Taoism, which also has a very long history: religious Taoism and philosophical Taoism run along parallel lines, the first being the medium for the second for most of the time, but at the same time it also gives it a particular slant. There are a number of irrational practices and exercises, traditional arts and techniques, which do not directly contradict the thought of the system's founders, but are extensions of it, from the magical, hygienic or religious angle, which were not in the original plan.

The aim most frequently pursued by these schools of thought is immortality. A whole mythology has grown out of these quests, and studies are made of the celebrated immortal ones, saints of another age, role models for today's believers. Their legends are carefully gathered, read, and religiously meditated over. The canon of Taoist scriptures has therefore evolved greatly throughout its history. A number of other works have been added to the books of Lao Tzu, Chuang Tzu, and Lieh Tzu. In 745, 1464 had been compiled: they form the *Tao tsang*.

The Tao Te Ching

The 'way' and the 'virtue'

The principle of Taoism

As opposed to those philosophies which praise social values, the Tao Te Ching preaches an 'effective disengagement' (non-involvement).

The formation of the Ch'in Empire in 221 was long and painful. It was punctuated by terrible wars and important social changes.

The period of the warring kingdoms

From the 5th century onwards the growth in population became more noticeable (the country would reach 57 million inhabitants in AD 2, more than those of the Roman Empire at that time). The empty spaces between the different centres of civilization were gradually eaten into. The lands were cleared. New techniques were discovered: cast iron and the ox-drawn plough amongst others. Commercial and manufacturing classes appeared. The towns developed. States became centralized. The authorities subdued the feudal lords and extended their influence to every aspect of life. The peasants were conscripted and made into a powerful army with a strong labour force in reserve. Great irrigation schemes were undertaken. China shed its fragmented structure and became a great nation.

This did not happen without a struggle. Powerful rivals emerged in every region. Seven great kingdoms divided up the country and struggled for control and, within each of these noble families and newcomers, the rich and the workers all sought to increase their influence and power. Everything was being questioned: social hierarchies, authorities, traditions, techniques, life itself. In order to consolidate their power the despots set up councils of specialists (in government, war, diplomacy etc) whose positions were rather shaky. They established a body of paid officials who could be dismissed at any time.

In this turbulent process of civilization, where one unlawful leader followed another in successive power struggles, there was a desire for some spirit of wisdom which could bring stability to the situation.

The hundred schools

Close to the seat of power, there were scholars, often officials or advisers to the rulers, who tried their best to give some sort of sense to life in their society. But, as their origins were different and they each had their own concerns at heart, the ideas they developed were many and varied. They were called the hundred scholars. This intellectual activity, going on at the time of Socrates, gave birth to many controversial writings.

> **The schools**
> 'If custom demands that the word *chia* be translated as school, it is important to be aware that the Chinese give it a very wide range of meaning. They use it in relation to different Arts (the body of knowledge held, for example, by the teachers in mathematics, astronomy, divination, medicine ...) as well as using it in relation to different ways of behaving (the codes for living favoured by this or that teacher of wisdom). These codes are intended to regulate conduct and are taught through the adoption of particular attitudes.' (*La Pensée chinoise* (Chinese Thought), Marcel Granet, Paris, 1934)

K'ung Fu Tzu (Confucius) (551–479 BC) was the first of these sages. He tried to reconcile the traditional rules of life with the new social situation. Mo Ti or Mo Tzu (c. 480–420 BC) rose up against privilege and favoured an egalitarian society. The legalist school declared itself for the education of the people by a system of rewards and punishments. There were others, finally, who concerned themselves entirely with debate, becoming masters in the art of sophism, clever but useless argument. They formed what was called the school of Names.

All these theories were further developed and systemized to some degree by actual sects whose degree of organization ranged from the very strict to the quite lax. The teachers travelled around the country seeking protection and influence. They gained followers who then, going from one clique to another, became teachers themselves founding their own schools.

K'ung Fu Tzu (Confucius) and Lao Tzu

'When Confucius made ready to leave, Lao Tzu called him back saying: "I have heard it said that the rich and powerful man sends people on their way with riches and that the good man sends them on their way with words. I am in no way rich or powerful, but I humbly accept the title of good man; so I will give you a parting gift of words and this is what I have to say: The man who is intelligent and a keen observer is close to death, for he criticizes men honestly; he who has a very learned and penetrating mind puts himself in peril, for he exposes men's faults. The one who is a son or in a dependent position is no longer in control of himself."' (*Shih Ching*)

Emptiness

'Although 30 spokes converge on the hub, it is the emptiness between which makes the cart go. Clay is used to make vases, but they are of no use without the emptiness inside. There is no room which does not have doors and windows put into it, for again it is the emptiness within that provides the space for living. The physical has properties which the non-physical makes use of.' (*Tao Te Ching* 11)

Lao Tzu

Very different from these 'scholars', eager to influence the life of society, were the 'hidden sages' or wise old men, who abandoned the world of politics, business, and honours and withdrew to a life of solitude in the mountains. This made them less well known, but among them were some whose thinking was to have great repurcussions down through the centuries. One such was Lao Tzu.

In his 'Historical Memoirs', Ssu-ma Ch'ien says that he originated from Ch'u in southern China. His family name was Li and his name, Eh, but he came to be called Lao Tzu, the 'Old Teacher'. At first he was the archivist at the royal court of Chou and was already regarded at that time as a man worth listening to, an associate of the wandering philosophers. He was visited by Confucius, who said when leaving: 'Of the bird, I know that he can fly; of the fish, I know that he can swim; (…) but the dragon, I can know nothing of him: he rises to the sky on the clouds and the wind. Today I have seen Lao Tzu, he is like the dragon.'

Lao Tzu, seeing the approaching decline of the dynasty he served, withdrew to the West. When he arrived at the edge of the civilized world he met Yin Hsi who begged him to put his teachings down in writing. The master agreed to do this and drew the 5000 characters which make up the *Tao Te Ching*. So the legend goes.

The beginning of the text

The form and structure of the work seem to invalidate the legend. The *Tao Te Ching* is made up of a series of sayings and maxims with obscure or uncertain meanings, and of different dates and origins. The passages in verse are set out in fairly haphazard order. Contrasting rhythms follow one another for no apparent reason. Ancient quotations from the work sometimes differ from each other. So it seems likely that the whole thing is the result of thought processes maturing slowly within a tradition going back well beyond the time of its commitment to paper.

No doubt the text which has come down to us gives a poor impression of its development. However, it does allow us to imagine something of the complexity of this mixture of sayings, the honoured words of the sages, the popular dictums and memorable maxims which were produced by the trends of thinking which later come to be described as Taoist. It would not be too far from the mark to say that the *Tao Te Ching* is simply one part of this heritage which has been put down in writing, a part whose originality was immediately recognized and which soon came to be considered as sacrosanct. It does not present a strictly structured doctrine but it does bear witness to its emergence.

The text gives a full account of the life of the ancients, their thoughts, and the ideas borrowed from other schools and painstakingly incorporated. These long preludes explain the fragmentary nature of the work which no scribe can allow himself to touch because of its sacred character and the authority of the teacher who is supposed to be its author.

Structure

The *Tao Te Ching* is therefore written in the form of a collection of fairly short fragments which are in the nature of relics that are all the more precious in that they suggest more than they describe and question more than they assert. They give the impression that their mysteries have never been unravelled and yet it seems that a little more is understood at each encounter with them. The work is like a spring which one can draw water from continually without its ever drying up. The *Tao Te Ching* is like a prayer book, the daily reading of which will help in meditation.

Behind its pithy sayings the outline of a philosophy is in fact taking shape. In contrast to a strict and well-developed argument, the work wraps its doctrinal content in an original garb of poetry and paradoxes which can be interpreted in many ways. All things considered, it possesses a facade similar to that of a wise man whose casual words, spoken at chance encounters, will be retained but whose personality is so rich that it radiates through all these reflections.

However, the work has not remained entirely shapeless. It is traditionally divided into 81 short chapters and into two parts.

The first part deals with the *tao* (the way) and the second with the *te* (the virtue or power). The only justification for this division is the fact that Chapter 1 speaks about the *tao* and Chapter 38 about the *te* and has no real bearing on the understanding of the text.

'This book, translated and retranslated, is', says Michel Granet, 'actually untranslatable.'

The tao (the way)

It is true that, in addition to its fragmentary and puzzling form, the subject matter it treats cannot, by its nature, be translated in

---

Lao Tzu made divine

'Lao Tzu transformed his body. His left eye became the sun, his right eye the moon; his head became Mount K'uan-luan; his beard became planets and mansions; his bones became dragons; his flesh became four-legged creatures; his intestines became snakes; his stomach became the sea; his fingers became the Five Peaks; his hair became the trees and grass; his heart became the constellation of the flowering canopy; and his two kidneys together became the Father and Mother of the Real.'
(*Mélanges posthumes* (Posthumous Reminiscences), Henri Maspéro, Paris, 1950)

The heart at peace

'Do not attach great importance to rare things, they will always be being stolen. Do not flaunt anything that will arouse envy and the people will have peace in their hearts.
In governing the wise man says:
Make the hearts empty
Make the stomachs full
Sap the ambitions
Strengthen the bones
Keep the people from knowledge and desire
In short, ensure that the crafty ones dare not do anything.
Concentrate on doing nothing and everything will turn out well.'
(*Tao Te Ching* 3)

The Old Teacher, **Lao Tzu,** *flees decadence, travelling westwards and reaches the limits of the civilized lands.*
'Personnages chinois historiques ou mythologiques révérés en Chine'
(Historical and mythological Chinese figures revered in China) (18th century).
Bibliothèque Nationale, Paris.

words: the *tao* is indescribable and cannot be talked about. The communicable *tao* of other schools of thought, such as that of Confucianism, represents certain teachings, doctrines, and social values, whereas the ultimate *tao,* the *tao* of the *Tao Te Ching,* the supreme principle, is inaccessible to the senses, it is not open to change and cannot, properly speaking, be named: 'not knowing its name, I call it the way (*tao*); for want of anything better, I call it great' (*Tao Te Ching* 25).

Yet the *tao* is a womb from which the visible world is produced. It is *wu,* which means empty, but it has a method of being

visible: that is *you.* This opposition between *wu* and *you* is fundamental: the *wu* is not nothingness, the absence of being, it is a superior form of being, for it possesses all the potentialities; the *you* is the perceptible reality which can be seen and heard and touched. It is certain that when one moves from the *wu* to the *you* one distances oneself from the permanent, the ultimate *tao,* that transcendent reality which is older than the universe. 'This is why in the world's invisible mode (*wu*) we will contemplate its mysteries; in the visible world (*you*) we will contemplate its peripheries' (*Tao Te Ching* 1).

So, as the source of life, *tao* does have a

dynamic aspect: 'Tao gave birth to One; One gave birth to Two; Two gave birth to Three; Three gave birth to 10 000 beings' (Tao Te Ching 42). The two offspring of the One are Yin and Yang, the two constituent parts of all that is, constituent parts which are opposed, inseparable and complementary, like light and darkness, good and evil, life and death, male and female etc. The Three is their harmonious union which undergirds the whole universe.

The te (virtue)

So the tao is a force, an energy, a power. It is the energy from which all other energies are derived. 'The way never acts, but everything is done through it' (Tao Te Ching 37). It is the eternal principle, stable and, at the same time, always active in the world. It is the source of all activities. Yet everything that man does can only be relative, partial, and incomplete. His actions, in separating themselves from their common source, limit themselves, lose direction, forfeit their original purity, and lose the very thing that made them the tao. What good does it do therefore 'to act to no avail and bring misfortune on one's head?' (Tao Te Ching 10).

So it is useless, and in a way harmful, to become involved in the knowledge of this world, in science and social activities. These will lead to multiplicity and to change, they are merely relative, partial, and biased in one particular direction and therefore turn away from the permanent, essential tao. 'When the intellectuals appear, the great deceptions intervene. If we were to renounce wisdom and reject knowledge the people would be a hundred times better off' (Tao Te Ching 18).

The te, which is the effective power of tao is known to individuals first of all in a few key words: non-desire, non-passion, non-attachment, which move away from that which is relative; autonomy, equality, absence of value, judgment, which increase liberty. The te is identified with the stillness achieved by the old teacher: 'Everyone gets heated about things and swells up as if he were feasting. (…) I alone remain at peace, imperturbable, like a little child who has not yet laughed, detached like a homeless person' (Tao Te Ching 20). For people in

authority the te has the sense of leaving things to resolve themselves, non-intervention; 'The best leader is one whom people barely know, next comes the one whom the people love and praise, then the one they fear, and finally the one they defy' (Tao Te Ching 17).

The thought process does not stop there, however: the refusal of that which is not the tao leads to an even stronger involvement with the absolute. The te is the refusal to use the senses and reasoning powers, and instead to seek to experience emptiness and absence in the depths of one's own being and to concentrate only on the tao. The te is intuition set against reason, personal asceticism against positive action, it is a mystical experience which achieves a primitive kind of unity with life's origins in chaos. It is the kind of behaviour which can only be expressed negatively or paradoxically. It is a step towards the world of mystery. 'This obscure virtue is so very deep and distant! (The one who has it) returns with the beings (to the source); and so achieves great affinity (with the supreme tao)' (Tao Te Ching 65).

The superior man and the tao

'When a superior man understands the Way
He follows it with zeal.
When an average man understands the Way
He adopts part of it, but leaves the rest.
When an inferior man understands the Way
He bursts out laughing.
If he did not laugh the Way would not be the Way.'
(Tao Te Ching 41)

The excellence of the tao

'After the loss of the Way comes Virtue,
After the loss of Virtue comes Love,
After the loss of Love comes Justice,
After the loss of Justice come the rites.
The rite is the external form of sincerity and faithfulness, but also the source of disorder.
Foresight is the flower of the Way, but also the threshold of ignorance.
The Wise man depends on what is solid and not upon the passing flower; he take the fruit and holds on to that, mistrusting and rejecting the flower.' (Tao Te Ching 38)

Huang-ti and Lao Tzu

The great movement which spawned the mystique of the *Tao Te Ching* quickly found itself mingling with legends concerning Huang-ti, the so-called Yellow Emperor. He was one of the rulers of China's golden age (2852–2255 BC) who presided over the birth of the empire and saw it prosper. He once asked a devout Taoist called Kuang Ch'eng how to experience the *tao*: 'Be meditative' said the wise man. So the emperor withdrew and was like the first Taoist practitioner. Lao Tzu and Huang-ti became confused at some point, so much so that Huang-ti has sometimes been credited with writing the *Tao Te Ching* and mention has been made of *Huanglao*, a hybrid of the two names.

The confusion which led to Lao Tzu being absorbed to some degree into Huang-ti did give the Taoist themes a history reaching far back into antiquity. But, at the same time it brought in strange practices and techniques which were foreign to the *Tao Te Ching*. They were no doubt older, more traditional and particularly connected with the Yellow Emperor. The fact is that the *Tao Te Ching* was adopted by a movement which was far broader than its philosophy, but nevertheless found its spiritual basis in that philosophy.

Religious Taoism

From the 2nd century AD there grew up in China a mixture of crude superstitions, religious and magical traditions originating either with the people themselves or from abroad. This was all combined, with elements of the newly introduced Buddhist religion, into the philosophical school of the *tao* and made up what is called Neo-Taoism. This religious movement, with all its different elements, was dominated by the strong influence of Lao Tzu, seen as one of the first people dedicated to the pursuit of long life.

The Taoists began to produce numerous commentaries explaining the *Tao Te Ching*, and finding the bases of their practices in some of the obscure, impenetrable, and enigmatic passages of the text. It is true that criticisms could be made of the *Tao Te Ching*, but gradually this work became very important and proved to be an instrument of unity within *Taoism*, a religion made up of such diverse parts. It was a time of great literary production and from this a canon of scripture emerged. It comprised no less than 1464 titles. But since the 7th century Lao Tzu has been held to be the only source of revelation and all the sacred books are attributed to him.

Under the T'ang dynasty in the 8th century, Lao Tzu became 'Most high and heavenly emperor from the beginning of time', and his teaching was officially taught in the schools. Not all opinions are united about him, however: for some Lao Tzu is a divinity, if not the supreme divinity; for others he is simply an exceptionally gifted person. In many circles his book is read as part of the religious worship. So various sects have formed which, like those of the heavenly Masters, still living in Taiwan, continue to see the *Tao Te Ching* as a sacred book.

Translations and commentaries

The *Tao Te Ching* has generated great interest far beyond Taoist religious circles and is known throughout China, in Japan, and even in the Western world. It is certainly the Chinese book which has most often been translated into Western languages. It is also one of the most commented upon books: more than 200 commentaries were in existence in the 3rd century BC. The mysterious and puzzling meaning of the text provoked this flow of commentaries which has never ceased.

The Chuang Tzu

The 'Sacred Canon of Nan Hua'

The pinnacle of Taoist thought

Debate, irony, poetry, and a deep, mystical philosophy make this the basic book of Taoism.

According to the historians, Chuang Tzu lived during the 4th century BC. He came from the town of Meng in the present day region of Honan in China and probably lived at the time of the king of Liang, who reigned from 370 to 318 BC. He was married with a family; he had chosen to live modestly and was 'dressed in a robe of patched-up cloth with shoes tied to his feet with string'.

Chuang Tzu knew the sophist or philosopher Hui Shih who was Liang's minister from 343 to 322 BC, and they had some lively discussions. He used Hui Shih as an 'Aunt Sally', someone to bounce all his ideas off. When Hui Shih died Chuang Tzu missed having 'someone to work on' (24 E). He could speak with all the intellectuals of the day: K'ung Fu Tzu (Confucius) and Mo Tzu are often brought into play, usually to be argued against, and Lao Tzu is considered as a respected teacher.

The Chuang Tzu

No one knows for certain whether the *Chuang Tzu* was written by the wise man of the same name. The book is also called *Nan Hua Chen Ching*, the 'Sacred Canon of Nan Hua', from the name of the village Chuang Tzu retired to at the end of his life. But this does not really prove anything: the concept of the author had not really developed at that time.

However, the style does have the marks of a writer of genius: a lively mode of expression, a sparkling wit, and zest and an extravagant mocking tone throughout, all point to its having a single author. It is the work of 'an excellent writer of remarkable style and clear lively expression' said Ssuma Ch'ien in his *Shih Chi* (Historical Memoirs).

The book is no doubt the product of a school, compiled by disciples, redesigned and completed by successors all trying their best to imitate the style of the master. Being the work of successive generations it became one of the key documents of Taoism.

During the Han dynasty it was made up of 52 chapters, but now the book only has 33. Has the book been restructured or have 19 chapters been lost? We cannot tell, but it does not matter. The work is made up of a great many anecdotes and parables which are often controversial, intended to illustrate Taoist thought by comparing and contrasting it with the teachings of other schools.

The book includes neither long explanations nor philosophical arguments, but simply the facts, short stories either real or mythical. The art of the fairy tale is used to perfection: the characters are often crudely drawn, as caricatures; the plot is developed skilfully and clearly; the narration (or dialogue) is kept down to the minimum necessary to convey the meaning.

Distrust of honours

'A certain prince sent for Chuang Tzu to become his adviser. The philosopher replied to the envoy: "Have you seen the ox that is intended for the sacrifice? It is clothed in an embroidered cloak and is given food with herbs and beans. But one day it is taken to the great temple to be killed. Then it would really like to be a lonely calf, but can it? *Chuang Tze* 32, 1).

This method of explaining ideas does leave some areas rather unclear. It is not known, for example, what the author thinks about the popular ancestral beliefs, and mental and physical techniques aimed at securing a long life; he often refers to them without either criticizing or approving of them. Are they perhaps, as far as he is concerned, simply literary images and symbolic metaphors used in his writings, or should they be seen as part of his teaching and recommended behaviour as the old Taoist religion believed?

The book goes on step by step, revealing part of its truth in each new paragraph, outlining point by point the psychological and moral shape of the Taoist and inviting the reader on a complex metaphysical journey. It is not, in fact, easy to explain a doctrine which objects to the principle of logic itself, as demonstrating 'the uselessness of all opposing opinions, of oppositions or contrasts in general, especially those on which language is based' (*Encyclopaedia Universalis* vol. 18, Paul Demiéville).

The fundamental principle : the tao

Only one factor lies at the basis of the whole argument; it is a constant in all the stories, it is the key to each one, the essential framework: this is the *tao*. 'The *tao* is so great that it has no end, and so small that nothing escapes it. This is why it is present everywhere, in all beings. It is so vast that there is nothing which is not contained in it; it is so deep that no one can reach to the bottom of it' (*Chuang Tzu* 134).

But the *Chuang Tzu* gives no explanation of it, nor can it; for 'the *tao* explained is no longer the *tao*; reasoning and argument no longer arrive at the truth' (2 H). So it can be understood why any 'dogmatic' element is only tackled in a roundabout way and never directly addressed: words are simply not adequate for speaking of the *tao*; only the Taoist attitude can be described.

The Taoist

The holy man is free: he is bound to neither goods nor ideas, realities nor doctrines, power nor honours, values nor counter-values, not even to life or death, so many

mean, worthless things which would distance him from the *tao*. 'The wise man lives according to the movement of heaven ... he creates neither happiness nor misfortune, he merely reacts to the stimulus and only moves under pressure' (15 B), under the influence of the universal principle. This is how he travels along the way, the *tao*, and comes back to the natural truth: not feeling, not being moved, not taking action, but letting things be, that is the wise man's attitude.

It must be said that the world is not as it seems: each person holds definitive opinions; what is seen as good in one place, is considered bad elsewhere; what is black for one is white for another; as soon as there is somebody who will say yes, there is another ready to say no. The wise man will not be drawn into this; he is neutral, he is empty: he makes no distinction between true and false, between affirmation and denial, between life and death. He does not seek to impose his will or oppose another's will. He identifies himself with the centre line of the *tao*.

There is no point, for instance, in speaking about a great instigator, a creator. In fact, 'if I say: there is an instigator, I am only considering the tangible realities; if I say:

Where is the tao?
'Where is the tao?
Everywhere says Chuang Tzu.
– You have to localize it
– In this ant says Chuang Tzu
– Lower than that?
– In this blade of grass
– Lower still?
– In this tile
– And still lower?
– In this manure says Chuang Tzu.
Tung Kuo-tzu is silent. Chuang Tzu says:
Asking questions as you have just done leads you nowhere.' (*Chuang Tzu* 22 F)

Knowledge
'Our life is limited but the field of knowledge has no limits. It is dangerous to pursue the unlimited with limited forces: so anyone who gives himself to the pursuit of knowledge is unwise.' (*Chuang Tzu* 3 A)

---

there is no creative force it means I am considering only invisible emptiness (...) We can talk about and reflect upon these problems, but the more we talk, the further we are from the mark' (25 J).

Stillness

The *tao* is the only thing that matters to the wise man. Far beyond the disordered phenomena is something which does not change. 'Whoever experiences great unity, great obscurity, great sight, great fairness, great law, great trust, and great balance will reach supreme understanding. For great unity links everything; great obscurity breaks everything up; great sight penetrates everything, great fairness encompasses everything; great law governs everything; great trust wins everything, great balance sustains everything' (24 M).

Condemnation of detailed knowledge acquired by means of the senses and the intelligence, and promotion of a rounded knowledge achieved through stillness and intuition seem to be the ideal suggested in the *Chuang Tzu*. With illumination as the goal on the mental level and ecstasy as the ultimate practical expression, we are certainly dealing here with a world which knows nothing of reason and will, a world which reason is incapable of understanding and in whic the will is ineffectual, or even harmful. Not surprisingly, religious Taoists have been able to find pretexts in this book for numerous traditional and irrational practices to which Chuang Tzu refers without ever condemning them.

Mystical ecstasy

However, an account is given by a man who 'understood the *tao*': 'After three days I managed to leave the external world behind. I went on. Seven days later I could leave behind external things. I continued for nine more days and could leave behind my own existence. One fine morning I had a vision of the unique. That vision allowed me to get beyond the past and the present. I could then enter the realm where life and death no longer exist' (6 B).

One is irresistibly reminded of the words of Saint John of the Cross in 'The Dark Night of the Soul': 'The mind must be simple, pure, devoid of all natural affections, whether lifelong or of the moment, in order to be able to communicate freely with the fullness of the divine wisdom', or again: 'The one who arrives there is truly weakened: all that he knew until then appears very flimsy. And his knowledge increases so much that he remains not knowing, transcending all knowledge. (*Poems*, trans. Jean Baruzi, Yggdrasill, Paris, 1936).

It is therefore very much the description of a mystical experience comparable to those mentioned by the Christian and Muslim mystics. But, as Jean Grenier says in his *Esprit du Tao* (Spirit of the Tao), there is a great difference: Christians and Muslims achieve the contemplative state with the help of God, Taoists reach it by their own efforts; and again the Westerner aspires to the fullness of being whereas the Taoist aspires to emptiness, the destruction of the personal being (quoted by Etiemble in *Les Philosophes taoistes* (The Taoist Philosophers), Encyclopédie La Pléiade, Paris, 1985).

Innocence

"An old man was busy watering his vegetables with an earthenware jar. Hard work for little result.

"If only you had a machine of hollowed out wood, heavy at the back and light at the front which lifts water as if it was being drawn by hand, as quickly as the broth overflows the pot." The gardener got angry, changed colour, snorted and said, "This is what I learned from my master: whoever uses machines uses mechanics and his mind becomes mechanical. Whoever has a mechanical mind no longer has the purity of innocence and so loses peace of mind. The *tao* is no help to the one who has lost his peace of mind."' (*Chuang Tzu* 12 K)

Theft

'Whoever steals a clip is put to death; whoever steals a principality becomes its lord, the keepers of humanity and justice will live under his protection. Does that not prove that one steals with goodness and justice, wisdom and prudence?' (*Chuang Tzu* 10 D)

However, in a truly Taoist paradox, Chuang Tzu describes the island where the genies live. These are beings beyond human knowledge, 'white as snow, fresh as children, they do not take any kind of food but breathe the wind and drink the dew. They walk in the air, the clouds are their chariots and dragons are their mounts. Through the flow of their transcendence they keep men from disease and ensure fruitful harvests' (1 D). In short, a paradise in which one can recognize a fullness of being, a flowering of human nature.

Influence

This thinking from beyond the grave, in praise of a disregard for the things of this world could only take off like this during a period of fairly serious political unrest. This

---

The butterfly

'Chuang Tzu once dreamed that he was a butterfly, fluttering about content with its lot and quite unaware that he was Chuang. He woke up suddenly and was astonished to realize he was Chuang. He no longer knew whether it was Chuang dreaming he was a butterfly or a butterfly dreaming he was Chuang. Between him and the butterfly there was a difference. That is what is called the change of beings.' (*Chuang Tzu* 2 J)

The perfect man

'The perfect man is supernatural. The great fire on the plain is not enough to make him feel heat; the freezing of the rivers does not make him feel the cold, the thunder which splits the mountain and the hurricane which stirs up the sea cannot frighten him. This is how he dominates the clouds, sits astride the sun and the moon, and travels beyond the four seas. He is indifferent to life and death. How then could the difference between what is useful and what is harmful bother him in any way?' (*Chuang Tzu* 2 J)

---

was the case at the time of warring kingdoms when the hundred schools were all striving to impose their particular doctrine on the frequently changing and widely scattered ruling powers. In these circumstances the field was left open for the anti-authority ethic of Taoism and its principles seemed to be the ultimate explanations.

But then came the unification of China under the Ch'in dynasty (221-206 BC), the centralization of powers and the birth of imperialism. The favoured moral code could not be allowed to oppose the pragmatism or practical compromises necessary for material progress, nor the legalism required by the state authorities. Taoism lost out in influence to Confucianism and the *Chuang Tzu* suffered five centuries of decline.

It was after the fall of the Han dynasty during the 3rd century with the return of unrest and the barbarian invasions, that people again turned to the *Chuang Tzu*, reading and commenting on it. Kuo Hsiang (died around 313) is the author responsible for the text we know today, but a number of reflections have been added which spoil its purity. No doubt his Confucianism could not allow him to accommodate the full force of Taoist thought in all its extravagance.

Taoism and Buddhism

It is difficult to confuse the Taoist notion of the *tao* with the Buddhist notion of *boddhi*, the awakening which frees men from transmigrations (the change to another being after death). However, the two doctrines have followed a somewhat parallel route in China: the apparent disorder of Taoism has been able to make some kind of progress through the 'vehicle' of Buddhism, since the two are brought together in their similar emphasis on self-denial and the search for illumination. There is no shortage of teachers of *Zen* who quote from the *Chuang Tzu*.

The Lieh Tzu

The 'True Classic of Complete Emptiness'

A Taoist rhapsody
(or collection of unconnected items)

Lieh Tzu examines the different approaches to life in ancient China from the Taoist perspective.

Very little factual information is known about the life of Lieh Tzu, the author of the 'True classic of complete emptiness' which is called the *Lieh Tzu* in Chinese. It is said that he was born c. 450 BC. We are told that he declined to live under the patronage of any of the rulers and lived off the gifts of disciples and followers in the greatest deprivation. Nothing is known of his death: he was a 'hidden sage' in the best Taoist tradition.

However, other scholars since the 17th century have gone so far as to deny his existence: they claim that he is a character created by Chuang Tzu. It is true that in the work attributed to him, he himself is only mentioned 18 times and the great historian Ssu-ma Ch'ien (c. 145–90 BC) does not mention him at any time.

Even if, as is now believed, the compila-

tion of the tales in the book was completed c. AD 300, most of it is made up of very ancient texts. The material used is the same as what lies at the origins of the *Tao Te Ching* and the *Chuang Tzu*, it is in the same vein, bears witness to the same historical context, and adopts the same 'technique of life'. Moreover, many of the little stories it contains are also recorded in the *Chuang Tzu*.

A collection of fables

The *Lieh Tzu* is a collection of chosen pieces: it contains many parables, tales, and legends. They are short pieces, accounts of various deeds, stories on the subject of which master and disciples exchange thoughts, discussions which compare different ideas of what life is about. It is full of stories about influential people, especially great characters like emperors, ministers, and wise men of ancient times like K'ung Fu Tzu (Confucius) and the hedonist (pleasure seeker), Yang Zhu who are not at all in the same mould. Both are welcome in this book. Lieh Tzu does not dispute their prestige, he uses it. He explores their point of view, makes some concessions and, in a way, claims them for Taoism.

The book includes 'games that are purely verbal' (Benedykt Grynpas), quibbles worthy of the most pedantic philosophers, calling into question established customs, rival schools of thought and reasoned argument but all of them are used to serve the Taoist cause in that they form a dialogue of understanding against a background of restrained humour, rather than a dialogue of conflicting views.

The text has a light touch: there is nothing here of the terse, abrupt style of the

The hidden sage

'Lieh Tzu lived in a cottage in the principality of Cheng for 40 years with no one taking any notice of him; with the prince and his ministers and officers seeing him as just another common peasant. When famine struck the land he made ready to leave for Wei. His disciples said: Master, you are going to leave without anyone knowing if and when you will return. Will you instruct us before you go ...?' (*Lieh Tzu*)

Tao Te Ching. It is conciliatory, considered and relaxed: there is no trace of the rigid controversial force of the *Chuang Tzu.* It is examining practices rather than theoretical teaching. It works through examples of different attitudes whilst remaining within the traditional sphere of the Taoist masters.

An illustration of Taoism

One hundred and twenty three self-contained items have been grouped together in eight chapters of varying importance. They have been placed in no apparent order under a single title. The title of each chapter gives an indication of the main idea of it or the person responsible for it, although this arrangement is not always strictly adhered to. Some of the major themes will give us an idea of the work as a whole.

The 'heavenly jade' first spoken of by Lieh Tzu is a decoration conferred by the emperor on important officials in order to bring them to the notice of others. It gives an opportunity to show that appearance is not reality: Lieh Tzu, seeing an age-old skull says, 'He and I both know that the distinction between life and death is merely imaginary, he knows by experience and I know

through reasoning. He and I both know that clinging to life and fearing death is unreasonable, life and death simply being two phases, the one following inevitably on the other' (*Lieh Tzu*).

Non-action, which is dear to the Taoists, is called emptiness in this work. 'Why do you hold emptiness in such esteem?' the sage is asked, — 'Emptiness cannot be esteemed for itself. It is estimable for the peace to be found in it. Peace in the emptiness is a state which cannot be defined ... Alas, people now prefer to do good and be fair, which does not give the same result' (1 L).

We also see men who perform extraordinary feats quite naturally through non-action, such as the man who swims in a 240 foot waterfall, or another who goes into an inferno without being burned or singed: 'I acted according to my complete and undivided natural instinct. There is nothing which can stand against whoever acts like this' (*Lieh Tzu*).

No doubt there are holy men, Taoist saints, who know how to establish the continuum, the greatest law of the world': Chan Ho the fisherman, using a line made of natural silk, a needle, a simple rod and half a grain of wheat, would pull out enormous fish from a deep gorge because his mind, which was empty of all other thoughts, could go straight to the fish establishing a continuity between them, and as a result the fish was caught. (*Lieh Tzu*)

Leave things alone and everyone will have what is due to him: that is one of Lieh Tzu's favourite themes. A certain Yin was living a life of luxury and pleasure while an old servant, bent and frail was having a tough time. But every night the old man dreamed that he was a prince enjoying all life's pleasures: 'Why would I complain? he used to say. I enjoy myself half the time.' During this time the master used to dream that he was a servant, weighed down with toil. A friend said to him: 'This must be because you are enjoying far more pleasure than is your due during the day' (3 D). This then is the *Lieh Tzu*, the 'True Classic of Complete Emptiness'.

> **Keeping feelings in check**
>
> 'A child born in the principality of Yen had been brought up in the kingdom of Ch'ou where he spent his whole life. As an old man he returned to the land of his birth. Half way there, as he was approaching the main town of Chin, his companions said, in fun, "this is the main town of your homeland, Yen" ... The man believed them, turned pale and looked sad ... "This is the burial mound of your native village." The man sighed in grief ... "Here is the home of your ancestors." The man burst into tears ... Then his companions laughingly revealed their trickery. The man was very confused and when he arrived at Yen and really did see his old home town, he experienced little or no emotion.' (*Lieh Tzu*)

Vedism

Of the ancient Aryans who were based in the north of India c. 1000 BC, there remains neither monuments, nor treasure, nor any inscription. Our only clues as to their beliefs, traditions, and worship are to be found in their sacred books, the *Vedas*. Comparisons made between the *Vedas*, the Roman religions and that of the *Avesta* have revealed a common source. It seems clear that the tribes who invaded northern India came from the Iranian plateau from where other clans also set out in different directions. Georges Dumezil has found in each of them evidence of a similar concept of society founded on three orders: priests, warriors, and producers.

The similarity between the *Vedas* and the *Avesta* is so strong that one comes across the same words being used in each: the first one addressed to the Aryans, the second to the Arya; they have two groups of higher powers, but over the centuries they have developed along separate lines, the devas becoming gods in India and demons in Iran; the asura (or ahura) becoming demons in India and gods in Iran.

Although it is useful to note these similarities, they by no means settle the matter. What we know of the importance given to sacrifice and ritual, the many names given to the gods and the leading role of the priestly class, the Brahmins, comes essentially from the *Vedas*.

The heart of the worship is the sacrifice: an offering is given up to the god, either plants or animals, raw or cooked, ceremoniously poured out or thrown into the fire. It is intended as the object of an exchange between the person making the sacrifice and the particular god, who grants his favours in return. The sacrifice is a vital and urgent duty involving very complex requirements. So each Aryan has to apply to specialists who know all the obscure details of the ritual and are in fact professionals in this field. The sacrifices are long ceremonies with secondary offerings, special dedications, and the reciting of hymns and songs. Some may last for days, weeks, months, even years.

It can be seen, therefore, how important the influence of the Brahmins is: they are the ones who authenticate the texts and conduct the ceremonies, and by virtue of that fact, it is they who give the community a sense of stability, security, and belonging. The sacred literature, for which they are responsible, is the source of the Vedic civilization. Even though they have lost some of their significance for most Hindus, the *Vedas* have remained as the mysterious and sacred monuments which have inspired many practices and traditions.

The Vedas

Knowledge

The most ancient songs of the Brahmins

A divine revelation, these writings are the expression of the ideology, practices, and social life of the Aryans of India.

The ancestors of the Hindus settled, certainly as early as 2000 BC, in the Indus valley. These were Aryans of a white race who came, it is thought, from the Siberian Steppes. Some of them stayed at the time of their journey to Iran; this is why we speak of Indo-Iranians.

They were primitive peoples who feared the darkness which attracted wild beasts, the drought which made the earth barren and the clouds which blotted out the sun. To each of these scourges they gave a name, a face, and a will of its own: these were the *asura* (*asu* means 'life force'), fearsome spirits coming from powerful gods, holders of magical power.

On the other hand, there were those natural forces which gladdened their hearts and brought great benefits. The sun, the dawn, fire were all considered to be good spirits, the gods, *devas*, the shining ones. So everything that governed men's lives was made divine. In such a world full of powerful spirits it was important to discover good procedure and practices as methods of obtaining wealth, long life, and many descendants.

The word

'I am the one who spontaneously proclaims what is pleasing to gods and humans. Whoever I like, I make him powerful: I make him a bearer of formulae, a visionary, a wise man.' (*Rig Veda* 10, 125).

Over thousands of years customs grew up, rituals and prayers were instituted, and people with special functions related to these practices emerged. These were the Brahmins or priests who gradually defined the actions which were to be performed, developed a moral code, and organized a form of public worship, with established rituals and a body of appropriate chants.

In order to reinforce the sacred nature of the texts it was said that they had originated with the Rsi, a semi-godlike class of being who came down to earth in exceptional circumstances and, when they died, became stars (seven of them forming the Great Bear for instance). The *rsi* received the text from Brahma and revealed it to men without alteration. The whole process is called *sruti* (hearing).

The Brahmins are the guardians of it. Even today they can recite the essential part of this tradition by heart: they learn it in the original language, Sanskrit, from the age of seven as part of their initiation and apprenticeship in their calling. In most cases they do not understand the ancient language of this literature, it is the sounds rather than the meanings of the words that they must retain; the sounds have powers, they are *sabda-brahman* (the energy made of sounds) and are linked with the eternal unchanging energy of the cosmos.

The texts

But then came a period when these texts, linked with the power of the Brahmins, began to lose their authority. Jainism, Buddhism, and finally Hinduism attempted to change their practices and overturn their beliefs. There was now an urgent need to give some tangible form to what had, until now, been purely oral traditions. A group of priests who specialized in the practical expression of worship and the religious customs met together and began to decide on a canon of scriptures. The establishment of the canon took several centuries: between the 18th and 6th centuries BC.

The oldest Vedic texts appear in four forms which probably correspond to four different groups of scribes and certainly relate to the particular purposes for which they are intended.

The hymns or the Rig Veda

The hymns are the heart of the Veda. In fact the liturgy or form of worship is made up of a deed and a word, the one is no good without the other and the attention paid to the fine print of the Vedic religion indicates how much importance is given to the reciting of the text. Sometimes an entire hymn has to be repeated if the ritual is to be effective.

Every hymn of the Veda praises a divinity and each one is at pains to give the god concerned pride of place in the assembly of gods. So each of the 33 gods mentioned in the work finds itself, in turn, described as 'the greatest, the chief of the gods'. For each one of them represents some essential constituent part of the universe, without in any way denying the essential nature of the things represented by the other gods.

The school of religious thought which results from a combination of polytheism (belief in many gods) and monotheism (belief in one god) has been termed 'henotheism'. It holds to an idea of worship in which name, image and poetry are more important than theological point of view or rational thought. In the Veda, the power of transformation of beings and of the world is considered as a characteristic function of gods and demons. The aim of the worship is to identify each guise that the god might assume, to give him the correct name, to call upon him and implore his aid by means of precise formulae, and so achieve his good graces.

The prayers, invocations and beseeching of the gods often allude to mythical tales, the remains of a vast literature of legend which must have existed, at least in oral form, in very ancient times, and which it is very difficult to untangle from the few historical recollections which the hymns are thought to contain. The hymn VII, for instance, praises the priest Vasistha, hymn VI recalls the victory of Abhicayamana and recounts the Battle of the Ten Kings in which Sudas, helped by Indra, puts the allied princes to flight.

When celebrating the gods responsible for creation, the hymns become theories on the creation of the universe, several versions of which are offered. Sometimes Agni, the fire, plays the principal role, sometimes it is Savitar, the Sun, or again Tapas, the creative Passion. The world springs from a primordial sacrifice, one made at the beginning of time, or from the dismemberment of primitive man. Moving away from mythology, book X becomes speculative: 'Neither non-being nor being existed then. The air around us did not exist then, nor the firmament beyond. What was the great power that moved? And where? And under whose care? Was it the water so unfathomably deep?' (*Rig Veda* 10, 90).

Some of the poems are like parts of a conversation between several speakers, as if we were dealing with a play whose setting had disappeared. For instance, we have

The Sages
When the sages had formed the word in their soul, as grains are cleansed through a screen, so friends experienced true friendship, beauty impressed itself on the language. They followed the path of the word through the sacrifice; they found it entering the poets. They shared out the remainder in many ways: the seven sages made the word ring out all around.' (*Rig Veda* 10, 71).

The sacrifice
'It is up above that human poets were fashioned, that is where they were fashioned, human poets, our fathers, when the original sacrifice was born. I seem to see with my mind's eye those who first offered this sacrifice. The actions are turned to the songs, turned to the rhythm: the seven divine visionaries themselves agree on the model. When the sages refer to the way of the ancestors they take the reins in their hand like the drivers of a chariot.' (*Rig Veda* 10, 130)

Lopamundra's complaints to her husband, the ascetic Agastya, who rejects her (I, 179), the attempted seduction by Yami of her brother Yama (X, 10), and the domestic scene involving Indra, his wife Indriani, and the ape couple.

The hymns are written in a studied style. In most cases the structure is the same: after an initial verse aimed at arousing curiosity, the account goes on at some length describing the great qualities of the god, before ending with a prayer. However, within this framework the style can be quite daring, using bold symbolism and double meaning, exaggeration and paradox, questions and declarations. The 'language has been pressed into service to express all the subtleties of mythical and ritual imagination' (*L' Inde classique* (Classical India), L Renou, Paris, 1947).

The Yajur Veda

This version of the Veda relates more directly to the actual sacrifice; it is intended for the experts in the performance of the ritual, the *adhavaryu*. The texts are arranged in such a way that they follow the unfolding of the ceremonies. They give extremely detailed instructions for observing the rites, the formulae to be recited, the *mantras* with the relevant mythical or theological explanations.

A distinction is made between the *Black Yajur Veda* which includes prayers and comments, and the *White Yajur Veda* a document which includes fewer commentaries: it is a matter of different schools compiling the material in different formats.

The *Yajur Veda*'s originality lies mainly in the use it makes of short phrases (*yaju*) of quasi-magical power: 'You, says the priest to the ground intended to bear the altar, you are a lioness who triumphs over her enemies' and the earth becomes invested with that power. 'You for Indra' becomes the required formula for the sacrifice. By using this kind of incantation the attribute of a particular god can be reinforced further: 'Agni is light, light is Agni'.

The Sama Veda

This Veda belongs particularly to the cantor, the *udgatr* who has a very important role in the rituals. It repeats the hymns of the *Rig Veda* but with the addition of music.

It is made up of two main parts: the *arcika*, which contains unconnected verses with their own specific tune, and the *uttararcika*, which is the collection of all the songs whose first verse has been given in the *arcika* and which are set out in the order in which they occur in the ceremonies. It is the officiating priest's manual.

Some new words have been introduced into the *Sama Veda* in order to make the text more easily set to music. These are exclamations or complete phrases, usually short, called *stobha* which are more like magic spells or mystical formulae than intelligible expressions.

Some of these songs are also imbued with such power that they go far beyond the scope of the human senses and become too sacred or too dangerous to be heard among men. So we have the *gana* 'to be sung in the villages' and the *gana* 'to be sung in the forests' etc.

The sowing

'Grow, develop, swell, O seed! Be strong in yourself, seed! Break the pots you are put into, lightning will not strike you! Since we call on you, O seed, and since, God, you listen to us, you will be as great as the Sky, as indestructible as the Sea! May the people who serve you never perish! nor their barns! May those who offer you never perish and those who eat you never perish!' (*Atharva Veda* 6, 142)

Yami and Yama

'What desire has come over me, Yami, for Yama, to lie with him in the same bed. Such a wife to her husband, I want to give my body to you; let us leave it to be broken as under the wheels of a chariot! They do not stop, or close their eyes, those spies of the gods who go around this place. O wanton girl, go quickly to someone else, let him break you as under the wheels of a chariot!' (*Rig Veda* 10, 10)

Initiation ceremony
The teacher pours some soma mixed with melted butter on the statue of the god: 'Spread quickly, O soma, for Indra ... Rouse us for combat, O clarified butter. You are the intelligence of the gods, their loved ecstasy, strike the enemies who alarm us, drink the soma, O Indra, bring down those who despise us' (Rig Veda 9, 85).

The Atharva Veda

This collection, only a seventh of which is a new version of the *Rig Veda* seems to be intended for the domestic priest. It is a fairly free mixture of prose and verse and was not accepted as the fourth Veda until relatively recently, and then only by some schools. Its divisions are called recitations, readings or decades.

They are hymns, some short, some longer, which are more like incantations than real prayers: they are charms used to obtain healing, long life or release from demon possession; they include curses against devils, sorcerers and other enemies; magic formulae used to secure the love of a beautiful woman, peace in the community or prosperity in business. Many of them are concerned with protection for the king or the Brahmin.

We are no longer dealing here with the form of worship or ceremonial, or with gods and divine power; the key thing now is an individual action, an exercise in straightforward causality with formulae which are powerful in themselves. Louis Renou says that the *Atharva Veda* is 'almost a manual for the laity (the ordinary believers)'.

Influence

The Vedas still have great authority in the eyes of many Hindus: they are the inspiration behind present day marriage and cremation ceremonies, and are the founding principle of all Hindu scriptures, rather like the way that the Old Testament is an integral part of the Bible.

Plea to death
'O Death, pursue the road down there that is your own, separate from the way of the gods! I say to you, you who have eyes, you who hears, do not harm our children or our men.' (*Rig Veda* 10, 18)

To win the love of a woman
'Embrace me as the creeper embraces the tree, clinging all round it: be my lover and never leave me! As the eagle taking flight beats his wings on the ground, I beat on your heart: be my lover and never leave me! As the sun in a day encircles the sky and the earth, so I encircle your heart with love: be my lover and never leave me.' (*Atharva Veda* 6, 8)

The Brahmanas
Sacred knowledge

Legends and myths

The Brahmanas bring an explanatory and descriptive style to the poetic conciseness of the Vedas.

Works as serious and detailed as the *Vedas* have generated a mass of literature over the centuries. Different schools have confronted each other over necessary justifications, useful illustrations, possible explanations. Was there one a single Brahmana, or Ur-Brahmana, from which others have derived? The versions which remain, although largely in agreement all differ from each other to some degree.

So there are various Brahmanas, the most famous being the *Jaiminiya Brahmana*, the *Taittiriya Brahmana*, and the *Aitareya Brahmana.* The main point of the argument is almost always the same: taking the details of the ritual one by one, it shows that none of them is optional and that its place has not been fixed arbitrarily. The sacrifice performed by the humans is similar to that celebrated by the gods and each of them contributes to the operating of cosmic energy.

Summaries of ritual

The *Brahmanas* therefore include long passages of recipes or formulae for the sacrifice. If there are 36 ways of cooking the wheat or the barley, the text will emphasize every detail with reasons given for every decision: why oats rather than wheat, a spoon of fig wood rather than a spoon of acacia wood etc?

They turn to theology for the replies: Varuna wants barley because he is the god of Ploughing, Mithra wants wild cereals 'because he harms no one and no one harms Mithra' (*Catapatha Brahmana* V, 2, 3). For the same reasons, 'that which has been cut with an axe belongs to Varuna and that which gets broken by itself belongs to Mithra: so the container dedicated to Mithra must be made from a branch which has come down by itself' (*Catapatha Brahmana* V, 2, 3).

So many explanations give ample opportunity for recalling a number of mythological tales, the bases of the rites: they are often mentioned in the *Vedas* but are gone into in more detail here. We see, for instance, the goddess Urvaci marry a mortal, King Pururavas, but when he violates their agreement Urvaci returns to heaven; or again, we see Varuna grant a child to King Hariccandra, who had no descendants, on condition that it be sacrificed as soon as it is born, but for Rohita, the king's son, is substituted a Brahmin's son who himself is saved by the goddess Usas.

The *Brahmanas*, which must have been composed between the 10th and 7th centuries BC, are of the greatest importance in any attempt to understand Indian thought.

The Flood

'The fish says to Manu: "Keep me, I will save you ... This year such a great flood will come: prepare a boat and watch over me." Manu kept the fish. (...) When the flood struck he got into the boat, the fish rushed up, he fixed the boat's cable to his fin and reached the mountain of the north that way ... Then he said to him: "Now I have saved you, tie your boat to a tree and take care that you are not cut off by the water while you are on the mountain." (...) The flood carried off all the creatures and Manu remained alone down here.'
(*Catapatha Brahmana* I, 8, 1)

Zoroastrianism

Two thousand years BC there were some Aryans living in the north of India and others in Iran. Originally these were the same people. They had similar traditions and social set-ups and parallel religions. Here and there the priests held the dominant positions, rituals were extremely detailed, with a great many sacrifices and there were many different gods. This was the era when Vedism was at its height in India.

Sometime around the 7th century BC there appeared in Iran a man named Zoroaster (or Zarathustra) who was to overturn everything. He was born into a priestly family in the Herat region on the borders of Afghanistan. He studied for many years and when he grew up he held the office of *zaotar*, the priest responsible for the offerings made and the singing of hymns. His duties meant that he had to learn an incredible number of prayers by heart, just as the Brahmins in India did. This particular skill was much sought after by those noblemen and rulers who went in for holding sacrifices with complicated rituals. Zoroaster was highly regarded for his knowledge and was often asked to take part, so that he travelled widely in the land.

When time permitted he would write hymns and prayers for the occasion and this caused him to reflect on his subject. Fairly soon he became convinced of the need for reform in the official religion. His meeting with Vishtaspa, one of the minor kings who had invited him, proved to be decisive. At that first meeting he explained to him his horror at the bloody sacrifices and stifling formalism of the ritual, his doubts about the multiplicity of gods and his faith in moral values. The prince reacted enthusiastically. No doubt there was also a strong reaction against him, but gradually the doctrine took shape, habits were changed and a priesthood was instituted. Wise men, coming no doubt from a tribe in Media, adopted the reform, made themselves watchful guardians of the new orthodoxy and became its principal propagandists.

Zoroaster was named chaplain to Vishtaspa and had the pleasure of seeing his teaching spread from one person to the next throughout the whole country. Soon the whole of Iran was won over to the new religion and under the Sassanid Emperors it became the state religion. According to tradition Zoroaster spent 40 years with his host and died during an unfortunate war that the prince embarked upon against his neighbours.

The Avesta

The doctrine

The Law against demons

The revelation made by the Wise Lord to Zoroaster and his followers is contained in the Avesta.

In ancient Iran, as in ancient India, priests had to know numerous hymns and prayers. It was also part of their duty to recite them at appropriate moments, adapt them to particular circumstances and indeed to compose new ones. Zoroaster was a famous zaotar and he fulfilled these tasks with skill and care. Long after the reforms he introduced into the Iranian religion, his compositions were remembered. They were recited at ceremonies and revered like sacred words. Priests passed them down from one generation to the next without altering them at all.

Nearly 900 years after the prophet was preaching, at the time when Zoroastrianism was made the official religion of the empire, it seemed to be necessary to make

a collection of all the sacred Scriptures. The oldest texts, memorized in their original ancient tongue were not understood by the people of the time; so there had to be a complete translation of these. The *Avesta* therefore, is made up of words of Zoroaster, hymns and prayers used in worship, and the oldest explanations of Zoroastrian doctrine.

Unfortunately the collection was lost at the time of the rise of the Muslims when the Zoroastrians were reduced to a small nucleus in Iran and a group of immigrants in India. Only the parts pertaining to the ritual, the parts which the priest learned by heart and were the most sacred, have been preserved. This is the *Avesta* as we know it today.

The Yasna

The first part of the book, called the *Yasna*, relates to the ritual sacrifice, the Haoma. It concerns the pressing of a plant, the juice of which is then drunk, mixed with water or milk, by the faithful. This symbolic action is intended to restore creation and Zoroaster is seen as the ideal celebrant.

The form of worship consists of the recitation of the *Gatha*, very ancient poems calling on God's help, which seem to give an idea of early Zoroastrianism.

In the beginning there existed two twin spirits, one the principle of Good, the other of Evil; of the two 'Neither the thought, nor the teaching, nor the minds, nor the wishes, nor the words, nor the acts, nor the laws, nor the souls are in agreement' (*Gatha* XLIV, 2). The Good Spirit is called Ahura Mazda; he is the creator of the world and sees the secrets of the heart.

Angra Mainyu, the Evil Spirit, and the *devas*, his evil demons, are in control of the world. But Ahura Mazda has given his law to men: this commands them to give love and respect to the Wise Lord and to his helpers,

---

The deva

'But you, deva, you are all from the race of the Evil Spirit, you proceed from him, you and everything which honours you, such as lying and deceitfulness and all the deceptions by which you are known in the seven regions of the earth. For it is you who have produced and spread these doctrines which cause men to commit the greatest crimes and say what pleases you, deva: having fallen far below the Good Spirit, these men are far from the Spirit of Ahura Mazda and from Truth.' (*Gatha* XXXI, 3–4)

*Children, adults, and old men carry to **Ahura Mazda** and to Arhiman bundles
of palm leaves, the symbol of power over the universe.
Silver plaque from Louristan (Iran) 8th–7th century BC.
Art Museum, Cincinnati.*

the Amesha Spenta, to practise purity, to
encourage knowledge of the law, to devote
themselves to cultivating the fields and caring for the cattle and to maintaining the
worship ceremonies.

Ahura Mazda's moral teaching is summarized in the *Gatha* I: 'The holy man is the
one who, by wise thoughts, words, and actions, develops his holiness according to
the law and his power according to the
good spirit'. The text does not give many
other precise instructions, apart from rec-
ommending marriage: 'One person should
receive another according to the holy rules
and so have a happy life' (*Avesta* LII, 5), and
giving the order to punish the wicked: 'Put
the wicked to death by the sword' (*Avesta*
XXXI, 18).

Respect for the law allows one to hope for
a reward. 'Ahura Mazda has created the

pinnacle of integrity and immortality, of
fullness and purity, of sovereign power and
the rank of Good Spirit for the one who is
dear to him through thought and act' (*Avesta*
XXXI, 21).

> ### The dog
> The dog has eight characters of its own,
> that of a priest, that of a warrior, a
> ploughman, a musician, a thief, a
> werewolf, a courtesan, and a child: it eats
> the left-overs like a priest, (...) it walks on
> ahead like a warrior, (...) it is watchful and
> only ever half asleep like a ploughman, (...)
> it likes to sing like a musician, (...) it likes
> darkness like a thief, (...) it roams the
> night like a werewolf, (...) it hurts whoever
> comes near it, like a courtesan, (...) it
> sleeps like a child.' (*Vendidad* XIII, 44–8)

Zoroaster does not appear anywhere in the book as the miracle-working prophet who performs great wonders and converses with the creator. It is true that he does ask questions, but the Wise Lord is very wary of giving a direct answer. It seems that this might simply be a style of writing which allows the founder of Zoroastrianism to represent the whole of humanity and express its desire to know the answers.

The *Vispered* returns to the development of the ceremonies, incorporating the *Gatha* and adding a number of prayers to the spirits which preside over different classes of beings: 'I offer and make this sacrifice in honour of the master of the heavenly spirits, the lord of the earthly creatures, lord of sea creatures, the lord of the inhabitants of Empyrea (heaven), in honour of the lord of the winged creatures, of those which move along the earth, of the hooved and horned animals, in honour of those holy and pure lords from the pure world.'

The Vendidad

The book goes into more detail with the *Vendidad*. The stated aim of this part is to develop the rules to be observed for driving away the deva, the evil spirits, and these rules are set out in unusually detailed form. They describe how one should cut the nails and the hair, how to care for one's dog and,

in particular, how to perform the great ceremony of purification.

But it also records the creation by Ahura Mazda and the counter-creation by Angra Mainyu, the Spirit of Evil. It tells of the legend of the shepherd-king, Yima, who presides over a golden age but is condemned for having observed some wicked practices, and the story is also told of Zoroaster's temptation when Angra Mainyu offers him dominion over the whole world if only he will abandon his mission.

The *Vendidad* also gives a very moving description of the happiness of the true saint. According to the *Avesta*, happiness is 'there where a faithful man prays ... then where he builds his household, with his priest, his cattle, his wife, his son, his fine flock: and later in this household there is growth and increase in cattle, in virtue, in fodder, in the dog, the wife and the child, in warmth and in all the good things of life' (*Vendidad* III, 12).

The Yasht

The word yashta means 'religiously recited'. The *Yasht* are prayers addressed to the different Amesha Spenta, the seven immortal benefactors, to the different gods and goddesses, Anahita, goddess of Fertility, the spotless one; Mithra, the great god of Agreements who rises before the sun: Fravashi, the pre-existing spirit who is called upon in every area of procreation from sexual intercourse to breastfeeding, and many others.

No doubt it often happened — with relics of the pre-Zoroastrian era or the rediscovery of ancestral forms of worship — that prayers to these multiple divinities were adapted to the new doctrine. Hence this continual repetition after each being is invoked: 'created by Ahura Mazda': all have been created and the only Creator is the Wise Lord. Monotheism (belief in one god) is an essential characteristic of this religion.

Hymn to Mithra

'Ahura Mazda said to the holy Zoroaster: When I produced Mithra in the wide countryside, I made him as worthy of honour and praise as myself, Ahura Mazda. The perverse man who lies to Mithra destroys the whole land he lives in; a faithful man who cheats him damages as much as a hundred evil men ...' (*Yasht* X, 1–2)

The Epics

These are by no means sacred books. No religion, civilization or grouping of people has considered them as such. However, age alone speaks on their behalf and some of them tell us so much about the worlds of the gods, they have had such a great impact on the religions of their country and their time, and in many cases can easily be taken for sacred books, that it seems appropriate to devote a few lines to them here. Moreover, the literary styles of the two groups are so close that it is practically impossible to distinguish one from the other. It is often simply by tradition and the authority they are given in certain societies and at certain times that some books are acknowledged as sacred texts, while others are not.

It would be stating the obvious to speak about the links between mythology and religion but the links between religions and their Writings are not so apparent. They represent a whole world of beliefs: the Writings, whether they are seen as the sacred vehicles for particular revelations and recognized as such, or simply the results of a life of faith and the portrait of a civilization, bear witness to religion and demonstrate its constant presence through all the ages.

We will look here at just three examples: Northern Europe, Greece, and Mesopotamia (now Iraq), because they are the best known and perhaps the most representative of these religious-type epics which have appeared in most literate societies.

Northern Europe

We know very little about the religion of the ancient Germanic and Scandinavian peoples apart from what has come down to us through the Edda: a very elaborate concept of the sacred, an important mythology, belief in destiny, and a highly developed sense of honour, or one might say, of glory. It is only a short step from this to the conclusion that the work is the source of their religious activities. It is certainly a reflection of them, and therefore a witness to what they held as sacred.

The manuscript of the *Edda* (the *codex Regius*) was discovered in 1643 by Bishop Brynjolfur Sveinsson. It dates from the end of the 13th century, but it has been proved that it is only a copy of an original going back to around 1210 and that some of the fragments from which it is made up are much older. It is a mixture of sacred texts and heroic poems all of which have their roots in the oral tradition and form a fairly coherent whole, as much through their form as their content.

Many of these poems were used in the 13th century by Snorri Sturluson in writing his *Gylfaginning*, a prose text so explanatory and dogmatic that it is called the *Sturluson Edda* to distinguish it from the *Poetic Edda*. The author, one of the most influential Icelandic chiefs of his time, was trying to revive the ancient traditions and mythologies and strengthen the spirit of the people.

From among the texts of the *Poetic Edda*, we should mention the *Rigsthula* which shows how the god Heimdallr instituted the division of men into three classes: slaves, free men, and king; the *Grimnismal*, which tells how the god Odin had to undergo a series of tests before acquiring supreme knowledge; the *Havamal*, which explores the philosophy of life and moral code of the ancient Scandinavians; and finally the *Voluspa*, a sacred poem which traces the history of the gods and the world from their origins to the final catastrophe, the Ragnarōk, and proclaims the establishment of a new golden age.

All these poems are of exceptional literary quality, have an obvious sense of humour, and show unbounded admiration for shrewdness and cunning. They are full of ingenuity and largely made up of dialogues, creating a sense of combat, which is generally confined to the speeches and a mounting tension. They amount to a moving account of the pursuit of a high ideal, a battle against the forces of Evil, a conquest from the sacred value of existence to the victory of the gods over the giants.

Though the texts are comparatively recent (11th, 12th or 13th century), they nonetheless bear witness to a much earlier and no doubt exclusively oral civilization, in which the sacred and profane were inextricably mingled. At his birth the child would be dedicated to the Power of Destiny (Disir) who would give him a chance to succeed. It was a contract of a sort, a contract with obligations, yes, but also one based on good relationships with the gods, who were often called *vinr*: friend, or *astvinr*: very dear friend.

So these people, who, according to the evidence we have (in Caesar, Tacitus, Boniface, and others) had no temple or formal priesthood and whose language had no term for religion, faith or prayer, were steeped in the presence of the sacred, were aware of their links with a world beyond their own.

Greece

The Greek gods are illiterate. They are not interested in saying who they are or recounting their adventures or explaining their relationships. They live in an almost autonomous society, quite independent of anyone else and act as they please: Hades is an underground and hidden realm, Pan and his nymphs appear at night, Asclepius inhabits dreams, Dionysus reveals himself in disconcerting manifestations. They have no need of any man-made aid to perpetuate their memory.

Writing is not their responsibility; men are the ones who invented it (Palamedes, Orpheus), who exploit it and make a memorable work of it. In it the gods are named, classified, and assigned to their domain, they are honoured and glorified; they are feared or thanked. But the words and the celebrations are all man-made. The speech writers and myth-makers are recording the common history which affirms the identity of the Greek people.

Homer is without doubt the greatest of the myth writers. It is true that the *Iliad* and the *Odyssey* cannot be said to be sacred books, but they are the most ancient books in Greek literature; their origins are lost in the mists of time. They recount a history of man which is constantly interacting with the history of the gods; they mix the sacred and the everyday in the struggles of the nation's life. They are the source from which Greek mythology springs.

Plato was to say that Homer was the Greeks' teacher (*The Republic* X, 606). His texts were the basic ones used by private tutors, his heroes were held up as examples to the children, his tales formed the basis of the nation. So Nikoratos is able to make this allegation: 'My father, anxious for me to become an accomplished man, forced me to learn the whole of Homer. As a result I am still able to recite the *Iliad* and the *Odyssey* by heart today' (Xenophon III, 5).

This should not of course be seen as a form of catechism, a method of teaching religious doctrine by learning answers to set questions. If Homer teaches a kind of golden legend of gods and heroes, a theogony or study of their relationships, he does not give any instructions regarding man's duties towards the gods, nor the rituals to be performed in worship nor even any religious ethics. His objective is a civil one rather than a religious one, just as the whole of Greek society has a secular, civil basis, and his ideal is a chivalrous or gentlemanly one, shared by the gods.

So, are the *Iliad* and the *Odyssey* sacred books? Only in the Greek sense, within the framework of the Greek way of thinking.

The *Theogony of Hesiod* is much more of a holy book. The poet says that it was the Muses, the daughters of Zeus, who taught him this 'fine song' while he was tending his lambs near the divine Mount Helicon. But it simply gives a genealogy of the gods and celebrates the glory of Zeus on Olympus. It is, in short, a religious poem similar to the *Hymns of Pindarus*. Greece has nothing to compare with that body of sacred writings accepted by a people which constitutes a bible. And yet all its poetry, epic, lyrical or thoughtful and all its prose, historical, persuasive or philosophical are full of religious references.

Mesopotamia
(modern Iraq)

The Mesopotamian religion had a history spanning 1500 years between the third and second millenia BC. Each of the gods, Enlil, Enki, Ashur, and Marduk in his time enjoyed a moment of glory, usually related to the dominant period of the city of which he was the patron. There was an evolution of ideas, from those of the Sumerians who made the association between everyday reality and the divine to the divination or foretelling of the future as practised by the Babylonians. The discovery they made was that it is in ordinary everyday life that the existence of the sacred is revealed.

This then was a mark of Mesopotamian civilization and, as soon as writing came into use, even if, because of its great complexity, it was restricted to a small number of specialists, it was felt that the mythology which appeared to be the foundation of life and society should be set down on paper. So epics, prayers, and calls to the gods, reflecting the beliefs of the time were created. Some of them became holy books by virtue of the honour given to them and the power that reciting them was supposed to have.

One of the oldest of them is *Atrahasis*. It tells how 'when the gods were still mere men', they were obliged to provide for themselves. In order to relieve this burden, humankind was created. But this turned out to be a bad idea for the new creatures made such an uproar that the decision had to be made to kill them off. So there was the Flood and the destruction of humanity. Only 'the very intelligent Atrahasis, the Babylonian 'Noah', was successful in his damage limitation.

The myth of *Atrahasis* was eclipsed in the 11th century BC by *Enouma Elish* which recorded the Creation from the separation of Apsou, the sweet waters, from Tiamat, the bitter waters, to the time of Marduk's coming to power. Then came the *Myth of Auzu*, on the rivalry between the gods Nergal and Ereshkigal and the *Myth of Era* on the underworld, and many others.

There is no absence of a spiritual quest in this mythological literature. *The Epic of Gilgamesh*, the *Myth of Adapa* and the *Myth of Etana* all describe the search for immortality which seems to be inaccessible for some reason or another in every instance.

But any list of the fragments of poems, and various inscriptions on tablets, and so on, which have religious echoes would be very long indeed. They did not, of course, all have the same authority and power. They are now simply a sign of the permanence of the sacred in this civilization so closely related to the first books of the Bible.

All these texts convey an idea of the sacred which is best described in three parts: firstly, there is that which is primordial or existed before all things at the origin of the world and gave rise to the creation tales of the *Enouma Elish*; then there is that which is transcendent, going beyond man's experience, essentially the relationship between the divinity and men (and objects), which gave rise to the tales of conquest or rivalry between gods like the *Atrahasis* and the *Myths of Auzu* and of *Era*; finally there is something which is also found in a number of biblical passages, namely that which touches on wisdom and has produced the *Gilgamesh Epic* and the *Myth of Adapa*.

Index

Note: Entries in **bold type** refer to articles headed with the name shown.